# 'His Majesty's Loyal Opposition'

# LIVERPOOL HISTORICAL STUDIES
published for the
Department of History, University of Liverpool

1.    Patrick J. N. Tuck, *French Catholic Missionaries and the Politics of Imperialism in Vietnam, 1857-1914: a documentary survey*, 1987, 352 pp. (OUT OF PRINT)

2.    Michael de Cossart, *Ida Rubinstein (1885-1960): A Theatrical Life*, 1987, 244pp.

3.    P. E. H. Hair, ed., *Coals on Rails, Or the Reason of My Wrighting: The Autobiography of Anthony Errington, a Tyneside colliery waggon and waggonway wright, from his birth in 1778 to around 1825*, 1988, 288pp.

4.    Peter Rowlands, *Oliver Lodge and the Liverpool Physical Society*, 1990, 336pp.

5.    P. E. H. Hair, ed., *To Defend Your Empire and the Faith: Advice on a Global Strategy Offered c. 1590 to Philip, King of Spain and Portugal, by Manoel de Andrada Castel Blanco*, 1990,304pp.

6.    Christine Hillam, *Brass Plate and Brazen Impudence: Dental Practice in the Provinces 1755-1855*, 1991, 352pp.

7.    John Shepherd, *The Crimean Doctors: A History of the British Medical Services in the Crimean War*, 1991, 2 vols, 704pp.

8.    John Belchem, ed., *Popular Politics, Riot and Labour: Essays in Liverpool History 1790-1940*, 1992, 272pp.

9.    Duncan Crewe, *Yellow Jack and the Worm: British Naval Administration in the West Indies, 1739-1748*, 1992, 352pp.

10.    Stephen J. Braidwood, *Black Poor and White Philanthropists: London's Blacks and the Foundation of the Sierra Leone Settlement 1786-1791*, 1992, 288pp.

11.    David Dutton, *'His Majesty's Loyal Opposition': The Unionist Party in Opposition 1905-1915*, 1992, 336pp.

DAVID DUTTON

# 'His Majesty's Loyal Opposition'

## THE UNIONIST PARTY IN OPPOSITION 1905-1915

Published for the
Department of History
University of Liverpool

LIVERPOOL UNIVERSITY PRESS
1992

*Front cover:* Balfour's resignation as Leader of
the Conservative and Unionist Party in 1911,
as depicted in *Punch* (15 November 1911)

Liverpool Historical Studies, no. 11
General Editors: C. H. Clough and P. E. H.
Hair

First published 1992
by the Liverpool University Press
Senate House, PO Box 147, Liverpool, L69 3BX

**British Library Cataloguing in Publication
Data**
A British Library CIP record is available
ISBN 0 85323 447 7


Printed in the European Community by
Redwood Press Limited, Melksham, England

# TABLE OF CONTENTS

For Christine

# PREFACE

This book has taken a long time to reach fruition. The delay reflects less the author's indolence than the intrusion of a variety of other projects and commitments. That it has finally been published owes much to others and it is only right that these debts should be acknowledged. Philip Bell and Patrick Buckland made lengthy and helpful comments on an earlier draft. The text has been substantially re-written in the light of their constructive criticism. Paul Hair encouraged me to resurrect the whole project and produce a typescript and has done much as editor to improve it further. I should like to thank the members of the Publications Committee of Liverpool University Department of History, and particularly Cecil Clough and Alan Harding, for their advice and assistance. Robin Bloxsidge of the Liverpool University Press has been a most efficient publisher. The generous support of the University's Research Development Fund assisted my many visits to archives and libraries up and down the country. There, the staff were invariably cooperative and tolerant of my needs. Lengthy visits to archives in Birmingham and Edinburgh gave me the opportunity to enjoy the hospitality of my mother and my late cousin, Ronald George. The whole book has been typed by Alison Bagnall. Her rare combination of high competence and unwavering cheerfulness is much appreciated. But the final stages of production would not have been possible without the encouragement and support of my wife, Christine. It is only fitting that the book should be dedicated to her.


**David Dutton**                                                    October, 1991
**Liverpool**

## ACKNOWLEDGEMENTS

For permission to quote from material in their possession, or of which they hold the copyright, the author is pleased to thank the following: the Rt. Hon. Julian Amery; Lord Ashbourne; the Earl of Balfour; Dr. B. S. Benedikz and the University of Birmingham; the Bodleian Library, Oxford; the British Library; Cambridge University Press; Curtis Brown Group Ltd., London on behalf of the Estate of R. S. Churchill; the Clerk of the Records, House of Lords Record Office and the Trustees of the Beaverbrook Foundation; the Earl of Crawford and Balcarres; Lord Croft; the Dowager Countess of Cromer; the Earl of Derby; the Viscount Esher; Guardian News Service Ltd.; Mr. T. R. Hartman; David Higham Associates; Professor Anne Lambton; the Marquess of Lansdowne; Macmillan Publishing Company, New York; Mr. A. J. Maxse; Methuen, London; John Murray (Publishers) Ltd.; the Duke of Northumberland; the Viscount Ridley; the Marquess of Salisbury; Mr. J. E. Sandars; the Earl of Selborne; *The Spectator*; the Hon. Mrs. A. Stacey; Mrs. Gay Stafford; the Warden and Fellows, New College Oxford; the Duke of Westminster.

# INTRODUCTION

The Conservative party can reasonably regard itself as the natural governing party in twentieth-century Britain.[1] The century began auspiciously for the party with a triumphal victory in the Khaki Election of 1900 during the course of the Boer War, a conflict which saw the Liberal opposition in disarray over the attitude it should adopt. Lord Salisbury, the victorious Prime Minister, noted that 'the dual character of the English parties is for the moment destroyed' and expressed the magnanimous hope 'that our opponents will get into fighting trim before long', because 'it is bad for us, and it is bad for the country, if they continue to occupy a position so little conspicuous and effective as that which they occupy at the present time'.[2] As he died in 1903, Salisbury could have had no knowledge of the troubles that lay ahead for his own party. The boost to the fortunes and morale of Unionism given by the Boer War proved to be shortlived. It had, after all, taken about half a million troops to overcome something like a tenth of that number of Boers. Such statistics had shaken the confidence of the country in the government's capacity to rule the Empire and defend the state. By the end of the war the last vestiges of enthusiasm for victory were being swamped in an atmosphere of intellectual criticism and popular discontent. While the middle classes complained of rising inflation and increased taxation, those beneath them saw their real wages declining after several years of improvement. Continued electoral success for the government was by no means assured. But the defeat sustained in 1906 was no passing setback. It stands as one of the blackest moments in the whole history of the party, ranking beside the electoral disasters of 1832, 1945 and 1966. Indeed, because of what followed, it towers above them. For no period since 1915 has the party been out of power for a longer continuous number of years than after the resignation of Balfour's government in December 1905. When it is remembered that the two decades prior to 1905 had seen only three years when the Unionists were not governing the country, then the enormity of the defeat of 1906 becomes apparent.

Yet even in 1906 there was some cause to suppose that the return of a Unionist government would not be unduly delayed. The statistical returns of that year's election were open to misinterpretation. A significant feature of the voting was that it took a swing of only 10.5 per cent to bring about a net transference of 38 per cent of the parliamentary seats and that the victorious Liberals took 71 per cent of the seats with barely half the votes cast in a high, 83.7 per cent, turn-out at the polls. Put another way, in terms of the popular vote, and leaving out Ireland and the University seats, the Liberals and the emerging Labour party captured 56.4 per cent of the electors to the Unionists' 43.6 per cent. Had these percentages been reflected in a simple system of proportional representation in 1906, this would have resulted in 316 seats for the government and their supporters and as many as 244 for the Unionists. Furthermore, the Unionists' vote for each opposed candidate was, at around 4,300, much the same as it had been in the successful Khaki Election of 1900. Indeed, it was a feature of the Liberal party's electoral support between 1885 and 1910 that its vote fluctuated sharply, while by contrast that of the Unionists remained relatively stable even in 1906. The Unionist percentage of the poll thus varied in inverse proportion to the size of the turnout - the smaller the turnout, the larger was the Unionists' share of it. [3]

All this suggests that the startling turnover in seats in 1906 was not caused by any mass conversion from Conservatism to Liberalism. In purely statistical terms the party was perhaps less shattered in 1906 than has sometimes been depicted. In the circumstances Joseph Chamberlain, attributing the result to the natural swing of the electoral pendulum, could be forgiven for having predicted that the new Liberal government would last no more than two to three years. [4] Yet in fact it would be 1922 before the Unionists, standing alone, would win another general election.

The period 1905-15 may be seen as a watershed in the Unionist party's history between the dying years of aristocratic paternalism in late Victorian Britain and the party's successful transition into the age of mass politics and full democracy in the present century. Apart from the Khaki Election no special political significance need be attached to the year 1900 itself. But the death of Queen Victoria in January 1901 and the resignation of Lord Salisbury just over a year later appear in hindsight as symbolic breaks with the immediate past. Queen and premier had for so long been the focal points of national life that their departure emphasises the passing of stable landmarks in a rapidly changing political, social and economic landscape. Despite the apparent strength of the Unionists' position in 1900, it is clear that key long-term factors did not augur well for the party's future. Mr. Cornford has concluded that 'the chief factor in Conservative success [between 1885 and 1906] was lack of enthusiasm among the Liberals, on the assumption that a low poll reflects Liberal abstentions.' Overall Unionists appeared to be most successful in those elections with the largest number of uncontested seats. Furthermore, there was little evidence that the party was succeeding in significantly widening its power-base. The distribution of Unionist support remained in 1906 much what it had been in 1885. Yet with the late nineteenth-century extension of the franchise, 'class was becoming the most important single factor in deciding political allegiance'. Vulnerable, therefore, to the emergence of a party such as Labour with a broader appeal than its own, this was the crucial nettle which Unionism needed to grasp in the first years of the new century. [5] The main theme of the Unionists' two preceding periods in opposition had been the defence of the Union with Ireland - the very factor which gave the party its name, cohesion and identity - and Unionists stressed this same theme during their 1906 campaign. But the ensuing *débâcle* suggested that the electorate cared little for Ireland and perhaps indicated the growing irrelevance of the Unionists' traditional stance. This issue too would call for fresh thought.

In the longer term, the emergence of a third political party on the British mainland would work to the Unionists' advantage. In the first place, an eventual effect of Labour's arrival would be to squeeze out the Liberals from a viable position within the British political spectrum. This would be important for Unionists after World War One since the clarification of twentieth-century politics into a class-based struggle meant that they and the post-war Liberals were increasingly forced to dispute too much of a common ground for both to be able to survive as viable parties of government. In the second place, the emergence of a party of the left which paid at least lip-service to the tenets of international socialism opened up for the Unionists a golden opportunity to mould themselves into the only credible vehicle to resist this threat - as a substantial section of the British electorate would always regard it. Again, the squeezing out of the Liberal party may be seen as a by-product of this development. These trends did not, however, come to fruition until the First World War had delivered a massive catalytic jolt to the whole British political system. Thus the years 1905-15 were years of transition, during which Unionists staggered, for the most part unknowingly, towards the electoral Elysian fields they were later to enjoy.

Robert Rhodes James has written that 'the Conservative Party does not show up to advantage in Opposition. Regarding itself as the natural governing party, it views years in opposition as unnatural interludes.' [6] There may be something in this sentiment. Nonetheless, taken as whole, the experience of the twentieth century suggests that the party can usually conduct itself in a spirit of practical commonsense during its periods out of power. Not normally beset by ideological crises of conscience nor stricken by moods of self-doubt, this party - 'the great exemplar of political pragmatism'[7] - generally sets about the tasks of reorganisation, policy-reformulation and internal consolidation in a business-like manner. Most would agree, for example, that the periods 1945-51, 1964-70 and 1974-79 were characterised by the careful preparation for a return to office. Indeed the shock of electoral defeat and the loss of office have often had a beneficial effect in pushing the party from a rather negative view of change to a more positive commitment to new initiatives. Periods of opposition usually witness a reappraisal of existing assumptions and innovation, in the quest for electoral success at the earliest possible opportunity. Opposition tends to illustrate the party's great strength that, unlike some other political movements of the right, it has never been totally committed to reaction and a merely negative defence of the *status quo*.

Yet against this norm the decade under examination stands out in sharp contrast. Then the Unionists 'came nearer than at any time in their history to resembling a continental party of the Right ... and to neglecting their wider responsibilities to the nation as a whole'.[8] The picture is that of a party that had lost its way and which was failing to respond to the changing social, economic and political climate of the new century. The party's greatest single attribute - its adaptability - seemed to be in abeyance, a fact which threatened to cast it into that same pattern of long-term decline which was destined, but by no means predetermined, for its great rival, the Liberal party.

For a country which lacks a formal written constitution the political conventions of Great Britain are defined with remarkable clarity. This certainly applies to the concept of political opposition. 'The Opposition is office-seeking, in that its role is not merely to criticise those who are in power, but is also to seek to replace them.'[9]    Yet for most of the period 1905-15 the Unionist party bore little more than a passing resemblance to a viable alternative government. This usually least doctrinaire of parties, intent it now almost seemed on political suicide, was 'consumed by ideological passion'.[10] Again, according to convention, 'Opposition is loyal, in that it is concerned with achieving office within the established constitutional framework. The Opposition is thus essentially non-revolutionary.'[11] In the period under consideration, on the other hand, 'opposition was fractious, inflamed, and, under ... Bonar Law, unconstitutional. From 1906 to 1914 the Conservative Party in opposition betrayed itself and came close to betraying its country.'[12]

The decade of Unionist party history under consideration is thus one full of paradoxes. The pages which follow are an attempt to understand and resolve these paradoxes, while providing a study of the workings of a major political party in opposition during the last age of 'amateur' politics. The first years of this century were still the era of the political amateur. Politics remained a leisurely activity to which even the minority of committed and ambitious practitioners would not think of devoting the whole of their energies. Such a state of affairs would not, however, last. Indeed there were clear signs of a growing belief that politics and government could and should play a bigger part in the life of the nation than had been accepted in the late Victorian period. The aim of this study will be to examine how Unionists tried to cope, or in some cases tried to avoid coping, with the new problems and situations thrown up in the early twentieth century. Being in opposition and wishing to return to government, Unionists concentrated their attentions on three specific, if inter-related, issues - leadership, policy and organisation - and these will dictate the shape and structure of the present work. It will be necessary to explain why, after the electoral disaster of 1906, the party incurred two further rejections at the hands of the voters in 1910 and why, even at the outbreak of European war in 1914, the party's recovery was at best partial and fragile. Thus the subsequent rise of the party to a remarkably successful career in the following decades will be placed in clearer perspective. The study will thus move towards an assessment of the direction in which Unionism was heading at the moment when events in the wider European arena intervened to disrupt the course of British political development. In doing so, it will make a contribution towards the on-going debate on the nature of the party political structure in the Edwardian era.

## NOTES

1.   The party is described throughout this study as 'the Unionist party' in order to emphasise that it was in fact a coalition of the Conservatives and the Liberal Unionists. The term 'Conservative' is reserved for the more specific meaning which excludes the Liberal Unionists, although

contemporaries often used 'Conservatives' and 'Unionists' interchangeably.

2.    Speech to Primrose League 10 May 1900, cited G. Butler, *The Tory Tradition* (London, 1914) p.127.

3.    A. K. Russell, *Liberal Landslide: the General Election of 1906* (Newton Abbott, 1973) p.164; J. A. Thomas, *The House of Commons 1906-1911* (Cardiff, 1973) p.6.

4.    J. Chamberlain to Lord Northcote 24 Jan. 1906, Northcote MSS, Public Record Office, P.R.O. 30/56; Chamberlain to A. Deakin 26 April 1906, Joseph Chamberlain MSS [JC], University of Birmingham Library, 21/2/43.

5.    J. P. Cornford, 'The Transformation of Conservatism in the Late Nineteenth Century', *Victorian Studies* 7 (1963), pp.37, 53, 54-5, 66.

6.    R. R. James, *The British Revolution: British Politics 1880-1939* (2 vols, London, 1976) vol.1, p.233.

7.    N. Blewett, 'Free Fooders, Balfourites, Whole Hoggers : Factionalism within the Unionist Party, 1906-10', *Historical Journal* 11 (1968), p.95.

8.    I. Gilmour, *Inside Right: A Study of Conservatism* (London, 1977) p.32.

9.    R. M. Punnett, *Front-Bench Opposition* (London, 1973) p.10.

10.   Blewett, 'Free Fooders' p.95.

11.   Punnett, *Opposition* p.13.

12.   Gilmour, *Inside Right* pp. 32-3.

# 2

# PRELUDE TO DISASTER

The Unionists' decade in opposition began on 4 December 1905 when Arthur Balfour tendered his government's resignation, making way for a minority Liberal administration under Sir Henry Campbell-Bannerman. Any analysis of the years of opposition, however, requires at least a brief survey of the period which began with Joseph Chamberlain's famous speech in Birmingham on 15 May 1903, in which he called for the end of the prevailing system of free trade and the imposition of a regime of imperial preference. The debate over tariff reform dominated the last two and a half years of Balfour's government. It was also the central issue at the election of January 1906, at least within the Unionist party; and it continued to obsess Unionists to the virtual exclusion of all other issues during the first years of opposition.

Chamberlain was unequivocal about the advantages offered to the Unionists by his new policy initiative. 'You have an opportunity,' he announced, 'you will never have it again.'[1] Chamberlain might well have been addressing his remarks to the Liberal opposition. Once he had challenged the sacred tenets of free trade doctrine, Balfour's government never again possessed the internal unity and cohesion necessary for an effective administration. Campbell-Bannerman, leader of the Liberals, commented, 'This reckless - criminal - escapade of Joe's is the great event of our time. It is playing old Harry with all party relations .... All the old warhorses about me ... are snorting with excitement. We are in for a great time.'[2]

Soon after his initial pronouncement at Birmingham, Chamberlain left the cabinet, the more effectively to preach the new gospel throughout the country. There is, however, evidence that, at the time of their offical parting, Balfour expressed himself as being in fundamental sympathy with Chamberlain's views; and that Chamberlain's withdrawal was accompanied by a private understanding about a future public reconciliation once the former Colonial Secretary's oratory had won popular opinion to his cause.[3] The fact that Chamberlain's son, Austen, remained in the government, and indeed was promoted to the senior office of Chancellor of the Exchequer at the early age of forty, supports this view. However, staunch free traders within the Unionist ranks reacted sharply to Chamberlain's campaign and by the end of 1903 the so-called free food movement had developed into something resembling a new party. Its adherents had issued a manifesto, had undertaken to publish literature to further their cause, and had begun to organise themselves at constituency level.[4] Policy differences on issues other than free trade, such as education and labour policy in South Africa, precluded any formal fusion between Unionist free traders and the Liberal opposition, but by the end of the Balfour government as many as thirteen free fooders had crossed the floor of the House of Commons.[5]

If Chamberlain had left the government only after reaching an informal understanding with Balfour, the latter's failure in the months which followed to bring the party into line on the question of tariff reform helps to explain the change in character which overtook Chamberlain's campaign. Starting from a critical analysis of Britain's current and future economic and political difficulties, for which there was considerable sympathy over a wide political spectrum, Chamberlain moved towards the total subordination of all other considerations to a fanatical crusade which not only threatened the Unionist party with lasting schism, but also undermined that national consensus which he professed himself committed to maintain.[6] Despite mounting ill-health, Chamberlain spared no effort to spread his message. One Unionist M.P. recorded:

> Anxiety or overwork is beginning to tell upon his physique: his
> colour, a luminous sallow hue, does not connote good health,
> while a certain hesitation in the selection of words, and an
> occasional lack of grammatical construction, showed that
> preoccupation or excitement were disconnecting the structure of
> his remarks .... Some of the old stagers say a thorough holiday
> is imperative, or else he may lose the ear of the House.[7]

Chamberlain's frustration can only have been increased by the short-term economic climate of the country which seemed to undermine the intellectual case for his fiscal theories. The prevailing period of prosperity made a mockery of his argument that free trade was ruining the country. Apart from iron and steel, the major industries continued obstinately to prosper under the existing system.[8] Chamberlain's difficulties in winning over popular support were vividly illustrated by the defeat of tariff reform candidates in four by-elections in January and February 1904. As a result, at nine subsequent by-elections no Unionist candidate was prepared to declare openly for Chamberlain. But these candidates too were defeated, giving the Chamberlainites the opportunity to claim that the party's lack of success derived from Balfour's refusal to embrace tariff reform with their own whole-hearted enthusiasm.

If the country as a whole resisted his arguments, Chamberlain nevertheless enjoyed considerable success within the Unionist party itself. By the end of 1904 he had not only captured control of the Liberal Unionist Association, but had secured, through branches of his Tariff Reform League, a constituency organisation to rival that of the official National Union. In addition he had attempted, though without success, to implant a representative of the Tariff Reform League inside the Central Office, traditionally the stronghold of the party leader.[9]

Growing party divisions were reflected in the divergent opinions of the Unionist press, whose divided voice helped create a widespread image of a disordered party, while undermining the advantages which the party traditionally derived from its dominant influence in Fleet Street during the crucial period before a general election. Balfour might suggest to Austen Chamberlain that, apart from the fiscal issue, 'the agreement between your views and mine on the present political situation is ... nearly complete'[10], but in reality Chamberlain's maverick campaign had opened up a basic divide in political philosophy within the party's ranks. One leading free trader, Balfour's cousin, Lord Robert Cecil, commented regarding the Chamberlainites: 'It is not by any means only the Fiscal Question upon which I differ from them, it is their whole way of looking at politics. It appears to me to be entirely sordid and materialistic, not yet corrupt, but on the high road to corruption ....'[11] Chamberlain's opponents believed they were fighting to protect not only free trade but also the whole fabric of Conservatism as they understood it.

While the schism within the Unionist party became progressively deeper, the feeling that the time had come for the Prime Minister to go to the country also grew apace. It was probably first and foremost considerations of national policy which determined Balfour to hold on to the reins of office for as long as he did. But Balfour's perception of himself as a party leader was also important. Determined not to be another Peel and to maintain at all costs the semblance of party unity, Balfour attempted to paper over the divisions among his nominal followers with a veneer of verbal and intellectual gymnastics which left no one very sure as to where he himself stood on what was evidently the crucial political issue of the day. Not surprisingly, this attempt to chart an ill-defined middle way served only to alienate both camps in the fiscal debate. Characteristically, Balfour made an important speech in

Edinburgh on 3 October 1904 which revealed little more than a policy of deliberate and calculated procrastination. He announced that there would be no change in the fiscal system during the life of the present parliament but that, if the Unionists won the next general election, the colonies would be invited to a fiscal conference and that any decision there reached would be submitted to the voters at another general election.[12]

But for all Balfour's mental and verbal skills few Unionists seemed happy with the present state of affairs. One junior whip predicted:

> We shall lose more by-elections, and the Free Food element
> will become more restive, and will gradually fall into the way
> of voting against us on non-fiscal questions: all this must
> weaken the government....[13]

Exasperated by the attempts of the Tariff Reform League to purge the party of free traders, Robert Cecil thought it only fair that Balfour should be asked whether he, as leader, approved of such activities. Cecil knew, however, that this was not a question to which he would receive any reply, since an answer would be 'a censure on Joe's League and it appears to be the corner-stone of the Prime Minister's policy that he will not have an open breach with Joe'.[14] Cecil believed that the source of all evil was Balfour's attempt to combine under one formula men of totally divergent opinions. 'Such leadership', he prophetically noted, 'can only end in disaster.'[15] On the other wing of the party Austen Chamberlain complained of 'weakness and flabbiness which kill enthusiasm'. What was needed, he felt, was a great appeal for a great end - an appeal to a cause which would touch men's emotions and rouse their sympathy.[16] Even Balfour seemed to weary of his thankless task, despairing of both wings of the party which he had 'the melancholy privilege of leading'.[17] Not surprisingly, he turned down Joseph Chamberlain's offer, made in May 1905, to return to the cabinet without portfolio or salary.[18]

By the summer of 1905 it was evident to most observers that Balfour's government could not survive for much longer. The government saw the foreshadowing of future electoral defeat in a series of catastrophic by-election results, but still the strife-torn party refused to coalesce. Any hopes that the Unionists might once have had of winning the election were giving way to concern over the internal balance within what would remain of the parliamentary party after the expected Liberal victory, and hence to speculation as to whether Chamberlain would use the coming defeat to topple Balfour and become leader himself.[19] One estimate of the Unionist ranks prior to the dissolution suggested that the party in the Commons contained 172 out-and-out Chamberlainites, 73 'preferentialists' who would support the whole policy if it were recognised as the policy of the government, 98 Balfourian 'retaliationists', 27 free traders, and 4 who could not be classified.[20] But behind Chamberlain there was emerging a band of tariff reformers more militant than himself, eager that the kid-gloves and strained courtesies with which the controversy had so far been conducted should be cast aside. By July 1905 Chamberlain had himself become eager to see parliament dissolved, confident that, once in opposition, Balfour could not fail to follow the path along which he, Chamberlain, desired to see the party move.[21] His speeches were becoming increasingly abrasive and alarming to Balfour's inner circle.[22] His was now the style of an old man in a hurry. 'Hence perhaps a certain acerbity which is moreover more or less excusable in a man of seventy who feels that time is slipping away', noted Lord Balcarres.[23] As late as September Balfour was still firmly opposed to an autumn dissolution and was supported in this determination by influential colleagues such as Walter Long and Lord Selborne.[24] By November, however, Chamberlain, having exhausted his toleration of Balfour's fiscal sophistries, proceeded to lash out in a series of speeches which made it impossible for the Prime Minister to hold his government together any longer.

On 3 November, from the security of his power-base in Birmingham, Chamberlain publicly declared that he would 'rather be part of a powerful minority than a member of an impotent majority', and he demanded a dissolution. Lord Hugh Cecil, brother of Robert and a fellow free trader, gloomily interpreted the speech to mean that:

> Unity is to be achieved by elimination. All free traders and free
> fooders, all weak-kneed and timorous persons are to depart; and
> a purged and regenerated party is to hold high the flag of Tariff
> Reform.[25]

As his own senior ministers began openly to join in the fiscal controversy, Balfour commented in desperation that his was 'the most extraordinary cabinet that this country has ever seen!' Every other cabinet of which he had heard carried on its internecine conflicts behind closed doors, but at least put a decent face upon matters in public.[26] Then, at a meeting of the National Union in Newcastle on 14 November, Henry Chaplin's motion calling for imperial preference and a general tariff was carried overwhelmingly, while an amendment in support of Balfour's own line - the so-called 'half sheet of notepaper'[27] - was emphatically defeated. To rub salt into the leader's wounds, a resolution critical of the party organisation and evidently directed against its present management by Balfour and the Chief Whip, Sir Alexander Acland Hood, was also passed. Encouraged by these successes Chamberlain followed up with what was virtually an ultimatum at another great speech in Bristol a week later. In this he insisted that the Unionist party must fight the election, when it came, on the fiscal question. While professing continuing loyalty to Balfour as leader, indeed stressing that there had been no widening of the breach between them and that their personal friendship was unaffected, the Birmingham leader pronounced that 'no army was ever led successfully to battle on the principle that the lamest man should govern the march of the army'.[28] With his eyes fixed far more upon Chamberlain than the Liberal opposition, Balfour finally tendered his resignation to the King on 4 December 1905.

The Unionists now had no hope of entering the coming election campaign as a united force. For some time a feeling of gloom had pervaded the government. Austen Chamberlain had 'never felt so low about our prospects' and he watched with a feeling of extreme anxiety the growth of a situation which he had foreseen, but which he was powerless to prevent.[29] Isolated moderates such as Balfour's brother Gerald might still search earnestly for a compromise broad enough to satisfy all shades of fiscal opinion, but in fact no ground for compromise really existed. Gerald Balfour feared that, unless some basis of unity could speedily be discovered, the party would drift into disruption and disarray, causing grave danger to those interests which Unionism existed to defend,[30] but many leading Unionists seemed ready to contemplate this prospect rather than move towards some illusory middle ground. On the one hand Arthur Balfour was convinced that nothing he could now do 'short of denouncing Joe and all his work' would prevent the free fooders continuing their disruptive tactics,[31] while for his part Chamberlain could see no point in approaching Balfour again, since 'he seems determined to do all in his power to maintain the Free Fooders as an essential part of the Conservative party.' There was therefore no purpose in further discussions until the election had established a new balance of forces within the Unionist party.[32] Indeed Chamberlain was against any reconciliation with the free fooders which would lead to a watering down of the pure doctrine of tariff reform. 'If a formal reconciliation were patched up', he pointed out to his son Austen,

> some of the leading Free Fooders would have to be ... treated
> as probable members of a future fiscal reform government. Are
> there any of them whom you could trust? Would you like Hugh
> Cecil for instance in such a Cabinet? [33]

Using the agency of the Tariff Reform League, Chamberlain showed the extent of his hostility to Unionist free traders by creating difficulties for certain candidates in their own constituencies. [34]

Balfour's closest colleagues urged their leader to make his own position, and his differences with Chamberlain, entirely clear. Whatever the merits of his existing policy of ambiguity, such equivocation could not be presented to the electorate with any hope of success. Not only the electorate as a whole, they argued, but also many active Unionists were unaware that there were sharp differences of view between Balfour and Chamberlain, especially while the latter continued to proclaim that in substance he and the Prime Minister were in agreement. [35] Betty Balfour, the Prime Minister's sister-in-law, argued that Balfour's line that it was no use defining policy in detail until the matter could be taken up as a working policy had led to both wings of the party misunderstanding him and becoming entrenched in their own positions. He could still, she believed, get an enthusiastic response from the rank and file, but only if he seized the initiative without further delay. It would be 'quite fatal for Arthur's whole future that he should merely drift out of this crisis and shut his eyes to facts'. [36] Similarly both Hood, the Chief Whip, and Lord Lansdowne, the Unionist leader in the House of Lords, were emphatic that the time had come for Balfour to define his position, without qualification or equivocation. Unless it were defined, the majority of the party would follow Chamberlain, the minority Hugh Cecil, and Balfour would be left as a general without an army. [37]

Yet Balfour still calculated that his best strategy was to play down the divisions within his own party. He embarked therefore on a conventional election campaign, stressing his party's defence of the Union with Ireland and warning against the dangers posed by a majority Liberal administration. [38] Such tactics could not conceal the reality of the situation. 'Our modern political history', wrote a Liberal politician of long experience, 'shows no exception to the rule that a party which goes to the polls with open and serious divisions in its own ranks is doomed to defeat.' [39] Seldom in British electoral history can a party have been so pessimistic about its prospects at a forthcoming poll. As early as August 1904, Austen Chamberlain had been

convinced that the Unionists could not win.[40] His fellow tariff reformer, Lord
Selborne, agreed that they must focus their hopes on the next general election
but one, an election which they could win on a commitment to Imperial
Preference, provided that the agreement of the Dominions could be
secured.[41] St. John Brodrick, the former Secretary for India, feared that 'we
shall get hideously beaten', while Joseph Chamberlain privately predicted a
combined Liberal-Irish majority of something like 120.[42] In these
circumstances of gloomy expectation the main concern of the party's free trade
wing was to keep the party organisation out of Chamberlain's clutches.
Edward Carson was among those who feared the outcome if the majority of
Unionists returned were Chamberlainites, for in such a situation he could not
see how Balfour could stay on as leader.[43]

These forebodings of disaster soon proved to be well-founded. As the
election results came in, it became clear that the Unionists had not simply been
decisively beaten, but that their parliamentary ranks had been devastatingly
depleted. Many former ministers, including Balfour himself, had lost their
seats. Looking at the picture in the North-West, the *Manchester Guardian*
commented with only slight exaggeration:

> A candidate had only to be a Free-trader to get in, whether he
> was known or unknown, semi-Unionist or thorough Home
> Ruler, Protestant or Catholic, entertaining or dull. He had only
> to be a Protectionist to lose all chance of getting in, though he
> spoke with the tongues of men and angels, though he was a
> good employer to many electors, or had led the House of
> Commons, or fought in the Crimea.[44]

Not surprisingly, tariff reformers now argued, almost to a man, that had
a united Unionist party been able to fight the election on the fiscal issue alone,
the margin of the Liberal victory would have been greatly reduced if not
entirely eliminated. George Wyndham told Chamberlain that he had won
solely on tariff reform, while among the defeated candidates Andrew Bonar
Law asserted that he would not have got even as many votes as he did but for
his fiscal views.[45] Detailed analyses of the election have shown, however,
that such views are simplistic.[46] The sober conclusion of the historian of the
1906 contest is that 'there is no evidence, either statistical or historical, to
demonstrate that either one or the other set of fiscal views might, if adopted
by all the party, have been more successful'.[47] One contemporary assessment
of the causes of the Unionist *débâcle* listed 'fiscalitis' only fourth behind the

scandal of Chinese slavery in South Africa, the organisation of the labour vote, and the recovered solidarity of Nonconformity on behalf of the Liberal party.[48] Such an analysis emphasises the way in which, after a decade in government, the Unionists had inevitably succeeded in alienating a wide range of electors on a variety of different issues.

Taken at a different level, however, 'fiscalitis' was the primary cause of the Unionists' defeat, not so much because of the electorate's fear of food taxes and the so-called 'dear loaf', but because of the paralysis it had engendered in the Unionist administration ever since Chamberlain's first pronouncement on the fiscal question almost three years earlier - a paralysis which certainly undermined the Unionists' credibility as a party of government. Three years of internecine dispute, patched over only by Balfour's deliberate obscurity, had shattered the morale of the party organisation and destroyed the confidence of the public. In particular, the existence of an articulate minority of committed free traders provided the electorate with testimony of the deep divisions within the party.[49]

The Unionists, then, were consigned to a period of opposition. Yet few in 1906 would have predicted that their return to government would be so long delayed; that two further successive general elections would be lost; that the internal troubles which had beset the party in government would smoulder on unresolved for almost another decade; that a leader as respected as Balfour would be virtually forced out of office; and that under his successor the party would stretch the constraints of constitutional opposition to their very limit in its attempt to force the Liberal government from office. As the dust settled on the party's electoral disaster, Winston Churchill - a former and future Unionist - commented with mischievous frivolity that 'it would be great fun to be a Tory now!'[50]

## NOTES

1. L. S. Amery, *My Political Life* (3 vols, London, 1953-5) vol.i, p.235.
2. H. W. McCready, 'The Revolt of the Unionist Free Traders', *Parliamentary Affairs* 16 (1963) p.188.
3. D. Judd, *Balfour and the British Empire* (London, 1968) p.118.
4. McCready, 'The Revolt' p.188.

5.  Ibid, pp.203,205.
6.  G. R. Searle, *The Quest for National Efficiency* (Oxford, 1971) p.155.
7.  J. Vincent (ed.), *The Crawford Papers* (Manchester, 1984) p.70.
8.  R. Rempel, *Unionists Divided: Arthour Balfour, Joseph Chamberlain and the Unionist Free Traders* (Newton Abbott, 1972) p.97.
9.  Judd, *Balfour* p.127.
10. Sir A. Chamberlain, *Politics from Inside* (London, 1936) pp.27-8.
11. Cecil to Balfour 25 Jan. 1906, Robert Cecil MSS, British Library, Add. MS 51071.
12. Viscount Chilston, *Chief Whip: the Political Life and Times of Aretas Akers-Douglas, First Viscount Chilston* (London, 1961) p.329.
13. Vincent (ed.), *Crawford Papers* p.77.
14. Cecil to Salisbury 21 Feb. 1905, Salisbury MSS, Hatfield House, S(4)56/7.
15. Ibid, 2 March 1905, S(4)56/13.
16. A. Chamberlain to Selborne 3 Sept. 1904, Selborne MSS, Bodleian Library, 73/27.
17. Balfour to Hugh Cecil 11 July 1905, Balfour MSS, British Library, Add. MS 49759.
18. H. Maxwell to Chamberlain 2 Feb. 1906, JC21/2/63.
19. Balfour of Burleigh to St. Loe Strachey 28 Feb. 1905, Balfour of Burleigh MSS 11.
20. Undated note, Balfour MSS, Add. MS 49780.
21. M. V. Brett and O. Brett (eds), *Journals and Letters of Reginald, Viscount Esher* (4 vols, London, 1934-38) vol. ii (1934) p.91.
22. G. Wyndham to Balfour 8 July 1905, cited J. W. Mackail and G. Wyndham, *Life and Letters of George Wyndham* (2 vols, London, 1924) vol.ii, p.510.
23. Vincent (ed.), *Crawford Papers* p.81.
24. Balfour to Selborne 21 Sept. 1905, Selborne MSS 1/66; Long to Balfour 20 Sept. 1905, Long MSS, Wiltshire County Record Office, 947/61; Sir C. Petrie, *Walter Long and his Times* (London, 1936) p.100.
25. *The Times* 7 Nov. 1905.
26. Balfour to Austen Chamberlain 3 Nov. 1905, Austen Chamberlain MSS [AC], University of Birmingham Library, 17/3/13.
27. Early in 1905, in answer to a taunt from Lord Morley to summarise

his ambiguous fiscal policy, Balfour did so on a 'half-sheet of notepaper'. It involved fiscal freedom, closer commercial relations with the Empire, an open colonial conference and no rise in domestic food prices.

28. Petrie, *Long* p.101; Rempel, *Unionists Divided* p.133; Chilston, *Chief Whip* p.330; Chamberlain to Lord Northcote 30 Nov. 1905, Northcote MSS, PRO 30/56.
29. Chamberlain to Balfour 25 Oct. 1905, AC 17/3/10.
30. G. Balfour to Lord Goschen 9 Nov. 1905, Gerald Balfour MSS 117.
31. Balfour to G. Balfour 9 Nov. 1905, ibid 108.
32. J. Amery, *Joseph Chamberlain and the Tariff Reform Campaign* (London, 1969) pp.771-2. The fact that on 9 December the committed free trader, Lord James of Hereford, confided to his diary that 'there is no tendency in Balfour to incline towards free trade, and so now, with the General Election immediately in front of us, we Unionist Free Traders have to go our own way' gives some indication of the confusion created by Balfour's studied ambiguity: Lord Askwith, *Lord James of Hereford* (London, 1930) p.291.
33. J. Chamberlain to A. Chamberlain 10 Nov. 1905, AC 17/3/46.
34. For example, G. F. S. Bowles in Lambeth, Norwood. Chamberlain 'would rather have a Liberal Free Trader in the House than X [Charles Seely, Unionist free trade M.P. for Lincoln] who fawns on me and stabs me in the back': H. Page Croft, *My Life of Strife* (London, 1948) p.70.
35. Goschen to G. Balfour 7 Nov. 1905, Gerald Balfour MSS 108.
36. Betty Balfour to G. Balfour 8, 23, 27 Nov. 1905, ibid 118, 273, 281.
37. Hood to Sandars 16 Dec. 1905, Sandars MSS, Bodleian Library, c.750/245; Sandars to G. Balfour 15 Dec. 1905, Gerald Balfour MSS 273.
38. 'The Unionist leaders made a disastrous error of judgement ... in believing that anti-radical opinion could be rallied in 1905 over the cry of the union in danger.' A. K. Russell, 'The Election of 1906', Oxford D.Phil. thesis 1963, p.528.
39. Viscount Samuel, *Memoirs* (London, 1945) p.49.
40. Chamberlain, *Politics from Inside* pp. 22-3.
41. Selborne to A. Chamberlain 1 Sept. 1904, AC 17/3/80.
42. St. John Brodrick to Selborne 24 Nov. 1905, Selborne MSS 2/118;

W. A. S. Hewins, *The Apologia of an Imperialist* (2 vols, London, 1929) vol.i, p. 155. See also J. Chamberlain to Mount Stephen 22 Dec. 1905, cited Amery, *Joseph Chamberlain* p.774.

43.   H. M. Hyde, *Carson: the Life of Sir Edward Carson, Lord Carson of Duncain* (London, 1953) pp.212-3.
44.   Manchester Guardian 15 Jan. 1906.
45.   J. Amery, *Joseph Chamberlain* p.794; Law to Chamberlain 19 Jan. 1906, JC 21/2/16.
46.   P. F. Clarke, *Lancashire and the New Liberalism* (Cambridge, 1971) p.375. Archibald Salvidge told Chamberlain that 'the democratic constituencies of Liverpool ... went solidly for those candidates who supported your programme in its entirety': S. Salvidge, *Salvidge of Liverpool* (London, 1934) pp.70-1. But, comments Dr. Clarke, 'this is disingenuous. Salvidge had, as usual, made Protestantism the issue, and to claim the result as one for Tariff Reform is nonsense'.
47.   Russell, *Liberal Landslide* p.181. The results in Manchester and Liverpool were particularly illuminating. Manchester's six seats previously held by four Conservatives, one Liberal Unionist and one Liberal, returned four Liberal and two Labour members in 1906, while in the traditional Unionist stronghold of Liverpool two seats were lost to the Liberals.
48.   'Some thoughts upon the Present Discontent', Feb. 1906, Sandars MSS c.751/139.
49.   Rempel, *Unionists Divided* p.164.
50.   Churchill to Law 6 Feb. 1906, Bonar Law MSS, House of Lords Record Office, 18/8/13.

# 3

# LEADERSHIP 1906—1910

There has been general recognition of the crucial importance of the weeks immediately following the catastrophic election defeat of 1906 in determining the development of Unionist politics until at least 1910. Most historians have, however, emphasised that questions of policy were at the centre of the struggle which took place at this time within the party's ranks. The official biographers of the two leading participants went far to establish this consensus of interpretation. Mrs. Dugdale asserted that any rumours of disputed leadership were 'ludicrous' in the light of the correspondence that was passing in private between the two men, while according to Mr. Amery, Chamberlain was staking 'everything on policy'.[1] Yet it is possible to argue that, important though this period was for the formulation of party policy, a greater prize - the leadership itself - was at stake in the struggle which now ensued. Whilst historians have tended to argue that Chamberlain was throughout constrained by an underlying personal loyalty towards the party leader, many contemporaries recognised another Chamberlain - one whose ruthless ambition knew no bounds. Even within the ranks of the Unionist party there were those who would have agreed with the socialist Keir Hardie in his assessment of 'this Brummagem upstart, who had no thought beyond his own personal ambition, [and] had neither sense of responsibility nor sense of honour'.[2]

Defeat at the polls failed to restore unity to the Unionist party's depleted ranks - but was bound to change its internal balance of power. Not surprisingly Balfour, now without a seat in parliament, and Chamberlain, returned once more in his rock-solid Birmingham constituency, drew contrasting conclusions from the outcome of the contest. As far as Balfour was concerned, the need was for continuing caution, that is, very much the policy he had pursued on the tariff issue since Chamberlain's initial pronouncement back in 1903. For Chamberlain, on the other hand, the lesson was clear. A campaign in which the party had embraced tariff reform with wholehearted commitment and enthusiasm would at least have stopped a defeat degenerating into a rout.[3] Tired of 'peddling with fine distinctions', he hoped that he could now induce those who formed the remnants of the parliamentary party to abandon their hesitation and start afresh, absolutely united on the only policy which, he believed, could arouse popular enthusiasm.[4]

The crucial factor would therefore be the allegiance of those Unionists who had escaped the recent electoral rout and who now constituted the party rump in the new parliament. The figures seemed clearly to strengthen Chamberlain's position within the party hierarchy. Out of a total of 157 members, it was said that 109 were Chamberlainites, 32 supported Balfour's compromise formula of 'retaliation', while only 11 were out-and-out free fooders, with a further 5 who were not firmly committed. It would be difficult to interpret these figures as in any sense a popular endorsement of the policy of tariff reform. It was, after all, not only Balfourites and free traders who had gone down to crushing defeat. It was noticeable that several well-known tariff reformers, including six members of the tariff commission, had also lost their seats. Such men had been just as energetic as Chamberlain in educating their electorates to accept the merits of tariff reform, but had still failed to convince them of their case. The prominent tariff reformer, Leverton Harris, had been beaten at Teignmouth, even though this constituency had never previously returned a Liberal. Interestingly, the journalist St.Loe Strachey expressed the hope that the former Viceroy of India, Lord Curzon, might now bid for the leadership of the party, on the platform that the electorate had rejected all manner of tariff reform.[5] In this he confirmed the judgement of Henry Fowler, Chancellor of the Duchy of Lancaster in the new government, who, 'sick of the twaddle of the defeated', looked upon the electorate's verdict as a national one against protection in every shape and form.[6] Be that as it may, there was an argument, which tariff reformers were not slow to use, that in so far as the electorate wanted Unionism at all, it preferred Chamberlain's brand to that of the official leadership. The Tariff Reform League had emerged from the election in an overwhelmingly strong position within the party, even though its policies had been rejected by the electorate as a whole. Now, with Balfour for the time being excluded from the House of Commons, was Chamberlain's best - and certainly last - opportunity to rise to the party leadership.

It was a conclusion which many contemporaries were not slow to draw. In the last fortnight in January, letters began to appear in the press urging that Balfour should now stand aside for Chamberlain as Unionist leader. Aretas Akers-Douglas, Home Secretary in the late government, was convinced that the press was being 'worked from B[irmingha]m', and that calls for a leader with more personality presaged a bitter struggle ahead.[7] Many of Chamberlain's closest supporters urged him to snatch the leadership in order to free the party from what they saw as the deadweight of Balfour and his clique. A group of disgruntled backbench M.P.s, dissatisfied with Balfour's leadership, held several meetings at the home of Sir Gilbert Parker.[8] Their intention was to run Chamberlain for the leadership, both on personal grounds and as the only means of getting his policy officially adopted by the party.[9] Lord Ridley, chairman of the Tariff Reform League, was convinced that it would be impossible for Balfour to continue as leader and that Chamberlain would have to be pressed to take over from him:[10] 'The present elections have in the main been a revolt against [Balfour] and all that he stands for. He has undone all the good that Randolph Churchill began and given socialism a new impetus.'[11]

It was essential for Chamberlain's purposes that he should not give the open appearance of challenging Balfour's authority. His best chance lay in the mounting pressure of events which might make his assumption of the leadership inevitable. He continued, therefore, as he had done before the election, to issue frequent denials of any intention to take over Balfour's position at the head of the party, most noticeably in a long letter to Lord Ridley on 6 February, intended for publication. Chamberlain had 'trumped the trick again by his admirably drawn letter', commented Sir William Bull.[12] But Chamberlain faced an enormous task if he were to fulfil his ambition. The same man who could command unquestioning loyalty among his followers was the object of intense animosity among other Unionists. He was not, it must be remembered, a Conservative. Chamberlain's presence within the Unionist hierarchy was entirely a function of the disruption of conventional party politics which followed the introduction of Gladstone's first Home Rule Bill in 1886. Indeed Chamberlain used his status as a Liberal Unionist to underline his public denial of any ambition to replace Balfour in the leadership of the party as a whole. At a very basic level Chamberlain was obviously a different sort of man from those who had traditionally dominated the Conservative party. A man whose fortune derived from screw manufacture in Birmingham sat somewhat uneasily amongst the landed rich of the Conservative ranks. The word 'Birmingham' was itself used almost as a term of abuse to symbolise all that was seen as most distasteful about Chamberlain's intrusion into British and Unionist politics. For an old-style Tory like Lord Salisbury, son of the former Prime Minister, 'Birmingham' meant 'the caucus and the wire pullers and the programme and the Morning Post and what is called the discipline of party'.[13] Similarly Gibson Bowles resented the 'Birmingham Mind which would run an Empire on the principles of Retail Trade ... as unworthy as it is unstatesmanlike'.[14] There existed a strong feeling that Chamberlain had introduced a profoundly ungentlemanly streak into British public life. Strachey noted that the Chamberlainite tradition 'is that you must give no quarter in politics and that the spoils are to the victors'.[15] Many still resented 'Radical Joe' - the exponent of disestablishment and the Jacobin who had once condemned the Tory peers as those 'who toil not neither do they spin'. It was difficult to forget that in the 1870s the Birmingham firebrand had looked forward to the early advent of a republic and the final end to social and political privilege in Britain.

In the circumstances Chamberlain was obliged to proceed with the utmost circumspection. One question which could legitimately be raised was that of the party's temporary leadership while Balfour sought a safe seat to return to the House of Commons. Yet the question was somewhat academic. On the depleted Unionist benches there was no-one, with the possible exception of Walter Long, to rival Chamberlain in terms of experience and seniority. Yet it was significant that Chamberlain wanted the issue to be settled at a party meeting, stressing that 'it is not merely a question of persons that is at stake but also an indication of future policy'.[16] Whether it would in fact be possible to separate the questions of leadership and policy was, however, another matter. Balfour's private feeling was that a party meeting, 'whose sole business would be to wash its dirty linen in public', would be absolute lunacy. Having fought the election on his own policy, he would feel considerable reluctance to remain leader if, as he feared, the party were to decide in favour of Chamberlain's policy.[17] Indeed, Balfour admitted that there might now be a serious movement to have Chamberlain replace him, and that the latter's extraordinary electoral achievement in Birmingham, against the swing of the national pendulum, would alone constitute an almost overwhelming claim.[18] The leader's only option was to seek to wrong-foot his rival. His public response was that only Chamberlain could possibly take his place in the present situation, but that a party meeting would be inappropriate unless the permanent leadership were in question. After so great an electoral disaster, he added, the feeling of the rank and file might well be that some alteration should be made.[19] Chamberlain, however, insisted that a party meeting was needed. He wanted it confined to the Unionist members of the new parliament, of whom 'no one can say as yet what are the views'. Surely, Chamberlain argued, it was desirable to ascertain whether the 150 or so surviving M.P.s were agreed on either his own policy or that of Balfour. The nettle had got to be grasped. It was absurd to go on claiming that he and men like Hugh Cecil were in any sense 'in the same boat'. Chamberlain pointed out that, if the will of the majority was to shift party policy away from tariff reform, then his assumption of even the temporary leadership was out of the question. Presumably the unspoken corollary was that, should the meeting declare wholeheartedly for tariff reform, Balfour's permanent leadership would become equally untenable.[20]

Chamberlain, then, had succeeded in striking an eminently reasonable stance. 'Everything depends on the views of the majority of those with whom we have to work.' But in fact he was not dealing with quite the unknown quantity which he described, for he was well aware of the fiscal views of most of the Unionist M.P.s in the new House, and had already described the parliamentary party as 'practically unanimous ... for Union and Tariff Reform'.[21] To a member of the shadow cabinet Chamberlain later wrote:

I believe, although Balfour does not, that the great majority of those who have been returned have been successful on these [tariff reform] lines and that they desire above all that Balfour and myself should unite in such a policy.[22]

In effect, therefore, Chamberlain was inviting Balfour to accept the verdict on future policy of a group of men whom he believed on the whole to support his own line - a line, of course, which would make it extremely difficult for Balfour to retain the party leadership.

Chamberlain claimed that he had no intention of standing against Balfour, but, on the other hand, he would not join him again without a more definite understanding as to policy than had been the case since 1903. He was convinced that unless the Unionists began their period in opposition as a homogeneous group they would never again emerge as a victorious party.[23] The parliamentary party would need to be animated by a single spirit. The most important thing was to establish a 'firm, definite and united policy'. Chamberlain could not contemplate a period in opposition at the end of which the Unionists would still find themselves 'at sixes and sevens on the main object of our policy'.[24] This meant no more 'nursing' of the free fooders. The minority of the party would have to be content to bow to the will of the majority or stand aside. Unless his line was accepted, Chamberlain was determined to sit as an independent member. He would not take a place on the Front Bench to continue indefinitely with a policy in which he did not

believe.[25] Thus, if Chamberlain had his way the party which would emerge
from the ashes of electoral disaster would be shaped in his own image and not
Balfour's. Free fooders soon recognised that Chamberlain was determined that
'the Unionist Party is to be exclusively a protectionist party'.[26]

Those close to Balfour eyed Chamberlain's manoeuvres with wary
suspicion. Jack Sandars saw sinister motives behind his actions. The idea that
a party meeting would settle only the temporary leadership was 'ridiculous' -
the permanent leadership itself would be at stake. Chamberlain had asked to
be consulted about the choice of party whips. This too Sandars resented. Every
precedent suggested that the outgoing whips should continue to hold their
positions in opposition. Chamberlain was evidently trying to oust Alick Hood,
the existing Chief Whip and a loyal supporter of Balfour. Akers-Douglas, a
former Chief Whip, agreed:

> Joe means to have his knife into [Hood] and to have a voice -
> if not more - in the management of the C[onservative] C[entral]
> O[ffice] and its funds.[27]

Lord Lansdowne was also unhappy about Chamberlain's actions. He admitted
that there was no alternative to Chamberlain as temporary leader, but
recognised that 'long faces will be pulled and malcontents will be worse
content than ever'.[28] Invited to a meeting of the Liberal Unionist Association
Council at which Chamberlain would preside, Lansdowne feared that the
Birmingham leader would nail his colours to the mast and invite everyone to
set to work to convert the country to his fiscal views. This, Lansdowne
believed, would be 'an egregious blunder'.[29] When Chamberlain rather
condescendingly asserted that Balfour ought to be present at the forthcoming
Unionist parliamentary dinner, 'either as host or chief guest', Sandars and
Akers-Douglas could only roar with laughter. Sandars was pleased that Balfour
chose to ignore Chamberlain's 'impertinence'.[30]

But Chamberlain's apparent determination to stage a trial of strength
between his supporters and those of Balfour before parliament met could not
be ignored. Alfred Lyttelton felt that Chamberlain meant business - his policy
or Balfour's, with his lead or Balfour's.[31] It was therefore essential for
Balfour to object to Chamberlain's suggestion that the party meeting should be
restricted to the newly-elected M.P.s. The presence of Unionist peers would
help correct the balance since most of these were known to oppose
Chamberlain. There were even rumours of a movement among some Unionist
peers to demand a specific repudiation of Chamberlain, failing which they

would be prepared to act with moderate Liberals and give general support to the new government.[32] In more general terms, Sandars argued that it was unwise to commit the party to a particular line of policy and engage its energies in this one direction when it was not even known what offensive legislation the new Liberal government might introduce.[33]

Chamberlain, of course, continued to deny that the aim of his strategy was to capture the leadership of the party. The furthest he appeared willing to go was to mention the possibility of a compromise, alternative leader, perhaps Walter Long.[34] His purpose, he stressed, was merely to restore the party to its old efficiency and predominance. This meant securing agreement with Balfour on a programme of more 'definiteness' than the party leader had hitherto been willing to adopt.[35] Chamberlain thus strove to present himself as someone whose sole desire was to strengthen the party's future electoral prospects. Yet, despite his seventy years, Chamberlain's personal ambition was far from spent. Before the election he had brushed aside all proposals for a last minute reunion with Balfour. The basis of Chamberlain's election strategy had not been an expectation of victory at the polls, but the conviction that the election would radically change the internal balance of the party in his favour, leaving him in a much stronger position to influence policy than hitherto. This, of course, is precisely what had happened. Chamberlain had calculated on confronting Balfour from a position of greater strength after the election and this he was now able to do. His longer-term strategy had been focused on a second general election, while his immediate task was to make the ground sure for the time when 'another swing of the pendulum will take place and when our policy will be accepted by the whole Unionist party'.[36] Indeed Chamberlain had recoiled from the idea of winning the recent election if this had meant having to take office again 'with the old lot and the old policy'.[37] He was quite happy with the progress made so far by the tariff reform campaign, while his vision for the future was clear. At a second general election in perhaps two or three years time he believed that a large majority would adopt the views of the tariff reformers, especially if the trade of the country were less favourable than in 1906.[38] The decline in the buoyancy of British commerce from around 1908 would later show that Chamberlain's calculations were not without substance.

Thus, far from being an old man who had given up all thoughts of personal advancement, Chamberlain should be seen in the first months of 1906 as a vigorous politician, apparently at the height of his powers and with a vision of the not too distant future which would witness the triumph of his policies. Furthermore, the logical, if not the only, sequel to pushing his own policy was leading the party. Henry Chaplin envisaged Chamberlain being forced 'by circumstances or the feeling of the party' into 'something more' than the temporary leadership. Indeed, even if Balfour held on to the leadership, the attribution of the temporary leadership would virtually settle the question of who would represent the party at any time in the future in case of his absence or illness. Similarly, should Balfour at some point decide to stand down of his own volition, Chamberlain's claims to the reversion would be correspondingly strengthened.[39] Such an eventuality was by no means impossible. Chamberlain felt that Balfour, undoubtedly under severe strain since at least 1903 in his efforts to hold his government together, looked unwell, and he expressed fears that he might breakdown.[40] This may have been a case of wishful thinking on Chamberlain's part. Be that as it may, Balfour was certainly not one for sustained political in-fighting, which he viewed with considerable distaste. The prospect of a prolonged period of opposition at the head of a divided party can have afforded him little sense of pleasure. Even when Balfour did manage to return to the Commons, he seemed to have lost much of his old parliamentary dominance. In one celebrated encounter he received a severe mauling from Campbell-Bannerman, the new Liberal Prime Minister, who had never previously been thought of as a match for the intellectually agile Balfour. According to one backbench observer, Balfour's performance in the Commons before the autumn session was 'very poor'.[41] New M.P.s voiced their astonishment that such a man had succeeded in retaining the leadership of the House over the previous ten years.[42] Walter Long noted that 'they laugh and jeer at him as if he was something let down from the skylight'.[43]

Unionist free fooders were concerned that Chamberlain should not even assume the temporary leadership of the party. Clearly for Chamberlain to return to the Front Bench after an absence of three years, during which time he had been out of step with official policy, would in itself be a significant indication of the direction in which the party was moving. Robert Cecil warned that even a day or two with Chamberlain in control would be widely seen as an admission that his was to be the official policy in future. Cecil could see 'no hope of permanently acting with the Birmingham school'.[44] He later recalled a meeting with Chamberlain at which he could only repeat, 'rather ungraciously', that he regarded Balfour as his leader.[45] His brother

Hugh argued that the free fooders would have to unite behind Balfour in an attempt to prevent Chamberlain from capturing the party and committing it to a policy of tariff reform.[46]

On the other side, Chamberlain's supporters were becoming increasingly active. On 3 February J.L.Garvin produced a leader in *The Outlook* which was calculated to stir up the leadership controversy within the party. He wrote:

> The Byzantine theory of Unionist leadership - the theory of speechless loyalty to an hereditary succession - is at an end. As a parliamentarian Mr. Balfour has shown extraordinary gifts. But he has shown no power whatever of moving and holding the country. Unless the ex-Premier can show himself capable of receiving and communicating inspiration by rising to the height of Mr. Chamberlain's policy, the Unionist party will never return to power under his leadership.[47]

Garvin repeated his attack a week later. Balfour's leadership would continue and the talent, which had been employed to plunge the party into a worse ruin than the rashest of tactics could have brought about, would again be exerted in the name of reason to postpone its recovery.[48]

Throughout this period the Carlton Club was a hotbed of intrigue, with tariff reformers and free fooders gathered in small groups, the former accusing Balfour of wanting to renounce their policy and the latter alarmed at the prospect of Chamberlain emerging as the leader of the Unionist opposition. Great efforts were made by the party whips and some defeated ex-M.P.s to argue against a party meeting, but even among members loyal to Balfour the prevailing opinion was that the meeting would have to go ahead.[49] In the circumstances it was no surprise that a meeting between Chamberlain and Balfour on 2 February proved unfruitful.Both men held their ground, with Balfour unwilling to move on from the policy he had felt to be adequate ever since 1903. The atmosphere at the meeting was strained and at times heated, with Chamberlain's wife at one point dissolving into tears. Observers now feared that a complete break was inevitable. 'If Joe is able to be so unreasonable', argued Betty Balfour, 'the time has come when it will be better for him to break with Arthur - even if temporarily it is disastrous to the party.' Chamberlain seemed ready to sacrifice everything to his policy of tariff reform, and the man who had once shattered the Liberal party was now ready to do the same to the Unionists.[50]

Balfour's failure to make any concessions convinced Chamberlain that the former had now decided to stand with the free fooders rather than with the supporters of tariff reform.[51] Yet Chamberlain remained determined to force a party meeting and a division. Although recognising that a party meeting would reveal considerable differences of opinion, he believed that it would be best to bring the matter out into the open. According to *The Times*, Chamberlain's subsequent intention was to form all those who supported his views into a parliamentary tariff reform party, whose members would not refuse to receive the official whip but would also have their own whips and weekly or fortnightly meetings.[52] Thus, Chamberlain proposed to form a party within the Unionist party, when he was already confident of the adherence to his views of the majority of Unionist M.P.s. If he succeeded, it was difficult to envisage how Balfour could possibly continue as party leader. The hope expressed by Walter Long and others that Chamberlain and Balfour could still come together to enable the opposition to 'do great things' appeared increasingly unrealistic.[53] The veteran former Lord Chancellor, Lord Halsbury, gave voice to the mounting anxiety felt over the question of the leadership and warned that in the current atmosphere the only result of a party meeting would be the extinction of all chance of united action.[54] As *The Times* commented:

> if ... the party ... proves to be as strongly in favour of Mr.
> Chamberlain's policy as he believes, we cannot see how he can
> honourably decline the leadership.[55]

Opposition to Chamberlain now began to gain ground. St. John Brodrick felt that the Birmingham leader had damaged his reputation by his uncompromising adherence to his policies and that he had thereby lost the support of many committed tariff reformers within the party.[56] At a meeting on 2 February of Unionist leaders, including Long, Hood, Lansdowne, Halsbury and St.John Brodrick, it was agreed that Chamberlain's terms should be rejected, although the party meeting would have to go ahead, since otherwise Chamberlain would hold a caucus of his own.[57] Lansdowne urged Balfour to stand his ground. He warned Balfour that any compromise which the Chamberlainites were likely to accept would inevitably be seen as a surrender on Balfour's part and an admission that he had been insincere when he had claimed that his policy was a self-contained one, different from Chamberlain's. If the latter wrecked the party by his activities, so be it. He would have to accept the consequences and lead what remained of the party in the House of Commons, with one of his supporters leading in the Lords.[58]

Balfour too recognised that if Chamberlain refused to modify his position all hope of unity had to be abandoned. It would then be difficult to say whether the position occupied by the party 'partakes more of the tragic or of the comic'.[59]

. Sensing that the tide might now be moving against him, it was at this point that Chamberlain issued his public denial of any ambition for the leadership in his letter to Lord Ridley. It would, said Chamberlain, contradict 'the stories of hostility and exaggerated differences which have been manufactured by indiscreet friends on both sides'.[60] More importantly, it would improve Chamberlain's public image among moderate Unionists. Because Chamberlain now played down the possibility of independent action by the tariff reformers and was no longer talking in terms of excommunicating the free fooders, Gerald Balfour suggested that the Ridley letter was a climb-down. Chamberlain's power for mischief had, he felt, now largely disappeared.[61] It may, however, also be interpreted as a tactical move on the part of the Birmingham leader. Chamberlain stressed that he would in no circumstances be a candidate for the party leadership, partly because he was a Liberal Unionist in an electoral coalition dominated by the Conservatives.[62] But Chamberlain failed at this point to mention that he had already raised with Balfour the possibility of fusing the two wings of the Unionist alliance. Indeed he had recognised that in the new House of Commons there were probably more Conservative Chamberlainites than those who called themselves Liberal Unionists.[63] In fact, party reorganisation was the other half of Chamberlain's long-term strategy, a strategy which ultimately pointed to his own personal control, whatever his expressed intentions.

Balfour now saw that the time for equivocation was over. If the party decided in favour of Chamberlain's policy, he asked, how could Chamberlain, whatever his stated position, refuse to become its leader?[64] It was an argument designed to place Chamberlain in a difficult situation. To continue with his existing strategy would now give the clear appearance that he was prepared to claim the leadership. But this was a step for which he was not yet fully prepared. Chamberlain was committed to a gradualist approach precisely because an open clash with the party leader would almost certainly damage his already delicately poised position within the party and perhaps destroy his longer-term hopes. He explained his attitude to Garvin:

> It would be better to my mind to allow the point of difference
> to accentuate itself gradually rather than to emphasise it in the

first instance. I want to get as large a majority as possible of
Unionist members to join our group from the first and this can
only be done by showing that their cooperation will not be
incompatible with personal loyalty to the official leader.[65]

In a necessarily conciliatory reply to Balfour, Chamberlain now
emphasised his desire to reach a compromise solution. He sent Balfour a
proposed resolution to put to the party meeting which stated that while fiscal
reform was and had to remain the first constructive work of the Unionist
party, it was at the present moment not necessary to prescribe the exact
methods by which it would be implemented, although a moderate general tariff
on manufactured goods and a small duty on foreign corn should not in
principle be seen as objectionable.[66] Though Chamberlain expressed doubt as
to whether Balfour 'in his present mood' would accept even this declaration,
he had in fact succeeded in putting the ball firmly back in Balfour's court,
since the draft resolution was largely based on a composition of Balfour's own
pronouncements on the subject of tariff reform, which it would be difficult for
him to reject.[67] Even so, leading Balfourites, including Lansdowne, Hood
and Douglas, regarded the latter part of the proposed resolution as
unacceptable and an impasse seemed once again to have been reached.[68] A
further difficult meeting took place, which lasted for 'two mortal hours', with
Balfour, Lansdowne, Gerald Balfour, Douglas and Hood objecting to a
resolution and Chamberlain and his son, Austen, refusing to accept anything
less. Finally, it was Austen who broke the deadlock by suggesting an exchange
of letters, based on the proposed resolution, and this was at length accepted
by all present.[69] The compromise was made public in an exchange published
on 14 February and known, not surprisingly, as the Valentine Compact.

The important point, of course, was the effect of this compromise on the
balance of power within the party. Contemporaries were divided in their
judgements. Loyally, Gerald Balfour claimed that he had not expected the
Chamberlains to yield so much. 'It is a great thing gained to have no
resolution at the [party] meeting except one of confidence in Arthur.'[70] But
others took a different view. According to Lord Salisbury, 'the world - at least
the world with which I am in contact - thinks these letters are a surrender by
Arthur .... The free fooders are in despair.'[71] His brother, Hugh Cecil,
complained that Balfour had now identified himself with Chamberlain and
predicted that free trade Unionists would soon be driven out of the
parliamentary party.[72] Shortly afterwards the leader of the Unionist free

traders, the Duke of Devonshire, declared in the Lords that the publication of the correspondence was a step far in advance of anything hitherto heard on the issue of tariff reform from the leaders of the party. He felt obliged to state that he was opposed to the 'constructive policy ... announced by the leader of the Unionist party'.[73] But perhaps the most revealing comment was that of Balfour himself. His inclination was 'to throw up the leading part in what is too petty to be called "tragedy" and too dull to deserve the name of "comedy"', and he only refrained from doing so out of the feeling that 'to abandon my post now would be little short of desertion'.[74]

Chamberlain had not won his battle in the sense of forcing a resolution through a party meeting in terms which would have been humiliating for Balfour. But in practice he had done even better than this. The fact that the Valentine letters contained nothing which Balfour had not previously said in public speeches was very much to Chamberlain's advantage, since it deprived the party leader of any pretext for precipitating a crisis by offering his resignation and thereby forcing Chamberlain to show his hand in relation to any ambition for the leadership. Indeed it was difficult for anyone to attribute sinister motives to Chamberlain when 'the Resolution proposed is practically made up entirely from his [Balfour's] own speeches and declarations'.[75]

It was in this situation that the party meeting finally took place, with its tone providing a clear indication of who now held the initiative. The economist, W.A.S. Hewins, noted interesting details which were omitted from the published accounts of the meeting. These included the great reception Chamberlain received as he moved to his seat, the stumbling and hesitating style of Balfour's first speech, and the fact that the free fooders slipped away and did not even vote when the motion was put.[76] Chamberlain, who had 'an extremely alert, smiling and triumphant air', still insisted that he could never become leader of the party.[77] But 'the meeting was his and he could play with it as he liked'.[78] Lord Newton recorded:

> My recollection is that the audience appeared to be almost
> wholly in favour of Tariff Reform; that the proceedings were
> amicable and that Mr. Balfour appeared somewhat in the
> character of a captive, it being the general belief that he had
> yielded at the last moment in consequence of the pressure put
> upon him by numerous members of the party. Certainly the
> general impression was that Mr. Chamberlain had practically
> got his way.[79]

William Bridgeman, then a backbench M.P., confirmed this impression, noting that 'the feeling of the meeting was clearly strongly for Tariff Reform'.[80]

As his biographer records, Chamberlain had 'achieved as much as was possible while Balfour remained leader'.[81] But whether Balfour could continue as leader in these circumstances for very much longer was in considerable doubt. He would, thought Hewins, 'no doubt suffer in reputation and authority from the incidents of the last few days'.[82] The day before the party meeting Balfour had ensured his early return to the House of Commons when he was adopted for the City of London seat. But it was noted that at his adoption meeting he was 'very nervous and hesitating, could not frame his sentences and trembled much. He got through the brief speech and the reading of his address with difficulty.' His candidature was run by Sir Joseph Lawrence who persistently interpreted Balfour's words in a Chamberlainite sense.[83]

*          *          *

Having effectively triumphed in terms of policy, Chamberlain concentrated his attention over the next few months on questions of party organisation.[84] By the early summer he was riding high. Only his age seemed possibly to stand between himself and ultimate success. Yet, despite his years, Chamberlain seemed to have acquired a new vigour. To his Parliamentary Private Secretary he stated: 'My motto is never complain, never explain, always attack; and I propose to put it into practice in this Parliament.'[85] Much of course remained to be done. In some respects he was disappointed at the amount of progress made since the Valentine letters were exchanged.[86] But there could be no doubt that it was Chamberlain and not Balfour who was dominating and setting the tone of the Unionist opposition. This was particularly evident in relation to the Liberal government's ill-fated Education Bill. Much to Balfour's discomfort, Chamberlain often failed to give advance warning before launching his initiatives.[87] In April he described with relish the relatively poor performance of the new Liberal ministers, thankful that already 'the gilt is off the radical gingerbread'.[88] By July Beatrice Webb was wondering whether Balfour would ever recover his position as leader - 'at present there is a note of contempt in most persons' opinions of him'.[89] Chamberlain was listened to 'with respect and attention', but as regards

Balfour the feeling was one of 'deepening bewilderment and repugnance'.[90]

What finally stood in Chamberlain's way was less a sense of personal loyalty to Balfour than his own human frailty. In early July Chamberlain celebrated his seventieth birthday in Birmingham amid scenes that bordered on adulation, as thousands of the city's inhabitants packed their municipal parks to pay homage. On 11 July, however, he suffered a severe stroke. For a while the Chamberlain family attempted to minimise the nature of the illness, stressing that all that was needed was complete rest.[91] By the autumn of 1906, however, many were coming to realise that it was now doubtful whether Chamberlain would be able to take any further part in public affairs. Though his brain remained lucid, his body was partially paralysed and his speech permanently impaired. Never again would Chamberlain be able to address a political meeting. Indeed, for the remaining eight years of his life, Chamberlain was reduced to the status of backstage observer of the political scene, still desperately trying to affect the course of events, but with his power of influence immeasurably reduced.[92] In practice Chamberlain's illness marked the end of any serious challenge to Balfour's leadership of the party until after the general election of 1910. Quite simply there was no obvious rival. Balfour himself was not prepared to take any chances. He now went to the length of commissioning a doctor to analyse a photograph of his stricken rival. The medical conclusion thus reached was that Chamberlain's recovery was 'very, very doubtful'.[93] When Balfour met Chamberlain in November 1907 he noted that the invalid was unable to shake hands with his right hand and that his speech was almost incomprehensible. It was 'quite clear that he [had] had a paralytic stroke'.[94]

In this situation the leadership of the Chamberlainite faction passed nominally to the younger Chamberlain, Austen. The latter's loyalty to his father's political creed and to his father personally was unflinching. Indeed over the next eight years Austen succeeded in alienating most of those Unionists who had previously opposed his father. But there were very marked differences between father and son. Austen once wrote:

> I will pick primroses and forget politics for a week. I believe
> that last sentence sums up the difference between Father and me
> in our outlook on politics. Did he ever want to forget politics?
> I doubt it, but I constantly do.[95]

Lacking the vast ambition, ruthless determination and insatiable political appetite of his father, Austen lacked also the ability to inspire. Deep down he

probably wanted to play the role of mediator between the extremes of opinion
within the party rather than take on the leadership of one side in the debate as
his father's illness demanded. To Walter Long he confided in 1907:

> Through my father's illness I am necessarily forced more into
> the position of a protagonist. I cannot be so much the 'link'
> between the more and the less advanced as I was while he was
> active.[96]

Though kinder and more honourable than his father, Austen was also less
effective. So despite the great name which he bore he never succeeded in
inheriting the unqualified endorsement of all those Unionists who would have
followed his father wherever the latter had led them.

The fact that many prominent tariff reformers now looked outside the
Chamberlain family for an alternative leader was a clear indication that Austen
was never seen as an entirely satisfactory substitute for his stricken father.
During the second half of 1906 and into the following year Leo Amery tried
to persuade Lord Milner, the former High Commissioner in South Africa, to
come forward as the champion of a constructive Unionist policy based on the
Chamberlainite programme.[97] In particular, Amery wanted to see Milner
replace Lord Ridley as chairman of the Tariff Reform League - a proposition
which Austen vigorously resisted.[98] Nothing, however, could induce Milner
to descend from his Olympian detachment to take up the uncongenial activities
of party politics. Apart from Milner other tariff reformers floated the name of
Lord Curzon who, having returned from the Indian viceroyalty, was anxious
to recommence a domestic political career. J.L. Garvin even toyed with the
idea of Lord Northcliffe, the newspaper proprietor, as a potential standard-
bearer of the cause.[99] But as none of these alternative saviours really threw
his hat into the ring, Austen Chamberlain was left - much to Balfour's
advantage - as the nominal leader of an increasingly disgruntled and restless
section of the Unionist party.

None of this, of course, necessarily did anything to make Balfour an
effective leader of his party in opposition. He had, it must be conceded, many
admirable qualities. His intellectual prowess was unquestioned, as was his
debating skill in the House of Commons. He had after all led his party in the
lower house since 1891. But his attributes were more than matched by
corresponding weaknesses. His attitude towards his party was one of
paternalistic aloofness which looked back to a political era that was all but
over. Balfour's critics felt that he adopted a *de haut en bas* manner towards

his supporters and that he neither knew nor cared who they were. As the veteran parliamentarian Jesse Collings put it, 'He seems to me like a dweller in a back-water of a river, unheeding the passing stream and unheeded by it'.[100] There was always a clear limit to Balfour's commitment to political life. He was not, thought Leo Amery, really interested in politics, except when in the House face to face with a speech from the other side. The idea of encouraging young M.P.s by engaging in political conversation with them was quite foreign to his nature, and he could never have created a kindergarten of admiring acolytes.[101] One Unionist M.P. of fifteen years experience claimed never to have exchanged one word with his party leader, not even a 'good morning'.[102] But Balfour's problems were not confined to the House of Commons. Many Unionists felt that he had no rapport with the ordinary voter, partly because he selected his friends from among a restricted and far from typical section of London society.[103] The rank and file inevitably tired of the ingenious formulae, the dialectical subtleties and the elaborately qualified arguments of their leader. So while no-one could dispute the excellence of his mind, this attribute sometimes proved a disadvantage, since he seemed unable to deal with complex issues in simple terms. The result was that his pronouncements, when they did not go above the heads of his audience, were so contorted in their argument or encumbered with reservations that his party was left dissatisfied or bewildered.[104] Thus Balfour often seemed slow in coming to a decision, even when political necessity demanded rapid action. Austen Chamberlain once commented: 'he is in my opinion a bad leader ... because he doesn't and can't understand the working of his countrymen's minds.'[105] The editor Leo Maxse was equally forthright:

> What I don't like about Balfour is that he always seems to me
> to be trying to evade the issue. He gets screwed up to a certain
> point and we all imagine it is all right and then he inevitably
> plays into the hands of the enemy and discourages his own
> friends by some piece of mental gymnastics, which may be
> very ingenious but which is getting most wearisome. [106]

As a leader of his party in opposition Balfour's studied vagueness irritated those followers who looked primarily for something positive at which to grasp. He proved incapable of acting as a standard-bearer around which his party could group. 'Somehow', noted a former cabinet colleague, 'he does not inspire ... and his leading is simply the public expression of his family affections and his personal preferences.'[107] As the head of a national government Balfour had shown great ability, but after 1906, with their parliamentary strength shattered, the Unionists needed to consider themselves as a mass movement and it was as the supposed spearhead of this that Balfour was found wanting. One back-bencher commented that 'he never concerned himself with the Party, its management and organization, the machine and the sinews of political war'.[108]

Only in part was Balfour's tortuous equivocation explicable in terms of the complexity of his mind. There was equally an element of deliberate ambiguity. It had been as a result of the deep splits in the party over the question of tariff reform that Balfour had withdrawn behind 'elaborate qualifications and autocratic forms', becoming, as one historian has put it, 'a kind of constitutional monarch who, while his subordinates freely advocated conflicting policies on the fiscal question, only made a pronouncement when forced to do so'.[109] After the great split of 1903 Balfour had taken a line of compromise and conciliation, which had already done much to undermine his personal authority, while the warring factions fought about him for control of the party. But for Balfour party unity had become an end in itself, to which even party principles might have to be sacrificed. If there was one thing that Balfour feared above all else it was that he would go down in history as a second Peel, presiding over the crippling division of his party. Compromise had at least the virtue of postponing an irremediable rupture. But from what began as a natural, perhaps unavoidable, manoeuvre while the party was still in power, there followed the steady erosion of Balfour's control over those whom he nominally led. His behaviour was widely interpreted as vacillating and lacking in backbone.[110] In fact it was in many ways realistic. Under the provisions of the Septennial Act it was not impossible that the Liberal government would remain in power until 1913 without a further general election. As Balfour himself said when discussing the clamour for a 'constructive' policy:

> by [this] I suppose, is meant some cut and dried scheme - and
> this in the first year of a Parliament in which we are in a
> minority of 300! Truly it is not a wise world![111]

But while Balfour's tactics may have been necessary to keep a Unionist government in being during its last two years in office, many felt that with the coming of opposition it was imperative for the party to take a forthright line on policy and to decide in which direction it was travelling. It was unfortunate that for the remaining five years of his leadership Balfour appeared more defensive, lugubrious and vulnerable than ever before. The fact was that, although his career would witness an astonishing revival after 1916, he was now a tired man and the years after 1906 saw him at his lowest ebb.

With the party in opposition those close to Balfour sought to alert him to the dangers which he faced. His trusted private secretary, Jack Sandars, warned in somewhat muted terms of the effect his attitude towards leadership was having on the morale of the party. The rank and file, suggested Sandars, were clamouring for a broad line of policy above and beyond that of resisting the government, 'no matter how pernicious it may be'.[112] Walter Long was also afraid that, unless Balfour changed his methods, he would never regain his hold upon the party. He would then either have to go, or be left as a leader without the real confidence of his followers, and 'either would be disastrous'.[113] In similar vein Austen Chamberlain appealed to his leader for guidance and direction. Stressing that he was not calling upon Balfour to spell out a detailed programme, Chamberlain wrote:

> Can we not have a definite lead and clear guidance not merely as to what we will not do but, in a broad outline at least, as to what we will do on certain great questions. Meanwhile [we] are like sheep without a shepherd.[114]

Yet in so far as Balfour was aware of the criticisms being made of him, he seemed curiously indifferent to their effects. He could do nothing, he wrote, to put an end to them. He was certainly not going to go about the country explaining that he was 'honest and industrious like a second coachman out of place!' If people could not find this out for themselves, he insisted, they would have to remain in ignorance.[115]

Balfour found himself coming under constant attack in the press for his apparent inactivity. Some felt that the criticism was unfounded. 'They little realise', argued Lord Balcarres, a junior whip, 'how profound would be our chaos and how overwhelming our impotence would become were AJB to retire from the leadership ... for a single month.'[116] Such a judgement may or may not have been valid. But Balfour certainly succeeded in giving an impression of indolence and indifference which could not but damage the morale of those beneath him. Towards the end of 1907 Walter Long noted:

> There is no real improvement in the ranks of the Party, who believe that there is disunion in the councils of the Party which the Leader ought to put an end to. You know his temperament as well as I do. You know how incapable he is of doing

anything disagreeable to anyone. You know how much he will
put up with rather than say unpleasant things ... He knows my
views, but he thinks I am too severe in my methods and he
hopes that things will come all right. In the meantime we are
undoubtedly failing to take advantage of the improved condition
of things in the country, which if it were properly made use of,
would enable us, I believe, to turn the Government out.[117]

Part of the problem, as many saw it, was that Balfour was too effectively
sheltered from the full blast of his critics. Even those men who should have
been his closest political colleagues during the years of opposition found that
their leader was encased beneath a protective wall of family and staff, while
lesser figures had little chance of actually meeting their party leader. Joseph
Lawrence, M.P., complained that the practice of being seen through a
secretary or a whip did not apply to other countries with which he was
familiar. He reflected ruefully that in recent years he had had more
conversations with Presidents McKinley and Roosevelt than he had had with
his own political chief in London. Even Balfour's constituency party chairman
more usually saw Balfour's secretary than the leader himself.[118] One newly
elected M.P. tried to open Balfour's eyes to the strong feeling that it was his
private entourage which, intentionally or not, was preventing the views of the
most energetic of the party's workers in the country from reaching his
ears.[119]

As Balfour's trusted private secretary, Jack Sandars inevitably emerged for
many as a particularly despised *éminence grise*, exerting undue influence over
his master.[120] Writing to Walter Long, Sandars admitted that 'men don't
speak pleasantly about the Leader, and not enthusiastically about the chief man
on his staff'.[121] To the former cabinet minister, Arnold-Forster, Sandars was
'an intriguer of ability whom nobody trusts'. No good could be done until
Sandars and Acland-Hood, the Chief Whip, were permitted to devote their
energies to work other than running the Unionist party.[122] St. John Brodrick
proposed in 1907 that Balfour should appoint a 'sort of chief of staff' to keep
him in touch with the party and he specifically excluded Sandars from
consideration for the post.[123] Even Walter Long guardedly admitted that 'it
would help us all immensely if the Private Secretary element were not so
constantly in evidence'.[124] Certainly Sandars appears to have acted as the
filter through which much of the party's criticism of Balfour was passed before
it reached the leader's ear, and he also seems to have encouraged him to

persist in that style of leadership which avoided the spelling-out of future policy commitments.[125] By 1910 Lord Balcarres sensed 'something in the nature of a concerted attack'. on Sandars, who was blamed for Balfour's inaccessibility and his aloofness from the feeling of the party.[126] Yet, despite such hostility, Sandars survived as Balfour's right-hand man, beyond the latter's resignation as party leader and until disagreements over the formation of the first coalition, in May 1915, brought about a breach between the two men.

Significantly, when Austen Chamberlain felt compelled to bring the mounting disaffection within the party to Balfour's attention, it was to the latter's brother, Gerald, that he appealed.[127] But Balfour's close family could be just as protective as his private secretary. His sister-in-law, Betty, though listening in October 1907 to a lengthy recital by Walter Long of Balfour's failings, their effects upon the party and Long's proposed remedies, argued that the greatest danger ahead was that Balfour might grow sick of his task and retire. Nothing, she suggested, could be worse for the party or the country and 'perhaps, therefore, the less he hears of party disloyalty the better'. [128] Long, who felt that 'he could say things direct to [Gerald] that he could not say to Arthur', was persuaded by Betty to leave out from a proposed speech in Wolverhampton all criticism of Balfour and to adopt a tone of total loyalty.[129] Even a relative such as Lord Salisbury, Balfour's cousin, could spend a week with his leader and have 'no word with Arthur on the position of the Party ... a significant and rather melancholy circumstance'.[130]

Yet whatever the problems associated with his leadership, the major safeguard which Balfour enjoyed was the failure of his critics to unite behind a credible alternative leader. Joseph Chamberlain might have emerged into such a position, but his illness precluded this possibility. 'If this is so,' Sandars was assured, 'we need not fear, as he is the one strong man to be considered, the rest not being worth a row of pins.'[131] Yet in the longer term Balfour's attitude towards the task of leading the party in opposition was bound to weaken his own position. At no time did opposition to him become strong enough to force him from the leadership against his wishes. But the residue of good-will upon which any political leader ultimately depends was being progressively eroded. By 1911 one successful Liberal candidate could declare that the Liberal party had no greater benefit than the hesitating, ambiguous, skilful, philosophic speeches of the leader of the opposition. 'He has been our greatest asset and I hope he will long be so.'[132] More importantly, by the time that Balfour actually resigned, the conviction that his continued presence at the head of the party could only damage its future prospects was gaining ground in almost all sections of Unionism, even among elements previously loyal to the leader. But while dissatisfaction with Balfour grew apace, he himself, hesitant at the thought of again taking office, became increasingly contemptuous of the contending factions over which he had to preside and of the political infighting for which he had no taste. The prospect of giving up his post was always one which Balfour was likely to approach philosophically. As George Wyndham explained: 'He knows that there was once an ice-age and that there will some day be an ice-age again. This makes him indifferent.'[133]

## NOTES

1.    B. E. C. Dugdale, *Arthur James Balfour* (2 vols, London, 1936) vol.ii, p.22; J. Amery, *Joseph Chamberlain* p.800.
2.    Speech at Preston 28 Sept. 1900.
3.    Sir C. Petrie, *Life and Letters of the Rt. Hon. Sir Austen Chamberlain* (2 vols, London, 1939-40) vol.i, p.178.
4.    Chamberlain to E. Goulding 23 Jan. 1906, Wargrave MSS, House of Lords Record Office, A/3/2.
5.    Strachey to Curzon 3 Feb. 1906, Strachey MSS, House of Lords Record Office, S/4/17/3.
6.    Lord Askwith, *Lord James* p.293. Frances Balfour rejoiced at 'the crushing defeat of all Joe's programme and propaganda', while Edward Clarke, elected for the City, noted that 'but for [Chamberlain] we might have been defeated, but we should not have been destroyed': Frances Balfour to R. Cecil 16 Jan.1906, Cecil MSS Add. MS 51158; Clarke to Balfour 20 Jan.1906, Balfour MSS Add. MS 49858.
7.    Akers-Douglas to Sandars 5 Feb. 1906, Sandars MSS c.751/181.
8.    Lord Winterton, *PreWar* (London, 1932) pp.22-3.
9.    Lord Winterton, *Orders of the Day* (London, 1953) pp.16-17.
10.   Ridley to Law 5 Jan.1906, Law MSS 18/2/10.
11.   Ridley to J. Chamberlain 22 Jan.1906, JC 21/2/82.
12.   Petrie, *Long* p. 111.

13. Salisbury to Selborne 16 April 1910, Selborne MSS 6/53. When Joseph Chamberlain assumed the temporary leadership of the party after Balfour lost his parliamentary seat, Salisbury wrote, 'Altogether I deprecate Joe as deputy unless he is first tamed': Salisbury to Balfour 24 Jan.1906, Balfour MSS Add. MS 49758.

14. Bowles to Sandars 11 Nov.1911, Balfour MSS Add. MS 49862.

15. Strachey to Curzon 1 Aug.1911, Curzon MSS, India Office Library, Eur. F112/89.

16. Chamberlain to Balfour 23 Jan.1906, JC 21/2/2.

17. Balfour to Sandars 26 Jan.1906, Sandars MSS c.751/124.

18. Ibid, 20 Jan.1906, Sandars MSS c.751/99.

19. Balfour to Chamberlain 24 Jan.1906, JC 21/2/3.

20. Chamberlain to Balfour 25 Jan.1906, JC 21/2/4.

21. Chamberlain to Colonel G. Denisen 24 Jan.1906, cited Amery, *Joseph Chamberlain* p.792.

22. Chamberlain to Lord Halsbury 5 Feb.1906, Halsbury MSS, British Library, Add. MS 56372.

23. Chamberlain to J. Boraston 26 Jan.1906, cited Amery, *Joseph Chamberlain* pp.806-7.

24. Chamberlain to Long 30 Jan.1906, cited Petrie, *Long* p.110.

25. Chamberlain to Evelyn Cecil 26 Jan.1906, JC 21/2/17.

26. T. J. Spinner jnr., *George Joachim Goschen: the transformation of a Victorian Liberal* (Cambridge, 1973) p.234.

27. Akers-Douglas to Sandars 5 Feb.1906, Sandars MSS c.751/181.

28. Lansdowne to Sandars 22 Jan.1906, ibid c.751/106.

29. Lansdowne to Balfour 28 Jan.1906, cited Lord Newton, *Lord Lansdowne: a Biography* (London, 1929) p.348; Amery, *Joseph Chamberlain* pp.808-9; P. Fraser, 'Unionism and Tariff Reform : the Crisis of 1906', *Historical Journal* 5 (1962), p.157.

30. Sandars to Balfour 26 Jan.1906, Balfour MSS Add. MS 49764.

31. Ibid, 29 Jan.1906, cited Amery, *Joseph Chamberlain* p.798; Fraser, 'Unionism' p.157.

32. Sir A. Fitzroy, *Memoirs* (2 vols, London, 1923) vol.i, p.279.

33. Sandars to Balfour 27 Jan.1906, Balfour MSS Add. MS 49764.

34. Chamberlain to J. L. Garvin 5 Feb.1906, cited Amery, *Joseph Chamberlain* p.815; Chamberlain to Long 5 Feb.1906, cited Petrie, *Long* pp.110-1.

35.  Chamberlain to Mrs. Endicott 30 Jan.1906, cited Amery, *Joseph Chamberlain* p.799.
36.  Chamberlain to Lord Mount Stephen 22 Dec.1905, cited Amery, *Joseph Chamberlain* pp.773-4.
37.  Chamberlain to H. Chaplin 9 Jan.1906, JC 21/2/22.
38.  Chamberlain to A. Deakin 26 April 1906, cited Amery, *Joseph Chamberlain* p.889; Chamberlain to Northcote 29 March 1906, Northcote MSS PRO 30/56; Chamberlain to L. S. Amery 27 March 1906, JC 21/1/12.
39.  Chaplin to Chamberlain 1 Feb.1906, cited Amery, *Joseph Chamberlain* pp.810-1.
40.  Chamberlain to Chaplin 16 Feb. 1906, JC 21/2/33.
41.  Bridgeman diary, review of 1906 parliament.
42.  L. Masterman, *C. F. G. Masterman: a Biography* (London, 1939) p.72.
43.  Amery, *Joseph Chamberlain* p.861.
44.  Cecil to Balfour 25 Jan.1906, Balfour MSS Add. MS 49737. See also Betty Balfour to G. Balfour 17 Jan.1906, Gerald Balfour MSS 263.
45.  Viscount Cecil, *All the Way* (London, 1949) p.102.
46.  H. Cecil to Duke of Devonshire 11 Feb.1906, cited Rempel, *Unionists Divided* p.169.
47.  Amery, *Joseph Chamberlain* p.810.
48.  Petrie, *Long* p.116.
49.  Bridgeman diary 2, 5 and 10 Feb.1906.
50.  B. Balfour to Alice Balfour 4 Feb.1906, cited Judd, *Balfour* p.136; Lord Wolverton to Devonshire 5 Feb.1906, cited Rempel, *Unionists Divided* p.167; Amery, *Joseph Chamberlain* p.813.
51.  R. Pound and G. Harmsworth, *Northcliffe* (London,1959) p.298.
52.  Chamberlain to Halsbury 5 Feb.1906, Halsbury MSS, British Library, Add. MS 56372; Chamberlain to Boraston 3 Feb.1906, cited Fraser, 'Unionism' p.158; Bridgeman diary 3 Feb.1906.
53.  Long to Chamberlain 4 Feb.1906, JC 21/2/60.
54.  Halsbury to Chamberlain 4 Feb.1906, cited Amery, *Joseph Chamberlain* p.818.
55.  *The Times* 5 Feb.1906.
56.  Brodrick to Selborne 9 Feb.1906, Selborne MSS 2/131.
57.  ? to Sandars n.d., Sandars MSS c. 751/75.

58. Lansdowne to Balfour 4 Feb.1906, Balfour MSS Add MS 49729.
59. Balfour to Lansdowne 6 Feb. 1906, cited Newton, *Lansdowne* p.351.
60. Chamberlain to Halsbury 7 Feb.1906, Halsbury MSS Add. MS 56372.
61. G. Balfour to Betty Balfour 8 Feb.1906, Gerald Balfour MSS 118.
62. Chamberlain to Ridley 6 Feb.1906, cited Amery, *Joseph Chamberlain* pp.821-4.
63. Chamberlain to Balfour 25 Jan.1906, cited ibid p.803.
64. Balfour to Chamberlain 8 Feb.1906, cited ibid pp.832-3.
65. Chamberlain to Garvin 5 Feb.1906, cited ibid pp.814-6.
66. Chamberlain to Balfour 10 Feb.1906, JC 21/2/8.
67. Chamberlain to Ridley 10 Feb.1906, cited Amery, *Joseph Chamberlain* p.838.
68. Hood to Balfour 12 Feb.1906, Balfour MSS Add. MS 49771.
69. G. Balfour to Betty Balfour 14 Feb.1906, Gerald Balfour MSS 118; Fraser, 'Unionism' p.163.
70. Ibid.
71. Salisbury to Selborne 25 Feb.1906, Selborne MSS 5/128. Robert Cecil was told that 'those Unionists ... who have especial cause to regret recent events in the Party should be enabled ... to consider their new and difficult position': Bowles to Cecil 16 Feb.1906, Cecil MSS Add. MS 51072.
72. H. Cecil to Devonshire 16 Feb.1906, cited Rempel, *Unionists Divided* p.169.
73. B. Holland, *The Life of Spencer Compton, Eighth Duke of Devonshire* (2 vols, London, 1911) vol.ii, p.398.
74. Balfour to Goschen 15 Feb.1906, cited Spinner, *Goschen* p.235.
75. Chamberlain to Ridley 10 Feb.1906, cited Amery, *Joseph Chamberlain* p.838; Fraser 'Unionism' pp.161,163. Stressing that Balfour had not made fiscal reform 'party orthodoxy', Mr. Fraser argues that 'since the Unionist party had not pronounced on the fiscal issue, there was no question of the free fooders being cast off'. When, however, Hugh Cecil raised the matter at the party meeting, Balfour pointed out that, as leader, he could not be expected to give his blessing to a candidate who refused to accept the fiscal policy he had announced: Bridgeman diary 15 Feb.1906.
76. Hewins, *Apologia* i, 169.
77. Masterman, *Masterman* p.174.

78.   Hewins, *Apologia* i, 169.
79.   Newton, *Lansdowne* p.352.
80.   Bridgeman diary 15 Feb.1906.
81.   Amery, *Joseph Chamberlain* p.851.
82.   Hewins, *Apologia* i, 169.
83.   Ibid, p.167.
84.   See below, pp. 126-130.
85.   Winterton, *Orders* p.15.
86.   Chamberlain to A. Chamberlain 4 May 1906, cited Fraser, 'Unionism'
      p.164.
87.   Balfour to Hope 24 May 1906, Balfour MSS Add. MS 49858; Balfour
      to Betty Balfour 28 June 1906, ibid 49831.
88.   Chamberlain to Chaplin 4 April 1906, JC 21/2/35.
89.   B. Webb, *Our Partnership* (London, 1948) p.345.
90.   Masterman, *Masterman* p.72. R. F. Mackay, *Balfour: Intellectual
      Statesman* (Oxford, 1985) pp.228-9.
91.   Beatrice Chamberlain to Betty Balfour 6 Dec.1906, Gerald Balfour
      MSS 273.
92.   V. Chirol to Curzon 27 Sept.1906, Curzon MSS F112/13; D.J.Dutton,
      'Life Beyond the Political Grave', *History Today* 34 (1984), pp.23-8.
93.   Sandars to W. Short 4 March 1907, Balfour MSS Add. MS 49765.
94.   Balfour to Sandars 19 Nov.1907, Sandars MSS c. 754/125; Betty
      Balfour to G. Balfour n.d., Gerald Balfour MSS 271.
95.   A. Chamberlain to Mary Chamberlain 6 April 1914, AC 4/1/1113.
96.   Sir C. Petrie, *The Chamberlain Tradition* (London, 1938) p.22.
97.   L. S. Amery diary 28 Sept.1906.
98.   A. Chamberlain to Amery 23 Jan.1907, cited J. Barnes and D.
      Nicholson (eds), *The Leo Amery Diaries* (2 vols, London, 1980-88)
      vol.i p.58.
99.   A. M. Gollin, *Proconsul in Politics* (London, 1964) pp.111-4; A. M.
      Gollin, *The Observer and J. L. Garvin* (London,1960) p.18; D.Ayerst,
      *Garvin of the Observer* (London,1985) p.67; Amery, *Political Life* i,
      298-9; V.Chirol to Curzon 27 Sept.1906, Curzon MSS Eur. F112/13.
100.  Collings to J. Chamberlain 3 Aug.1911, JC 22/52.
101.  Barnes and Nicholson (eds), *Amery Diaries* i, 62.
102.  Vincent (ed.), *Crawford Papers* p.79.
103.  Lord Winterton, *PreWar* p.17. Selborne noted: 'Arthur's ideas of

leadership out of the House of Commons are as scanty as his power of leadership in the House is wonderful': M. Egremont, *Balfour* (London, 1980) p.233.

104. R. B. Jones, 'The Conservative Party 1906-11', Oxford B. Litt. (1960), p.11.
105. A. Chamberlain to L. Amery 21 Feb.1907, Amery MSS c.32.
106. Maxse to Law 5 June 1908, Law MSS 18/4/66.
107. H. Arnold-Forster to Law 24 April 1906, ibid 18/2/16.
108. Lord Swinton, *Sixty Years of Power* (London, 1966) p.26.
109. P. Fraser, 'The Unionist Debacle of 1911 and Balfour's Retirement', *Journal of Modern History* 35 (1963), p.355.
110. Sandars to Akers-Douglas 11 Jan.1907, Douglas MSS, Kent County Record Office, c.601.
111. Balfour to Sandars 2 Jan.1907, Sandars MSS c.753/19. Compare this with Arnold-Forster's fear that Balfour might 'return to power before the Tariff question had been thought out and worked out': Diary 20 July 1908, Arnold-Forster MSS, British Library, Add. MS 50353.
112. Sandars to Balfour 22 Jan.1907, Balfour MSS Add. MS 49765; Dugdale, *Balfour* ii, 43.
113. Long to Sandars 7 Nov.1907, Douglas MSS c.346/14.
114. A. Chamberlain to Balfour 24 Oct.1907, Balfour MSS Add. MS 49736.
115. Dugdale, *Balfour* ii, 35-6.
116. Vincent (ed.), *Crawford Papers* p.99.
117. Long to Selborne 25 Nov.1907, Selborne MSS 73/57.
118. Lawrence to Long 22 Dec.1910 and 4 Jan.1911, Long MSS 445/9.
119. P. Williamson (ed.), *The Modernisation of Conservative Politics* (London, 1988) p.30.
120. For a perhaps exaggerated view of Sandars' influence, see Sir C. Petrie, *The Powers behind the Prime Ministers* (London, 1958) esp. p.84.
121. Sandars to Long 16 Oct.1906, Long MSS 947/126.
122. Arnold-Forster to Law 24 April 1906, Law MSS 18/2/16.
123. Vincent (ed.), *Crawford Papers* p.104.
124. Long to Lawrence 7 Jan.1911, Long MSS 445/9.
125. Sandars to Akers-Douglas 7 and 10 Nov. 1907, Douglas MSS c. 478/8,9.

126. Vincent (ed.), *Crawford Papers* p.168.
127. A. Chamberlain to G. Balfour 7 Oct.1906, Gerald Balfour MSS 273.
128. Betty Balfour to G. Balfour 20 and 23 Oct.1907, ibid 271.
129. Ibid 22 Oct.1907.
130. Salisbury to Selborne 3 Oct.1907, Selborne MSS 5/195.
131. ? to Sandars 23 Jan.1907, Sandars MSS c. 753/80. After Chamberlain's death in 1914 Maurice Woods confidently asserted that, had the Birmingham leader's health held out, he would have seen the triumph of his cause in 1909: *Fortnightly Review* 1 Aug.1914.
132. R. Hunt to A. Chamberlain n.d., AC 8/7/16.
133. W. S. Blunt, *My Diaries* (2 vols, London, 1919-20) vol.ii, p.353.

# 4

# POLICY : TARIFF REFORM
## 1906—1909

The general election of 1906 made little difference to the policy preoccupations of the Unionist party in the first years of opposition. Rather unusually for a party of opposition, these preoccupations were largely determined by the agenda of the Unionists themselves rather than by the programme of the incumbent government, and, as had been the case since 1903, the focal point of attention remained the issue of tariff reform. Such a development did not, however, become immediately apparent. Balfour made good use of the first months of uncertainty following Chamberlain's illness to re-impose his own priorities upon the party. In the autumn session of 1906 his parliamentary performance was 'excellent',[1] but the secret of his success lay primarily in his ability to make the government's Education Bill and not the question of tariff reform the main object of Unionist attention. Balfour stressed that he did not want the Unionists to become a party of one idea, 'for if we become a party of one idea we shall fail to carry even that idea to a successful issue'.[2]

The tactic of allowing the parameters of political debate to be set by the Liberal government was one that was less futile than the Unionists' weak position in the House of Commons might imply. At an early stage Balfour determined that the real thrust of Unionist opposition to the new government should come from their control of the upper chamber. As he told Lansdowne, there had never been a period in history in which the House of Lords had been called upon to play a part that was 'so important, so delicate and so difficult'. Believing that the Lords, in selectively amending government legislation, would be acting in a manner not unwelcome to the more moderate members of the Liberal cabinet, Balfour advised that the party should fight all points of importance as stiffly as possible in the Commons, while making the House of Lords the theatre of compromise.[3] Particularly if the government applied the closure mechanism in the lower house, Lansdowne's peers would be waiting to exact their revenge,[4] even though Lansdowne himself seems to have had serious misgivings over the possible implications of the full use of the Lords' powers.[5] Publicly Balfour justified the use of the unelected authority of the upper chamber as imposing caution upon the government's legislative

'adventures'.[6] The Education Bill was the first measure to fall victim to the
opposition's tactics, with Unionists such as Walter Long calculating that
education would not be the sort of issue upon which the government could
safely argue a case for the limitation of the Lords' powers.[7]

In these circumstances the Valentine agreement on tariff reform appeared
to many as something of a dead letter. In late October 1906 Leo Amery found
his fellow tariff reformer, Edward Goulding, 'intensely depressed' by the
belief that Balfour and the Central Office were at heart irrevocably opposed
to the Chamberlainite policy.[8] Strachey later wrote that Balfour had 'crossed
the Rubicon, or shall we say appeared to have crossed the Rubicon or was
generally believed to have crossed it'.[9] But the party leader's tactics could not
indefinitely persuade committed tariff reformers to forget that only a few
months earlier the Valentine compact had appeared to mark the triumph of
their views within the party. Balfour was being wildly optimistic if he thought
that the tariff issue would simply die a natural death. In fact it would, with
intervals of respite and remission, divide and haunt the Unionists for nearly
three decades, becoming for them what Home Rule had been for their Liberal
rivals in the late nineteenth century. Hindsight suggests that this was a question
which the party should have grappled with and resolved at an early date. At
the end of his long political life Leo Amery reflected that it had been a fatal
error of the Unionist leadership to allow the question to be 'again and again
side-tracked and damped down'.[10] As the first general election of 1910
approached, Leo Maxse blamed this evasion of the issue for the fact that the
party had 'drifted into a mess'.[11] Certainly from the beginning of 1907 until
the opening of the constitutional crisis at the end of the decade, tariff reform
was again the foremost issue of internal Unionist politics.

   Yet surprisingly enough for a question that was so hotly contested, the
economic arguments for and against protection were seldom properly thought
out. Lord Lansdowne's confession of ignorance was revealing:

> Then what about the effect of Tariff Reform on the shipping
> industry? And what about the allegation that in order to get five
> or six million, we shall take fifty million from the pockets of
> commoners? ... I imagine that there are rejoinders to all these
> assertions. Would it be desirable for me to put myself into
> communication with Hewins on the subject?[12]

The economic climate of the country at any given moment remained the single
most important determinant of the relative strength of the party's tariff reform

and free trade factions. Many defenders of the *status quo*, even learned ones, showed an alarming readiness to regard free trade as an article of faith, a piece of holy writ, the questioning of which bordered on blasphemy. Correspondingly, some proponents of tariff reform produced arguments that were robust rather than accurate, suggesting that their policies offered an instant panacea for both present and future economic ills. Balfour himself had grave misgivings about lending his name to those crude promises which suggested that tariff reform offered an easy cure for unemployment.[13]

Balfour's first biographer judged that by the end of 1906 internal dissension in the party was 'beginning to perturb the Whips and Party Managers'.[14] Contemporary observers were somewhat more forthright. Curzon felt that the fiscal question had 'driven a spear-point' into the party's heart and, as a result, saw no signs of the Unionists recovering either their own or other people's confidence.[15] Sandars, while warning Balfour that the disquiet in the party was causing a general weakening of his authority throughout the country, predicted a forward move by the tariff reform faction within the next few months.[16] The Chief Whip's view was that there would be a 'serious revolt' unless Balfour showed himself in favour of a cautious and moderate policy of fiscal reform in line with the Valentine letters.[17] Another observer noted that the clouds 'were growing blacker in the fiscal heavens' and predicted a collision before very long.[18] But Hood's hope that the tariff reform faction could be induced to 'go slow' to preserve party unity looked increasingly over-optimistic.[19] The Tariff Reform League had arranged for the appointment of a committee to confer with Austen Chamberlain and Bonar Law on the possibility of repeatedly raising fiscal questions in the House of Commons to keep the issue on the political agenda and of sending an influential deputation to Balfour to urge him to talk more about tariff reform in his speeches.[20] Meanwhile the more extreme tariff reformers such as Leo Maxse had already decided that Balfour was 'utterly discredited - that is the ABC and the XYZ of the political situation'. The party's present plight filled Maxse with dismay and he was even becoming impatient with Highbury, where the attitude seemed to be that nothing needed to be done while Joseph Chamberlain was *hors de combat*.[21]

Enough of these rumblings reached Balfour to induce the leader to make an important speech in Hull on 1 February 1907. This contained a somewhat grudging reiteration of the Valentine policy, together with a warning to the tariff reform extremists of the foolishness of any detailed policy formulation at this stage and of the dangers which would arise from a split in the party's ranks. Reactions to the Hull speech varied enormously. Sir Almeric Fitzroy, Clerk to the Privy Council, recorded that it had not done much to unify the discordant elements in the party. Indeed, confusion and paralysis were invading every branch of its activity and it was 'only in silence that there is safety'.[22] Austen Chamberlain was more sanguine, but wanted to tie Balfour down by committing the party to a fiscal amendment to the Address in the House of Commons.[23] For Chamberlain this was particularly important in view of the forthcoming conference of the Prime Ministers of the self-governing colonies which, he hoped, would afford the opportunity of progress towards commercial union with the colonies on a preferential basis. With the firm backing of his father, Chamberlain was opposed to any watering down of the party's tariff reform commitment.[24] Balfour was opposed to the idea of a fiscal amendment, on grounds which epitomised his whole attitude towards his position as party leader:

> Everything which induces people overtly to proclaim themselves in different camps, everything which drives them into different lobbies, everything which tends to the formation of sharply defined and antagonistic sub-organisms within the greater organism of the Party must, in my opinion, militate against the ultimate triumph of Fiscal reform, as well as against every other policy to which we wish to give effect.[25]

Whatever their fiscal views, the overwhelming majority of the Unionist front bench were, at this stage, still loyal supporters of Balfour, and at the meeting of the shadow cabinet on 12 February Chamberlain found himself in a minority of one in pressing for a fiscal amendment. But the real strength of the tariff reform faction lay on the Unionist benches in the House of Commons, and, with Austen Chamberlain and Bonar Law taking the lead, forty-three carefully chosen tariff reform M.P.s met separately to try to force the hand and change the mind of the shadow cabinet. Chamberlain made little effort to acquaint his followers with Balfour's strong feeling against a fiscal amendment, with the result that when the shadow cabinet met again it was clear that an amendment was going to be moved from the back benches whatever the leadership decided. In the circumstances Balfour had little alternative but to adopt the amendment on behalf of the front bench. It was clear that Chamberlain was determined to pursue his own course, even at the expense of splitting the party.[26]

This particular trial of strength and its outcome did much to convince

Balfour that he could no longer maintain his equivocal stance on the whole question of tariff reform. [27] It did little, however, to help the cause of party unity. Salisbury noted that loyal Balfourites such as Akers-Douglas and Walter Long were in a state of seething indignation at Chamberlain, Law and other tariff reformers, while George Wyndham complained that there was 'nothing magnanimous or generous in the whole show of petty intrigue and sheepish cowardice'. [28]

\* \* \*

A combination of the irritation and mistrust engendered by Balfour's ambiguous leadership and frustration at the lack of progress made by tariff reform in the period immediately after Chamberlain's illness accounts for the emergence of the notorious, yet still rather mysterious, 'Confederacy' - the supreme example of the intolerance and ideological passion with which extreme tariff reformers defended their cause against those within the party who did not share their convictions. [29] Described variously as the 'inquisitorial arm' of the tariff reform movement and as 'a nine days wonder in Edwardian politics ... frankly designed to ... appear more important than it was', the Confederacy's chief significance probably lay less in its efforts to purge the Unionist party of sitting free trade M.P.s and candidates than in its capacity to sustain that atmosphere of mistrust, suspicion and animosity which characterised the party in the first years of opposition. [30] Robert Cecil, a free trader who found himself particularly harassed, noted bitterly that the justification put forward for the Confederacy was the same as for many of the other tariff reform tactics. Tariff reform was all that mattered politically and therefore any political action in its support was justified - 'the familiar defence of every tyranny'. [31] Yet on the other side of the fiscal debate Leo Amery did not remember the Confederacy amounting to much more than 'a few of us getting together from time to time, usually over dinner, as particular constituency problems cropped up'. [32] Even Henry Page Croft, the leading figure within the organisation, conceded that, at their prime, the Confederates numbered only fifty and that their principal successes were due to the fact that no-one knew who they were. All anyone did know was that the six or seven candidates who actually entered the lists against sitting Unionist free traders had the support of the Confederacy. This, apparently, was enough to put fear 'into the hearts of all local Unionist Associations'. [33]

The Confederacy's secrecy was undoubtedly its strongest weapon. No-one was ever completely sure who actually belonged to the organisation. E. G. Brunker, secretary of the Unionist Free Trade Club, discovered that its secretary was Thomas Comyn Platt and that it had come into existence because the advanced tariff reformers were so dissatisfied with Balfour's methods of dealing with the fiscal question.[34] It probably did the Confederacy no harm that Joseph and Austen Chamberlain were frequently listed among its members although there is no evidence that either took any part in its activities.[35] Even Balfour wrote to Austen Chamberlain remonstrating at the behaviour of the Confederates in terms which suggested that Chamberlain was in a position to curb their actions. His supposition was that the Confederates were only an extremist branch of the Tariff Reform League.[36] Both Chamberlain and Ridley, however, denied any connection between the Confederacy and the League. Chamberlain had heard that Leo Maxse was one of the Confederates, but insisted that he had never been able to discover other names or find out whether they had any headquarters or organisation.[37] Maxse himself claimed to be amused when named by the *Contemporary Review* as the organiser of the Confederacy.[38] Much of the confusion appears to have arisen from the fact that the Confederates were only seeking under a veil of rather ominous secrecy to achieve essentially the same ends as the Tariff Reform League. Indeed it seems likely that the original organisation, of which Page Croft and Comyn Platt were the leading lights, was absorbed by the League with the result that the distinction between Confederates and other tariff reform activists had ceased to have much meaning by early 1908.[39] By 1909 Strachey was urging reprisals against the twelve most violent tariff reformers on the assumption that they were Confederates.[40]

While the Confederacy as such may be of limited historical significance, the anxiety at its activities felt by free traders in the Unionist ranks was real enough. Robert Cecil feared that the Confederates had sufficient financial backing to challenge sitting Unionist free trade members in as many as twenty parliamentary seats.[41] Balfour was concerned that their tactics would not only destroy the hopes of tariff reform, but also the Unionists' chances of returning to power, while the party's Prinicipal Agent wrote cautiously of their 'injudicious zeal'.[42] Brunker felt confident that Balfour would not tolerate the Confederates' 'methods of barbarism',[43] but the problem was that the period of their activity coincided with Balfour's own steady movement towards the tariff reform position. This made disciplinary action by the leader increasingly unlikely. Thus, when the Central Office intervened in the North-West Manchester by-election of April 1908 to insist upon the tariff reform credentials of the Unionist candidate, it was widely supposed by free traders that the official leaders of the party had effectively joined the Confederacy.[44] Robert Cecil was quite convinced that the Central Office could have put an end to the activities of the Confederates had it so wished.[45] These developments did not help the efforts of moderate tariff reformers such as Walter Long to persuade their more ardent colleagues to abandon Confederate tactics.[46]

Yet it did not require the activities of the Confederates to ensure that there would be no internal party harmony during the first years of Unionist opposition. Despite Joseph Chamberlain's removal from the political stage, the division between his followers and those of Balfour and, more particularly, the out-and-out free traders, was an enduring one that went beyond any personal differences between the two men. In general, the more advanced the views of the tariff reformer the greater was his propensity to favour a policy of progressive state intervention over a broad range of political matters. This inevitably tended to distance Chamberlainites from the more traditional Tory stance epitomised by the party's landholding interest.[47] Inevitably, then, the years of opposition saw not only a struggle about the adoption of a particular policy, but also one which had the soul and future direction of the Unionist party as its prize. Though Balfour might succeed in keeping the party entrenched in the centre of the political spectrum, it was likely that the representatives of one or other wing - advanced tariff reformers or committed free traders - would find their position increasingly untenable. Walter Long felt that both the extreme wings of the party were deluding themselves - the tariff reformers by blinding themselves to the fact that their doctrines were frightening away many moderate men; the free traders by always blaming the party leadership for what was happening to them at constituency level.[48] But once Balfour's personal stance began to shift in the direction of the tariff reform camp, it was inevitably the free traders who found themselves progressively more uncomfortable within the Unionist coalition.

Certainly the Unionist party's prospects of re-emerging in the foreseeable future as a vigorous and coherent opposition did not look good in 1907. Lord Salisbury believed that the forthcoming Colonial Conference might well make matters worse:

The extreme Tariff Reformers will beat the big drum till we are

deaf. They will probably formulate their proposals to the
Colonial Premiers. We shall hear of nothing but taxes on food.
The Free Traders in the party will become profoundly irritated.
The agricultural labourer and the poor generally will become
gloomily suspicious.[49]

In fact the year would witness a major redefinition of Balfour's attitude
towards tariff reform, but one which left him still in control of the party and
even of the tariff reform movement itself.[50] Under the growing influence of
the arguments of Professor Hewins about the need to increase national
revenue, Balfour indicated a significant advance in his thinking in a speech to
the National Union at the Savoy Hotel on 15 February, an advance which he
confirmed in a better publicised speech at the National Union Conference in
Birmingham at the end of the year. Gradually in the course of 1907 the claws
of all but the most extreme tariff reformers were drawn, as the conviction
grew that Balfour was placing himself at the head of the movement with some
sign of positive enthusiasm.[51] Tariff reform spirits were further raised by the
onset of a mild economic depression which, long predicted, seemed to give
additional weight to protectionist arguments.

This is not to say that the year of Balfour's conversion progressed without
incident. The Colonial Conference stimulated the enthusiasm of the tariff
reformers with its indications that there was a willingness within the
self-governing colonies to support schemes of imperial preference.[52] But in
the House of Commons Balfour was much embarrassed when his front-bench
colleague Alfred Lyttelton proposed a resolution regretting the government's
failure to take up the unanimous invitation of the colonial Prime Ministers to
consider favourably measures of imperial preference. This manoeuvre, for
which the stricken Joseph Chamberlain was in part the inspiration, did less to
discomfort the Liberal government with its immense Commons majority than
to reveal again the latent divisions within the Unionist ranks.[53]

Nonetheless, at Birmingham Balfour handled the issue of tariff reform on
the 'plain, emphatic lines' which Long and others were now recommending.[54]
Balfour claimed that the impossibility of maintaining the country's existing
basis of taxation was becoming so obvious that he did not think he would find
any important section of the party difficult to move in the direction of fiscal
reform.[55] A backbench M.P. commented on the 'electric' effect on the party
of Balfour's conversion, after a year in which the opposition had seemed to
lack method and in which 'generally it was a sort of go-as-you-please style of

warfare'.[56] The impact was soon translated into success at the polls, in the form of an encouraging victory in a by-election in Mid-Devon. Austen Chamberlain was heartened to think that Balfour's great speech had finally shown him to possess the powers needed in a constructive statesman: 'He has made a pronouncement to his party and to the country which will rally us all to his support.' [57] Even Joseph Chamberlain was happy to note that Balfour was now a declared tariff reformer.[58] By the time of a further speech in Devonport in December, Balfour was almost unrecognisable as the same politician from whom the Valentine compromise had been reluctantly extracted less than two years before:

> Fiscal reform ... in a few months will no longer be ... a subject of division ... but will rather be an animating motive, a deep-rooted, patriotic and national conviction which ... is predestined to make the next Unionist Administration memorable in the history of this country.[59]

Thus, by the end of 1907, Balfour had unequivocally identified his party's fortunes with the cause of tariff reform. In this movement he had been encouraged by his closest advisers. Sandars and Hood had become convinced of the necessity for Balfour to consolidate his leadership by conciliating the Chamberlainite faction, and they were pleased that the Birmingham declaration committed the party to a full policy of tariff reform.[60] It was, however, a transformation in which Balfour, by stressing the revenue rather than the imperial aspects of the policy, still held the reins firmly in his own hands.[61] The worsening economic climate encouraged this approach. As Walter Long argued:

> What the people really want is that a policy of Fiscal Reform should be adopted which will give the country freedom to collect the largest amount of revenue as it thinks best with the least discomfort to the community.[62]

Hitherto tariff reformers had laboured under the handicap of having to expound their gospel during a period of comparative prosperity. At that time unemployment had been falling, giving the man in the street little reason to see why there should be a change in the country's fiscal system.

In view of earlier attitudes, the Unionist free traders continued for some while to look to Balfour for protection and support. Balfour's calculated ambiguity together with his family connections with some of the most prominent free traders encouraged this approach. But Balfour had a shrewd appreciation of the balance of power within his party and did little to curb the excesses of the advanced tariff reformers. Central Office had become particularly exasperated by the activities of Austen Chamberlain, who appeared to think 'it his business to dictate the Chief's policy'.[63] Older Conservatives alleged that Chamberlain would be prepared to sacrifice the Church, the Constitution and the Union itself to achieve his fiscal goal.[64] Sandars warned Balfour that prominent Unionists such as Lord Derby and the Duke of Devonshire might even leave politics altogether if the leader did not repudiate Chamberlain's attacks on the Unionist free traders.[65] Balfour's apparent weakness towards Chamberlain had not only caused immense annoyance among Unionist free traders but was also the object of pointed comment among leading Liberals.[66] Long feared that Chamberlain's methods would lose the party many seats, thereby actually postponing the advent of tariff reform. Unless he were stopped, great harm would be done to the party and the country.[67] Long found that he had personal cause to resent Chamberlain's methods when it became clear that the latter was keeping a watchful eye over Long's speaking engagements. Chamberlain was 'rather sorry' to see that Long was going to speak for the free trader, Abel Smith - 'a good fellow and in many ways a good party man ... but ... not a fiscal reformer'. Long complained to Balfour that there were some things that he would only take from his leader. 'I am sure you do not realise how many unpleasant things we have had to put up with at the hands of those who appear to claim a special authority derived from you.'[68] Long became particularly alarmed on learning that Chamberlain intended to take Balfour to see his father. Balfour was 'so good natured and easy-going : he is no match for all these intrigues'.[69] But while Balfour said he could quite understand how Chamberlain's speeches had produced irritation, he did not feel that it was within his power to stop them. Similarly, though he expressed alarm at the attempts of the Tariff Reform League to capture the local party organisations, 'how this is to be prevented I cannot even imagine'.[70]

By the beginning of 1908 Lord Balfour of Burleigh was complaining that the tariff reformers had renewed their claim to exclude any Unionist free trader from the House of Commons. But it was in vain that he looked to the party leader for support and a clear denunciation of the policy of proscription.[71] Balfour insisted that it was not within his power to try to influence the selection of a parliamentary candidate by a local Association. His hope, he stressed, was that if the matter were not pressed too hard, agreement on fiscal policy would ultimately be possible. Yet he recognised that 'this answer embodies a wisdom which does not commend itself to more ardent spirits and they will insist on pressing the question in its logical form'.[72] Hugh Cecil and other free traders were not convinced that Balfour was as impotent as he tended to suggest, and in consequence began to explore the idea of a rapprochement with the Liberals. 'It is putting it very mildly', wrote Cecil, 'that Bob and I are more in agreement and sympathy with Grey than we are with Austen and Bonar Law.'[73]

The difficulty for the free traders was to know what strategy they could pursue with any effect. Many years later Lord Robert Cecil recalled that he had begun to wonder whether he would not be happier in the Liberal camp.[74] Cecil got to the point of enquiring of Asquith whether the Liberals would oppose Unionist free trade candidates in constituencies usually won by the Unionist party, in the event of the sitting member being challenged by a tariff reformer. He thought it better, though, for Unionists not to go on to the same platform as government supporters.[75] Similarly, by the summer of 1907, his brother Hugh had reached the conclusion that the best and perhaps the only chance for Unionist free traders lay in co-operation with moderate Liberals.[76] Dispirited by Balfour's reluctance to help him return to parliament, Lord Hugh asked: 'Can you wonder that I think with longing of the chance of joining Rosebery and Grey?'[77] Probably in an attempt to bring Balfour and the leadership back into line, Robert Cecil revealed to Long that approaches had been made by several Liberals and that these were being seriously considered in some quarters.[78] But the problem was, as Long fully recognised, that it was by no means certain that the advanced tariff reformers wanted compromise and reunion except on terms of complete surrender by the free trade minority.[79] Even Long's argument that Unionist free trade candidates could for the time being be safely tolerated because there was no imminent likelihood of the party's return to power was unceremoniously brushed aside by Bonar Law.[80] By the time that Cecil confided the news of Liberal approaches to Long, negotiations between Lords Cromer and Lansdowne, designed to bring about a reconciliation, had already broken down. Strachey supposed that the tariff reformers were determined to block anything in the way of reconciliation and that the central section of the party around Balfour, though in favour of compromise, was too much afraid of the tariff reformers even to discuss it.[81] The Unionist free traders' bargaining position was an unenviably weak one and in any case after 1908, as Lloyd George's radicalism increasingly took hold of the Liberal party, the latter's attraction for them, whatever their horror of tariff reform, rapidly diminished. Forced to choose between the twin evils of what was rather misleadingly often called 'socialism' and tariff reform, the vast majority of Unionist free traders would unhesitatingly opt for the latter.[82] By the autumn of 1909, for example, Strachey had made up his mind that even free trade might have to be sacrificed in order to get rid of 'this Lloyd George and Winston-ridden Government'.[83]

If accommodation within the Liberal ranks was not for long a serious possibility, a further alternative for frustrated and disillusioned free traders was the creation of a new centre party. With this end in mind, Strachey, Cromer and Hugh Cecil entered negotiations with Lord Rosebery, the former Liberal Prime Minister, whose own position within the Liberal ranks had become increasingly uncomfortable over a long period of time.[84] As the attitude of the Unionist hierarchy hardened against the free traders, men such as Strachey came to think that a centre party was their only chance of salvation, 'though it is a consummation not to be hurried'.[85] As so often, however, the chimera of a new force in British politics rapidly disappeared when its political base was seen to be unviably narrow.

The option for the Unionist free traders of standing their ground within the party and even counter-attacking the onslaughts of the tariff reformers was one which scarcely existed in practice. As the Chief Whip remarked: 'I don't think there is much chance of the Free Fooders running men in opposition to Tariff Reform candidates'.[86] This was particularly the case once Balfour and more especially the Central Office had made significant moves towards the tariff reform side of the fiscal debate. As Hood put it to one prominent free trader:

> surely you do not suggest that where an Association might be loyal to the Member personally but unwilling to support the policy advocated by the Leader and accepted by the Party in the Country, the Central Office should give support to that Association?[87]

He would not use the Central Office to return to parliament a group of men who would either refuse to support, or who would oppose, the chief measure on which a majority had been secured.[88] Central Office reacted quickly to a Unionist free trade plan that the Unionist candidate, Joynson-Hicks, should run against Churchill in a by-election in North-West Manchester by enunciating the view that tariff reform was not an urgent question in the present parliament and might be left on one side until after the next general election. Hood bluntly informed Hicks that if he stood on the proposed basis he would not be recognised nor receive any assistance from headquarters. In such circumstances the plan soon collapsed.[89] By January 1909 the Central Office had even published a blacklist of M.P.s who would be denied official support at the next election because of their failure to endorse the fiscal policy spelt out by Balfour in Birmingham in 1907.[90]

Even had the free traders had the capacity to strike back against Confederate and Tariff Reform League attacks, many would have been hampered in doing so by a residual loyalty to the party leader. Balfour's steady drift towards the tariff reform camp made such an attitude unrealistic. By the end of 1907, A.R.D. Elliot realised that if for all practical purposes Balfour was to lead the protectionists, free traders would have to fight him too.[91] Elliot confessed that he could now see little practical difference between Balfour and Austen Chamberlain:

> and I am tired of all this talk of Balfour as 'our leader'. He is
> certainly not mine on what he calls the chief constructive policy
> of the coming government.[92]

Continued loyalty to Balfour was no longer compatible with effective action by the Unionist free traders to protect their position. Strachey argued that Balfour would have to be shown that the free traders could fight back and proposed that they should run third candidates in selected constituencies, unless the official Unionist candidate was prepared to pledge himself to take no steps in relation to tariff reform until a Royal Commission had been appointed to consider the whole question of free trade, preference and protection.[93] But this strategy was essentially one of bluff. Its aim was to frighten the Unionist party away from the position of the extreme tariff reformers.[94] If their bluff was called, however, the free traders would not have had the resources or the machinery to make their threats effective, even though attempts to improve organisation and raise a fund were made early in 1908.[95]

The position of the free traders became no easier in the course of 1908 as the continued worsening of the economic situation appeared to confirm the earlier warnings of Chamberlain and his disciples. With some justice Lansdowne told the annual meeting of the Liberal Unionist Council in November that 'we shall be driven to it [tariff reform] by the exigencies of the financial situation'.[96] In an atmosphere of declining trade and mounting unemployment the buoyancy of the tariff reformers was confirmed by the news

that the government was in an 'awful mess' and at its 'wits end' over the
national finances for the following year.[97] By June unemployment stood at
7.9%, and as the summer progressed the position deteriorated still further, so
that the monthly average for the year as a whole was worse than for any year
since the depression of the mid-1880s.[98] Marked electoral advantage for the
Unionists soon became obvious. The party won by-elections in South
Hereford, Peckham, Manchester, Pudsey, Haggerston and
Newcastle-upon-Tyne, and only narrowly failed to see the prominent tariff
reformer, Leo Amery, returned for Wolverhampton. Sandars noted that the
tariff question was making rapid strides in the country and that the party as a
whole was becoming daily more enthusiastic on the subject despite the
opposition of what he called 'the Cecilian cousinhood'.[99] Austen Chamberlain
felt able to reassure his father that every day that passed gave him increasing
confidence of the early success of his cause, while even in traditionally
free-trade Lancashire the local Unionist leadership was coming out firmly in
favour of tariff reform.[100] With a little tact and forbearance on the part of
the tariff reformers, thought an opposition whip, even the most intractable of
free traders would come to support a general tariff.[101]

The growing problems faced by Unionist free traders are well illustrated
in the experience of three figures - Hugh and Robert Cecil and G.F.Bowles.
Lord Hugh Cecil had lost his parliamentary seat in the 1906 landslide, but it
is clear that pressure from the tariff reform camp was instrumental in delaying
his return to the House of Commons. Bonar Law, speaking on behalf of the
Tariff Reform League, told Robert Cecil quite frankly that the League would
rather lose twenty seats than allow his brother to be returned.[102] Even the
Chief Whip thought it best not to have Lord Hugh inside the Commons for the
time being, since his presence there would act as a rallying point for free trade
discontent, while the Confederacy was active in trying to prevent his candidacy
for Oxford.[103]

Although Robert Cecil was entrenched as the sitting member for
Marylebone, his position was hardly less difficult than that of his brother.
During 1907 Cecil became the object of a concerted campaign by the Tariff
Reform League to oust him from his constituency. He narrowly survived a
meeting of his local association, only to find that a tariff reform candidate had
been started against him, a development which was likely to result in splitting
the Unionist vote. 'Am I expected', Cecil enquired, 'to devote my best
energies to the success of the Party in Parliament and at the Poll and as a

reward to be opposed by another Unionist candidate at the next Election?'[104] Faced with a three line whip enjoining him to support an unequivocal tariff reform amendment in the Commons, Cecil warned his cousin, Balfour, that his position was becoming increasingly untenable.[105] But the party leader had by now resolved to enter into no further correspondence with the Cecil brothers on the question of fiscal reform. On this particular issue they had either 'completely lost their heads or ... they want to find an excuse for leaving the party and joining themselves to some fresh political organisation'.[106] He was not moved by Lord Selborne's urging that Cecil should be allowed greater tolerance and latitude than his case intrinsically merited.[107] From his sick-bed Joseph Chamberlain also brushed aside any suggestion that special allowance should be made for the Cecils in view of the services rendered to the party by their father, the late Lord Salisbury.[108] In the circumstances, Lord Robert concluded that Balfour's attitude could only result in the 'political annihilation' of the Unionist free traders.[109] By March 1909 Cecil was again being pressed by his local party chairman for an assurance that his fiscal views were compatible with those of Balfour.[110] Garvin wanted Cecil to agree not to stand again if he felt unable to support a future tariff reform budget,while the Chamberlains were clearly ready to provide financial backing for a protectionist candidate to oppose Cecil.[111]

Similar constituency difficulties faced Bowles in Norwood. In December 1907 the Chief Whip told Bowles that a great change had come over the party since the Colonial Conference and that he could no longer expect backing from the Central Office. The general situation, thought Bowles, was 'rapidly reaching a point of absurdity'. In fact he was formally repudiated by a meeting of his local party association in April 1908.[112] By the beginning of 1909 it was clear that Bowles, still maintaining his opposition to a preferential tariff and unwilling to accept the terms of the Tariff Reform League, would not be able to stand as the party's official candidate at the next general election.[113] Under pressure from Robert Cecil and Balfour, somewhat half-hearted negotiations continued into the late summer of 1909 to try to devise a 'formula of appeasement', but to no avail.[114] In these circumstances both Cecil and Bowles accepted invitations to abandon their own constituencies and stand for Blackburn as Unionist free traders. This they duly did, only to be rejected by the electorate.[115]

The actions taken against Bowles and the Cecils were part of a determined push made by the protectionist faction in 1909 to bring the whole party into line on tariff reform, on the basis of Balfour's Birmingham speech of November 1907. This assault was signalled by an article in the January issue of the *National Review* and a list of 'blacked' M.P.s published in the *Morning Post* on 18 January with, it was claimed, the sanction of the Chief Agent.[116] The Confederates vowed to set up tariff reform candidates against these M.P.s at the earliest possible opportunity. As Austen Chamberlain argued:

> When we come into Office, we have a very difficult task before
> us ... The one danger which I think we must guard against is
> a majority containing sufficient Members hostile to us on the
> Fiscal question to destroy our policy in that matter and so to
> destroy, as they would do, the Unionist Party and its whole
> policy for a generation at least. [117]

Though Strachey attempted to retaliate on behalf of the Unionist free traders through the pages of the *Spectator*, the cause was a forlorn one.[118] The campaign against the free traders appeared to be almost entirely successful, with only Hugh Cecil, unopposed following the intervention of Lord Milner, being returned to parliament in January 1910. Even he was by then a passive free trader whose chief political interests were rapidly moving in other directions.[119]

More generally, the political winds were now producing new issues which appeared, at least for the time being, to marginalise the internecine struggle over tariff reform which had, for so long, scarred the body politic of the Unionist party. As Lord Cromer remarked:

> The more I see of the political situation, the more I am inclined
> to think that Free Trade versus Protection is falling into the
> background, and that the real fight before long will be Socialist
> versus anti-Socialist. [120]

The vast majority of free traders were, like Cromer, ready to retreat back into the party fold to prepare to fight the grave dangers posed before them by a Liberal government whose policies seemed to be becoming increasingly radical. As Strachey argued: 'nothing will ever persuade me that predatory socialism plus demagogy of the most reckless and unscrupulous description are not worse than tariff reform'.[121]

In such circumstances the tariff reformers had little difficulty in consolidating their hold over the party. In February 1909 Austen Chamberlain attended a meeting of the shadow cabinet,

> prepared for a fight and for another of those long uphill collar

strains by which our Tariff Reform van has been pulled along. Not a bit of it! ... Wyndham pressed manfully for a tariff reform amendment and hey presto! the thing was done! [122]
Now the tariff reformers looked forward confidently to an election, and were even meeting together weekly to thrash out the details of a protectionist budget. [123] On 8 October Joseph Chamberlain wrote to Garvin: 'I do not fear the result ... I am certain that if we play rightly and with plenty of "go" and ardour we shall win!' [124] Assuming victory, Sandars insisted that Balfour would at once formulate his tariff reform proposals, submit them to parliament and press them to enactment with all the parliamentary strength he could muster. He would not wait for another Colonial Conference, but would drive ahead and stake his political future and that of his followers on the issue. [125] But what some had already sensed as the changing ground of political debate now intervened, to transform the whole political situation, as the government's ill-fated Finance Bill of 1909 moved haltingly along the parliamentary course that would make it famous in constitutional history.

## NOTES

1.  Bridgeman diary, review of 1906.
2.  Balfour to Sandars 24 Jan.1907, cited Dugdale, *Balfour* ii, 45.
3.  Balfour to Lansdowne 13 April 1906, Balfour MSS Add. MS 49729.
4.  On Lansdowne's tactics see Fitzroy, *Memoirs* i, 327.
5.  Fitzroy, *Memoirs* i, 310. Over the Education Bill Balfour opposed any concessions by the upper house: A. Chamberlain to M. Chamberlain 27 Nov. 1906, AC 4/1/121. One Unionist peer described the Lords' veto of the Education Bill as a 'ridiculous exhibition of [a] majority consisting of ignoramuses': Lord Newton diary 30 Oct.1906, cited D. Southern, 'Lord Newton, the Conservative Peers and the Parliament Act of 1911', *English Historical Review* 96 (1981), p.835.
6.  Speech in Manchester 22 Oct.1906, *The Times* 23 Oct.1906.
7.  Memorandum by Long 9 July 1906, Balfour MSS Add. MS 49776.
8.  Amery diary 26 Oct. 1906.
9.  Strachey to H. Cecil 19 Nov.1906, Strachey MSS S/4/3/9.
10. Amery, *Political Life* i, 330.

11. Gollin, *Observer* p.114.
12. Lansdowne to Sandars 9 Dec.1909, Balfour MSS Add. MS 49730.
13. B. Webb, *Our Partnership* p.436.
14. Dugdale, *Balfour* ii, 41.
15. Curzon to Selborne 30 Jan.1907, Selborne MSS 10/147.
16. Sandars to Balfour 22 Jan.1907, Balfour MSS Add. MS 49765.
17. Hood to Short 14 Jan.1907, ibid 49771.
18. Short to Sandars 19 Jan.1907, Sandars MSS c.753/75.
19. Hood to Sandars 9 Jan.1907, ibid c.753/33.
20. Petrie, *Austen Chamberlain* i, 202-3.
21. Maxse to Law 2 Jan.1907, Law MSS 18/3/28. A. Sykes, 'The Confederacy and the Purge of the Unionist Free Traders 1906-1910', *Historical Journal* 18 (1975), p.352. On the dissatisfaction of advanced tariff reformers with Austen Chamberlain, see also Garvin to Amery 13 June 1907, Amery MSS c.32.
22. Fitzroy, *Memoirs* i, 312.
23. Chamberlain to Balfour 4 Feb.1907, Balfour MSS Add. MS 49780.
24. Chamberlain to Hewins 17 Jan.1907, Hewins MSS, University of Sheffield Library, 50/92.
25. Balfour to Chamberlain 9 Feb.1907, Balfour MSS Add. MS 49780.
26. Chamberlain to Ridley 16 Jan.1907, cited Petrie, *Austen Chamberlain* i, 203-4.
27. A. Sykes, *Tariff Reform in British Politics 1903-13* (Oxford, 1979) pp.125-9; A. Chamberlain to M. Chamberlain 13 Feb.1907, AC 4/1/137; 'The Fiscal Question in February 1907', Balfour MSS Add. MS 49780.
28. Salisbury to Selborne 2 March 1907, Selborne MSS 5/146; Mackail and Wyndham, *Wyndham* ii, 567.
29. Sykes, 'Confederacy' pp.349-66.
30. Blewett, 'Free Fooders' pp.117-8; W. D. Rubinstein, 'Henry Page Croft and the National Party 1917-22', *Journal of Contemporary History* 9 (1974), p.130. Lord Winterton, an avowed member of the Confederacy, later asserted that 'it did good': Winterton, *Orders* p.66.
31. Cecil, *All the Way* p.107.
32. Amery, *Political Life* i, 273-4. Amery's diary account for January 1909 is even more dismissive : 'Dined with the Confederates, at this moment a very notorious body. First time since an inaugural dinner ...

two or three years ago. Had not bothered about them as I did not like the rather silly and theatrical ways of Comyn Platt, the secretary.'

33. Croft, *Life of Strife* p.43.
34. Brunker to R. Cecil 9 Jan.1908, Cecil MSS Add. MS 51072.
35. This is not to say, however, that they were not broadly sympathetic towards its aims.
36. Balfour to A. Chamberlain 23 Oct.1907, AC 17/3/19.
37. A. Chamberlain to Balfour 24 Oct.1907, AC 17/3/20; Ridley to Balfour 1 Nov.1907, Balfour MSS Add. MS 49859.
38. Rubinstein, 'Page Croft' p.130.
39. Sykes, 'Confederacy' p.358. See also E. T. Broadhurst to R. Cecil 21 April 1908, Cecil MSS Add. MS 51158 : 'the Tariff Reform League - Confederacy or whatever you call them ....'
40. Strachey to R. Cecil 3 Feb. 1909, Strachey MSS S/4/4/2.
41. Cecil to Long 14 Jan.1908, Long MSS 444.
42. Balfour to A. Chamberlain 23 Oct.1907, AC 17/3/19; Hughes to Sandars 29 Oct.1907, Sandars MSS c.754/30.
43. Brunker to R. Cecil 6 Jan.1908, Cecil MSS Add. MS 51072.
44. Broadhurst to Strachey 4 March 1908, ibid 51158.
45. Cecil to Hood 14 Nov. 1908, ibid 51158.
46. See correspondence in Long MSS 444.
47. Sykes, *Tariff Reform*, esp. chapters 6 and 9; Blewett, 'Free Fooders' pp.98-102.
48. Long to P. Magnus 14 Dec.1907, Long MSS 444.
49. Salisbury to Milner 5 Feb.1907, Salisbury MSS S(4) 60/64.
50. Sykes has written of a 'Balfourite capture of tariff reform as much as a tariff reform capture of Balfour': Sykes, *Tariff Reform* p.144. See also W. Runciman to W. Churchill 13 Dec.1907, cited R. S. Churchill, *Winston S. Churchill* vol.2, companion pt.2 (London, 1969) p.720 : 'The Tariff Reformers set out to capture Arthur Balfour but he evades these simple creatures.'
51. Among those not fully satisfied with Balfour's new credentials were Leo Maxse and Jesse Collings: Maxse to Law 5 June 1908, Law MSS 18/4/66; Collings to J. Chamberlain 8 Nov.1908, JC 22/44.
52. J. Chamberlain to Northcote 24 May 1907, Northcote MSS PRO 30/56.
53. J. Chamberlain to Halsbury 12 May 1907, Halsbury MSS Add. MS

56372; P. Rowland, *The Last Liberal Governments* (2 vols, London, 1968-71) vol.1, p.119.

54.  Long to Balfour 31 Oct.1907, Balfour MSS Add. MS 49776.

55.  Balfour to A. Chamberlain 23 Oct.1907, AC 17/3/19.

56.  Bridgeman diary, review of 1907.

57.  Speech in Birmingham 15 Nov.1907, *National Union Gleanings* Dec.1907.

58.  Chamberlain to Northcote 24 Dec.1907, Northcote MSS PRO 30/56.

59.  *Gleanings* Jan.1908.

60.  Hood to Short 14 Jan.1907, Balfour MSS Add. MS 49771; Sandars to Balfour 17 Nov.1907, ibid 49765.

61.  Sykes, *Tariff Reform* pp.132-44.

62.  Long to Selborne 25 Nov.1907, Selborne MSS 73/57.

63.  Hood to Sandars 1 Feb.1907, Sandars MSS c.753/97.

64.  Vincent (ed.), *Crawford Papers* p.102.

65.  Sandars to Balfour 2 April 1907, Balfour MSS Add. MS 49765.

66.  Long to Sandars 10 Nov.1907, Sandars MSS c.754/109.

67.  Ibid 23 Nov.1907, c. 754/149.

68.  Petrie, *Long* pp.129-30.

69.  Chilston, *Chief Whip* p.339.

70.  Balfour to Sandars 5 April 1907, Balfour MSS Add. MS 49765.

71.  Lady F. Balfour, *A Memoir of Lord Balfour of Burleigh* (London, 1924) pp.130-1; Balfour of Burleigh to Long 18 Dec.1907, Long MSS 444.

72.  Balfour to Long 9 Jan.1908, Long MSS 444.

73.  H. Cecil to Lord Desborough 12 April 1909, Balfour MSS Add. MS 49860.

74.  Cecil, *All the Way* p.111.

75.  Cecil to Balfour of Burleigh 8 Feb. and 11 Feb.1909, Balfour of Burleigh MSS 13, 20.

76.  H. Cecil to Curzon 2 Aug.1907, Curzon MSS Eur. F 112/14.

77.  H. Cecil to Long 12 June 1907, Long MSS 444.

78.  R. Cecil to Long 24 Feb.1908, Cecil MSS Add. MS 51072.

79.  Long to Balfour 29 July 1907, Balfour MSS Add. MS 49776. Nor was the attitude of the free traders conducive to compromise. Selborne complained about their adoption of the 'extreme dogmatic attitude of the Cobden club': Selborne to Salisbury 23 May 1907, Salisbury MSS

S (4) 60/125.
80. Memorandum by Long 1 Dec.1907, Law MSS 18/3/49; Law to Long 3 Dec.1907, ibid 18/8/5.
81. Strachey to Hicks 3 Feb.1908, Strachey MSS S/16/2/8.
82. Strachey to R. Cecil 3 Feb.1909, Cecil MSS Add.MS 51159.
83. Strachey to H. Cecil 30 Oct.1909, Strachey MSS S/4/3/16.
84. Strachey to R. Cecil 5 March 1908, ibid S/4/4/1; Sykes, *Tariff Reform* chapter 7.
85. Strachey to Broadhurst 5 March 1908, ibid S/16/2/22.
86. Hood to Sandars 11 Jan.1908, Balfour MSS Add. MS 49771.
87. Hood to Bowles 30.Dec.1907, Cecil MSS Add. MS 51072.
88. Hood to Sandars 11 Jan.1908, Balfour MSS Add. MS 49771.
89. R. Cecil to Long 8 March 1908, Long MSS 444; Broadhurst to R. Cecil 14 April 1908, Cecil MSS Add. MS 51158.
90. Clarke, *Lancashire* p.288; Blewett, 'Free Fooders' p.113.
91. Elliot to Strachey 27 Nov.1907, Strachey MSS S/16/1/20.
92. Elliot to Strachey 15 and 19 Jan.1908, ibid S/16/2/4.
93. Strachey to Elliot 28 Nov.1907 and 18 Jan.1908, ibid S/16/1/21 and S/16/2/4.
94. Strachey to Balfour of Burleigh 14 Jan.1908, ibid S/2/5/8.
95. Clarke, *Lancashire* p.285.
96. *The Times* 21 Nov.1908.
97. Chamberlain, *Politics from Inside* pp.126-7.
98. N. Blewett, *The Peers, the Parties and the People: the General Elections of 1910* (London, 1972) p.50.
99. Sandars to Miss Balfour 20 March 1908, Balfour MSS Add. MS 49832.
100. Chamberlain, *Politics from Inside* p.129; Clarke, *Lancashire* p.274.
101. Vincent (ed.), *Crawford Papers* p.119.
102. R. Cecil to Magnus (draft) 18 Dec.1907, Cecil MSS Add. MS 51158.
103. Hood to Sandars 16 Dec.1907, Sandars MSS c.754/280; Amery diary 7 May 1909.
104. R. Cecil to Long 31 Jan.1908, Long MSS 444.
105. R. Cecil to Balfour 4 March 1908, Balfour MSS Add. MS 49737.
106. Balfour to Selborne 6 March 1908, Selborne MSS 1/68.
107. Selborne to Balfour 16 April 1908, ibid 1/82.
108. Chamberlain to Goulding 21 June 1909, Wargrave MSS A/3/2.

109.  R. Cecil to Long 18 April 1908, Long MSS 444.
110.  Ludlow to Cecil 30 March 1909, Cecil MSS Add. MS 51159.
111.  Garvin to Northcliffe 20 July 1909, ibid; J. Chamberlain to Goulding 27 July 1909, Wargrave MSS A/3/2.
112.  Bowles to Cecil 13 and 28 Dec. 1907, Cecil MSS Add. MS 51072.
113.  S. Hunt to Balfour 10 Feb.1909, Balfour MSS Add. MS 49860; Goulding to Law 30 Jan.1909, Law MSS 18/5/88.
114.  R. Cecil to Balfour 21 Aug.1909 and Sandars to R. Cecil 23 Sept.1909, Cecil MSS Add. MS 51071.
115.  P. Clarke, 'British politics and Blackburn politics, 1900-1910', Historical Journal 12 (1969), pp.319-23.
116.  Rempel, Unionists Divided p.187.
117.  Petrie, Long p.131.
118.  Gollin, Observer p.98.
119.  R. Rempel, 'Lord Hugh Cecil's Parliamentary Career 1900-14: Promise Unfulfilled', Journal of British Studies 11 (1972), p.127. See also A. Mejia, 'Lord Hugh Cecil: Religion and Liberty' in J. A. Thompson and A. Mejia (eds), Edwardian Conservatism: Five Studies in Adaptation (Beckenham, 1988) pp.11-37.
120.  Cromer to R. Cecil 28 May 1909, Cecil MSS Add. MS 51072.
121.  Strachey to H. Cecil 30 Oct.1909, Strachey MSS S/4/3/16.
122.  Chamberlain, Politics from Inside pp.144-5; Fitzroy, Memoirs i, 375.
123.  Amery diary 7 May 1909.
124.  Gollin, Observer p.123.
125.  Sandars to Amery 21 Nov.1909, Amery MSS c.34.

. 5 .

# POLICY : THE CONSTITUTION
# 1906-1911

Conservatives profess a devotion to the British constitution and the concept of parliamentary government. Writing in 1912 Lord Hugh Cecil argued that:

> so ancient and so splendid a fabric must be reverently touched even by restorers' hands and it would ill become those who, under the protection of the Constitution, have long enjoyed liberty and far pursued civilisation, to spoil that to which they owe so much by careless, impatient or even unnecessary change.[1]

Throughout the years of opposition after 1906, however, the Unionist party came close to breaching and at times almost certainly did breach accepted conventions of constitutional propriety. The problem grew out of the frustration of impotence engendered by the party's overwhelming defeat in the general election of 1906. The Liberals' landslide victory did nothing, of course, to alter the Unionists' built-in domination of the hereditary House of Lords. It thereby brought into focus a debate about the constitution which had not been fully resolved by the time that the outbreak of the First World War pushed consideration of almost all issues of purely domestic concern to one side.

It was with the Unionists' strength in the upper chamber in mind that Arthur Balfour made the cavalier pronouncement in the immediate wake of electoral defeat that his party 'should still control, whether in power or opposition, the destinies of this great Empire'.[2] Yet only to a limited extent was this proposition fulfilled in the first years of the Liberal government. Though no serious challenge was made to the powers of the Unionist dominated House of Lords, these powers were used with some discretion by the party hierarchy. The Unionists were extremely circumspect in their selection of those government bills which the Lords should amend or reject, and showed in this instance an uncharacteristic understanding of the likely popular reaction to proposed legislation. As Dr. Ramsden has noted, 'legislation that was of prime interest to Labour was passed with little opposition while Bills that appealed only to Liberals and Irish Nationalists were remorselessly opposed in the Commons and mutilated in the Lords'.[3] As a result, while the Liberals' Education and Plural Voting Bills were wrecked, the Trades Disputes Act of 1906, which had the overwhelming backing of the Trade Union movement, was allowed to pass on to the statute book with little resistance.

Notwithstanding these signs of judicious moderation, by 1908 Lord Salisbury judged that 'the Lords seem to be masters of the situation'. He was confident that if the Unionist peers continued to use their powers with discretion - 'as in Lansdowne's hands is certain' - they had nothing to fear.[4] In contrast to his own better known and more belligerent public pronouncement, Balfour had proposed to Lansdowne a reasonable and considered line of action for the upper chamber:

> I conjecture that the Government methods of carrying on their legislative work will be this: they will bring in Bills in a much more extreme form than the moderate members of the Cabinet probably approve : the moderate members will trust to the House of Lords cutting out or modifying the most outrageous provisions : the left wing of the Cabinet ... will be consoled for the anticipated mutilation of their measures by the reflection that they will be able to appeal at the next election for a mandate to modify its constitutions. The scheme is an ingenious one, and it will be our business to defeat it as far as we can. I do not think the House of Lords will be able to escape the duty of making serious modifications in important Government measures, but, if this is done with caution and tact, I do not believe that they will do themselves any harm.[5]

By the end of 1908, however, there were signs that this delicate balance between the effective use of the Lords' powers and a straightforward abuse of their constitutional position likely to furnish the government with a compelling electoral cry was beginning to collapse. The Liberals had attempted little important legislation in 1907. But in the struggle over the Licensing Bill of 1908 it became clear that the Unionist peers were split over the policy which the party should adopt. At the annual conference of the Conservative and Constitutional Associations held in Cardiff in November, delegates received printed cards warning that if Lansdowne allowed the bill to become law thousands of Unionists would never again vote for the party. A few days later Lord Milner wrote to Lansdowne of his great fear that the outright rejection of the bill would act as a check to the mounting tide of anti-government feeling in the country.[6] Thus when the Unionist peers decided on rejection, one observer concluded that Lansdowne had 'capitulated to the thinly veiled threat of a Tory revolt'.[7]

By the time, therefore, that Lloyd George introduced his famous budget of 1909, which brought the whole question of the powers of the House of Lords to a head, there were signs that the policy of discreet caution favoured by Balfour was giving way to the pressure of more extreme opinion. Few anticipated that the 1909 Finance Bill would occasion a political and constitutional crisis of the first magnitude. Jesse Collings, among the most experienced of contemporary parliamentarians, did not think that the budget would contain anything which might oblige the Lords to throw it out since this would compel a dissolution of parliament which he felt that the Liberals themselves feared. He expected that Lloyd George would 'fall back on borrowing and the sinking fund'.[8] After extensive debate in cabinet Lloyd George presented his proposals. He wanted to raise income tax and subject incomes of over £5,000 *per annum* to a supertax. Additional death duties sought to raise £4.8 million and stamp duty £1.25 million. There would also be additional duties of £1.8 million from spirits and £2 million from tobacco, new land taxes and a £2.25 million rise in the cost of liquor licences paid by publicans and brewers. The general consensus of recent historiography is that the Chancellor had no devious plan in introducing his budget to goad the Unionist peers into rejection and thus towards constitutional and electoral suicide.[9] Lloyd George, granted the anticipated budget deficit of £16-17 million, had no alternative but to introduce some startling measures. Such a conclusion is supported by the evidence of the Unionists' initial reactions to Lloyd George's fiscal proposals. It is true that *The Times* complained that 'the doctrine of social ransom [had] never been carried quite so far'.[10] But Austen Chamberlain, who as the party's last Chancellor had the task of leading the parliamentary opposition to the bill, responded far more moderately. It was, he conceded, 'certainly a "great" budget'.[11] Not until 3 May, when Balfour opened a debate on the budget resolutions, was there much evidence that the Unionist hierarchy might become at all vehement in its opposition. A Budget Protest League was formed at the end of June under the presidency of Walter Long. Even so, Lansdowne could still assure the National Union of Conservative and Constitutional Associations on 16 July that the Lords would do their duty and accept the budget, although not 'without wincing'.[12]

As far as the internal dynamics of the Unionist party were concerned, Lloyd George's budget encouraged the tariff reform wing to revamp their policies as a revenue raising alternative to the 'confiscatory socialism' now proposed by the Chancellor. If Lloyd George was able by means of ordinary taxation to raise the revenue needed for both social reforms, such as the recently introduced old-age pensions, and the expanded programme of naval construction, then one of the most powerful arguments in favour of tariff reform would have been decisively refuted.[13] As Lansdowne was later to explain: 'We opposed the Budget on its own account and we opposed it because we don't want the country switched off Tariff Reform and switched on to another policy which we believe to be suicidal.'[14] The budget was also a challenge to the cause of tariff reform in that it reflected the Liberals' long-standing cry that, by necessitating a tax on the people's food, protection was an essentially unfair device which now compared unfavourably with Lloyd George's more 'democratic' proposals.[15] Looked at from the other point of view, the budget could be held to vindicate tariff reform predictions of the collapse of free trade economics - and the substitution of socialism - under the double burden of trying to finance both social reform and imperial defence. As it was, Unionists had little on offer with which to counter Lloyd George's budget strategy apart from tariff reform - a fact which served to rally many previously sceptical free traders to the tariff reform cause. Many tariff reformers rapidly concluded that attack was the best means of defence and began to argue for the outright rejection of the Finance Bill. If the budget could be presented in its most lurid colours, their own cherished dogma would rekindle the enthusiasm of the converted while winning the allegiance of many of those who had hitherto wavered. The budget would have to be represented not as an attack on wealth but as an attack on wages, employment and trade, which the creation of wealth ensured. Thus the fiscal debate could be fought out in much clearer terms that at any time since the argument had begun.

On 27 July Balfour publicly endorsed tariff reform and challenged the government to fight an election on the rival merits of the fiscal policies of the two parties. In this way the external stimulus of the Liberals' budget provided Unionists with a coherence and unity over policy greater than three years of political in-fighting had managed to achieve.[16] Yet it is difficult to escape the conclusion that this unity was one of tactics rather than conviction. As the Unionist free traders were unable to suggest alternative sources of revenue, most of those who still remained found themselves compelled to trim, accept the lesser of two evils, and close ranks behind their tariff reform colleagues.[17] Typical among them was Lord Cromer, who reasoned that to support the budget simply because it rejected the philosophy of tariff reform was ultimately an untenable argument. Cromer posed the central question with impeccable logic and gave the only feasible answer:

> Are we ... to do what we consider an unwise thing and give a vote which will certainly injure Free Trade or ... are we to sever ourselves definitely from the Unionists and support a Government which is distinctly Socialist and violently hostile to the House of Lords? In spite of Free Trade and in spite of what I consider the unwisdom of the policy, I really do not think that I can adopt the latter alternative.[18]

The origin of the decision to defy a constitutional precedent of three centuries' standing and allow the Lords to reject the government's Finance Bill is clearly a matter of some importance. As Mrs. Dugdale concluded half a century ago, there is no firm evidence that the policy of rejection was forced upon the party leaders against their will.[19] The Budget Protest League appeared to show that rank and file Unionists were ready for a fight, while the leadership was not prepared to squander the party's new-found unity over tariff reform. Balfour, on his own understanding of the situation, appears to have concluded that he would do more damage to the party by allowing the bill to pass than by employing the Lords to reject it.[20] To refocus the central issue of the fiscal debate along the lines of tariff reform against 'socialism', rather than tariff reform against free trade, offered self-evident advantages to a leader who saw his primary aim in political life as the maintenance of party unity.[21] Asquith had himself conceded that 'if it could not be proved that Social reform ... can be financed on Free Trade lines, a return to Protection is a moral certainty'.[22] But the danger from Balfour's point of view was that party unity was being achieved on the terms of his erstwhile critics and that by abandoning the political centre ground, which he had championed since the fiscal debate began in 1903, he might not only deliver his party into the hands of extremists but also make the continuation of his own leadership untenable. The decision then, however difficult, was Balfour's own, though the support of the incapacitated but still influential Joseph Chamberlain for the policy of rejection was certainly significant. Indeed Chamberlain espoused this policy long before the party as a whole became committed to it.[23]

Since the case for tariff reform could only be given its chance if the

Finance Bill was stopped in its tracks, Unionist leaders moved inexorably, as the summer of 1909 progressed, towards rejection by the House of Lords. Some spurious justification for the use of the Lords' veto came from an unexpected quarter when the former Liberal Prime Minister, Lord Rosebery, pronounced that the budget was 'essentially and exclusively socialistic, and calculated to bleed the House of Lords to death without replacing it'.[24] With something short of total conviction, Unionists became advocates of a form of plebiscitary democracy, with their legal spokesman, Sir Robert Finlay, arguing that the one great function of the upper chamber was 'to secure that no new departure of capital importance is made until the country ... has been consulted'.[25] In similar vein the *Daily Mail* commented that the budget represented an 'audacious attempt to force socialism upon the country without consulting the people'.[26] Not all Unionists, however, were keen that the budget should be rejected. Lord Esher commented of the doubters: 'They seem haunted by the knowledge that the Radicals want a dissolution and the fear that they may be trapped into one.'[27] Finlay was himself worried that if the Lords amended the Finance Bill they would find their position 'constitutionally untenable', while Robert Cecil, perhaps seeing that the Unionists' stance would be less easy to defend than the simple Liberal cry of 'peers versus people', regarded the policy of rejection as 'little short of insane'. But his attempts to dissuade Balfour from the fateful step were unsuccessful.[28]

After Balfour had firmly committed himself in Chamberlain's own city of Birmingham, in a speech at Bingley Hall, to the cause of tariff reform, the die was effectively cast. A message delivered from Chamberlain himself, expressing the hope that the Lords would see their way to force a general election, further curtailed Balfour's freedom of manoeuvre. There could now be no turning back. Lansdowne, bluntly informed by the government that the Finance Bill must either be passed *in toto* or not at all, offered no alternative course of action. His fear was that 'the House of Lords will lose the hold which it now has on the country and entirely discourage the moderate men who look to us for support if we have to confess that we are impotent at such a crisis'.[29] If they failed to reject the budget, the Lords would forfeit their right ever again to resist the financial policy of a Liberal government, 'however outrageous [it] might be'.[30] But Lansdowne was able to predict the future course of events with remarkable accuracy. As he wrote to Lord Balfour of Burleigh:

We must, I think, assume that if there is a general election we

> may be beaten at the polls.The Radicals will no doubt do their
> best to confuse the issue and make out that a verdict in favour
> of the Finance Bill carries with it a carte blanche to deal with
> the H. of L. ... By the time the H. of L. is ripe for
> treatment,the popularity of the Budget will, unless I am
> mistaken, have greatly diminished. We shall not,in my opinion,
> get through the present crisis without two general elections.[31]

Never in recent times had a government's annual Finance Bill received
such a rough handling through its parliamentary passage. In the Commons the
Unionists, led by Balfour and Austen Chamberlain, did everything they could
to slow down its passage, regularly forcing the debate to continue throughout
the night.[32] Then, by September, it was the turn of the government to play
the game of parliamentary delay, their objective being, Austen Chamberlain
surmised, to tide the situation over until January 1910, so as to fight an
election on the new register.[33] On 16 November, in the Lords, Lansdowne
gave notice of the fateful amendment which would destroy the Finance Bill.
Sir Almeric Fitzroy, gravely apprehensive about the immediate future, 'could
not fail to gather that [Lansdowne] entertained grave misgivings upon the
course he was about to take ... Whig scruples have been ruthlessly sacrificed
to Tory passion and the petulance of wire-pulling demagogy'.[34] But even
those Unionists who regarded rejection as a hazardous option felt compelled
to rally round the leadership because they recognised that the House of Lords
itself might now become the object of the Liberals' attack. As Hugh Cecil put
it:

> Whatever we may think of the prudence of Lord L's tactics, we
> must nevertheless do all we can to strengthen his hands.
> Everything that is said against him or his motion ... will be
> quoted to aid the Govt. and their cry of 'Down with the Lords'
> .... Dissensions in face of the enemy on the eve of the
> dissolution might result in a triumphant Liberal majority.[35]

With the budget rejected, a general election became a constitutional
necessity and one which many Unionists approached with some optimism. As
Walter Long argued, 'Six weeks ago things looked bad, but the gilt is off the
gingerbread and now we have only got to keep ramming things home and I
believe we shall get the country with us'.[36] Yet, at least in the government's
presentation of the case, Lloyd George's Finance Bill had succeeded in forcing
the Unionists into a morally indefensible position as the defenders of a

reactionary alliance between food-taxers and hereditary peers opposed to the people of the country and their budget.[37] This was the reality of the situation which the constitutional niceties of Unionist apologists could do little to alter.

The Unionists' electoral campaign, though vigorous and energetic, seemed not altogether united in its presentation of the issues to the electorate. In one sense the party was back on safe and well-tried ground. With the emergence of a constitutional crisis the central issue of politics was once more the old one of resisting Radical calls for change and defending existing institutions.[38] But most Unionists recognised that merely to defend the *status quo* would not be enough, and in the quest for a positive alternative it was to the cause of tariff reform that they turned, and with far greater conviction than in 1906. Indeed the general election of January 1910 marked the high-water mark of 'whole hogger' influence within the Unionist party among both the leadership and the rank and file. It was curious, therefore, that Balfour's election address, which in the absence of a national manifesto carried particular weight, seemed preoccupied with constitutional matters and made only passing reference to tariff reform.[39] Lansdowne defined the leading issues as tariff reform, single-chamber government and the threat of socialism, while Austen Chamberlain was almost alone among the leadership in seeing the possible implications for the Act of Union arising out of the constitutional crisis. In general Unionists talked less of Home Rule than they had four years earlier, even though the issue would soon become far more a matter of practical politics.[40]

At this distance in time it is difficult to make much more sense of the ambiguous electoral results than did contemporaries. Though the Unionists had failed to maintain their by-election momentum of 1907-9, losing gains made in the three previous years, they did win 116 seats lost in 1906 and became the majority party in England. Overall the Unionists now held 273 seats compared with the government's 275. But crucially the Liberals could expect to rely on the 40 Labour and 82 Irish Nationalist members in the new house to safeguard their parliamentary majority. There was a widespread feeling that the cry of 'Peers versus People' had saved the situation for the government.[41] The fact that Unionists had gained seats in January 1910, particularly in the South of England, owed more to a general swing of the electoral pendulum back to the party in its traditional strongholds after the exceptional results of 1906 than to any great appeal exercised by tariff reform or the party's constitutional stance.[42] Not surprisingly, contemporaries drew differing conclusions from this first unequivocal submission of the policy of tariff reform to the

judgement of the electorate - conclusions which were predetermined by the
basic attitude of each man to the question of tariffs. From the undogmatic
centre Sandars perceived that 'the county elector is really more keen on Tariff
Reform than his urban brother' largely because the complaint about dear food
was more easily answered in the country districts.[43] A committed free trader
such as Lord George Hamilton, on the other hand, concluded that
Chamberlain's tariffs had prevented a Unionist victory: 'For the second time
Joe has upset the Unionist Party. As long as he is allowed to name trumps he
will always select the wrong suit.'[44] Strachey confirmed that if only the tariff
programme had been modified to exclude food stuffs, victory could have been
grasped. He was at least comforted that the Unionist free traders had no need
to reproach themselves, having subordinated their own convictions to the
common good of the party.[45] By contrast Austen Chamberlain unequivocally
concluded that tariff reform had been the party's trump card:

> Where we won, we won on and by Tariff Reform. Even where
> we lost it was the only subject in our repertoire about which
> people really cared.

Chamberlain admitted that food taxes had been the great difficulty confronting
Unionist candidates but argued that those who had faced this difficulty most
boldly had come off best. His conviction was that if the working man could
be shown that the issue was primarily one of employment rather than dear
food, the party would have no need to modify its policy.[46]

Chamberlain, however, was indulging in an exercise of self-deception.
Once the electoral dust had settled, it was evident that the cause of tariff
reform had suffered a severe set-back - a reverse that would be accentuated by
economic developments in 1910 as the sharp depression rapidly disappeared.
It was far from clear that tariff reform had won the fiscal battle against the
Liberals' budget, while its adoption as a tactical strategy to win working-class
seats had evidently backfired in areas such as London and Lancashire.[47]
Chamberlain had already been warned that the Central Office was looking to
'jettison the Imperial side' of his father's policy.[48] But it was Lord Salisbury
who initiated that policy discussion on tariff reform, and in particular food
taxes, which would come to a climax later in the year. In a letter sent to
Austen Chamberlain and Bonar Law, Salisbury argued that in the light of the
election results the policy of tariff reform should be maintained, but that food
taxes should be dropped. Sensing that the hung parliament made a further
election an imminent possibility, Salisbury posed the critical question: 'Is it

reasonable, is it possible, to ask us to enter into this struggle except upon the best ground we can find?' Thus was planted the seed which finally germinated ten months later as Balfour's referendum pledge.[49]

Just as the election left the whole question of fiscal policy in a somewhat ambiguous position, so too it was by no means clear what its impact had been upon the constitutional debate. There was some confidence, based partly on the reports of the royal confidant Lord Esher, that the narrowness of the Liberal victory precluded any possibility of the King being forced into ennobling enough peers to create a Liberal majority in the upper chamber.[50] But many Unionists recognised that, in the longer term, their position of power within the House of Lords was now vulnerable. As early as 3 January Lansdowne wrote to Balfour to describe the letters he had received 'pressing us for a strong declaration as to the House of Lords reform'. He was convinced that the shortcomings of the upper chamber could be corrected by reforms based on the scheme presented by the Rosebery Committee in 1908.[51]

On this issue Balfour's own views underwent a subtle change. Before the election he had opposed reform of the Lords, since any scheme of reform was likely to increase the power of the second chamber and thus make it more of a rival to the House of Commons.[52] A month later, however, he had come to the conclusion that for the Unionists to adopt a scheme of reform would strengthen the hand of the moderates within the Liberal cabinet and help resist 'unconstitutional pressure by the extremists'. Nonetheless, he fully recognised that it might not be easy to agree upon a scheme of reform which would be acceptable to the Lords themselves.[53] Indeed it was an important distinction that leading Unionists were now thinking in terms of a reform of the Lords' constitution rather than a limitation of their powers.

Austen Chamberlain immediately took up the stance of the future diehards in arguing that 'if they must die, they had better die fighting .... There is nothing to be gained by committing suicide and to consent to limit their veto to a single session would be suicide pure and simple.' Yet he recognised that in terms of electoral appeal the Unionists might well be taking on board a considerable liability: 'It is not the issue upon which I would choose to take the decision of the country if the choice were ours.'[54] The product of such thinking among the Unionist hierarchy was a host of novel schemes of constitutional reform concerned with the composition of the upper house and involving the introduction of life peerages and elected membership, with deadlocks between the two chambers being settled by referendums and inter-party conferences.

As Unionist leader in the Lords the attitude of Lord Lansdowne was naturally critical. His instinct was to show a readiness for reform, without pledging the party to any elaborate plan for remodelling the constitution of the upper chamber. Believing that reform was most likely to come through the co-operation of moderate men on both sides of the political fence, he was against any commitment to specific proposals at the present juncture.[55] Such caution was irritating to those Unionists who believed that the combined effect of Lloyd George's budget and the Liberals' election campaign had been considerably to lower the upper house in popular esteem.[56] The debate that ensued divided not only rank and file Unionists, but even members of the shadow cabinet. Throughout 1910 Unionists could not agree whether they should nail their colours to the preservation of the existing institution or whether they would be better advised to devise a scheme of reform and, if so, upon what basis the new chamber should be constituted. While some held firmly to the maintenance of the *status quo*, others argued eloquently that a purely hereditary chamber was an indefensible electoral handicap. The possibility of including an elected element in the hereditary Lords was an issue over which no consensus emerged. Curzon, St.Aldwyn, Onslow and Milner favoured such a mixture but found themselves opposed by Lansdowne, Salisbury, Cawdor and Halsbury, who believed that the position of hereditary peers within such a chamber would become untenable.[57] When Austen Chamberlain, supported by Lord Rosebery, began to move in the direction of elected and nominated peers, Balfour too reluctantly gave his support to this idea, though Lansdowne would still 'accept only a very small dose either of the nomination plan or of the electoral plan'. With such divisions of opinion Salisbury feared that the whole question was likely to be lost 'in the sands of generalities'.[58] But a general weakness of the various Unionist proposals was that all would have left the reformed House of Lords as a stronghold of Unionism and thus unlikely to win the support of the Liberal party.[59] At the back of all Unionist minds there was now the passionate conviction that any reformed house must still retain enough power to resist Home Rule.

The party which emerged from the first general election of 1910 was thus both confused and divided, again showing the shortcomings of Balfour's style of opposition leadership. In view of the party's continuing adherence to tariff reform, despite growing misgivings over food taxes, there were still those

prepared to believe that the stricken Joseph Chamberlain remained the effective
arbiter of Unionist politics. As Strachey bitterly complained:

> We have had the misfortune of a great party taking its orders
> from a man who necessarily lives in seclusion and only sees not
> merely his side but that side under favourable conditions. I hear
> that when people visit him the mot d'ordre is 'Oh, nothing
> must be said which will make the poor old fellow feel
> depressed or unhappy. Put the bright side of everything and
> cheer him up.' The consequence is orders have been issued by
> a man living in a fool's paradise. If he had been politically
> alive he would have been ready no doubt to tack and take in
> sail at the right moment. As it is he has sat deep down in the
> bowels of the ship and merely shouted out automatically 'Full
> steam ahead'.[60]

Not until March 1910, in fact, was there even a clear consensus within the
Unionist hierarchy that the party should aim to turn the Liberal government
out. Hitherto Balfour had been anxious to avoid taking office, assuring the
Liberals that he would assist in carrying on the King's government.[61]
Unionist policies were thrown into the melting pot in the course of 1910, but
the result was less synthesis and clarification than paralysis and confusion. As
one historian has written, the party 'spent 1910 tearing itself to pieces, unable
to decide either its policies on major questions in isolation, or the priorities
between those policies should it be forced to choose'.[62] Salisbury vividly
described the situation after a meeting of the shadow cabinet:

> all were satisfied we shall be defeated at the election ....
> Finally it appeared that there was nothing but a sort of
> Balaclava idea - mixed with a trace of Micawber. We were to
> fight our last ship, last shot, last ditch, but as to taking any
> steps to avert catastrophe, nothing.[63]

It was in this state of considerable uncertainty that the death of King
Edward VII on 7 May added an additional twist to an already complex
scenario. Both political parties were now dominated by the desire to avoid
presenting the new King with a constitutional crisis with which he was
untrained to cope. In such an atmosphere, and with Garvin leading the call for
a 'Truce of God' in the pages of the *Observer*, the two party leaderships
agreed by the middle of June 1910 to the unusual improvisation of a
constitutional conference.[64] But the Unionist leaders went into the conference

with the handicap of not having clearly agreed among themselves on their policy on constitutional issues. It was left to the four-man delegation of Balfour, Lansdowne, Austen Chamberlain and Cawdor to work out the party's ideas as the conference developed.[65] As Lansdowne predicted, 'no doubt each side will have difficulties of its own occasioned by the attitude of its supporters'. There had been 'a great deal of conversation, somewhat desultory I fear, as to the line to be taken in regard to the different matters which may come up for discussion'.[66]

Much mystery and speculation once surrounded the course of the ensuing inter-party discussions, largely because, though negotiations proceeded over several weeks, no record was published either at the time or subsequently, and perhaps also because of the intrusion of Lloyd George's dramatic and unexpected proposal for a coalition government. More recently, however, it has been possible to cut away the uncertainty and recreate the course of events from the contemporary notes of one of the Unionist delegation.[67] Earlier writers, suffering from a lack of archival material, made a number of assertions which it is now difficult to sustain.[68]

In the early sessions of the conference, before the break for the parliamentary summer recess, the Unionists' crucial debating point was their insistence on defining a category of constitutional legislation to which, in the event of a deadlock between Lords and Commons, a referendum should be applied as a means of resolution. Such a category would have to include the issue of Home Rule for Ireland, made more delicate and immediate as a consequence of January's election results. The Liberal delegates on the other hand showed a preference for joint sittings of the two houses to resolve constitutional deadlocks, but both the size of the Lords' representation at such sittings and the definition of constitutional legislation posed major problems. Additionally, the Unionists insisted upon reforming the House of Lords, despite their inability to sort out their own ideas on this issue earlier in the year. Indeed it was only Asquith's belated assurance that the government was not planning to exclude the idea of Lords reform from the final settlement which prevented the summer recess developing into the end of the whole conference.[69]

With the autumn session of the conference about to get underway, Lansdowne was pessimistic about its prospects:

I am not sanguine of the success of the Conference. There are marked divergences of opinion with regard to points which are

cardinal and we shall, I fear, be unable to secure agreement
except at a price which I am not prepared to pay.[70]
Balfour at this stage was equally realistic, but recognised that it was important
from a tactical point of view that the inevitable breakdown should be made to
appear the responsibility of the government. He was therefore receptive to
advice not to rock the conference boat with any provocative public
pronouncement, but was clearly alarmed by the rumour that the Liberals,
determined not to have an election before the Coronation, might try to keep
the conference going into the New Year.[71] Meanwhile, Austen Chamberlain
attempted to strengthen Balfour's resolve not to compromise on vital
principles:

> There is nothing new to say, but the old things must be
> repeated until they really sink into and fill the mind of the
> country .... Tariff Reform and Imperial Preference, Imperial
> Preference and Tariff Reform must be the burden of our
> song.[72]

One effect of the concentration of the party leadership on the progress of
the conference, the details of whose proceedings remained largely unknown to
the party at large, was the re-emergence of discontent among the rank and file.
In October and November backbench unrest crystallised into the formation of
the Reveille movement, in some ways a forerunner of the diehard revolt of
1911 and drawing its membership and support from the radical right in both
houses of parliament. Overall it was designed to bring about a change in party
policy from a negative defence of the *status quo* to the formulation of a
detailed policy programme. Reveille was an expression, 'if not of outright
rebellion, at least of dissatisfaction with the leadership'.[73] It inevitably made
Balfour more than ever wary of his own conduct in the resumed session of the
constitutional conference. Reveille's policies included the maintenance of
national defence, tariff reform and imperial union, small ownership and poor
law reform.[74] Only prompt action by the Chief Whip in associating the
leadership with the aims of the Reveille perhaps prevented the movement,
which saw the re-emergence of leading Confederates such as Page Croft and
Comyn Platt, from running out of control.[75]

It was against the background of these considerable internal difficulties for
Balfour and his colleagues that the conference which had reconvened on 11
October appeared to reach a point of impasse three days later. Though basic
agreement seemed to have been reached on the submission of deadlocked

legislation to a joint sitting of the two houses, the breaking point appeared to be whether, as the Unionists insisted, constitutional changes including Home Rule should be excluded from such a provision and submitted instead to a referendum. At this point, however, consideration of such constitutional niceties took something of a backseat in the face of Lloyd George's revolutionary suggestion - the proposed formation of a coalition government. During the summer recess, the Chancellor of the Exchequer had drawn up a memorandum, dated 17 August, proposing that many of the major areas of political dissension between the parties could best be resolved through compromise agreements imposed by a National rather than a party government. Lloyd George's motives for making such a suggestion remain an issue of debate. He may have been thinking in terms of easing the passage of the national insurance legislation to which his fertile brain had now turned, but at all events it seems likely that he shared the irritation periodically voiced throughout the preceding decade by radical politicians over a wide political spectrum at the sterility of the party political struggle. His attitude at other moments during his long political career certainly supports such a supposition. Now, with that party struggle apparently in danger of dissipating the country's energies, to the benefit of Britain's competitors and enemies, Lloyd George took up a theme that had at one time or another been espoused by tariff reformers, Liberal Imperialists, Fabians and Milner's circle of Imperialists, that the national interest of efficient and business-like government demanded the suspension of inter-party strife.[76]

Lloyd George and Balfour seem to have discussed these proposals no later than 11 October, with the Chancellor clearly believing that it was only with the Unionist leader himself that he could have useful discussions on such a crucial matter. 'Lansdowne was merely an ineffectual echo of him. Cawdor contributed nothing whatever and Austen Chamberlain, though independent, was such a slow and commonplace mind that he did not count,' commented one contemporary.[77] There is considerable evidence to suggest that Lloyd George played something of a double game in his presentation of the coalition proposal, putting forward rather differing versions of his plan to his cabinet colleagues and to Unionist opponents in order to sustain their interest. As Austen Chamberlain later recalled:

> As first put before us, it was more evident what we should get
> than what we should give .... I know that when Balfour first
> told us of the overtures we were astonished at George's

concessions and someone asked, 'but how can he justify such
a volte-face?' ... But ... later, when he had fully developed his
ideas, we said that it would be as impossible for us to justify
our acceptance of them to our people as it would be for him to
justify his acceptance of them to his people.[78]

It appears unlikely that any of the Unionist delegation saw the August
memorandum in October 1910. That memorandum would have put the
Chancellor's proposals in a less acceptable light from the Unionist party's
point of view.[79] As it was, the Unionist leaders were clearly led to believe
that the primary concern behind Lloyd George's suggestion was to put the
Royal Navy on to a satisfactory footing in view of the worsening international
situation. Additionally there was to be an impartial commission to enquire into
the question of tariff reform, whose report, to be presented within six months,
would be binding on the government.[80] The problem of Ireland would be
dealt with through a scheme of devolution, on lines that had been gaining
ground within certain sections of the Unionist party throughout the year.[81]
Garvin and F.S.Oliver were among those who had urged upon Balfour the
need to adopt 'federalism', or 'home rule all round', as a new departure in the
party's Irish policy. As Garvin warned Leo Maxse, 'some fundamental
alteration of the Unionist attitude on the Irish question is becoming
indispensable if we are to have a fair chance of saving anything'.[82] Austen
Chamberlain, perhaps recognising in these ideas parallels with an approach to
the Irish question with which his father had toyed in the 1880's, was by no
means hostile. In his opinion the idea of an agreement about devolution should
not be dismissed as impossible: 'there is a great deal to be said for it and
much is possible and safe as a national settlement which would be disastrous
if passed as a party measure under party conditions'.[83] Even Sandars
appeared interested:

Is home rule exactly what it was? In other words, is home rule
- Parnellite home rule - the issue and nothing else? If the larger
question of federation is in any way a matter for consideration
and debate,is it not possible to get on to this new ground?[84]

Though the decision on how to react to Lloyd George's *démarche*
belonged necessarily to Balfour, advice was not wanting from his Unionist
colleagues. F.E.Smith, speaking the language of 'efficiency' that had been
prominent at the time of the Boer War, argued that he could not

in twenty years remember a time when so many men in

England were sick of mere party cries and faction. A great sigh of relief would go up over the whole of business England if a strong and stable government were formed .... It might at best give us a national government for ten years; at the worst it would enable us to fight against opponents whose most formidable leaders were discredited and under circumstances which might lead to another period of Tory ascendancy.[85]

But, as the correspondence columns of *The Times* coincidentally showed, there were many Unionists who were at this stage unwilling to sacrifice their party label in favour of the broader national interest.[86] Balfour, moreover, apart from a natural suspicion of Lloyd George's motives (especially as it was not clear how Asquith viewed the proposals) was not, as his previous career illustrated, a leader ready to risk the unity and coherence of his party in order to clutch at the intangible chimera of national government. The haunting spectre of being another Peel was ultimately sufficient to prevent Balfour from embracing Lloyd George's proposals, as became clear at a meeting of the two men on 2 November.[87] This meeting served to bring the whole episode of Lloyd George's coalition proposals to an end.[88] In reality Balfour was not willing to agree to any significant alteration to traditional Unionist policy on Ireland, partly because of his conviction that federalism was not compatible with the preservation of the Union, and partly because he was aware that such a policy change would not receive the whole-hearted support of the party.[89]

It was probably only the excitement engendered by the coalition proposals that kept the Constitutional Conference itself in being after the deadlock reached on 14 October, even though no mention was made of the coalition at the formal sessions of the conference by any of the eight delegates.[90] Lord Esher found Balfour in retreat at Whittinghame, convinced that the government was in collusion with the Irish Nationalists, in order to get Home Rule excluded from the category of constitutional legislation.[91] Lansdowne was anxious to remind his colleagues that the point of difference between the two sides was rather greater than perhaps appeared to be the case. In addition to the problem of constitutional legislation and the question of Home Rule, no agreement had been reached on the size of the Lords' representation at a joint sitting, nor on the conditions under which the joint sittings would take place, while the whole question of Lords' reform was still in suspense.[92]

When the government compromised to the extent of suggesting that a general election should intervene on the next occasion that a Home Rule Bill

was rejected by the Lords, but on this occasion only, and that subsequent
Home Rule Bills should be treated like ordinary bills, it was clear that the
Liberals would go no further.[93] But it was also clear that the Unionists would
not accept a settlement on such terms. As Lansdowne later recalled, 'none of
us treated Home Rule as an open question'.[94] Austen Chamberlain also
objected to confining the security of the Union to a single occasion and to the
absence of any general provisions ensuring that constitutional changes should
be specifically safeguarded.[95] Not surprisingly the conference proposals were
unanimously rejected by the shadow cabinet meeting at Lansdowne House on
8 November.[96] The Conference itself was formally wound up at its twenty-
second session two days later. Though Sir Almeric Fitzroy commented that
agreement had been 'within an ace of being concluded',[97] the essential points
of difference had remained fundamental and unbridgeable. In so far as Balfour
had ever given serious consideration to Lloyd George's proposals, it was
probably only because of his view that the equality of the two great parties in
the Commons gave 'undue Parliamentary power to Radical extremists and Irish
Nationalists', a state of affairs which he found 'very dangerous to the country
and the Empire'.[98]

The spirit of political partisanship which had played no small part in
ensuring that Lloyd George's coalition proposals failed was inevitably
strengthened by the breakdown of the Constitutional Conference itself. Even
Garvin, who had so vehemently championed the 'truce of God', now executed
a *volte-face* and abandoned the paths of moderation.[99] Lord Camperdown
assured Balfour that his position had been strengthened : 'You can now run
your Policy against the Government - your positive Policy'.[100] But the
failure of a conference which had attempted to chart a political middle ground
served also to signal to the party rank and file the failure of Balfour's own
quest for this same *via media*, which had been so characteristic of his
leadership of the Unionist opposition. The Chief Whip feared that the party
would now fall prey to right-wing extremists : 'I can only say I regard the
decision as fatal to the Party. The chief will be swept away with most of his
experienced followers and the party will fall into the hands of Goulding,
Maxse and Co.'[101] Amery hoped that the general election, which was now
inevitable, could still be made to turn in the party's favour on the issues of
'tariff reform, imperial preference and a strong navy', but Sandars was
probably nearer the mark in warning Balfour to expect 'our third consecutive
defeat'.[102]

In some ways, as far as the Unionists were concerned, it seemed that there had been no change since the electorate had last gone to the polls in January. The year's twenty-one by-elections produced no alteration in the party's strength in the House of Commons. Despite the intense debate over policy the party as a whole, apart from acquiescing in the passage of the budget, had not significantly modified the platform on which it had been beaten at the beginning of the year. Yet beneath this veneer of continuity it was apparent that Balfour was no longer master of the situation to the extent that he had been in January. The fact that during the course of the year Unionists had espoused the idea of a referendum as an acceptable constitutional device had encouraged those members of the party whose adherence to tariff reform had never been wholehearted to seize upon it as a means of watering down the party's commitment to this policy. Lord Robert Cecil saw the referendum

> not only as a protection from the Radicals but also as a safeguard against the wild projects which the extreme Tariff Reformers appear to entertain. They seem to me to regard Tariff Reform as only the first step in a policy which is distinguishable only in name from State Socialism and with the present leadership one never knows how far we may be committed on future occasions.[103]

His idea was to have a short statement of the case for a referendum drawn up, get it signed by a few well-known names and then circulate it among all members of both Houses of Parliament with a request for their support.[104]

It was in the context of the Unionists' prospects for the coming general election that Cecil's hopes began to prosper. Having made considerable gains in the South of England in January, the party was now anxious to consolidate this progress north of the Trent and particularly in Lancashire. Throughout the year the Protectionists had done their best to convert the county to their cause, holding the annual Tariff Reform League conference there in November. Balfour himself regarded Lancashire as 'the very key and centre of the next electoral battlefield', an opinion shared by Garvin and others.[105] Sandars felt that what was needed was for one of the front bench to take his life in his hands, fight Manchester and 'give the lead to the County'.[106] Such considerations led to pressure being placed on the supposedly staunch tariff reformer, Andrew Bonar Law, to stand for North-West Manchester and to Balfour's assurance that a safe seat would be found for him should he be unsuccessful there.[107] Ironically in view of the influence he was now to exercise in favour of the referendum, Law's candidature was welcomed by all local Unionists except for the rump of free traders.[108] Yet the traditional commitment of Lancashire voters to the principle of free trade convinced many observers that the county could not be carried unless a substantial part of Chamberlain's tariff proposals was jettisoned. In this way the attraction of postponing food taxes until the matter had been submitted for the country's decision through a referendum became apparent. Meeting on 14 November, a group of prominent Unionists including Law, F.E.Smith, Ridley, Carson, Sandars, Hood, Goulding and Garvin, tried to hammer out an agreement on the vexed question of food taxes, but in the end only Sandars, Carson and Garvin were prepared to speak out for their abandonment.[109] Garvin was convinced that with the impediment of food taxes the Unionists had no realistic expectation of success. The best chance for the whole policy of Imperial Preference, therefore, was 'to go to the country now upon this cry, "At this election your vote will tax the foreigner but will not tax your food."'[110]

The referenders had little chance of success unless more of the party's prominent tariff reformers could be converted to their cause. It was with this aim in mind that Strachey went angling for the biggest fish of all and in an editorial in the *Spectator* appealed to Joseph Chamberlain to

> save the Union a second time by making it clear to the voters that they might vote for tariff reformers on this occasion without having their votes used to carry tariff reform before it had been once more submitted to the people at a general election .... If something of this kind is not done, I look upon the election with the gloomiest forebodings.[111]

All the time pressure was mounting inexorably on Balfour to announce a change of policy, despite the efforts of Austen Chamberlain to preserve his father's vision intact. Though Chamberlain could assure his father on 16 November that Balfour 'stands firm ... so all is well',[112] in the days that followed the party leader began visibly to waver. While the *Morning Post* remained committed to the whole-hogger position and the *Birmingham Daily Post* faithful to the Chamberlainite cause, the vast majority of the Unionist press was now swinging towards the referendum.[113] Sandars was an enthusiastic convert to the proposal and reported that correspondence was pouring in to Balfour urging him to commit the party.[114] Garvin continued to press that the referendum was 'a heaven-born solution. Northcliffe longs for it but won't move until AJB gives the signal. Entreat him. Entreat him.'[115]

The crucial development came from Law's growing fear, as a result of his electioneering in Manchester and his subjection to the opinions of Derby and the local party managers, that Lancashire could never be won unless the referendum pledge was introduced. Tentatively, and supporting his contention with the opinion of the editor of the *Lancashire Textile Mercury*, he wrote to Balfour on 26 November:

> Of course if it is to be done it must be done quickly, or it would be of no use and I can hardly say that I feel that I have given enough thought to it even to recommend it; but I do think that it is worth your consideration.[116]

Lansdowne too became a late convert to the cause and began to exert his influence on the leader. 'If the Tariff Reformers really believe in their cause,' he asked, 'and if they also believe in the Referendum, can they reasonably object to test the one by the other?'[117] It was, however, upon Law's opinion, however cautiously expressed, that Balfour now leant in justifying his *volte-face*, particularly to Austen Chamberlain, to whom he wrote of 'Bonar Law's idea' and 'Bonar Law's proposal'.[118] Law after all had the reputation of being a staunch tariff reformer. Recognising that the tariff reform camp was itself no longer united on this issue, Balfour seized upon the tentative signs of Law's conversion to restate his own basically guarded attitude towards tariff reform, an attitude which he had been forced by the pressure of events over the previous two years to dress up as positive enthusiasm. That Balfour was deliberately exaggerating Law's own views on the subject is clearly revealed in the words of a telegram which the latter sent to Sandars on the very day that Balfour was to address an audience at the Albert Hall:

> All wealthy Unionists, even strong Tariff Reformers, would say such declaration would mean victory, but I find all working-class audiences only interested in Tariff Reform and declaration would do no good with them and might damp enthusiasm of best workers. Declaration would be excessively difficult to work in practice. On the whole think we should gain by it at election but doubt whether subsequent difficulties are not too great to make it wise. Would there be any use in saying if Government undertook in event of their obtaining majority not to pass Home Rule without Referendum we would give same undertaking regarding Tariff Reform?[119]

Nonetheless, on 29 November and only days before the country went to the polls, Balfour announced at the Albert Hall that, if the Unionists won the election, no taxes would be imposed upon food until the electorate had had the opportunity of expressing its views in a referendum on this single issue.

Though the whole party was in theory still committed to the full policy of tariff reform, reactions to Balfour's Albert Hall pronouncement were predictably varied. If a Unionist had accepted the unqualified text of tariff reform as holy writ handed down by the revered elder Chamberlain, then Balfour's backsliding bordered on sacrilege. As Beatrice Webb noted, 'It is the last move in his duel with Chamberlain; it is a final checkmate to tariff reform'.[120] If, however, a Unionist had adopted the policy as a purely political and tactical antidote to the radical excesses of Lloyd George and his colleagues, then the leader's *volte-face* was entirely consistent and proper. Unionist electioneering would no longer be weighed down by the ball and chain of stomach taxes. Garvin, who had, as the national press readily acknowledged, himself played no small part in Balfour's change of heart, was overjoyed at his leader's conversion: 'as for AJB I will fight for him all ways while there is breath in my body.... Men are shaking each other's hands and saying he is out and out and out a leader and a man.'[121] But by revealing that the party's recent unity over policy had been a matter of convenience rather than conviction, Balfour, unless his gamble proved an immediate success, was courting a renewal of internal disharmony and further criticism of his leadership. Though some whole-hoggers thought that Balfour had fallen victim to an Asquithian trap, the majority now recognised that their leader had accepted party unity under the banner of tariff reform for largely opportunistic reasons. Though others had been instrumental in bringing about his last minute change of course, it would be Balfour himself who would have to bear the brunt of criticism from such men as Goulding, Ridley and Milner, to say nothing of the Chamberlains, father and son. Others were alarmed not so much at the damage done to tariff reform as at the constitutional device which the Unionists were now adopting. For Lord Esher the referendum was democracy run mad. 'And democracy precedes the fall of Empire always.'[122] Furthermore, Balfour had compounded his difficulties through the manner in which this significant modification of policy was arrived at, without reference to his senior colleagues in the shadow cabinet.[123] Indeed it is by no means certain that, had a meeting of the party leaders been convened, the referendum would have been approved.[124] As it was, the Unionist hierarchy, presented with a *fait accompli*, could not but accept the party's new policy, since the alternative would have been to renounce Balfour's leadership - a step for which the majority was as yet unprepared.[125]

One section of the party which gave a particular welcome to the referendum pledge was the Unionist free traders, whose existing readiness to throw in their lot with the party was confirmed now that there were clear signs that the policy of tariff reform was to be emasculated. Overall, however, though Beatrice Webb could call the pledge a 'superlatively fine stroke',[126] its disruptive effects were pronounced and markedly in evidence before the election itself was over - a clear harbinger of the coming fragmentation of the party in 1911. Those elements most disillusioned now with Balfour's actions would be in the forefront of the diehard movement and the Halsbury agitation a few months later. It was not even clear precisely what impact Balfour's pledge had on the election results in December 1910, thus denying to both the supporters and the opponents of the referendum the telling cry that their hopes or fears had been justified by events. It seems likely that Balfour's Albert Hall commitment was too subtle a manoeuvre to change the voting intentions of the average working-class elector, and there is some doubt in any case whether there was sufficient time between the pronouncement and polling for its potential impact to sink into the country's electoral consciousness.[127] Derby preferred to ascribe Law's failure to win in Manchester not to any aspect of tariff policy but to the unusually large turn-out of voters - nearly 92% - on a register that was a year old.[128]

Such uncertainties did not prevent Unionists from expressing strong opinions on Balfour's decision both before the election was over and afterwards. Cromer was hopeful that what had been done would have a great effect in Lancashire and elsewhere.[129] For Austen Chamberlain, on the other hand, the Albert Hall pledge was 'a great discouragement and I do not see how you are going to give effect to it', while for Hugh Elliot it represented 'a betrayal of the Tariff Reform party'.[130] To Lansdowne Chamberlain confessed that it was the worst disappointment that he had suffered in politics for a very long time, and he was by no means assuaged by Balfour's expressed distress at having had to take a decision 'of the expediency of which I know you are doubtful' or by the leader's assertion that the new departure was best for tariff reform itself as well as for the other articles of the Unionist political faith.[131] As Chamberlain reflected:

> To have fought so long and so hard to keep Tariff Reform in
> the forefront of our programme and to prevent its being

whittled away or postponed, to have come so near, as it seemed
to me, to success and then to see this new obstacle suddenly
interposed in haste and at the last moment ... left me miserable
and exhausted.[132]

The declaration of the election results, leaving the Unionists' overall
parliamentary position essentially unchanged, inevitably added further fuel to
the debate. Only if the referendum had proved an unqualified electoral success
could further dissension within the party have been avoided. One defeated
Unionist unequivocally declared:

I should have won but for the disastrous Albert Hall speech -
this lost me hundreds of votes just in the districts where I stood
to gain most by my uncompromising advocacy of Tariff Reform
and where it is impossible to win on the House of Lords
issue.[133]

Leo Maxse agreed, asserting that the pledge was nothing less than a crime and
at the same time giving notice of what the Albert Hall speech had done for
Balfour in the eyes of advanced tariff reformers:

For a long time past Unionists have had to choose between
Tariff Reform and Balfour, as well as between Unionism and
Balfour, because Balfour so palpably means continuous disaster.
Up to now those who count in our Party have sacrificed the
cause and their principles to this sinister individual, but I feel
quite sure that this cannot last as the discontent is too profound
and widespread.[134]

Maxse estimated that the pledge had cost the party between forty and fifty
seats. 'It is unpardonable. Balfour must go, or Tariff Reform will go - that is
the alternative.'[135] Lord Ridley too was convinced that the referendum had
lost rather than gained votes and concluded that Balfour was 'a terrible
handicap to us'.[136] By contrast Lansdowne loyally maintained that the pledge
had saved the party from disaster. Without it he felt sure that Unionists would
have lost many seats which they held by small majorities.[137] Nonetheless
Sandars went to the trouble of getting the Chief Agent to collect evidence from
the constituencies in an effort to refute the allegations of the anti-
referenders.[138]

To this consideration of the immediate past there was added a further
element of controversy when Austen Chamberlain, speaking at Buxton on 14
December in the last days of the election campaign, asserted that Balfour's

pledge had been given for one election only and implied that it would not be repeated.[139] Somewhat ingenuously Chamberlain then suggested that the simple fact that the Unionists had not won the election left them free to reconsider the pledge, and he tried to win Lansdowne over to this point of view.[140] Whether or not Chamberlain's interpretation of Balfour's declaration represented an honest difference of opinion is unclear. It is however certain that the leader had not intended to restrict the application of the referendum in the way Chamberlain implied. On the contrary, in later speeches, as at Wrexham on 7 December, when the result of the election was practically decided, Balfour made no hint of limitation, describing the policy as relevant to the next appeal to the country.[141] Chamberlain's speech, coming from the man whom many regarded as having a strong claim to the succession whenever Balfour should retire, inevitably caused irritation, especially as it seemed to indicate a lack of discipline within the shadow cabinet, reflecting badly on Balfour's role as party leader. Derby immediately announced that he could not share Chamberlain's interpretation and that he hoped that the latter's outburst would have the effect of revealing how small his following was and how loyal the party as a whole was to Balfour.[142] Sandars' fury could not be disguised:

> What I care most about is the shocking example of disloyalty
> in high places; it is wholly indefensible .... How can discipline
> be enforced or loyalty preached if an intimate colleague breaks
> loose from the ties of political confidence and thrusts his own
> opinions upon the public without a word of notice to those who
> are in intimate relations with himself?[143]

Garvin too regarded the speech as an outrage. He felt that this 'well-meaning but most limited man ... vastly overrates his importance to the party' and wondered what was being done 'to prevent Highbury from rotting the party at this of all moments'.[144] But with F.E.Smith following Chamberlain's line the Buxton speech threatened to reopen the whole tariff reform debate within the Unionist party which Balfour's conversion and the developments of 1909 had seemed to close. Blumenfeld feared that the *Daily Mail* intended to campaign for the complete abandonment of food taxes, while the Tariff Reform League was ready to organise a campaign to relegate the referendum on the lines of Chamberlain's speech.[145]

Chamberlain's point was clearly more than a matter of detail and Walter Long was astonished to find a small but energetic and able section of the party following the Birmingham line over the referendum. He diagnosed a new split in the party's ranks, which could become serious if not immediately healed, and looked to Balfour to make a clear pronouncement on the matter 'as I know many of our good men are anxiously looking for a lead'.[146] Long himself was rumoured to be about to inaugurate a Referendum League - something he vigorously denied - and he certainly believed that the Unionists should adopt the device as part of their programme of constitutional reform. To abandon it as regards tariff reform would expose them to the charge that they had only produced it as an election gimmick.[147] Long was convinced that very great harm was being done to the cause of tariff reform, and therefore to the cause of Unionism itself, by the behaviour of those protectionists who, as long as they got tariff reform, did not care about anything else.[148] In the absence of clarification from Balfour, however, diverse opinions were bound to proliferate. Bonar Law, for example, maintained that only if the referendum became a regular part of the British constitutional system would tariff reform have to be subjected to it, an opinion shared by Derby.[149] As Lansdowne told Balfour:

> our colleagues are deeply divided among themselves. Have you
> made yourself aware, for example, of the views held on the one
> side by Austen and Curzon and on the other by Finlay and
> Selborne? and when I couple these names I do not suggest that
> either the first two or the second think exactly alike.[150]

Thus, as the new year opened, Unionists still seemed as concerned with fighting one another as they were with opposing the Liberal government. Only for transient moments since the defeat of 1906 had the party presented the electorate with the coherent image of a viable alternative government. The policy re-examination that had necessarily taken place after the electorate's decisive verdict on Balfour's government had been neither dignified, harmonious nor ultimately conclusive. Though the party's parliamentary position had in simple numerical terms been vastly improved by the two general elections of 1910, at another level its position had become more difficult than ever. By forcing the Liberals back into their old alliance with the Irish Nationalists, the country's equivocal decision of 1910 meant that the central principles of Unionism were now in graver danger than they had ever been in the years immediately after 1906, despite the improvement in the Unionists' parliamentary representation. In this atmosphere of heightened crisis the failings of Balfour as leader of a party in opposition became ever more apparent. If Unionists could agree among themselves on little else, this at least was becoming a point of growing consensus.

* * *

Continuing divisions within the Unionist ranks left the party in a particularly vulnerable position in view of the importance of the issues which 1911 inevitably brought forth. Far from the election of December 1910 marking the climax of a period of intense political activity, it was widely seen as a staging post along an intrinsically dangerous trail which led towards ultimate decisions on the constitution and the Union itself. As Sandars noted, 'this Election is only a prelude - that and nothing else - and a prelude to great things'.[151] It was then unfortunate that recent policies had chilled or alienated a large body of opinion in the party and damped the ardour of some of its most enthusiastic spirits.[152] An attempt to hammer out the party's strategy at a meeting at Lansdowne House early in the new year proved confused and inconclusive with only 'a general canter over policy'.[153] Little in fact had been achieved by the time that the new session of parliament began. Austen Chamberlain later recorded:

> The opening of Parliament found the Unionist leaders ill-prepared and their councils in much confusion. We had declared for the reform of the House of Lords, but there was no agreement as to the extent and character of the change to be made. We had adopted the Referendum but even among those who welcomed it there was no agreement as to the circumstances in which it was to be applied. The Budget dispute was ended and the Budget which had raised such fears had become law, but we were now to face the battle over the Constitutional issue which the rejection of the Finance Bill by the House of Lords had brought to a head.[154]

It was in this unpromising situation that the Unionist party had to respond to the government's introduction of the Parliament Bill on 21 February. The Bill proposed that the Lords should not in future be able to amend or reject a Money Bill; that if a Bill were rejected by the Lords it would become law automatically providing not less than two years elapsed between its introduction and third reading in the Commons; and that the maximum duration of a parliament should be reduced from seven to five years. Official

Unionist policy at this time in regard to the Lords amounted to a combination of Lord Rosebery's proposals for reform together with Lansdowne's ideas for settling differences between the two houses of parliament, ultimately through a referendum.[155] One M.P. noted a strong feeling among backbench Unionists that these measures were likely to be a source of weakness rather than strength to the party, while Lansdowne himself feared that his proposals would provoke an immense amount of criticism and yet excite no enthusiasm among Unionist voters.[156] Certainly when Lansdowne introduced the party's proposals for reform on 8 May the response of the upper chamber was ominously unenthusiastic. Sir Almeric Fitzroy left a vivid account of this occasion:

> The atmosphere had been raised by expectation to a state of tense feeling seldom observable and a solemnity that was almost ominous spread itself along the crowded benches as the pale and attenuated figure of the Opposition Leader, with balanced phrase, graceful diction and judicial restraint, pronounced what was in effect a sentence of death upon the oldest legislative Chamber in the world .... I hear so great was the exasperation on the Tory benches after Lord Lansdowne's exposition that, if the negative to the second reading of the [Parliament] Bill had been moved, it might very probably have been carried.[157]

The problem was that Lansdowne's compromise proposals were only likely to appeal to that middle ground in the political spectrum whose very existence, in the light of recent events, was beginning to be questioned. To limit the number of hereditary peers entitled to sit in the upper chamber was not calculated to appeal to many Unionists, while for the vast majority of Liberals the fact that in Lansdowne's scheme the House of Lords would still retain its perpetual, if much reduced, Unionist majority was plainly unacceptable.

Since Unionists could not raise much enthusiasm for their own constitutional proposals, the focus of their attention inevitably turned to the far more radical plans of their Liberal opponents. With the breakdown of the constitutional conference the previous autumn, Balfour's initial inclination had been to allow the government's Parliament Bill to pass through the Lords without forcing the mass creation of new peers. Though warned by Garvin and others that such a surrender might break up the Unionist party, Balfour's overriding concern was to leave the upper chamber in the strongest position to resist a future Home Rule Bill, which the party political balance resulting from the general elections of 1910 had made likely if not inevitable. This aim could best be secured, he believed, by a House of Lords with reduced powers rather than one whose Unionist majority had been swamped.[158] In view of the Unionists' own inability to secure a parliamentary majority in the Commons, Balfour had come to the conclusion that the King could not ultimately refuse to comply with a demand by Asquith, should it be made, for a mass creation of Liberal peers.[159] Though his concern may have been genuine and far-sighted, Balfour characteristically gave the impression that he was not sufficiently interested in the issue.[160] By contrast, and rather optimistically, Leo Maxse was not in the least afraid of the threatened creation of peers becoming a reality 'for the simple reason that they will come over to our side as fast as they are made', while those who would later be active in the die-hard movement were already beginning to organise themselves to stiffen Lansdowne's arm.[161]

Despite the results of the election, Lansdowne refused to believe that the Parliament Bill would be passed in anything like its existing form.[162] If it came to the worst, he argued, the Unionists on returning to office could themselves play the numbers game and embark on a second batch of creations to override the new Liberal majority.[163] It seems that, before his death, Edward VII had not finally decided what his attitude would be towards a request for a mass creation of peers, although he certainly believed that to embark on such an exercise at the behest of the Liberal government would involve a degradation of the royal prerogative. His inexperienced successor's problems were compounded by the receipt of contradictory advice from the royal secretaries, Lord Knollys and Sir Arthur Bigge.[164] Additionally, many leading Unionists were ready to assure the new King that, should the government press the matter, the position and prestige of the Crown would be exposed to unjustifiable humiliation.[165] When Lansdowne met the monarch at the end of January 1911, he got the clear impression that King George abhorred the idea of a mass creation. This gave strength to Lansdowne in his hope that talk of a royal guarantee having already been given to Asquith was nothing but a gigantic bluff. In fact, partly through the connivance of Knollys, a royal guarantee had indeed been given and the government was determined to get the Parliament Bill on to the statute book more or less in the form in which it was first introduced into parliament.[166]

By June the somewhat cautious attitude of the Unionist leadership, with Lansdowne resting his hopes on the idea of amending the Parliament Bill, was beginning to cause resentment among the rank and file.[167] Yet any alternative course of action was full of danger. Walter Long warned that if the Unionist peers fought to the last ditch the country would not back them in a fight which the bulk of the electors would regard as a repetition of the electoral contest of the previous December.[168] But the situation was inevitably transformed when, in conversations with Balfour and Lansdowne, Lloyd George revealed that the government had indeed already secured the royal guarantee of which the Unionist leaders had been so sceptical. The effect of this revelation was particularly shattering for Lansdowne. 'He looked utterly smashed.'[169]

The crucial point was whether the Unionist peers were going to insist upon Lansdowne's amendments and if need be reject the bill on third reading if those amendments were deleted by the Commons.[170] It was upon this issue that the diehard forces began to muster, with Willoughby de Broke advising the venerable former Lord Chancellor, Lord Halsbury, that 'forces are at work urging [Lansdowne] to abandon the position he has taken up; and I think you will agree with me that we should try to influence him in the opposite direction'.[171] From now on the diehards served notice on Lansdowne that a split among Unionist peers was inevitable if he failed to fight the Parliament Bill to a bitter conclusion. The choice of the ancient Halsbury, 'installed as a sort of tribal "Ju-Ju" before whom [the diehards] and the *Morning Post* burned incense daily',[172] as their standard-bearer and nominal leader at least helped the diehards to surround their protests with an aura of revered dignity. As someone born almost a decade before the passing of the Great Reform Act of 1832, he could not, at the age of eighty-eight, be accused of attempting to further his own political career. But his emergence at this juncture once encouraged historians to suppose that what now took place was a revolt of political backwoodsmen - men who spent most of their time on their country estates and whose general lack of interest in political affairs had only been shaken by the palpable threat to their hereditary positions posed by the Parliament Bill.[173] As Dr. Phillips has conclusively shown, however, this stereotype is incorrect - 'analysis of House of Lords' attendance lists, intervention in debate, committee membership, office holding and participation in political organisations reveals that the diehards, as a group, were actually more active politically than the rest of the House of Lords taken as a whole.'[174]

When the shadow cabinet met to consider the problem on 7 July a distinct division of opinion was already evident among those present, but the majority view was that it would be unwise to resist the government's threat to create additional peers. Diehard sentiment continued, however, to grow with Leo Maxse complaining of the 'sickly sentimentalism and the intrigues in our Party to help the Radical Government and the wretched nervelessness of our Front Benchers'.[175] Strachey, always prepared to exaggerate Joseph Chamberlain's continuing influence in the determination of Unionist politics, severely under-estimated the extent of the diehard movement in claiming that it was 'Joe and only Joe and his mad henchman Garvin' who were ready to force the creation of peers.[176] Yet Balfour's 'nervelessness' was not likely to be remedied by the receipt of formal confirmation that a royal guarantee to create peers had indeed existed since before the last election.[177] The moving of Unionist amendments to the bill in the upper house obliged Asquith to inform the King that no alternative now remained to the creation of new peers.

When the full impact of this revelation had sunk in, its effect was clearly shown in the more conciliatory attitude adopted by Lansdowne in the third reading debate on 20 July. But, somewhat surprisingly, when the shadow cabinet again considered policy on 21 July, eight votes were still cast for a policy of resistance.[178] Though the Balfour-Lansdowne line of accepting the bill commanded a clear majority, the minority represented a substantial element of dissent. If reflected in the party as a whole, it meant that the leadership was unlikely to secure its policy of surrendering to the inevitable, by allowing the unamended bill to pass, without a struggle or indeed a split in the party's ranks. Balfour seems to have sensed this danger in toying momentarily with a half-way stance. If the government were forced into the creation of up to 100 new peers, he suggested, this would be a matter of indifference - a line of argument which Lansdowne and Curzon quickly extinguished.[179] Somewhat ominously, on the same day that the shadow cabinet met, the diehards gathered at Grosvenor House, the home of the Duke of Westminster, to pledge themselves to stand firm in resisting the government's bill. In the face of an apparent lack of leadership from Lansdowne, the peers rallied behind Halsbury, Selborne, Salisbury and others who were prepared to raise the standard of revolt.[180] Maxse, arguing that 'the white flag still dominates our Party', thought that it was quite impossible for things to go on as they were with a total lack of confidence between the party leaders and their nominal followers.[181]

An unruly scene in the Commons on 24 July served to illustrate the depth

of Unionist feeling that had been aroused. The incident seems to have been
stage-managed by George Wyndham, F.E.Smith and Hugh Cecil, in an
attempt to force Balfour's hand by revealing that he had lost control over the
Unionist opposition in the House of Commons.[182] Leo Amery later recalled:

> My most vivid impression is still of Hugh Cecil,in the front
> corner seat below the gangway, shouting 'traitor' [at Asquith]
> and gesticulating violently with his long lean arms; of others
> calling for Redmond, as the real ruler, and of Asquith standing
> at the box flushed and angry, rubbing his palms up and down
> the front of his thighs ... before he gave up the attempt to
> continue his speech.[183]

The situation was scarcely helped by a somewhat weary circular letter sent
on the same day by Lansdowne to all Unionist peers, recommending
submission to the government's will on the grounds that their lordships were
no longer free agents. If Lansdowne's difficulties were not great enough, they
were further increased when it became apparent that, in order to counter the
resistance of the diehards, certain Unionist peers were now contemplating
voting for the Parliament Bill rather than simply abstaining as the leadership
advised.[184] As Selborne warned,

> We can bear with each other with perfect temper and fairness
> so long as it is a question between abstaining and voting
> against;but if it comes to Unionist Peers voting for, then I
> know that the indignation and feeling among the party in the
> country will be intense and you will appreciate as well as I can
> what that means.[185]

A significant development was the emergence of the former Viceroy of India,
Lord Curzon, as an unlikely champion of the policy of surrender. His *volte-
face* took observers by surprise. A junior whip commented:

> How Curzon after being one of the most pompous advocates of
> adherence at all costs to the Lords' amendments can now so
> unblushingly admit that a few days ago he was merely bluffing
> and using grandiloquent language which he did not mean is
> marvellous and it will be a long time before I can think him a
> statesman again.[186]

At this point Balfour's attitude seemed curiously contradictory. In a letter
to Lord Newton, designed for publication in *The Times*, Balfour appeared to
take a strong line by announcing that he was prepared to stand, or if necessary

fall, with Lansdowne and that his advice to peers, though he did not wish to dictate policy, was that they too ought to follow Lansdowne.[187] This letter which accused the 'ditchers' of 'abandoning [their] leader' caused Austen Chamberlain 'pain and more than pain' and seemed to reverse Balfour's earlier line that the matter was one to be decided by the conscience of each individual for himself. Chamberlain, writing as bitterly to his leader as he did at any time during their long political association, argued that Balfour's letter was less an answer to the diehards' point of view than a denunciation of their conduct, especially as it was delivered to the press.[188] This 'very unpleasant letter' had made the position of the diehards very difficult indeed.[189] Yet at the same time that Balfour apparently nailed his colours to the mast in support of the 'hedger' policy, he struck a rather different note in his response to the attempts of party dissidents to follow up their parliamentary fracas, when Asquith had been forced to give up his attempt to address the House. It was now proposed to hold a dinner at the Hotel Cecil in honour of Lord Halsbury, to whom, in the words of Joseph Chamberlain , 'the country owes a debt of gratitude ... because in this crisis of his country's fate he has refused to surrender his principles'.[190] Balfour's somewhat curious reaction was to say that he had no objection to anyone attending the dinner, even though others readily recognised in this event a direct challenge to his leadership.[191] Strachey wanted Balfour and Lansdowne to announce that they regarded attendance at the dinner as a vote of no confidence in themselves, while Steel-Maitland hoped that the leaders would take the even bolder step of attending the dinner themselves.[192] While Balfour's letter to Newton appeared to make it impossible for a loyal Unionist to attend the dinner, the whips, much to their amazement, were instructed to tell Unionist members that they could go to the Halsbury dinner if they wished and were even permitted to go themselves. Bridgeman commented: 'This order was not an easy one to carry out, as every one wanted to know what "standing or falling by Lansdowne" meant if Balfour did not regard it as the duty of the party to abstain from the Halsbury dinner.'[193] To Walter Long the attitude of the leadership seemed like 'madness'.[194] Balfour's intention can only have been to try to play down the importance of the dinner as a possible focal point of discontent over his own leadership by feigning indifference to its guest list, and even encouraging his own supporters to attend in order to dampen down possible criticism.[195]

With Long fearing that the policy of the leadership was in danger of going by default for want of vigorous action, it was the diehards who clearly held the initiative. To counter the growing weight of diehard agitation Curzon and St.Aldwyn began urging peers to vote, it necessary, with the government to secure the passage of the Parliament Bill.[196] The evolution of Curzon's views on this issue is one of the more curious aspects of the whole episode. In contrast to Willoughby de Broke who hoped to have at his disposal to resist the bill 'every weapon save personal violence' - and he would 'not be averse to using even that' - Curzon acted discreetly behind the scenes. Careful canvassing enabled him to assess the voting intentions of the majority of Unionist peers, so as to calculate as finely as possible the number of Unionist votes that would be needed to carry the bill.[197] Though he had earlier ridiculed the whole idea of a huge creation of peers, Curzon had become convinced that Asquith was not bluffing and that, in the changed circumstances, surrender was the only viable option.[198]

Though Lansdowne could appreciate the reasoning of those Unionist peers who were coming near to actually voting with the government, he was anxious that their number should not be great, since the result of such action would be to widen existing divisions within the party. Though reluctant to speak out against anyone prepared to vote for the bill, his advice remained that his followers should abstain on the third reading.[199] Long thought that it would break up the party if it were known that Lansdowne had allowed peers to be asked to vote for the bill and blamed Balfour's attitude over the Halsbury dinner for putting the party in a very awkward position.[200] Robert Cecil, though 'no admirer' of the existing Unionist leadership, feared that the defection of Unionist peers into the government lobby would create such a storm of opinion as would 'sweep away both Lansdowne and Balfour and shatter the remnant of the Unionist party'.[201] But it was Balfour who seems to have persuaded Lansdowne to take a firmer line against any peer who actually voted with the government. Meanwhile the diehards were lulled into the belief that at the very most only half a dozen Unionist peers would support the bill.[202]

The continuing adherence of Austen Chamberlain to the diehard cause, besides throwing an interesting light on the absence of any doctrine of collective responsibility within the shadow cabinet, inevitably added respectability to the Halsbury campaign. On 31 July Chamberlain published a letter commending the diehard stance for saving the party from disgrace and 'our cause from disaster', while his father Joseph added his not insignificant support.[203] Long found Chamberlain's letter 'abominable' and urged Balfour to react with prompt and decisive action. The Halsbury group were hard at work in the constituencies with a powerful organisation while the party leaders were doing nothing. 'A.J.B.'s followers will drift away from him if prompt steps are not taken.'[204] Part of the problem appears to have been that Balfour was less committed to the policy of surrender than were some of his senior colleagues, including Lansdowne. As late as 7 August he seemed willing to contemplate a small creation of peers, even though Lansdowne and Curzon had been insistent that a government defeat over the bill would lead inevitably to a mass creation.[205] The diehards' determination was further increased when, for the government, Lord Crewe stated that the King's pledge had been given with 'natural and legitimate reluctance' - a remark which encouraged the belief that at the last moment the King might still refuse to carry out his ministers' bidding.[206]

The ultimate outcome of this constitutional drama remained uncertain until the final debate in the Lords on 10 August. The diehard L.S.Amery, elected to the Commons only three months before, recorded his observations:

A few dull speeches and then as a wind up,after the [Lord] Chancellor rose to move the Question,a somewhat pompous oration from Curzon, followed by another short vigorous appeal from Halsbury. We thought the debate was over, but Rosebery got up and made a last effort in favour of surrender.He sat down and Selborne leapt to the table and in a short speech of amazing eloquence denounced Rosebery and asked the House not to perish in the dark by its own hand, but to die in the light at the hands of its enemies. It was the last speech made under the old order and a fine one. Then came the division. For a few breathless minutes we were all huddled together in the Lobby. The first we heard was that 111 peers had gone into the No-Surrender lobby and we thought ourselves safe, but a minute or two later came the news that the Government had won. First report by 11, afterwards corrected to 17. Apparently, over 30 peers, not counting a dozen bishops, had voted with the Government for the destruction of the constitution. Went home very angry.[207]

The long fight over the Parliament Bill was thus over. But the Unionist party's concentration upon constitutional issues was not. For beyond the Parliament Act there lay an even more fundamental question in Unionist thinking. The party's feelings about this first alteration to the constitution would not have been so passionate had its members not perceived that its passing reopened the whole issue of Irish Home Rule which for nearly two decades had lain dormant in the Liberal party's legislative portfolio. If Unionists had finally decided that they should not fight the Parliament Bill to the last ditch, it was by no means certain that they would reach the same conclusion in relation to a second fundamental challenge to the existing constitution.

## NOTES

1.    Lord H. Cecil, *Conservatism* (London, 1912) p.243.
2.    Unionist rally in Nottingham 15 Jan.1906.
3.    J. Ramsden, *The Age of Balfour and Baldwin 1902-1940* (London, 1978) p.28.
4.    Salisbury to Selborne 20 May 1908, Selborne MSS 5/207.
5.    Balfour to Lansdowne 13 April 1906, cited Newton, *Lansdowne* p.354.
6.    Newton, *Lansdowne* p.370.
7.    Fitzroy, *Memoirs* i, 368.
8.    Collings to J. Chamberlain 28 Feb.1909, JC 22/47.
9.    B. K. Murray, 'The Politics of the "People's Budget"', *Historical Journal* 16 (1973), pp.555-70; J. Grigg, *Lloyd George: The People's Champion 1902-1911* (London, 1978) p.180. But Lloyd George may well have foreseen that, by going so far to undermine the revenue motives for tariffs, his budget was likely to provoke tariff reformers to some sort of resistance.
10.   *The Times* 30 April 1909.
11.   Chamberlain, *Politics from Inside* p.177.
12.   Rowland, *Liberal Governments* i, 222. Lord Esher agreed that it would be preferable for Balfour to pledge to repeal the land clauses of the Finance Bill once the Unionists were returned to power, rather than allow the Lords to reject the bill: J. Lees-Milne, *The Enigmatic Edwardian* (London, 1986) p.200.
13.   See Balcarres diary entry for 15 Feb.1908: 'I fancy the bolder spirits in the government may be tempted to rush an early dissolution ... when the old age pension scheme has been outlined .... We should

certainly be strengthened in arguing for tariff reform to meet that liability': Vincent (ed.), *Crawford Papers* p.106. See also F. Coetzee, *For Party or Country* (Oxford, 1990) p.114.

14.  *Manchester Guardian* 2 Jan.1910.
15.  Murray, 'People's Budget' p.558.
16.  Grigg, *People's Champion* pp.202-3. 'The Unionist party was, temporarily, more united than at any point since the Boer War': Coetzee, *Party or Country* p.125. Yet there were dangers for Balfour in this situation. An electoral victory on this issue would be a Chamberlainite victory; a defeat would be his and would damage the whole party: B. B. Gilbert, *David Lloyd George: the Architect of Change 1863-1912* (London, 1987) p.388.
17.  Clarke, 'Blackburn' pp.318-9.
18.  Cromer to Balfour of Burleigh 29 Sept. 1909, Balfour of Burleigh MSS 33. It is, however, true that members of the upper house most strongly opposed to the policy of rejection also tended to be well known for their commitment to free trade.
19.  Dugdale, *Balfour* ii, 57. Neither, of course, was it a case of Balfour foisting the policy on a reluctant party. By the late summer Unionists, with a few exceptions, had developed a consensus about rejection which stood out in marked contrast to their recent history of division and dissension.
20.  Murray, 'People's Budget' p.567; Grigg, *People's Champion* p.216.
21.  In his Bingley Hall speech on 22 September Balfour posed the stark alternatives as the 'bottomless confusion of socialist legislation' and the 'hopeful movement of tariff reform'.
22.  S. Koss, *Asquith* (London, 1976) p.103.
23.  Amery, *Chamberlain* p.935. Chamberlain carried more weight than J. L. Garvin, editor of *The Observer*, whom some have portrayed as the almost omnipotent manipulator of Unionist politics at this time: Gollin, *Observer* pp.115-7. Like many men on the fringes of political power, Garvin tended to exaggerate his own influence in shaping Unionist policy. He did, though, record one interesting meeting with Joseph Chamberlain : 'More tragic than ever to see him and listen to his smothered words, but more inspiring than ever to be in contact with his cool and resolute will. "This Budget tries to knock the House of Lords out of the Constitution." "Hope the Lords will knock it out!"': Gollin,

*Observer* p.100.
24. Statement published on 22 June 1909.
25. Blewett, *Peers* p.99.
26. A. O'Day (ed.), *The Edwardian Age: Conflict and Stability 1900-1914* (London, 1979) p.73.
27. Brett, *Esher* ii, 409.
28. Finlay to Strachey 11 July 1909, Strachey MSS S/16/3/14; Cecil, *All the Way* pp.112-3.
29. Lansdowne to Curzon 6 Sept. 1909, Curzon MSS Eur. F112/16.
30. Newton, *Lansdowne* pp.378-9.
31. Rowland, *Liberal Governments* i, 229-30.
32. R. Jenkins, *Mr. Balfour's Poodle* (London, 1954) p.82.
33. Chamberlain, *Politics from Inside* p.182.
34. Fitzroy, *Memoirs* i, 386.
35. H. Cecil to Balfour of Burleigh 21 Nov.1909, Balfour of Burleigh MSS 8.
36. Gollin, *Observer* p.125.
37. Murray, 'People's Budget' p.568; Coetzee, *Party or Country* p.119.
38. Sykes, *Tariff Reform* p.215.
39. Blewett, *Peers* p.114.
40. Clarke, *Lancashire* p.378.
41. Bridgeman diary, 'Review of the Election'.
42. Blewett, *Peers* chapter 7; Coetzee, *Party or Country* p.130.
43. Sandars to Balfour 21 Jan.1910, Balfour MSS Add. MS 49766.
44. Hamilton to Strachey 23 Jan.1910, Strachey MSS S/8/4/3.
45. Strachey to Hamilton 25 Jan.1910, ibid.
46. Chamberlain to Balfour 29 Jan.1910, AC 8/5/1. As the Chief Whip put it: 'It's like this Austen .... We've just got to rub the food duties in - keep on pegging away at them, that's what I say': Chamberlain, *Politics from Inside* pp.201-2.
47. Blewett, *Peers* p.158; Murray, 'People's Budget' p.569.
48. F. Ware to Chamberlain 25 Jan.1910, AC 8/3/12.
49. Salisbury to Chamberlain 1 Feb.1910, AC 8/5/6.
50. Brett, *Esher* ii, 440.
51. Newton, *Lansdowne* p.385. The core proposal in Rosebery's scheme was that possession of a peerage should no longer automatically give the right to sit and vote in the House of Lords. Lords of Parliament

should comprise (a) peers chosen by their fellows and nominated by the crown; (b) peers sitting by virtue of their offices and qualifications; (c) peers chosen from outside.

52.  Balfour to Lansdowne 29 Dec.1909, Balfour MSS Add. MS 49730.
53.  Ibid 29 Jan.1910, Add. MS 49766.
54.  Chamberlain to Balfour 29 Jan.1910, AC 8/5/1.
55.  Lansdowne to Chamberlain 31 Jan.1910, AC 8/5/4; note by Lansdowne on Salisbury's memorandum of 28 Jan.1910, Salisbury MSS S(4) 67/20.
56.  Sandars to Garvin 15 Feb.1910, cited Gollin, *Observer* p.169; note for Balfour 1 March 1910, Balfour MSS Add. MS 49766.
57.  St. John Brodrick to Selborne 23 Feb.1910, Selborne MSS 3/105.
58.  Salisbury to Selborne 19 March 1910, ibid 6/44.
59.  R. Cecil to Lady Selborne 29 April 1910, ibid 74/25.
60.  Strachey to Rosebery 26 April 1910, Strachey MSS S/12/7/21.
61.  Chamberlain, *Politics from Inside* pp.226,255-9.
62.  Sykes, *Tariff Reform* p.232.
63.  Salisbury to Selborne 29 April 1910, Selborne MSS 6/55. Joseph Chamberlain shared the prevailing pessimism concerning the next general election 'if we went on as at present': Amery diary 5 July 1910.
64.  Gollin, *Observer* p.195; Ayerst, *Garvin* p.94.
65.  Leo Maxse was not impressed by the Unionist delegation and lamented that 'if we had a Joe to look after our interests we should be all right and this Conference would be turned to splendid purpose .... One feels his absence every hour of every day': Gollin, *Observer* p.198. From the pages of the June issue of the *National Review* Maxse warned: 'It is not time to talk compromise. Those who begin negotiating with Mr.Asquith will find themselves sold to the Molly Maguires before the end of the chapter.'
66.  Lansdowne to Curzon 16 June 1910, Curzon MSS Eur.F. 112/17.
67.  The present account follows C. C. Weston, 'The Liberal Leadership and the Lords' Veto 1907-1910', *Historical Journal*, 11 (1968). This article makes use of the contemporary notes of Austen Chamberlain and comments made on these by Lord Lansdowne: AC 10/2/35-65.
68.  For example, Lansdowne's supposed domination of the conference and his role in bringing about its failure: Jenkins, *Balfour's Poodle* p.159;

R. C. K. Ensor, *England 1870-1914* (Oxford, 1936) pp.423-4.
69.  Weston, 'Liberal Leadership' p.528.
70.  Memorandum by Lansdowne 10 Sept.1910, Sandars MSS c. 761/36.
71.  Brett, *Esher* iii, 25; Balfour to A. Chamberlain 20 Sept.1910, AC 8/6/11.
72.  Chamberlain to Balfour 23 Sept.1910, AC 8/6/16.
73.  G. D. Phillips, *The Diehards: Aristocratic Society and Politics in Edwardian England* (Harvard, 1979) p.133.
74.  Croft, *Life of Strife* pp.54-5.
75.  Hood to Sandars 10 Oct.1910, Sandars MSS c.761/170; Lansdowne to Willoughby de Broke 11 Oct.1910, Willoughby de Broke MSS, House of Lords Record Office, 1/8.
76.  Searle, *National Efficiency* p.198.
77.  Masterman, *Masterman* p.163.
78.  Chamberlain to Lansdowne 26 Aug.1912, AC 10/2/22.
79.  Searle, *National Efficiency* pp.177-98. An indication of Lloyd George's duplicity is given by the way in which he suggested to F. E. Smith that the conference itself was in danger of breaking up because of the Unionist delegation's refusal to consider a federal solution to the Irish question. In fact no such proposal was made: Chamberlain to Cawdor 21 Oct.1910, AC 10/2/15.
80.  This is how Lloyd George later portrayed his own actions: D. Lloyd George, *War Memoirs* (London, 1938) i, 20-23.
81.  R. Fanning, 'The Unionist party and Ireland 1906-10', *Irish Historical Studies*, 15 (1966), p.165.
82.  Garvin to Maxse 6 Oct.1910, cited Blewett, *Peers* p.162.
83.  Chamberlain to Balfour 19 Oct.1910, Sandars MSS c.761/222; Chamberlain to Cawdor 21 Oct.1910, AC 10/2/15.
84.  Fanning, 'Unionist party' p.167.
85.  Smith to Chamberlain 20 Oct.1910, AC 12/28.
86.  *The Times* 29 Oct., 4 Nov., and 11 Nov.1910.
87.  Searle, *National Efficiency* p.193; Balfour to Chamberlain 24 Oct.1910, AC 10/2/9. Lloyd George's curious suggestion (*War Memoirs* i, 23) that his proposals commanded widespread support among the Unionist hierarchy and that only the intervention of the former Chief Whip, Aretas Akers-Douglas, prevented their adoption is not supported by the surviving archival record. Either Lloyd George

was strangely ill-informed or carrying out a belated vendetta against Douglas.

88. R. J. Scally's interesting attempt to relate this episode to similar examples over the preceding decade of growing frustration with the straitjacket of party politics and to the apparent fulfilment of the ideals of business efficiency in government with the formation of the Lloyd George coalition in December 1916 is marred by the author's repeated inaccuracies and exaggerations. Scally is, however, right to stress the state of flux in party politics in the decade before 1914 which suggested that a major realignment of political allegiance was by no means out of the question: R. J. Scally, *The Origins of the Lloyd George Coalition* (Princeton, 1975).
89. Fanning, 'Unionist party' pp.168-9.
90. Chamberlain to Lansdowne 26 Aug.1912, AC 10/2/22.
91. Brett, *Esher* iii, 27.
92. Memorandum by Lansdowne 17 Oct.1910, AC 10/2/28.
93. Copy of Finlay's notes on a meeting of Unionist leaders 18 Dec.1910, AC 10/2/57.
94. Lansdowne to Chamberlain 27 Aug.1912, AC 10/2/23.
95. Note by Chamberlain 25 Dec. 1913, AC 10/2/57; Dugdale, *Balfour* ii, 61-2.
96. Note by Selborne 8 Nov.1910, Selborne MSS 74/41.
97. Fitzroy, *Memoirs* ii, 422.
98. Balfour to Garvin 22 Oct.1910, Balfour MSS Add. MS 49795.
99. Gollin, *Observer* p.235.
100. Camperdown to Balfour 12 Nov.1910, Balfour MSS Add. MS 49861.
101. Hood to Sandars 11 Nov.1910, Sandars MSS c.762/32.
102. Amery to F. S. Oliver 12 Nov.1910, Amery MSS c.35; Sandars to Balfour 9 Nov.1910, Balfour MSS Add. MS 49767.
103. Cecil to Balfour of Burleigh 2 May 1910, Balfour of Burleigh MSS 37.
104. Ibid 17 May 1910, 36.
105. Balfour to Derby 6 Oct.1910, Derby MSS, Liverpool City Library, 2/18; Gollin, *Observer* p.238; Clarke, *Lancashire* p.380. Much of Lancashire's importance derived from the contemporary practice of staggered elections. It was believed that early declarations in the North of England would affect voting behaviour in the South.
106. Goulding to Law 4 Aug.1910, Law MSS 21/3/10.

# 110 LOYAL OPPOSITION

107. Balfour to Law 15 Oct.1910, ibid 21/3/15.
108. Derby to Law 31 Oct.1910, Derby MSS 2/19.
109. Gollin, *Observer* pp.239, 245.
110. Garvin to Sandars 14 Nov.1910, Balfour MSS Add. MS 49795.
111. Strachey to Selborne 16 Nov.1910, Strachey MSS S/13/7/4; Blewett, *Peers* pp.180-1.
112. Chamberlain, *Politics from Inside* p.300.
113. Gollin, *Observer* pp.247,262.
114. Sandars to Garvin 26 Nov. 1910, cited ibid p.257.
115. Garvin to Sandars 27 Nov.1910, cited ibid p.260.
116. Law to Balfour 26 Nov.1910, Law MSS 18/8/14. As Gollin has shown, Lord Blake's assessment of Law's role in these developments is misleading: Gollin, *Observer* p.265; R. Blake, *The Unknown Prime Minister: the Life and Times of Andrew Bonar Law 1858-1923* (London, 1955) p.108.
117. Lansdowne to Balfour 25 Nov.1910, Balfour MSS Add. MS 49730; Sandars to Garvin 27 Nov.1910, cited Gollin, *Observer* p.261. Lord Cromer believed that Lansdowne's influence was decisive in influencing Balfour: Cromer to Derby 30 Nov.1910, Derby MSS 2/19.
118. Balfour to Chamberlain 28 Nov.1910, cited Chamberlain, *Politics from Inside* p.304.
119. Law to Sandars 29 Nov.1910, Law MSS 18/8/15.
120. Webb, *Our Partnership* p.466.
121. Gollin, *Observer* pp.265-6.
122. Brett, *Esher* iii, 37.
123. For Walter Long's objections on this point, see Long to Balfour 20 Jan.1911, Balfour MSS Add. MS 49777.
124. Blewett, *Peers* p.187.
125. As Austen Chamberlain wrote to Richard Jebb of the *Morning Post* : 'I will not allow myself to be run against Balfour for the leadership. As long as he likes to keep it, he stands a head and shoulders above the rest of us. I am bound to him by many ties of personal affection, Party allegiance and political regard, and though I see his faults as a leader I also know his strength and I will not join any movements, open or secret, directed against him, nor will I allow myself to be used in opposition to him': Petrie, *Chamberlain* i, 270.
126. Webb, *Our Partnership* p.466.

127. Selborne doubted the capacity of the British elector to assimilate a new idea in less than four weeks and was certain that, had the referendum been adopted immediately after the January election, 'the whole position would have been altered': Selborne to Balfour 24 Dec.1910, Selborne MSS 1/139.
128. Derby to Hood 4 Dec.1910, Derby MSS 2/19.
129. Cromer to Derby 30 Nov.1910, ibid.
130. Chamberlain to Balfour 1 Dec.1910, Balfour MSS Add. MS 49736; Elliot to Chamberlain 7 Jan.1911, AC 8/7/11.
131. Chamberlain to Lansdowne 18 Dec.1910, AC 8/7/6; Balfour to Chamberlain 30 Nov.1910, AC 8/7/3.
132. A. Chamberlain, *Politics from Inside* p.316.
133. Hewins to Chamberlain 15 Dec.1910, AC 8/7/14. Joseph Chamberlain argued that tariff reform had 'not been sufficiently worked .... Wherever we have put it in the forefront we have at least gained generally on the pollings': J. Chamberlain to Amery 12 Dec.1910, JC 21/1/19.
134. Maxse to Law 14 Dec.1910, Law MSS 18/6/145.
135. Maxse to Goulding 10 Dec.1910, Wargrave MSS A/3/2; Coetzee, *Party or Country* p.135.
136. Ridley to Law 27 Dec.1910, Law MSS 18/6/150; Ridley to Chamberlain 16 Dec.1910, AC 8/7/26.
137. Lansdowne to Long 19 Dec.1910, Long MSS 445/8; Lansdowne to A. Chamberlain 14 Dec.1910, Balfour MSS Add. MS 49730.
138. Sandars to Balfour 21 Dec.1910, Balfour MSS Add. MS 49767.
139. *The Times* 15 Dec.1910.
140. Chamberlain to Lansdowne 18 Dec.1910, AC 8/7/6; Lansdowne to Balfour 23 Dec.1910, Sandars MSS c.762/204. Lansdowne could not agree that Balfour's words bore this limited interpretation. 'If the Referendum is to be defended at all,' he maintained, 'and to find a place in our policy, it must to my mind be defended upon the ground that we are ready to resort to it whenever a new departure is made in reference to a "matter of great gravity" not yet "adequately submitted" to the country, and, I should say, even when both Houses are agreed. Tariff Reform seems to me to be obviously a "matter of great gravity"': Lansdowne to Long 23 Dec.1910, Long MSS 445/8.
141. Note by Sandars in a collection of press cuttings of Balfour's speeches,

March 1911, Sandars MSS c.762/130.

142. Derby to Sandars 15 and 19 Dec.1910, Balfour MSS Add. MS 49743. Derby expressed himself more cautiously but in the same sense to Law: Derby to Law 17 Dec.1910, Law MSS 18/6/147.

143. Sandars to Short 15 Dec.1910, Balfour MSS Add. MS 49767; Sandars to Akers-Douglas n.d., Douglas MSS, Kent County Record Office, c.478/10.

144. Garvin to Sandars 15 Dec.1910, Balfour MSS Add.MS 49795; Garvin to Goulding 16 Dec.1910, Wargrave MSS A/3/2; Gollin, *Observer* p.274; *The Observer* 18 Dec.1910.

145. Blumenfeld to Sandars 17 Dec.1910, Blumenfeld MSS, House of Lords Record Office, SAN7.

146. Long to Lansdowne 20 and 28 Dec.1910, Long MSS 445/8; Long to Comyn Platt 6 Jan.1911, ibid 449/17; Long to Balfour 29 Dec.1910, ibid 445/3.

147. Memorandum by Long 22 Dec.1910, Sandars MSS c.762/198; Long to 'John' 29 Dec.1910, Long MSS 445/2; J. Lawrence to Long 22 Dec.1910, ibid 445/9; Long to Lawrence 26 Dec.1910, ibid. Derby shared Long's belief that to abandon the referendum would be seen as 'political trickery' and confided his intention to withdraw from political life if Chamberlain's line were followed by the party as a whole. Derby's worry was that Balfour would not be strong enough to deal with Chamberlain: Derby to Long 4 Jan.1911, Long MSS 445/10; Derby to Curzon 11 Jan.1911, Curzon MSS Eur. F 112/18.

148. Long to Lawrence 20 Dec.1910, Long MSS 445/9.

149. Law to Derby 19 Dec.1910, Law MSS 18/8/16; Derby to Lawrence 14 Jan.1911, Derby MSS 4/39.

150. Lansdowne to Balfour 19 March 1911, Balfour MSS Add. MS 49730.

151. Gollin, *Observer* p.272.

152. Lawrence to Long 4 Jan.1911, Long MSS 445/9.

153. St. John Brodrick to Salisbury 18 Jan.1911, Salisbury MSS S(4) 69/12.

154. Chamberlain, *Politics from Inside* p.317.

155. For Rosebery's proposals, see footnote 51 above. Lansdowne's proposals included (a) a joint sitting to settle disputes arising out of 'ordinary' bills; (b) a referendum to deal with disputes involving 'a matter of great gravity' which had not been adequately submitted to the judgement of the people; (c) a joint committee presided over by the

Speaker to determine whether or not a bill was a money bill. Pure money bills would be exempt from interference by the upper chamber.
156. Robert Sanders diary 3 March 1911; Lansdowne to Balfour 19 March 1911, Balfour MSS Add. MS 49730.
157. Fitzroy, *Memoirs* ii, 443. Sanders commented two days later that 'Lord Lansdowne's scheme for reform of House of Lords has fallen very flat': Sanders diary 10 May 1911.
158. Balfour to Sandars 28 Dec.1910, Sandars MSS c.762/241; Gollin, *Observer* pp.311-3.
159. Brett, *Esher* iii,41.
160. W. S. Blunt, *My Diaries*, (2 vols, London,1919-20) vol.ii, p.353.
161. Maxse to Goulding 19 Dec.1910, Wargrave MSS A/3/2; A. Wilson Fox, *The Earl of Halsbury, Lord High Chancellor, 1823-1921* (London, 1929) p.235.
162. Lansdowne to Chamberlain 14 Dec.1910, AC 8/7/19.
163. Lansdowne to Strachey 10 March 1911, Strachey MSS S/9/7/4.
164. H. Nicolson, *King George the Fifth* (London, 1952) pp.129-30.
165. Ibid, p.149.
166. As he told Lord Esher, Balfour was unable at this stage to convince Lansdowne that the mass creation of peers might really take place: Brett, *Esher* iii, 55; note of conversation with Sir Francis Hopwood 21 May 1914, Gerald Balfour MSS 118.
167. Lansdowne to Salisbury 13 April 1911, Salisbury MSS S(4) 70/10.
168. Long to Lansdowne 22 June 1911, cited Petrie, *Long* pp.153-4.
169. Masterman, *Masterman* pp.200-1.
170. Lord Newton withdrew his amendment after Lansdowne 'begged [him] particularly not to divide': Newton to Strachey 17 July 1911, Strachey MSS S/11/1/5.
171. Willoughby de Broke to Halsbury 11 June and 10 July 1911, Halsbury MSS Add. MS 56374; Wilson Fox, *Halsbury* pp.232-3,5.
172. A. Clark (ed.), *A Good Innings: the Private Papers of Viscount Lee of Fareham* (London, 1974) p.118.
173. Winterton, for example, suggested that many of the diehard peers 'had never even been in the Chamber, except to take the oath': Winterton, *PreWar* p.177. George Dangerfield wrote of 'hereditary nobodies' living an 'obscure and doubtless a useful existence on their country estates': G. Dangerfield, *The Strange Death of Liberal England 1910-*

*1914* (New York, 1935) pp.22, 42.

174.   G. D. Phillips, 'The "Diehards" and the Myth of the
       "Backwoodsmen"', *Journal of British Studies* 16 (1977), p.108. See
       also G. D. Phillips, *The Diehards: Aristocratic Society and Politics in
       Edwardian England* (London, 1979) chapter 1. This misconception was
       shared by many contemporaries. Newton, for example, assessing the
       diehards' probable numerical strength at around fifty, surmised that
       'probably nearly all of them are quite obscure people': Newton to
       Strachey 17 July 1911, Strachey MSS S/11/1/5.

175.   Maxse to Blumenfeld 10 July 1911, Blumenfeld MSS MAXS 1.

176.   Strachey to Newton 18 July 1911, Strachey MSS S/11/1/5. See also
       Strachey to Stamfordham 18 July 1911, ibid S/13/5/1. Nonetheless,
       Chamberlain's views on the matter were unequivocal. The Lords, he
       thought, had made a mistake in spending so much time over the
       question of their own reform - they should have kept their energies for
       fighting the government's bill. 'Our men have all through been too
       polite to the Government when they ought to have been nasty':
       Conversation with H. F. Wilson 16 July 1911, JC 22/145. All who
       met Chamberlain at this time were left in no doubt about his adherence
       to a policy of 'no surrender'. See, for example, Amery, *Political Life*
       i, 378.

177.   F. E. Smith to Balfour 14 July 1911, Balfour MSS Add. MS 49861.

178.   Dugdale, *Balfour* ii, 68 gives the following pattern of voting. For
       resistance : Selborne, Halsbury, Salisbury, A. Chamberlain,
       Wyndham, Carson, Smith and Balcarres. Against resistance : Curzon,
       Midleton, Londonderry, Chaplin, Long, Bonar Law, Douglas (out of
       loyalty to Balfour), Lyttelton, Derby, Ashbourne, Steel-Maitland and
       Finlay.

179.   S. H. Zebel, *Balfour* (London, 1973) p.168; G. W. Balfour, 'Note of
       talk with Lord Balcarres', 10 Sept.1911, Gerald Balfour MSS 276. The
       belief that the government would be content with a fairly limited
       creation was shared by many of the leading diehards: Lord Willoughby
       de Broke, *The Passing Years* (London, 1924) p.286. Salisbury
       understood that the King would not consent to create more than the
       minimum needed to pass the bill: Chamberlain to Balfour 26 July
       1911, AC 9/2/1. Unless this reasoning is accepted, the apparent
       blindness of the diehards to the implications of their actions, which

would lead to a permanent minority status for the Unionists in the upper chamber, becomes difficult to comprehend.

180. Newton, *Lansdowne* p.423.
181. Maxse to Sandars 21 July 1911, Balfour MSS Add. MS 49861.
182. Blunt, *Diaries* p.371; R. Churchill, *Churchill* ii, companion pt.2, 1103.
183. Amery, *Political Life* i, 380.
184. Lady V. Hicks Beach, *Life of Sir Michael Hicks Beach* (2 vols, London, 1932) vol.ii, p.269.
185. Selborne to Steel-Maitland 28 July 1911, Steel-Maitland MSS, Scottish Record Office, GD 193/155/2.
186. Bridgeman diary 24-29 July 1911; D. Southern, 'Lord Newton, the Conservative Peers and the Parliament Act of 1911', *English Historical Review* 96 (1981), pp.834-40.
187. Bridgeman diary 24-29 July 1911.
188. Chamberlain to Balfour 26 July 1911, AC 9/2/1.
189. Chamberlain to Selborne 25 July 1911, Selborne MSS 74/143.
190. Balfour to Chamberlain n.d., AC 9/2/2.
191. Sanders diary 26 July 1911; Bridgeman diary 26 July 1911; Long to Halsbury 25 July 1911, Halsbury MSS Add. MS 56374; Balfour of Burleigh to Halsbury 25 July 1911, Balfour of Burleigh MSS 56. The *Evening News* wrote openly of 'the anti-Balfour dinner'.
192. Strachey to Lord Onslow 25 July 1911, Strachey MSS S/17/2/8; Steel-Maitland to Selborne 25 July 1911, Selborne MSS 74/142.
193. A. Boscawen to Law 26 July 1911, Law MSS 18/7/190; Bridgeman diary 26 July 1911; G. Balfour notes of talk with Lord Balcarres 10 Sept.1911, Gerald Balfour MSS 276.
194. Long to Steel-Maitland 31 July 1911, Long MSS 449/58.
195. Curzon regarded the Halsbury dinner as a failure. 'His exultation was great and his language only appropriate to the defeat of a political opponent': Sandars 'Diary of Events in Connection with the passage of the Parliament Bill', 12 Aug.1911, Sandars MSS c.763/162.
196. Bridgeman diary 24-29 July 1911.
197. Wilson Fox, *Halsbury* p.255; note by Curzon on his role in the Parliament Bill crisis, n.d., Curzon MSS Eur. F112/89.
198. Earl of Ronaldshay, *The Life of Lord Curzon* (3 vols, London, 1928) vol.iii, pp.55-6; note by W. Ormsby Gore of a meeting at Hatfield on

19-21 Dec.1910, 29 Dec.1913, Willoughby de Broke MSS 6/12.

199.　Lansdowne to Curzon 29 July 1911, Curzon MSS Eur. F112/89; Fraser, 'Unionist Debacle' p.359.

200.　Long to Lansdowne 30 July 1911, Long MSS 448/7.

201.　Cecil to Balfour of Burleigh 5 Aug.1911, Balfour of Burleigh MSS 56.

202.　Chamberlain, *Politics from Inside* p.342; Fraser, 'Unionist Debacle' p.359; Sandars 'Diary of Events'; Selborne to Salisbury Aug.1911, Salisbury MSS S(4) 70/125.

203.　J. Chamberlain to Halsbury 4 Aug.1911, Halsbury MSS Add. MS 56372; Fraser, 'Unionist Debacle' p.358; A. Chamberlain to Amery 2 Aug.1911, Amery MSS D44.

204.　Long to Lansdowne 2 Aug.1911, Long MSS 448/7. This episode is important for understanding the animosity which existed between Long and Chamberlain at the time of the contest for the succession to Balfour in November. Sandars wrote of Long's 'vendetta' against Chamberlain for his letter of 31 July: Sandars 'Diary of Events'; Vincent (ed.), *Crawford Papers* p.208; Long to St. Aldwyn 2 Aug.1911, Long MSS 448/29.

205.　Sandars 'Diary of Events'.

206.　Nicolson, *George V* p.154.

207.　Barnes and Nicholson (eds), *Amery Diaries* i, 81-2. See also Amery, *Political Life* i, 381. The King seems to have been greatly relieved that the need to create 400 new peers had been avoided: 'My dear Rosebery, I thank you with all my heart, Yours very sincerely, George RI', cited Lees-Milne, *Enigmatic Edwardian* p.233.

# 6

# ORGANISATION 1905-1914

In an age when even the majority of those in government did not look upon politics as a full-time occupation, the organisation of a party in opposition was inevitably somewhat rudimentary. To lose office and to face, at least before the Parliament Act of 1911, the possibility of up to seven years in the political wilderness, fulfilling a constitutional but largely impotent duty, was a daunting prospect. Most leading politicians placed in such a position tended to divert more and more of their time to extra-parliamentary interests. Many might realistically conclude that they were unlikely to hold public office again. Away from Westminster local party managers could often do little to prevent what were, at the best of times, only loosely constructed party organisations from fossilising or even disintegrating. There were, however, signs that this situation was beginning to change. As the expanded electorate ensured that politics became more of a full-time commitment, so the realisation increasingly grew that, even when out of government, a party needed to keep its machinery well oiled, both inside parliament and in the country, in order to convince the electorate and itself that it was a viable alternative administration, capable of resuming the reins of government whenever the opportunity arose. A party needed not only alternative policies but the apparatus to formulate those policies, to put them across, and to keep them in the public eye. As far as the making of opposition policy was concerned, the nineteenth century had seen the beginnings of an institutionalised practice whereby former ministers continued to meet together in subsequent periods of opposition as the 'ex-cabinet'.[1] Under Balfour, partly because of the extent of the defeat of 1906 and partly as a result of the prolongation of the years of opposition, the ex-cabinet developed a subtly different complexion and the phrase 'shadow cabinet' crept into common usage.[2] Sandars employed the term as early as March 1906, but many contemporaries continued to use the two titles interchangeably.[3] Certainly the shadow cabinet of these years was a less formalised institution than it has since become. A junior whip defined it with as much exactitude as was possible: 'the Shadow Cabinet is formed of ex-Cabinet ministers sitting on the opposition side and any others whom the leaders may wish to summon, and is usually attended by the Chief Whip'.[4] It met when the leader decided that the situation required it and on no fixed basis.[5]

But while the nomenclature employed by contemporaries may not always have reflected the fact, the distinction between an ex-cabinet and a shadow cabinet was potentially an important one, the one looking back to the last period of government and the other forward to the next. A junior whip gave expression to the confusion which continued to exist:

> I don't know whether the 'Shadow' is retrospective, or projecting - whether it is meant to indicate our next government or to pay compliments to those who have previously served. Anyhow, the room is half filled with ... excellent though discredited politicians whose inclusion in a future Conservative government would create dismay, perhaps revolt among the rank and file.[6]

The actual membership of the shadow cabinet in these years reflected the fact that the leadership never successfully grappled with this dilemma. Consequently, as a policy formulating body, it gave perpetual trouble. To omit individuals gave offence, yet to invite them might give rise to unspoken claims for office which would be difficult to evade once the party returned to power. In 1908 Balfour went to the length of inviting the seventy-seven year old Jesse Collings to a dinner of Unionist leaders, in order to make it clear 'to all mankind' that the people who dined should not necessarily be regarded as members-elect of a new government to be constituted in the dim and distant future - 'for no human being would put Jesse Collings into a Government'.[7]

As the years of opposition opened Lord Lansdowne suggested streamlining the normal practice of the ex-cabinet through the formation of a small committee, including four or five members from each house of parliament, which would hold at least weekly meetings. Balfour's answer, however, was that it would be very difficult to exclude any member of the previous cabinet who still had a seat in parliament.[8] This response determined the nature of the body with which Balfour had to deal during his years as Leader of the Opposition. Some figures were included who had not been serving in the Unionist cabinet when the government left office in 1905. The former law officers, Edward Carson and Robert Finlay, became regular members; Bonar Law, in 1905 still only Parliamentary Secretary to the Board of Trade, rose rapidly through the party hierarchy; and Steel-Maitland attended after becoming Party Chairman in 1911. But the most prominent of the younger generation was F.E.Smith, who was only elected to parliament in 1906.

Smith's rapid rise may be attributed to his performance in the Commons where he supplied the kind of devastating criticism of the Liberal government for which disheartened Unionists had vainly looked to Balfour. The dramatic years between the rejection of the People's Budget by the House of Lords and the passing of the Parliament Act were the making of Smith. By December 1910, Garvin was calling for his promotion to the front bench, to 'make the back benchers think with encouraged feelings that the "flow of promotion" - blessed thing - had begun again'.[9] Balfour too was anxious to secure Smith's membership of the shadow cabinet, but was correspondingly concerned at the offence this might cause to anyone who was now to be excluded.[10]

Smith, however, was an exception. On balance, membership of the shadow cabinet tended to reflect the last Unionist administration rather than look forward to the next, making it considerably harder for talented newcomers to make their way through the party's ranks. In other words, as the long years of opposition continued, the personnel of the shadow cabinet became increasingly elderly and less representative of the party's new blood. As Bridgeman noted in 1912: 'I am doubtful if such a Shadow Cabinet as now exists is ever likely to be much in touch with current opinion.'[11] Four years earlier Bonar Law had expressed the fear that in a future Unionist government Balfour would endeavour to 'bring back all the old gang'.[12] The average age of the shadow cabinet which Balfour handed on to Bonar Law in 1911 was 56. When Smith joined it at the beginning of 1912 he was, at 39, by far the youngest member and the only one with no previous experience of government. More revealing, however, was the presence in it of several figures who were most unlikely ever to serve in a future Unionist government. The former Lord Chancellor, Halsbury, was then aged 88. Lord Ashbourne, aged 74, had first served as Lord Chancellor for Ireland as long ago as 1885, while Aretas Akers-Douglas was still attending meetings of the shadow cabinet in 1914, even though his tenure of the Home Office between 1902 and 1905 was generally thought to have been disastrous.[13] Henry Chaplin, aged 71, had not served in a Unionist government since 1900. In 1911 the Unionist leadership tried to rid itself of Chaplin's embarrassing presence by putting his name forward for a peerage, but Prime Minister Asquith would not cooperate. Sadly Chaplin had 'no conception of his own uselessness' and always managed to find his way to meetings of the shadow cabinet even when his name was deliberately omitted from the written invitations.[14]

These difficulties no doubt encouraged both Balfour and Bonar Law to call

the shadow cabinet as infrequently as possible, and only when those important
and controversial issues were at stake upon which some sort of authoritative
pronouncement had become imperative. In August 1913, for example, Bonar
Law held a shadow cabinet in order to gain authority to make policy
declarations on the questions of payment for M.P.s and on female suffrage.[15]
Even then, major decisions were sometimes made without reference by the
leader to the consultative body. Balfour's decision to submit any future
Unionist tariff reform budget to a referendum is the most glaring example of
this - and one which caused untold resentment, not only among the
Birmingham wing of the party.[16] Similarly, in 1914 the decision to support
the Liberal government in its attitude to the developing international crisis was
taken by a small group of Unionist leaders meeting at Lansdowne House on
1 and 2 August, rather than by a full gathering of the shadow cabinet.[17] The
ill-defined authority of the shadow cabinet was particularly evident at election
times. It was not regarded as responsible for issuing the policy statement upon
which the party would fight the election. The manifesto remained the personal
appeal of the leader and was delivered as an address to his constituents. In
such circumstances the manifesto could not be regarded as the sole policy
pronouncement of the party's campaign. Party policy was taken to be not only
what the leader said but also what other prominent front-bench members of the
party said in speeches during the campaign, even though this might include
inconsistent or incompatible statements. The first general election of 1910 saw
the issuing of an unusual joint manifesto, amounting to a press handout on the
divisive issue of tariff reform, signed by both Balfour and Joseph
Chamberlain.[18]

The shadow cabinet appears to have been most frequently summoned
between 1909 and 1911 to discuss policy in relation to the People's Budget
and the Parliament Bill. Yet these regular meetings did nothing to endear the
institution to the party leader. One member noted that 'meeting after meeting
developed hopeless and inharmonious divisions'.[19] Balfour was hardly likely
to agree with Walter Long's assessment that the ex-cabinet ministers ought to
meet at least once a fortnight whilst parliament was sitting.[20] After his
experience over the Parliament Bill, Balfour confided that he would 'certainly
hesitate' before calling any further shadow cabinets.[21]

Part of the problem was that dissent among members was less likely to
result in resignation than was the case with a real cabinet. In a memorandum
prepared for Bonar Law when he became party leader, the Chief Whip pointed

out that the responsibility for differing from the decision of the majority was 'prescriptive' in opposition, as against the immediate outcome of such a difference in an official cabinet.[22] Similarly in 1911 Balfour complained to Austen Chamberlain that

the shadow cabinet showed irreconcilable differences of opinion. Had it been a real Cabinet one of two things would have followed. Either the dissentient minority would have resigned, or they would have silently acquiesced in the decision of the majority. There could, of course, be no question, in the case of a shadow cabinet, of resignation. There certainly has been no silent acquiescence.[23]

This meant that members of the shadow cabinet had more scope to deviate from the official line than has become the practice in more recent times.[24] Austen Chamberlain, in particular, took advantage of this laxity and enjoyed a freedom of expression which would now be regarded as unacceptable from a member of a shadow administration.[25] To the promptings of his staff that he should be less indulgent towards such excesses, Balfour could only reply that in opposition he had no authority and could only 'give good advice'.[26]

Bonar Law's succession to the leadership offered an opportunity to review the condition of the shadow cabinet. Bridgeman felt that 'when a new leader succeeds to an old one, he should undoubtedly be unhampered by any traditional obligation to consult any such body, but should be allowed to consult with those of his own choice be they few or many'.[27] The Chief Whip concurred. Now was the proper moment to review claims to membership and to modify personnel. He believed that the shadow cabinet should either be restricted to exceptional meetings or else be summoned 'with tolerable regularity'. His own advice to Bonar Law was to place greater reliance in future on 'restricted conference'.[28] This counsel appears to have been accepted and for some time the shadow cabinet virtually fell into abeyance.[29] In February 1912 Lansdowne attempted to avoid even the 'semblance of a "shadow cabinet"' by convening only a small group of Unionist leaders, while Bonar Law argued that the leading Unionist peers should meet separately to avoid reviving the institution.[30] When the two leaders actually got down to the names of those who should be invited to 'a kind of modified "Shadow"', the exclusion of given individuals presented as many problems as it had for Balfour. Lansdowne, with his greater experience of party management, complained that 'if the H of C "Shadows" are to number eleven, I don't see how I can leave out Londonderry (who is very touchy and, at this moment, on the war path) and I fear old Halsbury will be furious'.[31] The Chief Whip noted the meeting of February 1912 as the first since Balfour's resignation, and 'all the obsolete mandarins were present, Ashbourne, Chaplin, Lord Halsbury etc.'[32] Bonar Law's continuing reluctance to summon the shadow cabinet resulted partly from the conviction that such a gathering would inevitably provide a forum for open dispute between his two rivals for the leadership, Austen Chamberlain and Walter Long. 'Whatever the former says is immediately pronounced ridiculous and "I never heard such a proposal".' Though Law's attitude was perhaps understandable, it did little to expedite decisions on crucial policy issues. After Law had been leader for nearly two years, the Chief Whip was still complaining that no final decision had been reached on the National Insurance Act, Food Taxes, the referendum, or the constitution of the House of Lords.[33]

The organisation of the Unionists' opposition inside parliament also left much to be desired. In the Commons attendance was poor, even on the front bench. In the last parliamentary session under Balfour's leadership, Edward Carson, the former Solicitor-General, attended only 40 divisions out of a total of 340.[34] Even at the time of Lloyd George's famous People's Budget, the Liberal Charles Hobhouse noted: 'the debate was dull and at one time only one Tory was present in the House and on five occasions when a member addressing the House sat down, no Tory rose to speak'.[35] Though 157 Unionists were returned at the general election of 1906, the party's effective strength at Westminster in terms of reliable working M.P.s was probably no more than 40 or 45. 'It is really a disgraceful state of things', complained Lord Balcarres, 'and I am surprised how seldom the newspapers draw attention to our apathy.'[36] With such a large proportion of the parliamentary party 'ill, idle or incompetent', the strain upon those left to confront the government in the Commons was very considerable.[37] Even well-known front-bench figures such as George Wyndham, Arthur Lee, Alfred Lyttelton and Andrew Bonar Law were 'seldom seen except when some topic of personal interest arises' and their absence inevitably had a demoralising effect on enthusiastic backbenchers and party managers alike.[38] At the start of Bonar Law's leadership the Chief Whip urged that the front bench should be well occupied, even when no ex-minister was actually required to speak. He felt that Unionists lost more chances at question-time than during any other hour of the day. 'Ministers are slack because of our indolence.' Also disturbing was the reluctance of members of the Unionist front bench to dine in the Commons with their parliamentary rank and file.[39]

Even had its members been more assiduous in their parliamentary attendance, the Unionist front bench could not have put forward an array of talent to match that of the Liberal government, whose cabinet must rank among the most distinguished in twentieth-century British history. Balfour's shortcomings as a leader of the opposition have already been considered.[40] Balfour himself provided the most eloquent commentary on Lord Lansdowne, Unionist leader in the Lords. 'I shouldn't call him very clever', he later recalled. 'He was - I don't quite know how to put it - better than competent.'[41] Of those beneath them Austen Chamberlain seemed pedestrian, especially when compared, as he inevitably was, with his illustrious father. Walter Long was alarmingly unpredictable, able one day to appear as a champion of traditional Toryism and the next as an advocate of advanced social reform. His jealousy of colleagues made him 'an unbearable nuisance from time to time', but 'within a few minutes he embraces us all with the most fulsome assurances of affection, admiration and respect'.[42] On his infrequent appearances in the Commons, Bonar Law was developing a reputation as an effective and hard hitting debater. But few other leading Unionists made much of an impression. To make matters worse, the front bench was depleted by an unusual number of deaths in these years, including those of Arnold-Forster, George Wyndham, Earl Percy and Alfred Lyttelton. Indeed a Unionist electoral victory at any time before the outbreak of the First World War would probably have found the party ill-prepared to stock the Treasury bench. 'I do not see where ministers are to be drawn', confessed Lord Balcarres. 'The outlook from the point of view of ministerialisation is full of discouragement.'[43]

Several Unionist ministers from the government of 1905 had, of course, lost their seats in the *débâcle* of 1906. But the most senior of the defeated front benchers - Balfour, Long and Lyttelton - quickly returned to the Commons after by-election victories. The return of other former ministers was of doubtful benefit to the party. Henry Chaplin, elected for Wimbledon in 1907, 'won't be much use at Westminster' insisted a junior whip: 'his florid speech and rotund person will do no more than provoke laughter - while he is thoroughly lazy and can't be guaranteed to play the game'.[44] But 1906 had also cut a great swathe through the middle order of the party, removing figures who found it far more difficult to return to the Commons at by-elections. In such a situation M.P.s of obvious talent such as Bonar Law and F. E. Smith had the opportunity to make a rapid advance through the party's ranks, but new talent did not abound. It is striking that, apart from Smith, only two other future cabinet ministers came into the Commons for the first time in 1906 - Robert Cecil and William Bridgeman. Only in 1910 was there a major intake of new blood with clear ministerial potential.

On going into opposition Lansdowne had suggested to Balfour the creation of a number of small standing sub-committees to deal with various areas of policy.[45] This proposal was not put into practice, although the party occasionally made use of *ad hoc* committees of the shadow cabinet, as, for example, in February 1914 when the question was raised of amending the Army Annual Bill in the House of Lords.[46] Within the Commons only haphazard attempts were made to assign shadow portfolios, essentially on the basis of continuing specialisation in the affairs of an ex-minister's old department. This system tended inevitably to break down where the ex-minister had died, become a peer or left political life, and Balfour appears to have made little effort to groom successors by encouraging specialist spokesmen to fill the gaps.[47] The work for the most part fell into Balfour's own hands. 'Generally', noted Bridgeman, 'it was a sort of go-as-you- please style of warfare.'[48] Balfour perhaps feared the loss of a future Prime Minister's powers of patronage through the allocation of specific opposition duties in the House of Commons, even though this would have increased the party's efficiency in debate.[49] When Bonar Law became leader, the Chief Whip advised that 'the subjects for debate should be assigned where no representative or obvious ex-minister survives'.[50]

As the Unionists' last Chancellor of the Exchequer, Austen Chamberlain led the attack on the 1909 Finance Bill, while Walter Long, a former Chief Secretary for Ireland, was the principal spokesman in debates on the Home Rule Bill and on Ireland generally. But even this procedure was never entirely rigid. In 1909 Long complained that Edward Carson had been chosen to move the rejection of the government's Irish Land Bill, with George Wyndham winding up the debate. The Chief Whip had 'not even thought fit to tell [Long] of [his] decision, much less to consult [him] beforehand'.[51] Two years later, and with a new Chief Whip installed, Long complained with considerable anger of the hopeless way in which the work of the opposition was carried out in the House of Commons. He was convinced that 'if we go on in the old happy-go-lucky fashion nothing but disaster can follow'. The request that he should speak on Lloyd George's insurance bill was nothing but 'a haphazard arrangement' made apparently to suit the convenience of Austen Chamberlain. Being the most senior Privy Councillor on the Unionist front bench after Balfour, Long felt that the time had come to put an end to 'an impossible system and a most disagreeable one'.[52] Yet at the time of Balfour's resignation such major areas as the Home Office, foreign affairs and India all lacked official Unionist spokesmen in the lower house, while other subjects such as local government were inadequately catered for.[53]

Overall the impression is that the management of the party's parliamentary affairs was extremely unbusinesslike. A characteristic incident occurred at the end of 1910 when Lansdowne found himself having to insist that a meeting of the shadow cabinet should be held *before* Balfour went abroad for his Christmas holiday, rather than delaying the meeting, as Balfour suggested, to the very eve of the new parliamentary session, for which the opposition's tactics needed to be finalised.[54] Not surprisingly the opposition frequently found itself out-manoeuvred by the government's parliamentary managers. Earlier that year George Wyndham lamented to his wife that

until after Asquith and Arthur and others had spoken ... we - the Opposition front bench - did not know what line we were to take officially, or the order of Debate, or the Opposition amendment, or who was to move it, or when it was to be moved ... no one was prepared - and no one could have been prepared.[55]

Even Alick Hood recognised that it would be far better for party leaders to meet a couple of days earlier, consider the questions to be debated and arrange for speakers.[56] Yet many of the most glaring deficiencies resulted from the over-burdening of Hood and the consequent collapse of his control over the management of the Commons. Backbench Unionist M.P.s were among the chief casualties.[57] Lansdowne found the Chief Whip's behaviour towards the young men of the party 'most disheartening'.[58] As with their senior colleagues little effort was made to organise their parliamentary activity. There was no attempt to divide up work and give reasonable parliamentary opportunities to the ordinary backbench M.P. The result, noted Long, was 'a great deal of dissatisfaction and a present feeling of depression and misgiving'.[59] Liaison between the party hierarchy and the backbenchers was notoriously poor. Curzon was among those who commented on the need for more coordination and consultation between 'the framers of policies at the top and the supporters of policies below'.[60]

*   *   *

The organisation of the party outside Westminster displayed as many shortcomings as it did within the House of Commons. The problem was essentially two-fold. At a personal level a succession of inept Principal Agents had failed to sustain the well-oiled efficiency which had characterised the party machine in the 1890s. Lionel Wells presided over the party organisation during the crucial last two years of the Unionist government, but despite a reputation for administrative competence revealed little capacity for the practical side of political and party work. The problem was compounded by the presence in the Chief Whip's office from 1902 to 1911 of Alexander Acland-Hood, a man who was temperamentally ill-disposed towards radical reorganisation. Weakness at the top inevitably left more scope for the efforts of individual local agents than was usual in the Liberal party, but the limited circulation and relative failure of the Conservative Agents' Journal, launched in 1902, indicates the difficulty of coordinating such activity.[61]

Problems of personnel merely served to magnify a more deep-rooted malaise. In organisation, as in other spheres, the Unionists had not yet grasped the need for streamlined professionalism to cope with the modern party political system. Party organisation seemed still to presuppose a small electorate of loyal and easily manipulated voters and to have no concept of the need to convert opponents or win over floating opinions. Such a system was inevitably breaking down, based as it was upon suppositions that were a generation out of date. Illustrations of the party's failure to adapt to the realities of the twentieth century abounded, of which the unmanageable combination of parliamentary and constituency duties in the hands of the Chief Whip was probably the most glaring example. The fact that the Unionist 'party' was still a coalition of separate political forces did not make matters any easier. The concurrent and often wastefully repetitious activities of the Liberal Unionist Council and the Conservative Central Office created a major structural difficulty, exacerbated by their policy differences especially over education and tariff reform. Similarly, the ill-defined and somewhat uneasy relationship between Central Office and the National Union posed increasing problems in the first years of the new century.[62]

The question of party organisation outside Westminster occupied Joseph

Chamberlain's attention in the aftermath of the general election of 1906. It was indeed an important part of his strategy to capture the party in his own interest. Reorganisation and the ultimate triumph of tariff reform were inextricably linked in Chamberlain's mind, as his critics and opponents were quick to recognise. Chamberlain had once advised the young Lloyd George, 'whatever you are tempted to do in politics, be sure you have the party machine behind you'.[63] He obviously had faith in his own advice and even before the general election had made strenuous efforts to gain influence inside the Central Office.[64] Electoral defeat inevitably encouraged calls for a thorough overhaul of the party machinery.[65] But Mr. Fraser's comment that 'nothing came of the proposal to reform the Conservative central organisation. It petered out in a few inconclusive conversations' does less than justice to the almost frantic manoeuvres in which Chamberlain engaged after the party meeting in February.[66]

Chamberlain defined the problem in the following terms:

> The issue seems to me the same as that which was raised by Lord Randolph Churchill in 1883 and involves the decision as to whether the Central Organisation is to remain an autocratic and non-representative body or whether with a democratic electorate it ought not to be strictly representative and responsible to the Party as a whole.[67]

The old structure, Chamberlain believed, had been finally discredited and 'a great democratic and representative organisation' should now be substituted in its place.[68] Reorganisation would also involve the formal fusion of the Conservative and Liberal Unionist organisations. As a popular body, the reformed central organisation would inevitably fall under the grip of Chamberlain himself - the one contemporary politician who had successfully made the transition from patrician to popular politics. As Edward Carson had noted:

> The more I go about the more I see that Chamberlain has got hold of the bulk of our people. I don't mean so much our leading men as those of the working classes who follow us.[69]

In his desire that the party's representative associations should now be reviewed with the object of popularising them, and of securing working class involvement, Chamberlain was aiming to move the Unionists in a quite novel direction. But the cry of 'democratising' party organisation filled traditional Tories with alarm. Robert Cecil felt that Chamberlain - 'an impulsive and unscrupulous demagogue'- was indulging in 'American Bossism in its worst form'.[70] His brother Hugh warned Balfour , 'You will be mad if you consent - but you often are mad, alas!'[71] At the party meeting in February 1906 Balfour had committed himself to the setting up of a small committee to investigate the question of party organisation.[72] In May it was decided to set up a Standing Advisory Committee of seven, including the Chief Whip, to liaise between the National Union and the Central Office and to bring matters of importance to Balfour's attention. The balance of power on the Advisory Committee might become a question of crucial importance. Worried that Chamberlain might now succeed in moulding the party even further in his own image, the Unionist free traders had formally repudiated Balfour's leadership early in March.[73] Much to their dismay a committee set up by the National Union to look into the question of the reorganisation of the Central Office was composed almost wholly of tariff reformers and there were 'ominous paragraphs' as to the lines on which the reorganisation should take place.[74] The tariff reformers had already gained control of the National Union and had resolved in November 1905 that it was desirable to strengthen the central management of the party by the addition of a popular representative element in close touch with the constituencies. But the attack on Central Office was a vital part in Chamberlain's strategy, since the office was very much an expression of Balfour's control over the party. One ex-cabinet minister described it as 'a private club where all but Sandars and a few cronies are seen as intruders' under the 'well intentioned but imbecile direction of Acland-Hood'.[75]

After his interview with Balfour on 2 February Chamberlain commented:

His views about organisation seem to me equally unsatisfactory. He was not enthusiastic at the suggestion of a union of forces and indeed under the circumstances I cannot wonder . Why should he in any way weaken his control if he is determined to go forward on the present lines?[76]

The Chief Whip feared that Chamberlain intended to gain control of the party's election machine and noted that he was very active behind the scenes, 'working old Harry Chaplin for all he is worth' to block one suggested reorganisation proposal which would have deprived the Chamberlain faction of overwhelming power.[77] At this stage Chaplin was Chamberlain's chosen instrument to achieve his aims, and at the time of the Valentine agreement Chamberlain pressed Chaplin's claims to be the first of the defeated Unionists

for whom a seat in parliament should be sought.[78] The Unionist hierarchy
tried delaying tactics in an effort to thwart Chamberlain's ambitions. During
April and May there were constant meetings of the reorganisation committee
at which Chaplin put every obstacle in the way of progress, 'obviously in
order to produce chaos and to invoke the aid of Mr. Chamberlain to deliver
the Party from its embarrassment'. But Chaplin proved to be an unsubtle and
unsuccessful lieutenant and soon forfeited Chamberlain's confidence. Lord
Ridley commented:

> I am sometimes inclined to think that Chaplin has made his
> object a little too apparent and that we might have got our own
> way more if he had not so frightened all the old women.[79]

Thus, when Hood informed Chamberlain that in the event of a vacancy at
Worcester Chaplin would most likely be the Unionist candidate, Chamberlain
replied that Chaplin was 'useless and played out' and that he wanted a younger
man in his place.[80]

Chamberlain's official biographer has implied that after the end of May
1906 he took few further initiatives on the question of party reorganisation.[81]
In fact, with Chaplin's efforts frustrated, Chamberlain turned his attention to
the younger Unionist M.P.s, urging them to protest against the attitude of
Balfour and Hood and suggesting to them that they were receiving insufficient
attention and consideration. Hood was able to counter this manoeuvre by
holding a friendly conference with the young members whom Chamberlain had
approached. The latter next directed his attention to the Conservative peers,
while simultaneously inspiring articles in the *Morning Post*, *Outlook* and
*National Review*, attacking Balfour indirectly through Sandars, Hood and the
Central Office. At a specially arranged meeting at Sandon in Staffordshire,
Chamberlain urged the eight or nine young peers present to ask for a voice in
the selection of candidates and generally for control of the Central Office. He
also gave them the significant advice that if they failed they might consider the
option of joining the Liberal Unionist ranks. The details of this clumsy intrigue
reached Balfour via Lord Churchill, but despite the party leader's attempt to
allay their anxieties, the peers addressed him a letter demanding increased
powers on the Advisory Committee and the right to appoint the Chief Agent
of the party. This manoeuvre confirmed the opinion of Balfour's staff that
Chamberlain's aim was to devise measures to convert the Advisory Committee
into a committee for managing the party.

Chamberlain's stroke in early July largely put an end to the campaign for a major reform of the party's organisation. Not surprisingly no progress was made towards amalgamating the Conservative and Liberal Unionist organisations, despite Chamberlain's complaint that there had been 'a sort of competition' between the officials of Conservative headquarters and those of the Liberal Unionist and tariff reform organisations.[82] At a special conference later that month Leo Maxse complained that the Central Office was as autocratic as before, but his motion was withdrawn and approval given instead to a rather meagre list of reforms which left the Central Office still firmly under Balfour's control, though deprived now of some of its spending power.[83] Balfour's staff were easily able to counter further efforts by Maxse and Bridgeman to dominate the Advisory Committee in such a way that it could overrule the Chief Whip, assume most of his functions, and place itself between him and the leader.[84] Thereafter its importance declined and there is little evidence that the Advisory Committee played a significant role in the management of the party's affairs.[85] Though the National Union secured control over party propaganda, publications and the party's professional lecturing staff, this fell far short of what Chamberlain had sought. Separation of the National Union and the Central Office was now carried out at every level. Thus, rather than Chamberlain's envisaged professional machine, an even more amateurish and less centralised system emerged.[86] The division of functions between the popular and central organisations was ill-conceived. The National Union had always been designed as a servant of the party in parliament and was fundamentally unsuited for its new functions.[87] It was being used in 1905 and 1906 by the leaders of the tariff reform movement as a vehicle to propagate their own ideas and its enhanced status did not reflect a spontaneous upsurge of democratic control from the party's rank and file whom it nominally represented. After 1906 the National Union and the Central Office continued, as *The Times* put it, to resemble 'two motor cars driven side by side along a narrow road, with the attendant risks of collision'.[88]

\*    \*    \*

The combination of Chamberlain's illness and the slow reconciliation to the prospect of a lengthy period in opposition forced the question of party reorganisation into the background after the summer of 1906. Balfour's progressive acceptance of the policy of tariff reform during the course of 1907 also reduced pressure for any further action in this area. Behind the scenes, members of the Tariff Reform League continued to strive at constituency level to capture local associations, often cloaking their activities behind the respectability of the Liberal Unionist Council.[89] The League was potentially the strongest pressure group the Unionist party possessed, but because the party itself remained divided over tariffs the League was never wholly successful in mobilising local opinion, especially in areas such as Lancashire where opposition to food taxes remained entrenched.[90] Some organisational improvements followed the appointment of J. Percival Hughes as Principal Agent at the end of 1906, a nomination that was generally well received both within and outside parliament.[91] Lord Balcarres noted of Hughes:

> He made a good impression: seems a shrewd man and is certainly an expert on registration and election law which is a vast improvement on his two predecessors.[92]

Hughes did much to re-establish harmony between the Central Office and the National Union and also recruited a number of experienced agents to advise him and to watch over local organisation, he himself visiting constituencies and giving help where necessary.[93]

The dimensions of the problem were such, however, that changes of personnel at the top could never fully overcome organisational inertia, entrenched administrative practices and deep-rooted opposition to innovation. The Central Office remained the primary obstacle to reform. Long complained in 1910 that when local associations applied for help or guidance they either received no reply at all for a considerable time, or replies which when they did come were quite useless.[94] Similarly Sandars complained that many people formed a poor opinion of the Central Office because they were kept waiting in a room,

> or in an apology for a room, which would not answer the purpose of a small Attorney's office in the country. When a man has kicked his heels for a long time ... and at the end of it finds that he cannot have an appointment with the Chief Agent, he goes away and tells all his friends ... that the Central Office machinery has hopelessly broken down.[95]

At a local level the shock of defeat in 1906 induced many Unionist associations to review their positions and initiate change. Developments in Bolton in 1907 and 1908 were typical of local initiative. Minimum subscriptions were reduced, and wider representation was secured at General Council meetings, while the Executive Committee was broadened to include representatives from the association's council, the Workingmen's Association, the Primrose League, individual subscribers and, later, Junior Unionists.[96] Nonetheless the *National Review* could still claim in July 1909 that the majority of party agents were 'about as fitted for their duties as is a sergeant of marines to navigate a ship'.[97] It was of course these men who provided the recruitment material from which the Central Office was staffed. As Sandars put it:

> they are excellent men of their type ... but they have no sympathy with new ideas, no imagination, no elasticity of method, in a word they are old-fashioned.[98]

In general Balfour studiously avoided giving any attention to party organisation. But such an attitude was difficult to maintain after the jolting shock of two further general election defeats in 1910. It was not simply that the high hopes of parliamentary recovery were only partially fulfilled in January 1910. The tariff reformers had this time fought the contest far more on their policy terms than in 1906 and, unable any longer to place the blame on party policy, the hawks among them sought an institutional scapegoat. Having presided over two successive election defeats, Acland-Hood's position had become particularly vulnerable. Before long members of the shadow cabinet began to express their misgivings. Walter Long, content at this stage to depersonalise his criticisms, tried to persuade Balfour that the party was asking men to do more than they could do. 'A man', he stressed,

> may be the best Whip in the world and yet be unable to combine with it the very different work of organising the country. A man may do some of the work of the Head Agent with brilliant success and yet be unable to cope with the extraordinary difficulties which constantly arise in connection with the management of the Party's affairs.[99]

A few days later Henry Chaplin called for the ending of the dual responsibility that existed between the National Union and the Central Office.[100] Nearer to Balfour, Sandars was prepared to criticise Hood for his dilatory response to the evidence of organisational shortcomings revealed by the January election. Hood had disarmingly observed that 'Hughes might as well stay away until over Easter as there was really nothing for him to do'. Akers-Douglas, who like Sandars had hitherto been a loyal supporter of the Chief Whip, now scathingly remarked that Hood was totally ignorant of any of the details of provincial organisation outside his own electoral division of West

Somerset.[101] Subsequently Hood was moved to strengthen Hughes' staff by giving him a second-in-command and five additional district agents.[102]

On the backbenches Leo Amery felt the need to reconstruct the whole party organisation. Convinced of the 'utter badness' of the Central Office, he asserted that nothing could be done until Hood was either 'poisoned or pensioned'. Amery hoped to make use of the business expertise of the dynamic young Canadian, Max Aitken, but at all events the removal of Hood should not be long delayed.[103] By September 1910 an acrimonious correspondence on the subject of party organisation was passing between Hood and Walter Long.[104] The following month the *National Review* entered the fray, arguing that even if the Central Office were manned by archangels it would remain inefficient as long as it was centralised in the Whip's room of the House of Commons.[105] Sandars did his best to persuade the press to keep their hands off the Central Office and the question of organisation, but as the second election of 1910 approached was himself ready to think in terms of a redistribution of functions which would leave Lord Balcarres as Chief Whip, Hood trustee of party funds and Hayes Fisher director of the Central Office.[106] Others were as yet more cautious. R. D. Blumenfeld of the *Daily Express*, while recognising that 'the rusty old machine' was in need of attention, firmly believed that the shortcomings of the Central Office could not be remedied by a covert attack on its officials.[107] Akers-Douglas, who was soon to head the committee of enquiry into party organisation, at this stage believed that criticism of the Central Office was largely unfair. Arguing that 'the machine went well and smoothly', he believed that such defects as existed could be placed at the door of the National Union, and he remained convinced that the Chief Whip should retain overall responsibility for both parliamentary and constituency work.[108]

Inevitably, though, when it became clear that the election result of December 1910 was substantially the same as in January, the undercurrent of criticism burst out into a torrent. 'The more I hear of things the more convinced I am of the absolute rottenness of the whole Central Office', commented Lord Malmesbury.[109] Frustrated Unionists had no other scapegoat upon which to vent their spleen, apart from Balfour himself - a development for which the majority were as yet unready. Sandars got near to the heart of the problem:

> The Central Office has stood still for more than a generation.
> It lives the same cramped life; it employs the old methods; it

works with the same class of men ... and meanwhile the whole
face of the political world and the Party has changed.[110]
This third successive electoral setback was inevitably a mortal blow for
Acland-Hood. St.John Brodrick concluded that the time had come to take the
organisation of the party in the country out of the hands of the Chief Whip.
Despite Hood's many qualities, 'the Archangel Gabriel could not give
satisfaction in all these capacities under present conditions'.[111]

The case of Southampton was illustrative of the problems of organisation
and of the amateurishness of the Central Office. The local agent noted:

When I arrived here last Monday fortnight the place was
absolutely naked as far as organisation was concerned. No
agent had been here since last March, not a single voter had
been canvassed, all the old returns had been burnt or destroyed,
the local association was heavily in debt, the Ward Committees
might as well have been non-existent and a paralysing apathy
pervaded the whole Party in the Borough. That was the
situation which the Central Office had invited me to step into
at about a fortnight before the poll! [112]

Only in isolated areas was the party organisation anything like satisfactory.
Lancashire, and in particular Liverpool, was the outstanding example. In
Liverpool, under the guidance of Alderman Archibald Salvidge and the
patronage of Lord Derby, a professional efficiency existed, characterised by
the close intermeshing of parliamentary and municipal politics. This helped to
sustain party morale and prevent the machinery going stale between general
elections.[113] When Joynson Hicks, whose previous electioneering experience
had been confined to Lancashire, moved to Sunderland, he was 'astonished at
the difference'.[114] Salvidge would therefore be an automatic choice for
membership of the committee of enquiry that was soon to be appointed. The
investigations which he then undertook merely confirmed the isolated
superiority of his organisation in Liverpool. 'In only one instance', he
asserted, did he find 'even an elementary state of organisation.' Salvidge
continued:

When I entered upon this work outside Liverpool I did so with
a view to ascertaining whether it were possible to adopt our
plan of Workingmen's Associations in more Constituencies, but
I am now of the opinion that in most places before thinking of
starting auxiliary organisations the ordinary Conservative

Associations, which should be the parent Association in each
division, require overhauling and putting upon a thoroughly
representative and workable basis. [115]

It appears to have been Walter Long who first put the idea of an enquiry
into Balfour's mind. Confident that there would be no difficulty in finding the
right men for the main administrative posts, he put forward himself and Akers-
Douglas as two Conservatives - Liberal Unionists had to be avoided - upon
whom Balfour could safely devolve responsibility for conducting an
investigation. Long was convinced of the gravity of the situation and certain
that without action there was bound to be very serious trouble 'in our
unfortunate and distracted Party'. The existing system had broken down
because of a failure to recognise the changes that had taken place in political
life, both in the Commons and in the country, over the previous two
decades. [116] At the beginning of 1911 Long sent Balfour a petition signed by
a large number of Unionist M.P.s calling for a formal enquiry, and it was
probably his vehemence which caused Hood to object to Long's possible
chairmanship of such a body. [117] Long was also in touch with Comyn Platt,
the former organiser of the Confederacy, who was marshalling backbench
opinion for a 'thorough cleansing of the Augean Stables'. [118]

With pressure coming also from Lords Curzon, Salisbury and Derby,
Balfour had little option but to go ahead with a Unionist Organisation
Committee in February 1911. Balfour caused considerable offence to Hood by
not consulting him over the question of an investigative committee, but made
a wise choice in selecting Akers-Douglas to head the enquiry. [119] Douglas
was a widely respected figure, well versed as a former Chief Whip in the
question of party organisation, but having left the Central Office as long ago
as 1902 he could be relied upon to approach the question without prejudice.
His chairmanship was to be balanced by the selection of a cross-section of the
party's interest groups, designed above all to create confidence among 'the
younger and more ardent members'. [120] The committee which finally emerged
was perhaps disposed to be rather more critical of the *status quo* than Balfour
would have preferred, since it included Long and Willoughby de Broke , but
left out Curzon and Hayes Fisher from the leader's original selections. [121] St.
John Brodrick sensed 'every disposition to be drastic', but doubted the method
to be used, while the *National Review* and *Morning Post* voiced similar
misgivings. [122] The committee was free to range widely in its enquiries, but
there was general sympathy for Amery's conviction that an appropriate starting

point was that the so-called 'democratic' reforms initiated in 1906 were all in the wrong direction and that the division between Conservative and Liberal Unionist organisations had 'become an absurdity'. The great need was to make the organisation really effective and, through a proper system of decentralisation, ensure that it was in effective touch with the constituencies.[123]

The Organisation Committee met a total of 43 times, interviewed 103 witnesses and received written testimony from a further 289 others. By April 1911 it was ready to issue an interim report, which proved in the event to be the chief fruit of its deliberations. This concluded that the concordat of 1906, creating a system of divided control between the Central Office and the National Union, had been the chief obstacle in the way of an efficient central organisation. The 1906 arrangement seemed to have resulted in a complete paralysis of the Central Office; no serious effort had been made to overcome the difficulties thus created, nor, it was said, had any representations been made to Balfour that the machine created in 1906 was one which could not possibly work. The interim report recommended reviving the earlier practice whereby the Principal Agent also acted as Honorary Secretary of the National Union, and, most importantly, further recommended that the Chief Whip should no longer be responsible for the management of the affairs of the party in the country.[124] A renewed element of personal friction was introduced into the situation when Douglas refused to sign the committee's report if a paragraph, recommending that Hood and Hughes be not retained in office, was included. Eventually Douglas was obliged to write privately to Balfour conveying the terms of this paragraph.[125] Hood, taken into Douglas's confidence, now found his own position quite untenable:

> I have sacrificed time, health, money, estate, sport and family life for the sake of the Party .... When I have been anxious to go I have been asked to stay on and now I am to be summarily dismissed. No Chief Whip ... however unsuccessful he may have been has ever been treated like this and no man with an atom of self-respect would stand it for a moment.

He determined now to resign his seat in the Commons and take no further part in politics.[126] Meanwhile Long encouraged him to believe that it was largely the fault of Sandars that his troubles had become 'so damnable'.[127]

Under the reforms now carried out, organisation, finance and the provision of literature and speakers were vested in the Central Office, which was to be headed by a new official, the Chairman of the Party, who would carry cabinet rank. The National Union, which was to have been the vehicle of Chamberlain's reforms in 1906, now found its wings neatly clipped. It would revert to its function as a body to educate and reveal the views of the rank and file.[128] Problems of personnel again intervened to complicate the smooth introduction of these changes. Walter Long objected bitterly to the choice of Arthur Steel-Maitland as Chairman, both on account of his lack of seniority and because of his Birmingham connections.[129] Akers-Douglas, while recognising Steel-Maitland's capacities as an organiser, also doubted his suitability for the post and, after some difficulty, succeeded in conveying this opinion to Balfour.[130] The latter responded with tact and dexterity. On the one hand Maitland's appointment was appropriate since the major impetus for reform had come from the party's younger elements. Yet his youth was a positive advantage since it would remove any chance that he could exercise undue influence within the party. Moreover his Birmingham background was misleading, since his politics were Conservative rather than Liberal Unionist.[131]

Overall the new measures very considerably strengthened the Unionist party machine. In particular, the pruning of the Chief Whip's functions and the creation of the office of Chairman were landmarks in the party's transition into the world of modern politics. A system derived from less strenuous times had gradually resulted in placing upon the Whip a burden too great for one man to bear. Originally it had no doubt been intended that the Chief Whip's main work should be the management of the party in the Commons. But from the fact that he naturally became the ordinary channel of communication between the leaders and the rank and file, more and more duties had fallen upon him. For one man to keep every part of so complicated a machine in good working order was obviously impossible. A second advantage was that Balfour's position at the head of the party now seemed to have been strengthened. The administrative changes confirmed his control over the organisation through subordinates to be nominated by himself. They increased the flow of information available to him, while curbing the encroachments of the National Union. In short, business efficiency had triumphed over the democratic trend inherent in the 1906 reorganisation, since the National Union was now deprived of its nascent policy-making role and aspirations. In this way the possibility that a powerful extra-parliamentary body might develop inside the Unionist party, comparable to the modern Labour party's annual conference and National Executive Committee, was ended. But Balfour would ultimately suffer as a result of the removal or demotion of such loyal party functionaries as Hood and Hughes, while the newly appointed Chairman could only undermine Sandars' unofficial position as Balfour's means of communication with the party as a whole.[132] Additionally Walter Long, hitherto a loyal if sometimes critical supporter, was left disappointed and embittered. Though he exaggerated in suggesting that Balfour had adopted his own rather than the committee's recommendations, there were grounds for his irritation. Steel-Maitland's meteoric promotion from parliamentary obscurity was one source of resentment. In addition, the committee's proposal that the party's whips should be selected to represent the widest possible range of constituencies was largely ignored.[133]

An interesting postscript to the work of the Organisation Committee was provided by the rumour, reported in the press, that Hood was to be asked to stay on as party treasurer. Balfour's relationship with Hood had deteriorated considerably after the setting up of the Organisation Committee and the party leader may have seen an opportunity in the nomination for the treasurership of making amends.[134] Long, however, recognised that such a development could only undermine the committee's proposals and that it would be impossible for someone of Hood's seniority to work under Steel-Maitland.[135] In the face of mounting opposition - R. D. Blumenfeld even threatened the new Chief Whip with a party split unless Balfour withdrew Hood's nomination - the idea was dropped and Lord Farquhar emerged as the new party treasurer. Hood had had sole control of party funds since 1902. During this time Balfour had studiously avoided asking any questions about them, either as to the source from which they came, their amount or their expenditure. He had confined himself to the single question, 'Have you got enough to go on with?', and always declined to hear any particulars.[136] In the autumn of 1910 Hood noted that the party had £525,000 invested at nearly 4%, together with £25,000 on deposit and about £35,000 in the current account.[137]

Steel-Maitland was not slow in making his presence felt inside the party organisation. He attached particular importance to improving the contacts with local agents which Hughes had already begun, and did not hesitate to tread on toes inside Central Office itself. His initial attention focused on the lack of business expertise with which matters had previously been handled. His staff could not, he complained, 'tell you within £10,000 what the year's expenditure had been; probably not within £20,000'. Existing practice allowed for no proper classification of expenditure, no recovery of loans and no following up of lapsed subscriptions. In general 'work was done which could not be put off', but problems and responsibilities had been shelved if at all possible.[138] By the autumn of 1911 Steel-Maitland had assessed the limited value of the existing staff in the Central Office. With a single exception he found all his senior officials 'useless'. He determined to get rid of these as soon as he could find capable men to take their places, but recognised the difficulties he would run into and the unpopularity he would incur.[139] Over the next year or so substantial remedial action was taken. William Jenkins, district agent for the Midlands Liberal Unionists, became chief organising agent in 1911; John Boraston, an experienced political organiser and formerly chief agent to the Liberal Unionist Council, became Principal Agent in 1912; while Malcolm Fraser, a former newspaper editor, took over the party's press bureau and was soon involved in negotiations over the future of *The Globe*.[140]

It was particularly important that the Unionists should concern themselves with the press in the new age of popular politics, since newspapers were obviously the most important link with the world of politics for the vast majority of the population. After the divisions which had characterised the years of Balfour's government, Unionist newspapers had rallied to present a much more united front and by 1910 were overwhelmingly supportive of tariff reform.[141] Political involvement was clearly on the increase. In 1907 Hood had toyed for a while with the idea of loaning £100,000 to Arthur Pearson to buy *The Times* in return for general support for the party from that newspaper, while five years later Steel-Maitland was deeply involved in complicated negotiations over the future of the *Daily Express*.[142] The press bureau itself was set up by Hughes as a panic reaction to a press campaign in the Northcliffe newspapers, which convinced the Principal Agent that Northcliffe was hoping to take over the Central Office.[143]

Fusion of the Conservative and Liberal Unionist organisations had been demanded during the negotiations of January and February 1906, but Balfour had succeeded in diverting the issue to consideration by a committee of the National Union, where no progress was made. The appointments of Boraston and Jenkins may have made matters easier and fusion was achieved by 1912, despite the fact that the Organisation Committee of 1911 had concluded that the amalgamation of the two parties would not yet be possible. Indeed leading Liberal Unionists such as Austen Chamberlain and Lord Selborne appear to have been hostile to suggestions of fusion as late as the summer of 1911.[144] But in the autumn of that year Chamberlain secured the seal of Conservative approval and was elected to the Carlton Club, soon to be followed by several other prominent Liberal Unionists, while on 10 July 1912 it was formally agreed that Liberal Unionists should have the same privileges with regard to membership of the club as were enjoyed by Conservatives.[145] Shortly after becoming party leader, Law had called a meeting of leading Conservatives to discuss the desirability of fusion and from this initiative progress was rapidly made.[146]

Changes inside parliament following Hood's retirement were probably less marked than those observed in the Central Office, although the appointment of Lord Balcarres as Chief Whip was widely welcomed. Bridgeman, who became a junior whip at the same time, still felt that Balcarres's reduced functions left him with too much to do, while the seven junior whips were generally under-employed.[147] Balcarres was probably fortunate that during his tenure the focus of parliamentary attention shifted into areas where he had less difficulty in maintaining party discipline and unity than had been the experience of his predecessor. It is significant that Steel-Maitland was widely spoken of as a possible successor to Balcarres when the latter succeeded to the peerage as the Earl of Crawford in 1913.[148] But in the event the post of Chief Whip went to Lord Edmund Talbot.

In general, then, the party machine at Bonar Law's disposal during the first years of his leadership was a considerably more professional organisation than that available to Balfour. This was a direct result of the reforms of 1911. In the somewhat longer term, this revamped party apparatus, invigorated by new personnel, would help to carry the Unionists through the war and beyond, laying the foundations for the party's organisational superiority over its rivals which became a prominent ingredient in its recipe for electoral success in the twentieth century.

## NOTES

1.    Punnett, *Front-Bench Opposition* pp.4-5.
2.    Ibid p.46; G. D. M. Block, *A Source Book of Conservatism* (London, 1964) p.90.

3.  Petrie, *Powers behind Prime Ministers* p.79; Akers-Douglas was still writing of the 'ex-cabinet' as late as 1911: Akers-Douglas diary 23 March 1911.
4.  Bridgeman diary 30 Dec.1912.
5.  Punnett, *Front-Bench Opposition* p.221.
6.  Vincent (ed.), *Crawford Papers* p.191.
7.  Balfour to Sandars 6 Jan.1908, Sandars MSS c.756/31.
8.  Newton, *Lansdowne* p.354.
9.  Garvin to Sandars 21 Dec.1910, Balfour MSS Add. MS 49795.
10. Balfour to Sandars 2 Jan.1911, Sandars MSS c.763/11. Winston Churchill wrongly assumed that Balfour's hesitations over Smith's promotion reflected 'the fatuous and arrogant mind of the Hotel Cecil, wh. even at its last gasp would rather inflict any amount of injury upon the Tory party than share power with any able man of provincial origin': R. Churchill, *Churchill* vol.2, companion part 2 p.1089.
11. Bridgeman diary 30 Dec.1912.
12. Riddell, *More Pages* p.4.
13. Douglas diary 12 March 1914. As late as January 1914 Lansdowne regarded Douglas's inclusion in the shadow cabinet as 'inevitable'. He was also 'inclined to add ... St.Audries [Acland Hood]' despite the fact that the latter had in effect been ejected from the office of Chief Whip in 1911: Lansdowne to Law 30 Jan.1914, Law MSS 31/2/75.
14. Vincent (ed.), *Crawford Papers* p.191.
15. Law to Smith 31 July 1913, Law MSS 33/5/48.
16. Blewett, *Peers, Parties* p.187; Long to Balfour 20 Jan.1911, Balfour MSS Add. MS 49777.
17. Petrie, *Chamberlain* i, 370.
18. Block, *Conservatism* p.71.
19. Lord Midleton, *Records and Reflections 1856-1939* (London, 1939) p.270.
20. Long to Derby Sept.1910, Long MSS 449/6.
21. Balfour to W. Anson 18 Sept.1911, Sandars MSS c.764/47. Ultimately the shadow cabinet was to meet without Balfour immediately prior to his own resignation: Fraser, 'Unionist Debacle' p.307.
22. Memorandum by Balcarres Nov.1911, Law MSS 41/I/1a.
23. Petrie, *Chamberlain* i, 285.
24. One indication of this was the way in which front-bench Unionists felt

able to associate with the specialist organisations and ginger groups which proliferated during the last years of Balfour's leadership and whose policies were not always fully in line with those of the official leadership. 'All the splinter groups included at least one member of the shadow cabinet': Ramsden, *Balfour and Baldwin* p.41.

25.   Nonetheless, when F. E. Smith was invited to join the shadow cabinet he was apprehensive that this would seriously curtail his freedom of action : 'they clip my wings and make me responsible for their policy': Birkenhead, *F. E.* p.150.

26.   Balfour to Sandars 6 April 1907, Sandars MSS c.753/139.

27.   Bridgeman diary 30 Dec.1912.

28.   Memorandum by Balcarres Nov.1911, Law MSS 41/I/1a.

29.   In early 1914 when the shadow cabinet appears to have been revived, Lansdowne thought it 'not easy to decide who should be invited' and was not sure how widely Law intended to 'spread his net': Lansdowne to Law 30 Jan.1914, Law MSS 31/2/75.

30.   Lansdowne to Law 11 Feb.1912, Law MSS 25/2/13; Law to Lansdowne 7 Feb.1912, ibid 33/4/8. A year later Austen Chamberlain noted that Law 'rightly avoids summoning it as much as possible': Chamberlain, *Politics from Inside* p.527.

31.   Lansdowne to Law 23 Feb.1912, Law MSS 25/2/49, 52.

32.   Vincent (ed.), *Crawford Papers* p.265.

33.   Ibid p.281.

34.   Memorandum by Balcarres Nov.1911, Law MSS 41/I/1a.

35.   E. David (ed.), *Inside Asquith's Cabinet* (London, 1977) p.81. See also Churchill's description of a debate on the Parliament Bill, Churchill, *Churchill* vol.2, companion part 2 p.1078.

36.   Vincent (ed.), *Crawford Papers* p.108.

37.   Ibid p.101.

38.   Ibid p.160.

39.   Memorandum by Balcarres 28 Nov.1911, Law MSS 41/I/1b.

40.   See above pp.34-40.

41.   Dugdale, *Balfour* i, 335.

42.   Vincent (ed.), *Crawford Papers* p.182. One uncharitable critic suggested that 'the doctors must have taken Walter Long's brains instead of his appendix, they were both small and very swollen, so the mistake is quite permissible': Lowther to Blumenfeld 7 Sept.1909,

Blumenfeld MSS LOWT 1.
43. Vincent (ed.), *Crawford Papers* pp.122-3; see also ibid pp.99, 111.
44. Ibid p.100.
45. Newton, *Lansdowne* p.354.
46. Chamberlain, *Politics from Inside* p.605.
47. Memorandum by Balcarres 28 Nov.1911, Law MSS 41/I/1b.
48. Bridgeman diary review of 1907.
49. Petrie, *Long* pp.151-2.
50. Memorandum by Balcarres 28 Nov.1911, Law MSS 41/I/1b.
51. Long to Hood 17 Sept.1909, Balfour MSS Add. MS 49777.
52. Long to Balcarres 6 July 1911, Long MSS 449/59.
53. Memorandum by Balcarres 28 Nov.1911, Law MSS 41/I/1b.
54. Lansdowne to Balfour 28 Dec.1910, Sandars MSS c.762/247.
55. Mackail and Wyndham, *Wyndham* ii, 656.
56. Hood to Long 29 Jan.1911, Long MSS 449/36.
57. Sandars to Balfour 19 Dec.1910, Balfour MSS Add. MS 49767.
58. Ibid 24 Dec. 1910.
59. Memorandum April 1910, Long MSS 449/5.
60. Curzon to Balfour 23 Dec.1911, Sandars MSS c.762/210.
61. G. Jones, 'National and local issues in politics : a study of East Sussex and the Lancashire spinning towns, 1906-1910', unpublished Ph.D. thesis, University of Sussex, 1965 pp.209-10.
62. Middleton had acted as Honorary Secretary of the National Union as well as Chief Agent: Ibid p.211.
63. M. Thomson, *David Lloyd George* (London, 1949) p.22.
64. Hood to Balfour 22 Dec.1905, cited Rempel, *Unionists Divided* p.132.
65. See, for example, Maxse to Law 29 Jan.1906, Law MSS 18/2/12. Maxse himself feared that 'jealousy of Joe will prevent anything being done'.
66. Fraser, 'Unionism' p.164.
67. Chamberlain to Ridley 6 Feb.1906, cited Amery, *Chamberlain* pp.821-4.
68. Chamberlain to Hewins 16 Feb.1906, Hewins MSS 49/32.
69. Hyde, *Carson* pp.212-3.
70. Cecil to E. Clarke 29 May 1906, Cecil MSS Add. MS 51158.
71. H. Cecil to Balfour 14 Feb.1906, Balfour MSS Add. MS 49759; R.Cecil to Balfour 14 May 1906, ibid 49737.

72.  *The Times* 16 Feb.1906.
73.  R. Jones, 'The Conservative Party' p.42.
74.  R. Cecil to Balfour 24 May 1906, Balfour MSS Add. MS 49737.
75.  Arnold-Forster to Law 24 April 1906, Law MSS 18/2/16.
76.  Chamberlain to Boraston 3 Feb.1906, cited Amery, *Chamberlain* p.814.
77.  Sandars to Balfour 14 May 1906, Balfour MSS Add. MS 49764.
78.  'Notes on political events connected with Mr. Chamberlain's action', July 1906, Sandars MSS c.751/252. This document is the main source for the next two paragraphs.
79.  Ridley to Chamberlain 25 May 1906, cited Amery, *Chamberlain* pp.885-6.
80.  Compare this with Chamberlain's assurance to Chaplin that he had done his best to secure his selection for Worcester, but that the local party had insisted upon choosing Stanley Baldwin: Chamberlain to Chaplin 10 June 1906, cited Amery, *Chamberlain* p.886.
81.  Amery, *Chamberlain* p.886.
82.  Ibid p.803.
83.  R. B. Jones, 'Balfour's reform of party organisation', *Bulletin of the Institute of Historical Research* 38, (1965), p.96; *National Union Gleanings* Aug.1906.
84.  Note by Sandars on letter from Bridgeman of 2 Aug.1906, Balfour MSS Add. MS 49764.
85.  J. Lawrence to Long 4 Jan.1911, Long MSS 445/9.
86.  Ramsden, *Balfour and Baldwin* p.26.
87.  R. T. McKenzie, *British Political Parties* (London, 1963) p.146.
88.  *The Times* 30 Jan. 1911.
89.  Sandars to Balfour 2 April 1907, Balfour MSS Add. MS 49765.
90.  G. Jones, 'National and local issues' pp.322-5.
91.  Hood to Douglas 21 Dec.1906, Douglas MSS c.471/2.
92.  Vincent (ed.), *Crawford Papers* p.99.
93.  G. Jones, 'National and local issues' p.222.
94.  Memorandum April 1910, Long MSS 449/5.
95.  Sandars to Amery 2 Feb.1911, Amery MSS D44.
96.  G. Jones, 'National and local issues' p.223.
97.  Ramsden, *Balfour and Baldwin* p.52.
98.  Sandars to Balfour 25 Dec.1910, Balfour MSS Add. MS 49767.

99.    Memorandum by Long for Balfour 3 March 1910, Long MSS 449/4. At this stage Long stressed that 'unless our organisation is complete the best leader and the most carefully devised policy will fail'.

100.   Chaplin to Law 13 March 1910, Law MSS 18/6/118.

101.   Sandars to Balfour 18 March 1910, Balfour MSS Add. MS 49766.

102.   Hood to Douglas 17 Sept.1910, Douglas MSS c.471/3.

103.   Amery to Law 16 July 1910, Law MSS 18/6/146.

104.   Sandars to Balfour 14 Sept.1910, Balfour MSS Add. MS 49766.

105.   *National Review* Oct.1910.

106.   Sandars to Douglas Dec.1910, Douglas MSS c.478/10. See also Vincent (ed.), *Crawford Papers* p.150.

107.   Blumenfeld to Sandars 17 Dec.1910, Blumenfeld MSS SAN7.

108.   Douglas to Sandars 17 Dec.1910, Douglas MSS c.478/11.

109.   Malmesbury to Long 3 Jan.1911, Long MSS 449/28.

110.   Sandars to Short 19 Dec.1910, cited Jones, 'Balfour's Reform' pp.99-100.

111.   Brodrick to Balfour 22 Dec.1910, Sandars MSS c.762/190.

112.   G. Armstrong to Hughes 9 Dec.1910, Long MSS 449/21.

113.   C. Petrie to Derby 14 Dec.1910, Derby MSS 2/20. Derby was anxious to extend this practice to Manchester and 'if they won't have it, they must have somebody else to be their leader': Derby to Walter Russell 15 Jan.1911, ibid 2/18.

114.   C. Barlow to Derby 4 Jan.1911, ibid 4/39.

115.   Salvidge to Long 3 Feb.1911, ibid 449/19.

116.   Long to Balfour 22 Dec.1910 and attached memorandum, ibid 449/4; Long to Balfour 29 Dec.1910, ibid 445/3.

117.   Long to Balfour 3 Jan.1911, Sandars MSS c.763/14; Hood to Balfour 1 Jan.1911, ibid c.763/5.

118.   Platt to Long Jan.1911, Long MSS 449/17.

119.   Hood to Long 16 Jan.1911, ibid 449/36.

120.   Balfour to Douglas 17 Jan.1911, Douglas MSS c.22/21. The other members of the committee were Goulding, Long, Salvidge, Selborne, Steel-Maitland, Willoughby de Broke, Sutton Nelthorpe (National Union Lincolnshire Area Chairman), George Younger (Scottish Whip) and Ralph Glyn (Secretary).

121.   Balfour to Douglas 28 Jan.1911, Douglas MSS c.22/22.

122.   Brodrick to Salisbury 18 Jan.1911, Salisbury MSS S(4) 69/12;

Ramsden, *Balfour and Baldwin* p.58.

123. Amery to Steel-Maitland 31 Jan.1911, Steel-Maitland MSS GD 193/150/1; Amery memorandum, Balfour MSS Add. MS 49775; Amery to Long 10 Feb.1911, Long MSS 449/52. Amery's analysis of the situation was broadly shared by Sandars (Sandars to Amery 2 Feb.1911, Amery MSS D44) and bore a strong resemblance to the eventual recommendations of the Organisation Committee.

124. Interim report, Long MSS 450/13; memorandum by Long on the committee's recommendations 6 July 1911, ibid 450/17.

125. Sandars to Lansdowne 12 April 1911, Sandars MSS c.763/74. Dr. Ramsden in arguing that the committee 'concentrated on structures rather than personnel' perhaps overstates his case (*Balfour and Baldwin* pp.59-60.) There was much deep feeling about personalities. F. E. Smith urged Long not to 'give way about Alec Hood'. He thought that Long, Salvidge and two other unnamed members of the committee should 'threaten to resign if your recommendations are flouted': Smith to Long 28 June 1911, Long MSS 449/57.

126. Hood to Douglas 17 April 1911, Douglas MSS c.471/4.

127. Long to Hood 15 July 1911, Long MSS 449/36.

128. Jones, 'Balfour's Reform' p.101; Jones, 'Conservative Party' p.122. The committee's full recommendations may be found in Steel-Maitland MSS GD 193/80/4.

129. Long to Balfour 1 June 1911, Sandars MSS c.763/85.

130. Douglas to Long 9 June 1911, Long MSS 449/35.

131. Balfour to Long 2 June 1911, ibid 449/4.

132. Ramsden, *Balfour and Baldwin* p.100.

133. Memorandum by Long 6 July 1911, Long MSS 450/17.

134. Vincent (ed.), *Crawford Papers* pp.174-5.

135. Long to Hood 6 July 1911, Long MSS 449/36.

136. Hood to Law 18 June 1913, Law MSS 29/5/33.

137. Hood to Douglas 17 Sept.1910, Douglas MSS c.471/3.

138. Undated memorandum on the Central Organisation, Steel-Maitland MSS GD 193/108/3.

139. Steel-Maitland to Balfour 5 Nov.1911, ibid.

140. Ramsden, *Balfour and Baldwin* p.68; Armstrong to Long 4 March 1911, Long MSS 449/21.

141. G. Jones, 'National and local issues' p.124.

142. Hood to Douglas 7 Nov.1907, Douglas MSS c.471/1; correspondence between Steel-Maitland, Oliver Locker-Lampson, R. D. Blumenfeld and Max Aitken May-June 1912, Steel-Maitland MSS GD193/80/2.

143. Ramsden, *Balfour and Baldwin* p.56.

144. Douglas to Long 16 June 1911, Long MSS 449/35. In 1909 Chamberlain, believing that Jesse Collings was on the brink of death, declared that 'we will not surrender another L.U.seat in B'ham to the Conservatives for anyone': A.Chamberlain to M. Chamberlain 19 April 1909, AC 4/1/424.

145. Petrie, *Carlton Club* p.151.

146. Steel-Maitland to Derby 12 Dec.1911, Derby MSS 4/40.

147. Bridgeman diary 26-30 June 1911.

148. Ibid 18 Feb.1913.

PUNCH, OR THE LONDON CHARIVARI.—December 31, 1913.

## THE NEW BRUNSWICKER.

*(After Sir John Millais' "The Black Brunswicker.")*

Tariff Reform *(to Mr. Bonar Law, of New Brunswick and Bootle, Lancs.).* "DEAREST, MUST YOU LEAVE ME FOR THE ULSTER WARS?"

Mr. Bonar Law. "I FEAR SO, MY LOVE; BUT ONLY FOR A TIME, ONLY FOR A TIME."

# 7

# LEADERSHIP 1911–1914

With hindsight it is possible to see a steady erosion of Arthur Balfour's position at the head of the Unionist party throughout 1911. The party's third successive electoral defeat - all sustained under his leadership - could not be ignored. Balfour's adoption of the referendum had opened himself up to the charge that he was prepared to compromise on principles in order to attract votes. But those votes had not been attracted in sufficient numbers fully to justify what Balfour had done. The breakdown of the constitutional conference in 1910 and Balfour's reluctance to take a firm grip on his party continued to strengthen the position and power of the party's extremists - a development which would play its part not only in driving Balfour from the centre of the political stage, but also in shaping the style of leadership adopted by his successor. A feature of 1911 was the growth of splinter organisations, working largely outside official party channels which, ominously for Balfour, often numbered shadow cabinet members among their activists. But 1911 also offered Balfour the possibility of a reprieve. The growing focus of Unionist attention upon the constitutional crisis which was likely to result from the government's Parliament Bill forced dissidents to defer to his leadership. Such a reprieve was, however, likely to be no more than temporary if Balfour's handling of that crisis failed to give satisfaction. Once the dust of electoral disappointment had settled, there were already those who were prepared to question the leader's position. Joseph Lawrence doubted whether Balfour's prestige would ever recover from his third defeat. 'I meet no one', he noted, 'who forgives him his bad tactics.'[1] Rowland Hunt starkly posed the choice facing the party, as one between 'a very charming personality' and 'the future of our race and Empire'. He believed that 'a revolt and a bold decided policy [were] almost our only chance before it is too late'.[2] Similarly Leo Maxse, for whom the removal of the leader later became something of an obsession, was already convinced that Balfour would have to be driven out at no matter what cost.[3] Majority opinion, however, was probably prepared to give Balfour the benefit of the doubt until he had had a chance to show his qualities in response to the government's Parliament Bill.

Yet Balfour's handling of the unfolding constitutional crisis of 1911 did little to improve his position. The leadership's cautious tactics were widely interpreted as tantamount to acquiescence in the government's legislative designs. In June, Maxse complained that the opposition had so far put up a 'lamentable fight' and that Balfour, if not actually in league with Asquith, constantly behaved as though he were, appearing to obstruct any serious fight against the Parliament Bill. Providing only that Balfour and his colleagues kept out of the way, Maxse was confident that the bill could be defeated.[4] Part of the problem was that the party's rank and file were not privy to all the information upon which Balfour and Lansdowne shaped their policy. This was particularly true once Balfour had appreciated that Asquith was fully prepared to go ahead with a mass creation of peers to ensure the passage of the bill. Though the subsequent modification of Balfour's approach may now seem entirely explicable, the effect at the time was deplorable. A junior whip commented:

> In the meantime Balfour's opinion is unknown. Unionist
> members of the House of Commons are left to the last moment
> without a lead. Perplexity and growing differences of opinion
> have been allowed to ferment and the outlook to my mind is
> very serious unless Balfour goes in for no surrender.[5]

Leo Maxse, still confident that the Liberals were engaged in a 'gigantic bluff', felt that the Unionist peers had been placed in a difficult position by the character of Balfour's resistance to the Parliament Bill, which had given the impression that he was 'at heart a Single Chamber man'.[6]

By the summer divisions within the party were becoming as bitter as anything which divided Unionists as a whole from the government. What began as a question of tactics fast developed into an effective challenge to the leadership in which the opponents of Balfour and Lansdowne presented their leaders' tactical surrender to the Parliament Bill as a sacrifice of principle. In fact, Balfour and Lansdowne reached their conclusions on the basis of an assessment of the course of action likely to do least damage to the upper chamber and therefore to the long-term interests of the Unionist party.[7] Not for the first time, however, Balfour failed to carry his nominal followers along the logic of his own reasoned path. Maxse railed that the front bench might as well undertake to help the government to carry all its legislation. Then 'we can have a definite and decent split. The goats will all be together and so will the sheep.'[8]

The final passing of the Parliament Bill and the manner in which this government victory was achieved left the Unionist party indulging in an internecine feast of mutual recrimination. F. E. Smith needed time to assess 'the staggering calamity' of what had happened, but was 'profoundly convinced' that things could not go on as they were.[9] Bridgeman could not 'speak or write the disgust' he felt at this 'despicable surrender, just when I hoped that accidentally the consequences of bad and dilatory leadership were possibly going to be avoided by the action of Lord Halsbury and his stalwart colleagues'.[10] The *Daily Express* printed a list of those Unionist peers who had voted for the bill, framed in a white feather decoration, while Carson hoped that the list of 'Judas Peers' would be posted in every Unionist club in the country until their names became a byeword.[11] Sandars, trying to sound out party opinion for Balfour's benefit, could get little or no reassurance from any quarter. It was the common theme of the Liberal press that Lansdowne had arranged the final outcome in collusion with the government and that, while he had drawn off the greater body of his supporters from definite action, he had all the time left enough of his own men to go to the support of the government to ensure the bill's passage. Not surprisingly feeling against Lansdowne was particularly strong.[12]

Ultimately, however, it was the position of Balfour which suffered most damage, not so much because of the policy with which he had been associated as because of the way he had led, or failed to lead, his army. Many were shocked that Balfour, anxious to begin his summer break, had been absent from London between 3 and 7 August and had left for the continent before the final outcome of the vote in the Lords was known. 'I do not doubt', wrote Balcarres with some feeling, 'that our attitude towards public policy might well have been modified were today in the month of April instead of August.'[13] Calling upon his wealth of political experience the veteran M.P. Jesse Collings concluded: 'In this crisis he has left his place as leader, and "qui quitte sa place la perd" should apply.'[14] Balfour's dilemma was that what might have been good for himself would almost certainly have been bad for the party. Had he encouraged the Lords to stand their ground against the Parliament Bill, he might have refurbished his now tarnished reputation, but in doing so he would have led his party into the most dangerous waters - as he had recognised in advocating the line of surrender.

Certainly the whole session had been a bad one for the party - in the whips' office Pike and Talbot claimed they had 'never known things in such a bad way'.[15] Balcarres found the party's keenest men disheartened, dismayed and even disgusted. He could only hope that the Unionists' pent-up energies could be diverted into criticising the government rather than attacking one another.[16] Though the stance of the diehards over the Parliament Bill had no doubt been sincere, it clearly represented a repudiation of Balfour's style of leadership, characterised as it was by a kid-gloves approach to both the government and dissidents within his own ranks.[17] Bridgeman was now convinced that Balfour should resign quickly on grounds of ill-health. Selborne appeared to him the most likely successor. If Balfour tried to remain in place the danger was that within two months the party would fragment and Balfour would be hounded out of office.[18] Sandars heard that, whatever the feelings of the front bench, the rank and file of the parliamentary party were becoming profoundly anti-Balfourite.[19] For his part Balfour felt bitter, not just because so many Unionist peers had defied his advice, but 'the press campaign, and the speeches render their action unforgettable and unforgivable'.[20] Meanwhile his rapid departure for the continent to start his summer break encouraged hostile critics to allege complicity with the government. Though Balfour seemed happy to try to cut himself off from his party's internal wrangling, even declining to have mail forwarded to him, the transformation of his position at home could not be ignored. Joseph Lawrence commented:

> Neither Mr. Balfour or Lord Lansdowne will ever again be able to inspire the country. They are dead, for all useful political purposes .... Mr. Balfour's trip to Gastein, where his ears are stuffed with cotton wool, while Sandars withholds all knowledge of home truths, bears an ugly look to the man in the street.[21]

Bemoaning that 'single-chamber tyranny' would inevitably involve Home Rule in Ireland and Disestablishment in Wales, Wyndham was among the more charitable Unionists in dismissing the suspicion that Balfour and Lansdowne had connived at the tragedy that had been incurred. But he was ready to argue that they had been both blind and obstinate.[22]

Throughout the parliamentary recess rank and file opinion against Balfour did not subside.[23] But residual loyalty to a man who had led the Unionist party in the Commons for two decades was not going to disappear overnight, even though, as Lord Sandys argued, the line between criticism and hostility was rather a thin one.[24] For the time being, therefore, much of the opposition to Balfour's continued leadership was submerged within the Halsbury Club, which by formalising its existence at the beginning of October served as a focal point for diehard discontent. As Austen Chamberlain pointed out, though he sometimes 'despair[ed] of the fortunes of a Party so led,' he had worked very closely with Balfour for eight or nine years and was too attached to him ever to join any combination against him or his leadership.[25] Chamberlain's hope was that Balfour might at least have his eyes opened to the consequences of his recent actions. One such consequence was that the chairman of a leading Conservative Association had written to Steel-Maitland:

> I am a loyal man and will do what I am told, but don't, I beg,
> ask me to call my Association together to approve the leader's
> action or I shall have a contrary motion carried against me.[26]

The major task facing those who had dissented from the Balfour-Lansdowne line over the Parliament Bill was now to decide upon their future course of action and their position within the party. As Wyndham argued, the recent disaster was primarily due to the fact that the leaders would not decide upon a policy and announce it clearly. 'We must not err in the same way.'[27] It was important to take action and not neglect the ordinary party men, who were stunned and embittered by recent events.[28] It was also clear, as Carson put it, that 'milk and water won't satisfy the thirst of the party'.[29] Milner wanted a small group of younger and independent-minded Unionists to get together, agree on a common policy and advocate it in the Commons and outside, without bothering one way or another about Balfour and the party hierarchy. 'It was no good trying to turn Balfour out; the only thing was to let events take their course and go ahead with our own policy.'[30] He was above all keen that the diehards should not content themselves with a line of blank resistance, but should go ahead with a definite line of policy.[31] But while Rowland Hunt called for the formation of a 'new Patriotic Party' composed of Liberal Unionists, tariff reformers and those of the Conservatives who would join, and Comyn Platt felt that the idea of a new party could not be ruled out, majority opinion was that the dissidents should continue to work within official party channels.[32]

Lord Selborne's attitude was both typical and influential. Believing that the Halsbury stance commanded widespread support within the party, he placed priority upon ensuring that the diehards continued to speak with a united voice. He therefore proposed that sympathetic members of the shadow cabinet, together with Hugh and Robert Cecil, should meet to hammer out a consistent policy on the principal topics of current politics, although agreement with the Cecils on the question of tariff reform remained unlikely.[33] The proposal of a memorial to Halsbury for the purpose of forming a permanent

organisation of the 'No-surrender' group understandably filled the newly
appointed Party Chairman with alarm, and he urged caution upon Halsbury
before such a step was taken.[34] 'The object of the Association', he warned,
> stripped of verbal trimmings, can be nothing else than hostility
> to Mr. Balfour and Lord Lansdowne .... If it is an endeavour
> to obtain a more coherent and spirited action, the proper way
> to obtain it is by Mr. Balfour's colleagues using their legitimate
> influence to obtain it at Shadow Cabinet meetings etc., and not
> by an Association of this character.[35]

Yet, as set out by Selborne to Austen Chamberlain, the diehards' aims
seemed harmless enough:
> I do desire that we should have our proper weight in the
> councils of the party and our proper influence over the opinion
> of the party and I think that this can best be assured if we can
> agree to speak with one voice on all the important questions of
> current politics during the autumn campaign .... If we can
> agree on the general lines of the constitutional reform we desire
> to support, I should not be adverse to establishing an
> organisation within the party for the promotion of that special
> object .... It will tend to keep us together who have been
> working together in the crisis and so to increase our
> influence.[36]

To others, however, Selborne was more forthcoming. Eschewing the whole
idea of a new party, he had nonetheless set his sights on capturing the party
and the 'Unionist machine lock, stock and barrel'. The strength of the diehards
within the party hierarchy would, he predicted, enable their views to prevail
within the party, 'which is the same thing as capturing the Party'.[37] Aside
from the front bench he was also anxious that steps be taken to rally
parliamentary support in both houses. Great care would be needed in relation
to Balfour's position as leader, for while party opinion as a whole favoured the
diehard stance, personal loyalty to Balfour could not be discounted. He was
most 'deservedly loved personally by all those ... who have come into
personal contact with him'. The diehards would therefore need to act in a way
which avoided charges of intrigue and disloyalty. If such care were taken,
Selborne was confident of success at the next meeting of the National Union
Conference, one of his chief advantages being the support of the majority of
the party's platform orators.[38]

The attitude of the diehards towards the party leadership thus remained somewhat equivocal. Austen Chamberlain assured Sandars that his chief desire was to see the party close ranks behind Balfour's leadership, but though Selborne and Wyndham concurred that the time was not ripe for a vacancy in the leadership of either House, their longer-term commitment to Balfour was more open to question.[39] Willoughby de Broke, denying that he personally had ever been a rabid anti-Balfourite, recognised that a strong feeling that neither Balfour nor Lansdowne could ever lead the party to victory again underlay the whole of the present diehard movement. [40] As Northumberland put it:

> By all means let our leaders continue to lead us, but let us, if
> we can, put some fight into them and make them feel that if
> they will not lead us to fight we will fight without them!

His message to Balfour and Lansdowne was clear: 'If you won't lead us to the front but insist on making strategic movements to the rear, we will go to the front without you.'[41] Robert Cecil, grappling with the conflict between political principle and family loyalty which had obsessed him ever since the Chamberlainite intrusion into Unionist politics, saw the Halsbury Club as the last chance the party had of working together as a single coherent force in British public life. 'We are all agreed', he wrote,

> that we do not wish to turn A.J.B. out, still less Lansdowne.
> The idea is to induce them to lead better. I admit that this may
> not - probably will not - succeed and then we shall have to
> decide whether we will go on our own course or submit to their
> leadership .... I do not believe it is possible to make A.J.B.
> lead in the way we should approve and that if the Unionist
> Party is to be a force in the country he will have to go. But
> others are more sanguine and I don't like to quench smoking
> flax .... I could not be a party to a movement the object of
> which is to displace A.J.B. I had far sooner split off and have
> a party of my own. Indeed ultimately I believe and hope that
> such a split will take place. At present, however, the time is
> not ripe for separation .... If the H[alsbury] C[lub] succeeds it
> will show that there is sufficient agreement between the two
> Unionist wings to enable them to work as one party. If it fails
> it may dawn on some of them that the want of vitality in the
> party is due to the fact that the two wings neutralise each other

and the policy of neither of them is put forward with vigour.[42]

In such circumstances an attempt began to devise a coherent set of policies on the radical right of the party. Wyndham was anxious to bring the imperialist Lord Milner into the diehard councils at an early date and to put forward what he described as a true Tory policy.[43] Leo Amery later recalled a meeting with Milner and Wyndham at which it was agreed that the main issues of principle were imperial unity, defence and social reform, with tariff reform as the essential economic instrument. Agreement was also reached on the need to find some form of federal constitution for the United Kingdom once the government's Home Rule proposals had been thwarted.[44] During the winter of 1911-12 sub-committees of the club held a series of meetings to discuss questions of policy, with constitutional matters still to the fore.[45] Selborne, told that the Central Office was loath to touch the constitutional question because of the lack of public interest in the subject, determined on a campaign to educate the electorate as to its importance.[46]

At least for the time being the Halsbury Club was able to embrace both those who still hoped to keep the old leadership but change its attitudes and those who were convinced of the need to oust Balfour, even though this juxtaposition caused friction and led to threats of resignation. Austen Chamberlain, though in general sympathy with its objectives, only joined the club on the strict understanding that it was not to direct its activities against Balfour.[47] His presence was important in lending respectability to what might easily have been interpreted as an organised revolt. Probably with one eye on the ultimate succession to the leadership, Chamberlain's brother Neville had urged him to come forward and give the diehards a lead.[48] In fact, of course, the presence of senior members of the shadow cabinet such as Chamberlain, who had 'joined the train after it was in motion',[49] as promoters of an organisation from which Balfour and Lansdowne were excluded was anomalous in the extreme. At all events the club's formation was a development which could not be ignored.[50] Long suspected that, whatever the professed intentions of the club's leaders, it was being used as a centre for a determined attack on Balfour and Lansdowne.[51] He attempted to force Balfour into action by opening his eyes to the realities of the situation, but contrary advice was coming from the Party Chairman who, despite earlier misgivings, was now convinced that the club was not hostile to Balfour, but that it was 'muddleheaded'. There were, he believed, no positive proposals on which the diehards were more united than was the party as a whole.[52] At all events it was certainly true that, though Lansdowne regarded its proceedings as 'ridiculous',[53] the continued existence of the club gave little chance for the party's wounds, upon which the *débâcle* of August had poured further salt, to heal. As Salisbury argued, when justifying his resignation from the club in the middle of October,

> I feel strongly that a new spirit in the conduct of the Party is required - greater vigour in the country, greater decision in Parliament. But I think also, as many others think, that we must have a unified party and from that point of view I cannot believe that to keep alive the irritation of last August is wise. We must have vigour without, but we must have conciliation within. To secure this vigour we must be the leaven of the party but not its blister.[54]

In the early autumn Balfour's supporters made strenuous efforts to persuade him to call a party meeting to explain the lines of policy upon which he proposed to proceed and to secure the defeat of a hostile motion to be moved by Maxse at the meeting of the National Union in November. Lord Midleton[55] believed that unless something was done three-quarters of the party would drift into the Halsbury Club. Balfour needed to learn from Lansdowne's mistakes of the summer, when the latter had not done enough to make his own position perfectly clear to his fellow peers. 'If Balfour would say something of the same kind to the National Union meeting, the opposition to him there would collapse for all practical purposes.' But the problem was compounded by the fact that Balfour, drained and dispirited by the events of the summer, was by no means inclined to take active steps in his own defence.[56] As early as June he had privately indicated his readiness to step down from the leadership, while doubting whether any of his senior colleagues was capable of succeeding him.[57]

Protective instincts towards Balfour led a group of senior Unionists to meet at Devonshire House to work out the best means by which they could help him. Derby and Lyttelton stated their opinion that the leader's resignation might be anticipated at no very distant date, but neither of them believed that it would take place immediately, or that Balfour had absolutely made up his mind. Bonar Law and Long were deputed to interview Carson, whom some saw as the Halsbury Club's candidate to succeed Balfour, in the hope of extracting from the club a declaration of loyalty to the existing leader, but this meeting proved unfruitful. It was also noticeable that when, a fortnight later, at the club's first annual meeting, Chamberlain moved a resolution of confidence in Balfour and Lansdowne, there was determined resistance from the younger members who found such a gesture 'preposterous in the highest degree'. By this stage, however, senior party figures were probably aware of the imminent announcement of Balfour's resignation.[58]

No direct causal relationship can be established between the activities of the Halsbury Club and Balfour's final decision to resign the leadership in November 1911. It is not likely that at this crisis of his career the workings of Balfour's most complex mind can be so easily explained. Nonetheless two converging developments are evident. On the one hand, though not all its members were committed to Balfour's removal, the Halsbury Club did serve as a vehicle for that small but growing band of obstinate Unionists who, at least since the referendum pledge and the second general election of 1910, had seen a change in the leadership as a primary policy objective. At the same time the club was an expression of that growth of political extremism within the party which Balfour found so distasteful - a distaste which certainly played a major part in his ultimate decision to withdraw.[59]

Balfour had toyed briefly with the thought of resignation at the time of the abortive constitutional conference of 1910,[60] but it was the period after the passing of the Parliament Bill which proved critical for him. Though he had immediately escaped to the continent, upon his return to Britain Balfour never fully recovered his appetite for the political fray. By late September Lord Esher could record that Balfour was still smarting over the behaviour of the diehards in July and August: 'A.J.B. is very angry with his own people. He thinks that they behaved abominably to him, which they did.'[61] To Balcarres, who had believed that the leader's attitude towards the malcontents had hardened since the summer, Balfour confided at the end of September his inclination to stand down, though he denied that he had yet made a firm decision.[62] It was becoming increasingly clear that Balfour had no stomach for continuing to lead a party which, with only brief interludes since 1903, had spent more time in tearing itself apart than in fighting its political opponents. Granted Balfour's personality, the responsibility of leadership in such circumstances for a man of over sixty years of age, who had little immediate prospect of returning to government, was one that might be gratefully relinquished. In private Balfour confided: 'I confess to feeling I have been badly treated. I have no wish to lead a Party under these humiliating conditions. It is no gratification to me to be their leader.'[63] Balfour had been deeply wounded by developments within the party since the summer, especially as these involved figures who were either related to him or whom he had hitherto regarded as among his closest political allies.[64] At times he would try to rationalise his feelings by suggesting that after twenty years of leading the party in the Commons, the time had come for a change.[65] When Sandars told him that Selborne was requesting a meeting of the shadow cabinet to consider the question of the payment of M.P.s and the action of the House of Lords over the Naval Prize Bill, Balfour's emphatic response was that he did not intend to hold another shadow cabinet. The denial of collective responsibility in the summer still rankled with him:

> after full discussion, a minority decline to accept my advice which commanded the majority of votes at the Shadow Cabinet and the dissentient members have gone out into the world proclaiming their differences and have embarked upon a policy of active resistance.[66]

On returning to Scotland from the continent Balfour was greeted by a long and elaborate memorandum from the newly appointed Party Chairman, dwelling upon the disaffection within the ranks of the party and the need for drastic efforts to be made by the leader to bring his colleagues and followers into line. To this Balfour did not attach undue weight, but noted it as 'collateral to other circumstances which he thinks infinitely more important'.[67] Steel-Maitland was, after all, only a recent colleague and far more significant in influencing Balfour was a long letter received from Walter Long, the most senior of his active political associates. Long described the situation as so grave as to call for action on the part of those who were Balfour's personal supporters and to require a complete change in policy and tactics on Balfour's part. Criticising the party's recent handling of the Parliament and National Insurance Bills, Long called for the sort of decisive action from Balfour of which the latter was by now, in all probability, incapable:

> The Government must be attacked all along the line, no quarter must be shown, there must be no qualification as to the policy of the future, there must be a clear and definite statement that we mean to fight the government and that we offer as alternatives the policy of which we all approve.

Pulling few punches, Long moved inexorably towards his ruthlessly blunt conclusion:

I have only written thus strongly to you from a deep sense of
duty, and because I am convinced that unless prompt and
determined steps are taken to grapple with the situation, not
only will you find yourself with very few followers, but our
Party will, as a result of your leadership, be hopelessly broken
up, and cease to be the great instrument for public good which
it has always hitherto been, and which it must continue to be if
the safety of the country is to be secured.[68]

This 'extraordinary letter'[69] made a considerable and lasting impression
on Balfour's mind. He saw it as a bold and brutal invitation to retire and it
had come from his oldest colleague, 'my professed friend and upholder.
Nothing of the Diehards could be compared with this for what is called
disloyalty.'[70] The letter was likely to stiffen Balfour's opposition to Long's
election as his eventual successor, if he had not already come to the conclusion
that Austen Chamberlain should succeed him in the Commons.[71] Revealingly,
Balfour commented that Long was asking him to change 'and I cannot
change'.[72] Within a week he had told Sandars that he was extremely anxious
to retire. He had come to no final conclusion, but his present idea was to
announce the decision in Edinburgh towards the end of October.[73]

Over the next few weeks various influences were brought to bear in an
attempt to dissuade Balfour from the final step of resignation. A good
performance in the Commons over the government's Insurance Bill seemed
momentarily to strengthen his position.[74] Sandars and Derby both stressed the
vital contribution which Balfour could make in the forthcoming crisis over
Home Rule and the likelihood that his retirement would be followed by that
of Lord Lansdowne as Unionist leader in the upper chamber.[75] Derby's
appeal was couched in precisely those terms of flattery and the overriding need
for party unity which, in other circumstances, would have been likely to
overcome Balfour's depression:

If, as in your own case when Lord Salisbury resigned, there
existed somebody who everybody recognised as the fit
successor, I might agree with you, but you know better than I
do the jealousies that exist between our colleagues when it
comes to merely a question of leading the opposition. Your
resignation would inevitably lead to a split in the Party and that
just at a time when we wanted to be united in our opposition to
Home Rule ... if you go now before there is an obvious

successor to you, you will not only see the party split in two,
but you will find that scores of men will take no further part in
politics.

But while Derby tried to stress how small, if noisy, the opposition to Balfour
actually was, evidence was still growing that for some at least his removal
remained an important goal. Under Leo Maxse's influence the *National Review*
campaigned under the simple slogan 'Balfour must go', the initial letters BMG
becoming an ominous motif. In its October issue the *National Review* bluntly
concluded that 'the Unionist Party... is condemned to impotence as long as it
is led by Mr. Balfour'.[76] Maxse's contempt for Balfour had become total. His
belief was that the leader did not want to turn out the present government, as
he would then have the disagreeable task of forming a government of his own,
of discarding old friends and of having to grapple with difficult issues such as
tariff reform.[77] In fact Balfour no longer had the will to resist. The King was
informed on 7 November of his decision to resign and on the following day
this was made public in an announcement to his constituency association.[78]

Despite the emphasis which he placed upon his age, his indifferent health
and his length of parliamentary service, the objective conclusion must be that
Balfour had been driven from office by his own party. Though no one could
doubt the difficulties of the situation which had confronted him, his record as
leader of the party in opposition was not impressive. It was not simply that he
had led the Unionists to three successive general election defeats. Even more
seriously, only for brief periods over the preceding six years had they looked
even remotely like a potential party of government. Apart from the obvious
goal of returning to power, an opposition leader is likely to strive for success
in four areas. He will aim to influence government policy; to maintain the
enthusiastic backing of his parliamentary followers; to uphold morale among
party workers in the country; and to win the backing of the electorate as a
whole for particular party policies. In none of these areas is there much
evidence of Balfour's success. By temperament he was in any case ill-equipped
for the demands of leading a party in opposition and this was particularly the
case in the torrid political climate that existed after 1906. He simply could not
provide the sort of straightforward thrust and attack for which his followers
clamoured. Walter Long put his finger on the essence of Balfour's failings
when discussing the question of Irish Home Rule:

> You indicate that Home Rule must be opposed so long as we
> are entitled to assume that it is Gladstonian Home Rule. Now,

is it not inevitable that the inference drawn from this must be
that there is some form of Home Rule to which you as Leader
of the Party, would not offer relentless opposition? The
majority of your supporters are opposed to Home Rule in any
form; all your supporters hate the "splitting of straws": the bulk
of your followers in the country (the electors) have not the time
or the knowledge sufficient to enable them to discriminate
between one kind of Home Rule or another: and what they all
ask for ... is clear, distinct guidance: a plain policy and
straightforward statements appeal to the people and will win,
but qualifications and doubts "ifs and ands" mystify and make
them ask in their agony - for no other word describes it - for a
clear indication of what the leaders of the Party mean to do.[79]

When Balfour gave up the party leadership few could have imagined that
almost two more decades of distinguished public service at the highest level
were still before him. In that endeavour which he placed above all else, he had
apparently failed. The leader who was obsessed with the unity of his party and
haunted by the historical tragedy of Robert Peel, could claim in 1911 little
more than that a total internal rupture had been avoided. Yet, as perceptive
contemporaries were aware, it is difficult to see how Balfour could have
succeeded. As Wyndham pointed out:

It is certain that the Unionist Party will be divided not only
over Tariff Reform, but also over Defence and Social Reform.
You could not prevent this. Under these circumstances I feel
your choice is limited to resigning now or throwing the
enormous weight of your personality and intellect into the scale
of some one extreme group. Since that is my view I am driven
to the conclusion that you would waste the harvest of your
personality and intellect if you committed both to the doubtful
triumph of a faction or an isolated idea.[80]

Though the words were not his, Balfour probably accepted the logic of
Wyndham's argument. By resigning when he did and bequeathing his problems
to an as yet unknown successor, Balfour apparently concluded that, for him
at least, there was nothing to be gained from dying in the last ditch.

*    *    *

George Wyndham's first response to the news of Balfour's impending retirement was that 'we are in for a Dark Age'.[81] Though the language may have been somewhat melodramatic, many objective observers in November 1911 would have agreed with the sentiment that lay behind it. The election of a new leader might give hope of repairing some of the breaches in party unity and morale which Balfour's continued presence had served only to exacerbate. But it was unlikely to prove a panacea for all the ills from which the party had suffered during six years in the political wilderness. The bitterness engendered by the split over the Parliament Bill went deeper than anything attributable to Balfour's own failings at that time of crisis, while at the level of policy formulation the Unionists still needed to work out a coherent alterative strategy with which to challenge the Liberal government. Differences of opinion over specific issues of policy reflected a deeper divide as the contending factions of the Unionist coalition fought out a real, if often poorly articulated, battle to determine the character of the party as a political force in twentieth-century Britain. Curzon gave immediate expression to this fact in his fear that Balfour's resignation would 'throw the party into the hands of the extreme Birmingham school'.[82]

As if this problem were not serious enough, another lay immediately ahead. All Unionists knew that the survival of the Liberal government was now dependent less on its own vitality than on the support of the Irish members at Westminster - a support which was not freely offered but bartered in exchange for the promised introduction of a third Irish Home Rule Bill. This dark cloud on the legislative horizon threatened the major opposition party to its very core. To the Union with Ireland the party owed not only its name but its primary raison *raison d'être*, and now, unlike the situation in 1893, no omnipotent upper chamber lay reassuringly across the path of the government's proposed legislation. Whoever succeeded Balfour would thus take on the leadership at a crucial and perhaps decisive moment in the party's history.

Some, though not all, of these problems might have been alleviated had a single candidate stood out as the obvious and undisputed successor to Balfour. This, however, was not the case. While Lord George Hamilton could 'not see who [was] to keep the party together for the future',[83] the claims of Austen Chamberlain appeared to be the strongest and, had the choice rested with his shadow cabinet colleagues, his election would probably have ensued without too much difficulty. At the time of earlier rumours about the state of

Balfour's health, Jesse Collings had found that Chamberlain's claims to the reversion had not been seriously challenged, while Balfour himself had probably come to the conclusion that Chamberlain should follow him in the leadership of the party in the House of Commons.[84] At this vital moment in his career, however, Chamberlain suffered from a double disadvantage in being his father's son. For those who had opposed the elder Chamberlain and set their faces against his ascendancy within the party, it was easy to tar the son with the same brush, as coming from the despised and alien Birmingham tradition - 'that tribe who have no pretence to represent the Conservative side of politics'.[85] Though the fact of being a Liberal Unionist was by 1911 not quite the impediment it had been to his father, Austen was still widely seen as the champion of a particular faction within the party. This could not but be confirmed by his recent association with the Halsbury movement. Conversely, for those Unionists who had venerated, and indeed still did venerate, the great Joseph Chamberlain, the comparison between father and son was a painful and disappointing one. Though much has been made of the impact which the father had on the character and career of his elder son, this should not obscure the very real differences between the personalities of the two men. Lacking the vast ambition, ruthless determination and restless energy of his father, Austen Chamberlain managed to avoid the extremes of hatred which Joseph could arouse. But he also lacked the ability to inspire. As Lord Blake has put it, he was 'altogether kinder than his father, more likeable, more honourable, more high-minded - and less effective'.[86]

After the summer of 1906 radical Chamberlainites had not viewed Austen's succession to the leadership of the tariff reform movement with any great enthusiasm, and their fears that his respect for Balfour and scrupulous regard for political rectitude would allow the latter to set the rules of the political game had at least in part been borne out. Though both father and son repeatedly expressed genuine affection for Balfour, it was only Joseph who could put this into cold storage at times of major political importance.[87] So despite the great name which he bore Austen had not inherited the unqualified regard of all those Unionists who would have followed his father without question. Furthermore, his behaviour during the course of the leadership crisis merely confirmed the misgivings of those who had always doubted his suitability for the party's highest office. Leo Amery was later to comment: 'The trouble with Austen was not undue humility or diffidence. He had quite a good opinion of himself. But he had an exaggerated fear of being regarded as pushful.'[88] Lacking a real will for power, Chamberlain would accept the leadership only if he did not have to struggle to attain it. Yet, granted the hostility which his candidature would arouse, this situation could not occur.

For those who found Chamberlain unacceptable, the alternative candidate seemed to be Walter Long. A country gentleman of impeccable lineage and representative of that traditional Tory strain of the Unionist party which always mistrusted Chamberlain, Long had sat in the Commons since 1880. He had a long ministerial career behind him and had occupied the post of Chief Secretary for Ireland at the dissolution of Balfour's government in 1905. Though his following among the Unionist hierarchy was not great, he had such considerable support among the backbenchers that his claims to the succession could not be lightly dismissed. But he was almost ten years older than Chamberlain, volatile in his behaviour, an undistinguished debater and not renowned for his intellectual gifts or quick wits. As Balcarres put it, though Long had none of Chamberlain's disqualifications, he possessed 'every other conceivable one'.[89] Thus, although if the matter was left to a straight count of Unionist M.P.s Long's election was by no means out of the question, his leadership would be as little likely to unite the Unionist ranks as would Chamberlain's.

In such circumstances the emergence of a third candidate for Balfour's mantle was perhaps not quite as surprising an event as has sometimes been imagined. Andrew Bonar Law, though an M.P. only since 1900 and lacking any experience of cabinet office, was by no means an unknown quantity in 1911. Law had made a good impression during his first years in parliament and his defeat in the general election of 1906 had caused considerable dismay.[90] Soon re-entering the Commons as the member for Dulwich, Law rose rapidly within the Unionist ranks and by 1908 had established himself as one of the leading members of the parliamentary opposition. Early the following year Goulding described him, admittedly with some exaggeration, as 'second man to A.J.B.'[91] Then, at the beginning of 1911, he became one of the few 'new' members of the shadow cabinet, a body which was still largely composed of ex-cabinet ministers. Before the contest for the leadership actually got underway, Austen Chamberlain had recognised Law's claim to succeed Balfour should he himself prove too unpopular with one section of the party, 'and I have no doubt that he would like it in exactly the same sense as I should'.[92] Under pressure from his friend Max Aitken, the Canadian-born newly-elected member for Ashton, Law appears to have reneged on an earlier assurance to Chamberlain that he would not contest the leadership with him, since this would be likely to strengthen Long's chances of election.[93] Both Chamberlain and Law were widely regarded as committed tariff reformers and therefore likely to compete for the same votes, whereas Long's views on fiscal reform were rather more middle-of-the-road.

Since no formal procedure existed for the selection of a new leader in the House of Commons, it was the Chief Whip, Lord Balcarres, who seized the initiative. On 7 November he assembled the party whips and announced that Balfour had decided to resign. The Chief Whip then proceeded to discuss the steps necessary to choose a successor. He proposed to call a party meeting within the next week in order to avoid prolonged intrigue and to get the whole matter settled before the meeting of the National Union conference. The names of four possible candidates were mentioned, Chamberlain, Long, Law and Carson, of whom the whips unanimously favoured the first.[94] Balcarres believed that Long, if elected, would break down and be such a failure that he would be obliged to resign in less than a year, while he considered Law to be 'lamentably weak'.[95] Later that same day, however, Long intervened to say that it was not Balcarres's business to call a party meeting, but that the proper course of action would be to summon the Unionist Privy Councillors and see what their opinions were.[96] The postponement of the party meeting seemed to Balcarres and the other whips a potentially disastrous course and the former undertook to try to persuade Balfour to use his authority as out-going leader to insist upon a party meeting.[97]

Just before Balfour announced his resignation to his City constituency, the party whips advised Unionist M.P.s of the situation and it was the latter who insisted on a meeting of the party at as early a date as possible. Sensing that the party managers were manoeuvring for a Chamberlain victory, with Pike claiming that Long's health would not stand the strain, Long intensified his lobbying and, perhaps surprisingly, began to gain ground.[98] His behaviour towards Chamberlain became abusive and hysterical - a development that was scarcely justified in view of Chamberlain's continued reluctance to promote his own cause at all vigorously.[99] At this stage Chamberlain's somewhat cavalier behaviour during the years of Balfour's leadership appears to have been working against him. But it was becoming increasingly clear that neither of the front-runners was likely to achieve an outright victory and, more importantly, that the disgruntled adherents of whoever turned out to be the losing claimant would be unlikely fully to reconcile themselves to the victory of their opponent.

It was in this situation that Bonar Law's determination, backed by Aitken and Goulding - an erstwhile Chamberlain supporter - not to withdraw his own candidature began to assume significance.[100] Hitherto it had been generally assumed that Law was more interested in staking his claims for the future than in enhancing his prospects of the immediate succession. Now, however, having already shaken Chamberlain's grip over the tariff reform faction within the parliamentary party, he began also to appear a more attractive proposition than the unpredictable Long. His role in securing the party's commitment to submit tariff reform to a referendum had not been forgotten by those Unionists for whom the Chamberlainite doctrine had always been something less than holy writ.[101]

At this point Chamberlain took a step which did as much as any other single action in a long parliamentary career to assure his reputation for political rectitude. He refused absolutely to follow the advice given by Balcarres, and later by Law himself, that, if he were now to give way in favour of Long, the leadership would still be his within a matter of months, because of the certainty that Long would prove inadequate for the tasks demanded of him. Long's leadership was likely to prove 'a brief but disastrous fiasco'.[102] But what might foster Chamberlain's own personal interests could only damage those of the party in view of the enormity of the issues which lay close on the political horizon.[103] Accordingly, Chamberlain wrote to Long, stressed the serious divisions that would emerge within the party if the question of the leadership went to a vote, and proposed that both candidates should retire from the contest in favour of Bonar Law. This gesture placed Long in an invidious position in which his only viable course of action was to follow Chamberlain's lead and support the claims of Law.[104] For Chamberlain the pain of personal sacrifice was probably less acute than were his feelings for the disappointment which his decision would cause to his father.[105] But he showed that his confidence in Law's capacity for the leadership was not total by letting him know that, should the occasion arise, he, Chamberlain, would have no hesitation about standing again for the highest post in the party.[106]

Initially, Chamberlain's manoeuvre, which had been designed to preserve party unity, appeared likely to have exactly the opposite effect. From the whips' office Bridgeman noted 'a greater feeling of discontent ... than at any previous time', with many of the supporters of both Long and Chamberlain feeling that their man had been jockeyed out of the race. He feared that 'Monday's meeting may now be a stormy one'.[107] Maxse, on the other hand, assured Law that outside parliament his election would be greeted with unqualified enthusiasm.[108] The weekend of 11-12 November afforded a short period for reflection after the heated turmoil of the previous days with the result that by the time of the party meeting most members had come to the conclusion that the adoption of Bonar Law was by far the best way out of the party's difficulties. The gathering of 223 M.P.s at the Carlton Club, presided over by Henry Chaplin, 'supremely benign and calming in appearance and demeanour', passed without a discordant note. The tone was set by the first speech from Walter Long, 'a masterpiece of plain speaking and noble devotion to the best interests of the Party and Country'.[109] Thereafter the election of Andrew Bonar Law was a mere formality. Lansdowne agreed to stay on as leader in the upper chamber, thus minimising the impression that the leadership had been ousted by diehard agitation and making more likely the reunification of the party's warring factions.[110]

\*     \*     \*

Most Unionists must have been conscious at the end of 1911 that, in the choice of Bonar Law, they had made a definite and perhaps decisive change of direction. The new leader was recognisably different from his predecessors. In a comment which said as much about herself as about the object of her scorn, Margot Asquith noted that 'politically he is the most sophistical untrue unsound gerry-built quick clever affectionate vulgarian I've ever met'.[111] Certainly, the aristocratic grip of the Hotel Cecil, which had held firmly on to the reins of power within the Unionist party for a full three decades, had been decisively broken, replaced by the very different style of 'a self-consciously ordinary man, a politician who asked to be identified with as an equal rather than deferred to as a leader'.[112] The aristocratic bearing and courtly elegance of Balfour gave way to Law's commonplace and commercial appearance. Lord Lee of Fareham left a vivid and revealing account of Law's first official dinner for the Unionist front bench:

> The dinner was worthy of its setting. It was brought in - slightly congealed - from a neighbouring caterer's and the whole atmosphere of the occasion was more that of a 'wake' than a Tory festival. The faces of some of my more aristocratic

colleagues, and their faint disgust with the food and the Derry and Tom's furnishings, were a sheer delight to my soul and I was simply fascinated by the only 'objet d'art' to be seen in the whole house - a cast-iron bust on the sideboard of Robert Burns, with the ridge from the join of the mould vertically bisecting his forehead and nose.[113]

There was considerable irony in Law's emergence as Unionist leader. As Lord Blake has written:

A Presbyterian of Canadian origin, who had spent most of his life in business in Glasgow, had become leader of the Party of Old England, the Party of the Anglican Church and the country squire, the Party of broad acres and hereditary titles.[114]

Yet the man who was to lead the Unionist party for the next decade remains, despite the penetrating insights of his biographer,[115] something of an enigma. The man whose private life was sober and devoid of ostentation now helped induce into the political world a passion and violence which had not been seen since the 1880s. A man of few close friends, who probably never fully recovered from the sudden death of his wife in 1909, began to command a respect and following as a political leader which Balfour had never equalled.

There had already been signs, soon to be fully confirmed, that British politics were entering into a new era in which emotions would run higher and language become more bitter than had been seen for many years. In such a situation the continued presence of the sophisticated and urbane figure of Arthur Balfour at the head of the Unionist opposition would have appeared an anachronism. Most representative party figures were now glad, whatever their feelings of personal affection, to be rid of the complexities and complications, the philosophical subtleties and the dialectical niceties of their former leader. Balfour's rarefied approach had led to no appreciable party advantage. Unionists looked instead for someone who would pull no punches with the Liberal enemy and lead a direct frontal assault without qualification or hesitation. Bonar Law proved ready and willing to fulfil the role from which Balfour had almost always recoiled, seeing in a rumbustuous style of politics the best way, not only to attack the government, but also to heal the wounds within his own party. The bludgeon which Law employed not only frightened the other side but, more importantly, put heart into the troops in his own ranks.[116] Where Balfour had hesitated, Law struck.

Contemporaries were soon conscious of the change in the tone of the parliamentary opposition. With a note of contempt Charles Masterman recorded that

> the session had also been remarkable for what had been called the 'New Tactics'. This consists of nothing more subtle than a party of young bloods below the Opposition gangway shouting and interrupting and making a row whenever a front bench man gets up to speak.[117]

But this was not simply a case of parliamentary hooliganism. With genuine conviction many Unionists believed that the government, by introducing a measure like the Parliament Bill and employing the means which it had to ensure its passage on to the statute book, had strained the bounds of constitutional propriety to the point where the old rules of the political game were no longer valid and where they themselves were now justified in adopting tactics which might previously have been regarded as inadmissible.[118] Bonar Law accepted this rationale, whereas Balfour most likely did not.[119] It is difficult, for example, to imagine the episode when Unionist M.P.s hid in the washroom of the House of Commons in order to try to spring a surprise defeat on the government taking place while Balfour was leader.[120] It was Law's achievement to channel the enthusiasms and frustrations of his party into a coherent Unionist strategy in the years before the outbreak of the First World War, thereby succeeding in retaining within the party's parameters extremists who might otherwise have been driven into altogether more dangerous waters.[121] A significant development was the decision of the Reveille movement, only a fortnight after Law's election, to cease its activities as a mark of confidence in the new leader.[122] Law's style of leadership has thus been justly described as 'pragmatic extremism, extreme action and the threat of more extreme action to come, but used in the cause of more limited objectives'.[123] The dangerous corollary, however, was that Law might cross over the thin line which divided opposition pursued with the utmost vigour and aggression from behaviour that was unequivocally unconstitutional. In relation to the question of Ulster this frontier of legality was touched, if not actually transgressed.[124]

It was no easy task for Law to take over the leadership in November 1911 and suddenly assume seniority over a number of politicians who had already held high cabinet rank. The temptation for contemporaries to draw comparisons with Balfour was always strong. Derby could not help feeling that in six months time, when Balfour might well be taking the leading part in the fight against Home Rule, the party would want him back.[125] The Party Chairman, Steel-Maitland, was among those who never fully reconciled themselves to the change in the leadership or to the nature of Law's qualities.[126] Yet in the troubled times of the years 1911-14 Law proved for the majority of Unionists to be a far more effective leader of the party than Balfour, let alone Chamberlain or Long, could ever have been. Though not conclusive, the fifteen by-election gains, as against only two seats lost, in the period up to the outbreak of war, provide some evidence of Law's success. Certainly the new leader satisfied F. S. Oliver's maxim for a successful politician:

> The approval of his adherents is the breath of his nostrils, the
> wind in his sails; without it he can do nothing.[127]

Inside the House of Commons Law developed into a highly successful debater, having at his command a wide range of facts and statistics, making little use of notes but employing an armoury of hard-hitting phraseology. But he lacked Balfour's mastery of parliamentary techniques and sometimes revealed his inexperience.[128] Austen Chamberlain conceded that Law had 'plenty of pungency and pugnacity' which had been lacking in Balfour's speeches. But he was also

> rather rash and has not yet realised the difference between his
> old position and his new one. He is too much inclined to use
> any weapon against the government, as he would have done in
> former days when he was little reported and less studied,
> without considering that now he must be ready to support and
> prove any charge he makes.[129]

During the second reading of the Coal Mines (Minimum Wage) Bill on 19 March 1912, Law followed Asquith in the debate, but was put off his stride by an interruption and proceeded to suggest alternative courses of action, none of which he really supported.[130] Sometimes the asperity of Law's attacks proved too much for some of his own supporters. Fitzroy commented that it was 'his misfortune that he cannot make it hot for his opponents without lapses from parliamentary decorum'.[131] All in all, however, by the summer of 1912 a Unionist whip could record that, though Law tried too hard to make impromptu interjections, the party in the Commons had become warm admirers of the new leader.[132] As a result the whole tenor of parliamentary opposition was crisper and better sustained than at any time during Balfour's leadership. Even government bills about which Law did not necessarily feel

with the same intensity as he did over Home Rule were vigorously
opposed.[133] Perhaps it was Lord Riddell, the owner of the *News of the
World*, who best summed up the situation:
> The Conservatives have done a wise thing for once. They have
> selected the very best man - the only man.[134]


### NOTES

1. Lawrence to Chamberlain 14 Dec.1910, AC 8/7/23.
2. Hunt to Chamberlain 12 Jan.1911 and n.d., AC 8/7/15-16.
3. Leo Amery diary 28 Jan.1911.
4. Maxse to Steel-Maitland 15 June 1911, Steel-Maitland MSS GD 193/151/3.
5. Bridgeman diary 17-24 July 1911.
6. Maxse to Long 17 July 1911, Long MSS 448/10.
7. Similarly, Walter Long favoured allowing the Parliament Bill to pass since a swamped upper house would be unable to resist the immediate passing of a Home Rule Bill. A Unionist dominated House of Lords, even partially emasculated by the Parliament Bill, would at least allow the party the time to rally its forces. See correspondence in Long MSS 448.
8. Maxse to Sandars 24 July 1911, Balfour MSS Add. MS 49861.
9. F. E. Smith to A. Chamberlain 13 Aug. 1911, cited Lord Birkenhead, *Frederick Edwin, Earl of Birkenhead* (2 vols, London, 1933) vol.i, p.219.
10. Bridgeman diary 6-12 Aug.1911.
11. *Daily Express* 12 Aug.1911; Hyde, *Carson* p.288.
12. Sandars to Balfour 14 Aug.1911, Balfour MSS Add. MS 49767. Later in the year the annual meeting of the Liberal Unionist Conference had to be moved from Bedford to Derby because none of the local magnates in Bedfordshire would take the chair to Lansdowne: A. Chamberlain to Selborne 1 Sept.1911, Selborne MSS 79/67.
13. Vincent (ed.), *Crawford Papers* p.212.
14. Collings to J. Chamberlain 3 Aug.1911, JC 22/52.
15. Sanders diary 15 Aug.1911.

16. Vincent (ed.), *Crawford Papers* p.221.
17. As Dr. Phillips has argued, the idea that the diehard stance over the Parliament Bill was dictated by a desire to oust the existing party leaders is 'excessively Machiavellian'. 'Hostility to the Parliament Bill, not the very real frustration with Balfour and Lansdowne, was the diehards' primary motivation': Phillips, *Diehards* pp.134, 137.
18. Bridgeman diary 15 Aug.1911.
19. Ibid 16 Aug.1911.
20. Vincent (ed.), *Crawford Papers* p.215.
21. Lawrence to Willoughby de Broke 15 Aug. 1911, Willoughby de Broke MSS 3/37.
22. Mackail and Wyndham, *Wyndham* ii, 701.
23. Sanders diary 24 Oct.1911.
24. Sandys to Willoughby de Broke n.d., Willoughby de Broke MSS 3/80.
25. A. Chamberlain to M. Chamberlain 20 Aug.1911, cited Chamberlain, *Politics from Inside* p.352.
26. Ibid p.347.
27. Wyndham to Selborne 16 Aug.1911, Selborne MSS 74/178.
28. Mackail and Wyndham, *Wyndham* ii, 700.
29. Hyde, *Carson* p.293.
30. Leo Amery diary 17 Aug.1911.
31. Milner to Amery 24 Aug.1911, Amery MSS C25.
32. Hunt to Willoughby de Broke 14 Aug.1911, Willoughby de Broke MSS 3/34; Comyn Platt to 'Chief' Aug.1911, ibid 3/88.
33. Selborne to Halsbury 26 Aug.1911, Halsbury MSS Add.MS 56374. Neither, of course, was there complete uniformity of opinion among Halsbury's supporters as to the ultimate form of the constitution or the use of the referendum: Wyndham to Willoughby de Broke 19 Aug.1911, Willoughby de Broke MSS 3/50.
34. Steel-Maitland to Halsbury 11 Sept.1911, Halsbury MSS Add.MS 56374.
35. Memorandum by Steel-Maitland 2 Oct.1911, ibid.
36. Selborne to A. Chamberlain 4 Sept.1911, Selborne MSS 79/71.
37. Selborne to Willoughby de Broke 18 Aug.1911, Willoughby de Broke MSS 3/46 and Selborne to Wyndham 22 Aug.1911,ibid 3/62.
38. Selborne to Willoughby de Broke 25 Aug.1911, ibid 3/63 and Willoughby de Broke to Selborne 12 Aug.1911, Selborne MSS 74/176.

39.  Sandars to Balfour 17 Sept.1911, Balfour MSS Add. MS 49767;
     Chamberlain, *Politics from Inside* p.361.
40.  Willoughby de Broke to Selborne 17 Aug.1911, Selborne MSS 74/182.
41.  Northumberland to Willoughby de Broke 11 and 17 Aug.1911,
     Willoughby de Broke MSS 3/14, 43.
42.  Cecil to Salisbury 17 Oct.1911, Salisbury MSS S(4) 71/59. Cecil gave
     a rather different impression of his views when looking back on these
     events nearly forty years later: Cecil, *All the Way* p.118.
43.  Wyndham to Willoughby de Broke 15 Aug.1911, Willoughby de Broke
     MSS 3/40.
44.  Amery, *Political Life* i, 395-6. Significantly, Lord Balcarres, the Chief
     Whip, still maintained that 'our solvent must be found in aggressive
     and sustained criticism of everything the govt. proposes' rather than the
     formulation of alternative policies: Balcarres to Sandars 17 Sept.1911,
     Sandars MSS c764/43.
45.  See minutes of meetings in Selborne MSS 75/6.
46.  Selborne to Salisbury 6 Sept.1911, Salisbury MSS S(4) 71/6.
47.  Chamberlain, *Politics from Inside* pp.358-60; Gollin, *Observer* pp.354-
     5. An executive committee was elected on 6 November consisting of
     Amery, Astor, Carson, Hugh and Robert Cecil, Austen Chamberlain,
     Lloyd, Lovat, Milner, Ormsby-Gore, Pretyman, Smith, Winterton and
     Wyndham.
48.  N. Chamberlain to A. Chamberlain 7 Oct.1911, cited Petrie,
     *Chamberlain* i, 293.
49.  Chamberlain, *Politics from Inside* p.371.
50.  Vincent (ed.), *Crawford Papers* p.230.
51.  Petrie, *Long* p.170.
52.  Long to Balfour 19 Oct.1911, Balfour MSS Add. MS 49777; Steel-
     Maitland to Balfour 17 Oct.1911, ibid 49861.
53.  Lansdowne to Balfour 17 Oct.1911, ibid 49730.
54.  Salisbury to Selborne 14 Oct.1911, Salisbury MSS S(4) 71/54.
55.  Formerly St. John Brodrick.
56.  Midleton to Curzon 15 Oct.1911 and St.Aldwyn to Curzon 19
     Oct.1911, Curzon MSS Eur.F 112/18.
57.  Vincent (ed.), *Crawford Papers* p.186.
58.  Petrie, *Long* p.170; C. Petrie, *The Carlton Club* (London, 1972)
     p.166; Winterton, *Pre-War* pp.230-1.

59. Zebel, *Balfour* p.170.
60. Brett, *Esher* iii, 30.
61. Ibid p.59.
62. Balcarres to Sandars 26 Sept.1911, Sandars MSS c. 764/99; Vincent (ed.), *Crawford Papers* p.224.
63. Sandars 'Memorandum on events leading to Mr. Balfour's resignation' 8 Nov.1911, Balfour MSS Add MS 49767.
64. Vincent (ed.), *Crawford Papers* p.228.
65. Balfour to Lady Elcho 8 Oct.1911, cited Dugdale, *Balfour* ii, 83.
66. Sandars 'Memorandum on events'.
67. Balcarres to Sandars 2 Oct.1911, Sandars MSS c.764/118.
68. Long to Balfour 29 Sept.1911, cited Petrie, *Long* pp.165-7.
69. Note by Short Oct.1911, Sandars MSS c.764/113. Sandars found the letter 'more offensive on reading it again': Note by Sandars 21 Oct.1911, ibid c.764/126.
70. Sandars 'Memorandum on events'; Balcarres to Sandars 9 Oct.1911, Sandars MSS c.764/138.
71. Petrie, *Carlton Club* p.167.
72. Dugdale, *Balfour* ii, 88.
73. Balfour to Sandars 5 Oct.1911, Balfour MSS Add. MS 49767.
74. W. Bridgeman to C. Bridgeman 26 Oct.1911, cited P.Williamson (ed.), *The Modernisation of Conservative Politics: The Diaries and Letters of William Bridgeman,1904-1935* (London, 1988) p.52.
75. Sandars to Balfour 8 Oct.1911 and 2 Nov.1911, Balfour MSS Add. MS 49767; Derby to Balfour 5 Nov.1911, Derby MSS 4/39.
76. *National Review* Oct.1911.
77. Maxse to Garvin 11 Oct.1911, cited Gollin, *Observer* p.351. To Archibald Salvidge Maxse wrote: 'But I own to being simply appalled by the attitude of the people at the top of our party and above all by their total failure to realise that a continuance of Balfourism means general ruin .... I believe if we go on as at present, without drastic changes at the top, that Unionism will gradually "peter out"': Salvidge, *Salvidge* p.113.
78. Dugdale, *Balfour* ii, 89-90.
79. Long to Balfour 29 Sept.1911, cited Petrie, *Long* pp.166-7. See also Balcarres to Lady Wantage 22 Feb.1912, cited Vincent (ed.), *Crawford Papers* p.262.

80.  Wyndham to Balfour 8 Nov.1911, Balfour MSS Add. MS 49806.
81.  Ibid.
82.  Curzon to Balfour 4 Nov.1911, Balfour MSS Add. MS 49733.
83.  Hamilton to Balfour of Burleigh 9 Nov.1911, Balfour of Burleigh MSS 25.
84.  Collings to M. Chamberlain 20 March 1910, cited Amery, *Chamberlain* p.951. As the vacancy had arisen while the party was in opposition, there would be no leader of the whole party for the time being. It would be for the monarch to decide at the appropriate moment whether the leader in the Commons or the leader in the Lords should become Prime Minister and thus leader of the party. In practice, however, the chances of a peer becoming premier were starting to diminish. Though Law and Lansdowne generally cooperated well, the divided leadership could lead to problems. See Dicey to Strachey 27 May 1913, Strachey MSS S/5/6/12.
85.  Balfour of Burleigh to R.Cecil 5 Dec.1909, Balfour of Burleigh MSS 38.
86.  Blake, *Unknown Prime Minister* p.72; D. J. Dutton, *Austen Chamberlain: Gentleman in Politics* (Bolton, 1985) chapter 3. Concerning his position within the tariff reform movement, Austen Chamberlain wrote : 'I feel that I stand as Father's son in a very special way for T.R.: that men look to me to hold that citadel and yet (not unnaturally considering that I stayed in the Govt. when Father went out and considering all the concessions I have had to make to Balfour and party unity) that those who are Tariff Reformers before everything do not wholly trust me as they would trust Father': Chamberlain to M. Chamberlain 30 Oct.1911, AC 4/1/733.
87.  R. Jay, *Joseph Chamberlain: a Political Study* (Oxford, 1981) pp. 312-3, 316. On learning of Balfour's retirement, Austen Chamberlain wrote: 'There is the great news, sad news to me whatever happens for I love the man, and though as you know he has once or twice nearly broken my heart politically, I now can think of nothing but the pleasure of intimate association with him': Chamberlain, *Politics from Inside* p.378.
88.  Amery, *Political Life* i, 386.
89.  Vincent (ed.), *Crawford Papers* p.230.
90.  See, for example, Ridley to Law 5 Jan.1906, Law MSS 18/2/10.

91.  Blake, *Unknown Prime Minister* p.56.
92.  Chamberlain, *Politics from Inside* p.375.
93.  Aitken to Law n.d., Law MSS 18/7/198. Long later discovered that Garvin had tried unsuccessfully to induce Law to retire from the contest in order not to damage Chamberlain's chances: Long to Law 7 June 1912, Law MSS 26/4/12.
94.  Carson, in fact, declined to enter the contest. Williamson (ed.), *Modernisation* p.53.
95.  A. Chamberlain to M. Chamberlain 11 Nov.1911, AC 9/3/13.
96.  Long's tactics were somewhat surprising in view of the fact that his own strength derived largely from backbench support.
97.  Bridgeman diary 7 Nov.1911.
98.  Sanders diary 12 Nov.1911.
99.  A. Chamberlain to M. Chamberlain 11 Nov.1911, AC 9/3/13. Compare Chaplin's rather strange assertion that both leading candidates behaved with total propriety throughout the contest: Chaplin to Balfour 19 Nov.1911, Balfour MSS Add. MS 49772.
100. Goulding to Law 9 Nov.1911, Law MSS 24/1/1; Blake, *Unknown Prime Minister* p.74. Though greatly exaggerated at the time, there can be no doubt that Aitken's role as Law's 'Campaign Manager' left a bad taste in many mouths. Sandars wrote disparagingly of the 'little Canadian adventurer who sits for Ashton-under-Lyne': Sandars to Balfour 10 Nov. 1911, Balfour MSS Add. MS 49767.
101. Hamilton to Balfour of Burleigh 13 Nov.1911, Balfour of Burleigh MSS 25.
102. Chamberlain, *Politics from Inside* p.388.
103. Ibid pp.388-91.
104. Sandars to Balfour 10 Nov.1911, Balfour MSS Add MS 49767.
105. Gollin, *Observer* p.359; A. Chamberlain to M. Chamberlain 10 Nov.1911, cited Chamberlain, *Politics from Inside* p.381.
106. Sandars to Balfour 12 Nov.1911, Balfour MSS Add. MS 49767. Chamberlain, in fact, made no attempt to dislodge Law from the leadership, although he came near to breaking with him over the question of food taxes in the winter of 1912-13.
107. Bridgeman diary 10 Nov.1911.
108. Maxse to Law 11 Nov.1911, Law MSS 24/3/9.
109. Bridgeman diary 13 Nov.1911.

110. Sykes, *Tariff Reform* p.253.

111. M. Asquith to Strachey 1911, Strachey MSS S/11/7/39.

112. Ramsden, *Balfour and Baldwin* p.92. Austen Chamberlain later recorded that 'the fact that he [Law] had no experience of government did not trouble him when he took the leadership. What he was afraid of then was his want of birth. He was confident that he could lead without experience but afraid that the party might follow unwillingly because he had not blue blood in his veins': A. Chamberlain to Ida Chamberlain 25 March 1921, AC 5/1/195. Balfour himself commented of his successor, 'I think it quite possible that Bonar Law may surprise you': cited Lees-Milne, *Enigmatic Edwardian* p.234.

113. Clark (ed.), *Good Innings* p.120.

114. Blake, *Unknown Prime Minister* p.86.

115. Ibid pp.87-99.

116. H. A. Taylor, *The Strange Case of Andrew Bonar Law* (London, n.d.) p.170. Balcarres wrote : 'The Party, in its subconscious way, likes Bonar Law's attitude precisely because it lacks those very qualities which in a Gladstone or a Balfour would conform to high parliamentary tradition': Vincent (ed.), *Crawford Papers* pp. 262-3.

117. Masterman, *Masterman* p.219.

118. Carson to Law 27 Dec.1911, Law MSS 24/5/156.

119. Balcarres did not share this assessment of Balfour, arguing that had he remained leader he would 'himself ... have translated his resentment into speeches far more violent than any to which he has been accustomed': Vincent (ed.), *Crawford Papers* p.262.

120. Sanders diary 5 Aug.1913.

121. Ramsden, *Balfour and Baldwin* p.85.

122. Page Croft to Law 30 Nov.1911, Law MSS 24/4/92.

123. Ramsden, *Balfour and Baldwin* p.67.

124. See below pp.203-7.

125. Derby to King George V 16 Nov.1911, cited Churchill, *Lord Derby* p.156.

126. Lord Riddell, *More Pages from my Diary 1908-1914* (London, 1934) p.68; Chamberlain, *Politics from Inside* p.534.

127. G. Peele and C. Cook (eds), *The Politics of Reappraisal 1918-1939* (London, 1975) p.16.

128. Lloyd George commented at the beginning of 1913 : 'Bonar Law may

talk as his people talk in their clubs. He may reflect the Conservative mind and therefore please his followers in the country, but he doesn't know the Parliamentary game. He is almost invariably wrong. For real business give me old Arthur Balfour!': Riddell, *More Pages* p.118.

129.  Chamberlain, *Politics from Inside* p.415.
130.  Winterton, *Orders* p.65.
131.  Fitzroy, *Memoirs* ii, 538.
132.  Bridgeman diary April-Aug.1912.
133.  For example, the Welsh Church Disestablishment Bill. See Winterton, *Orders* p.63.
134.  Riddell, *More Pages* p.26.

PUNCH, OR THE LONDON CHARIVARI.—January 22, 1913.

NOT LOST, BUT LEFT BEHIND.

*(By request of the Ship's Crew.)*

# 8

# POLICY : TARIFF REFORM
## 1911—1914

The first issue of policy to confront Bonar Law when he became party leader was that of tariff reform. Granted the party's still equivocal stance on this question at the time of Balfour's resignation, this was by no means surprising. It was always likely that the brief interlude of consensus over this issue, achieved largely for reasons of tactics rather than conviction, would be challenged once more owing to the party's failure at two general elections in 1910 to win back the reins of government. The status of Balfour's referendum pledge of November 1910 in relation to future elections would have been in doubt even had Balfour retained the leadership. With his replacement the issue obviously became more acute. Bonar Law could not have relished the re-emergence of this issue which had caused such problems for his predecessor. Especially as the focus of political attention moved towards Ireland and with by-elections turning in their favour, Unionists at long last had some reason for optimism. Yet the party's internal history over the previous eight years must have suggested that Law would burn his fingers in trying to tackle this most divisive of questions. Conversely, if Law could unite the party behind an acceptable agreement on tariffs, he had perhaps a last chance to give Unionists a viable fiscal policy to set against that of the Liberal government. Law's own past suggested at first glance that under his leadership the party would take a more decisive stance in favour of tariffs than at any time before. When urged by the Chief Whip to allow some measure of latitude to the free trader T.G.Bowles as a Unionist candidate, the new leader stressed that the party could not afford to have many candidates who were not absolutely committed to support its programme.[1] In the months which followed, however, Law came to disappoint those who had looked to him finally to consummate Joseph Chamberlain's elusive vision. Ironically, Fabian Ware later recalled that when Law became leader Chamberlain himself had commented, 'He is not a Tariff Reformer.'[2]

The Canadian-American Reciprocity Agreement of 1911, coming after two general elections at which the success of tariff reform had been at best only qualified, caused serious splits within the tariff reform section of the Unionist party. Many now believed that the goal of Imperial Preference would have to be radically modified since the Canadians had made this important economic arrangement outside the closed imperial circle of which Chamberlain had dreamed. Bonar Law even went so far as to propose that the time might have arrived when preference should be abandoned.[3] The removal from office of the Canadian Prime Minister, Wilfred Laurier, in September, and his replacement by the Conservative, Robert Borden, did not fully heal this breach, which was still evident in the divided opinions of the tariff reformers over the choice of Balfour's successor in November. The developments which took place in the first year of Law's leadership are only comprehensible against this background of differing emphases and interpretations.

The new leader was scarcely installed before the various factions within the party set out to influence him in respect of future policy on tariffs. Playing upon the prejudices which Law had himself developed during his electioneering experience in Manchester in 1910, Lord Derby spelt out his views:

> Tariff Reform as at present advocated will not do for us here
> [in Lancashire] and by hook or by crook we have got to make
> some such alteration as will prevent our opponents having the
> very taking cry that we are taxing the people's food and I am
> in hopes that you may see a way out of the difficulty.[4]

Derby was no economist and his argument was the simple but telling one that food taxes would lose votes. 'Unless the difficulty is met in some way or other', he argued, 'it is hopeless to think of our winning.'[5] Law, doubting whether the party as a whole would swallow the abandonment of food taxes, felt that at this stage there was 'nothing for us but to go straight forward with the programme as it is'.[6]

Austen Chamberlain, arguing from the opposite point of view to Derby, had been even quicker in nailing his colours to the mast. While still a contender for the leadership, he made it publicly quite plain that, should the party choose him, they would do so knowing that a Unionist government under his premiership would 'without any further mandate, sanction or approbation' embody tariff reform in statutory form.[7] To Law he pointed out that Balfour's referendum pledge had been part of an attempt to persuade the government to submit its own constitutional proposals to similar plebiscitary examination. That attempt having failed, the Unionist party should not feel bound by its earlier commitment. Personally Chamberlain would not be party to a repetition of what he regarded as the mistake of the referendum, nor join a government which proposed to handle tariff reform in that way. Having 'burned my boats' Chamberlain could not 'unsay what I have publicly stated'.[8] Treading carefully, the most that Law would promise was that he would not change party policy on the question of food taxes without first obtaining Chamberlain's consent.[9]

In the early weeks of 1912 Law continued to receive a barrage of advice over future policy. Long protested that the party was committed to the referendum and that it must not be abandoned, while Lansdowne too showed a preference for continuing with Balfour's pledge, although he did not feel that the party was still bound by it.[10] Yet, partly because he was by no means anxious to drag his party's continuing divisions out into the open, and partly because as a new leader he still felt a little unsure of his position, Law did not bring this contentious issue to the shadow cabinet until March. Then it was the intense pressure of the Chamberlainite faction which prevailed and the shadow cabinet decided that food taxes should remain a plank of the party programme and that the referendum should be abandoned. The decision was not, however, made public for the time being. The delay may have reflected Law's hesitation at being seen to overthrow the policy of his predecessor.

As the Chief Whip argued, for many tariff reformers food taxes were an integral part of the policy as a whole and it was a point of honour that the party should not abandon them. Only in this way could preference be given to colonial products in the British market and only a policy of Imperial Preference could save the Empire from disintegration. As Law summed up the situation for the shadow cabinet: 'in short these taxes are a handicap, but we must carry our handicap and carry it boldly'.[11] Londonderry and Derby were the only members who actually dissented from the majority view, although Balfour was away at Cannes at the time of the meeting.[12] On his return Balfour confirmed that the decision was not inconsistent with the pledges that he had given, though he did nothing to conceal his extreme anxiety as to the result of giving up the referendum.[13] But it was the attitude of Lord Derby which was to assume crucial significance. According to Austen Chamberlain, Derby admitted that it was not possible to drop food taxes, though he would give anything to be able to do so.[14] In the account of F. E. Smith, Derby later gave Law a personal assurance that he would be loyal to the shadow cabinet's decision.[15] By September, however, he warned the Chief Whip that he was 'coming out against the Food Taxes. I can't stand them any longer.'[16]

Despite the decision of the shadow cabinet the debate continued throughout the spring and summer of 1912. 'Whatever you hear to the contrary', stressed Derby, 'there is still as great an opposition to the food taxes in Lancashire as there was when the proposal was first brought forward.' If the party came into government still committed to food taxes, Derby doubted whether he would be able to offer his support. Indeed so great would be the opposition within the House of Commons, no matter how large the government's nominal parliamentary majority, that the party might split completely and 'be in the wilderness for 20 years'.[17] Walter Long, investigating the position in Liverpool and Manchester at first hand, provided corroborative evidence to support Derby's conclusion. There was practically a unanimity of opinion that Tariff Reform had not made any headway since the last Election and 'nearly everybody I spoke to on the subject was convinced that there is great hostility to food taxes. The average Lancashire voter firmly believes the proposals of the Tariff Reform Party will cause an increase in the cost of living.'[18] Long concluded that although an election at the present time would probably bring the Unionists back into power, they would not be able to retain their popularity in the country unless there was a change in policy.[19] In a by-election in South Manchester the Tariff Reform League had attempted to make their policy a vital issue and had sent a large number of speakers and canvassers into the division. But Long was convinced that their actions had been of no assistance to the party and 'in fact, if we had been defeated, I should certainly have ascribed it to the work performed by the Tariff Reform League'.[20]

Robert Cecil, who had earlier absented himself from the Commons rather than face a Unionist fiscal amendment which he could not support,[21] stressed that, without seeking it out, he was constantly coming across evidence of the unpopularity of food taxes. He doubted whether Law's advisers were giving him accurate information on the state of opinion in the party.[22] His elder brother, Lord Salisbury, argued that by making the Unionists unpopular in the country food taxes were largely responsible for the continued survival of the Liberal government. If that government now proceeded to destroy the constitution, repeal the Act of Union with Ireland and disestablish the Welsh church, the policy of food taxes 'would probably rank as the most costly ... in history'.[23] Law, however, remained convinced that, though food taxes were a handicap, to change the policy now would increase the difficulty of winning the next election rather than diminish it. He was certain that any proposal to drop food duties or submit them to a referendum would provoke a large split in the party, which would be a greater handicap than anything else.[24] What, however, was significant in Law's response was that his continued adherence to food taxes was based not upon any belief in their intrinsic value (though he did anticipate 'a great advantage to small-holders and also to Ireland' from a small duty on food stuffs), and only secondarily on his general faith in the benefits of tariff reform, but primarily upon his calculation of the probable impact of any change in policy upon the internal dynamics of the Unionist party. Thus, were Law to receive clear evidence that his present assessment of the situation was not entirely accurate, the possibility of a fundamental alteration to party policy remained real, notwithstanding the conclusion already reached by the shadow cabinet.

As a result, the battle of the summer of 1912 to win over Law's mind was fought out largely in terms of the tactical advantages and disadvantages to be expected from changing the party's attitude to food taxes. Even under Law, supposedly a committed tariff reformer, the argument focused, as it had latterly done under Balfour, upon calculations of electoral and internal party benefit rather than upon basic questions of national economic advantage. Of course, from the outset of the tariff reform campaign only a minority of Unionists had shared the full vision of Joseph Chamberlain with its imperial and social reform dimensions. In this vein Hugh Cecil stressed that the prospects of electoral success were 'doubtful' if the party adhered to food taxes, while the announcement that Balfour's referendum pledge had been dropped would be 'electorally ruinous ... electorally impossible'. It could only end in 'vacillation, obloquy, disorganisation and panic'.[25] The debate, as the free trader Strachey recognised, was no longer being conducted on the old free trade-tariff reform divide. As he made plain to Law when asking for a reiteration of the referendum pledge on food taxes, Strachey was not seeking to preserve 'any scintilla of Free Trade. I am asking it simply and solely in order that the Unionists and so the Tariff Reformers shall win.'[26] For the time being, however, Law continued to insist that the party had no option but to go forward with the full programme. To repeat the promise of a referendum would occasion a revolt among the tariff reformers and 'I am inclined to think that it would be justified from their, or perhaps I should say from our, point of view'.[27] The hesitation in Law's response was perhaps significant.

Before the shadow cabinet decision of March was finally made public, Law sought out the opinion of the new Canadian Prime Minister, Robert Borden. The latter insisted that to go back on the party's full programme would be regarded by his supporters in Canada as a serious blow to the whole question of preference. Food taxes were seen in this most important of dominions as essential for an effective policy of imperial consolidation.[28] By the autumn of 1912 Lansdowne believed that an explicit statement on the issue had become inevitable and that the party would even gain from it. Since he had been consulted by Balfour when the original pledge was given and had often repeated it in subsequent speeches, it was agreed that Lansdowne should have the responsibility for clarifying the party's current policy.[29] As the rumour of an impending policy pronouncement gained ground, the opponents of food taxes launched a last effort to dissuade Law from this fateful step. Younger, the party's Scottish whip, warned of the serious consequences north of the border if party policy were changed,[30] while Hugh Cecil produced six pages of 'final protest':

> If there were no Union or Church or Ulstermen at stake, this
> would deserve to be called insanity. But when the highest
> national interests are involved, when those whom we are bound
> to succour and save by every consideration of honour and
> chivalry may have to pay the price of our folly, what word fitly
> describes our action? [31]

Nonetheless on 14 November Lansdowne, speaking at the meeting of the Conservative National Union at the Albert Hall, made public the repudiation of the referendum pledge decided upon by the shadow cabinet earlier in the year.

In the wake of Lansdowne's speech Austen Chamberlain breathed a premature sigh of relief:

> Lansdowne spoke admirably at the Albert Hall and disposed of
> the Referendum most neatly. So that is off my mind, but if you
> knew how often Law has doubted and hesitated since our
> decision was taken just after he was made leader, you would
> know what a weight is off my mind. These declarations were
> to have been made nearly a year ago and were very nearly not
> made this week.[32]

In other quarters, however, the Albert Hall declaration was less well received. A junior whip recorded the general view that it was most unwise to bring the question to the front again at a time when the party appeared to be making great headway simply by attacking the government. In Scotland and the North of England the effect was particularly bad.[33] Long had a 'disagreeable experience' when visiting Bradford. The local party chairman and all the Bradford candidates asked to see him to impress their view that the Albert Hall announcement had destroyed any chances they had of electoral success.[34] The reaction in Lancashire was swift and predictable. In the Manchester cotton trade the response was one of despair, 'followed in some by the complete political apathy of men who feel their cause lost and in others by rage at what they hold to be a betrayal'.[35] Archibald Salvidge, the party's political boss in Liverpool, was disappointed that the 'fanatical protectionists' had been allowed to exert undue pressure . Lansdowne's speech had robbed the party of all the advantages it had been gaining by concentrating upon the Irish question.[36] Feeling his party loyalty severely strained, Salvidge was particularly annoyed that so important a pronouncement had been made 'without any consultation or without advice being solicited'.[37]

Indeed, one of the most curious aspects of the whole episode was that, although Law and Lansdowne had scarcely made a hasty decision, having reflected on the problem over a period of months, the leadership was so markedly out of step with rank and file opinion in the party on this issue. Balcarres later commented on 'our lack of sound information'.[38] Though Law had consistently maintained that, in juggling to find the lesser of two evils, the balance of advantage lay in placating the Chamberlainite wing, and claimed to have gone to great lengths to find out what ordinary M.P.s felt on the matter, the fact was that by the end of 1912 the number of Unionist M.P.s still unswervingly committed to the full programme of tariff reform was relatively small.[39] As Strachey pointed out, it was the opposition of moderate tariff reformers to the Albert Hall speech rather than the predictable outcry of the free trade minority of which Law should take note.[40] Thus in making public the shadow cabinet's conclusion, Law and Lansdowne were in danger of fermenting precisely that rebellion in the party's ranks which the leadership's decision of March had been designed to prevent. As a result, when Austen Chamberlain noted that 'in a few weeks, almost in a few days, the revolt had become general; the panic had spread to all but a few stalwarts',[41] what he was observing was not so much a massive desertion from the tariff reform camp as the vociferous expression of what had for some while been majority opinion within the party - that the full policy of Imperial Preference, which included food taxes, was an insuperable electoral liability.

The press soon joined the fray and on 12 December the *Liverpool Courier* launched its 'Great Alternative' campaign calling for a reconsideration of

Unionist policy - a campaign in which much of the national press including *The Times* and the *Daily Mail* became quickly involved.[42] On 14 December the *Courier* announced that

> party loyalty has definite boundaries. It becomes mere servility when it is a support of leaders who are moving where their followers are unwilling to go, it becomes mere criminal folly when it is an endorsement of a policy condemned by every canon of sound thinking.[43]

But at this stage many important figures including Lord Derby, whose reaction could be decisive in shaping Lancashire opinion, held their fire in the knowledge that Law was about to make an important speech in Ashton-under-Lyne. Visited by George Lloyd, Rupert Gwynne and Leo Amery on 14 December, Law made light of recent developments and dismissed as ridiculous the idea that there could now be any change of policy from the Lansdowne declaration. Law's callers 'went out elated, feeling that here was somebody not in the least troubled by these petty alarms'.[44] Yet two days later when Law spoke at Ashton - without apparently consulting Chamberlain - their reaction must have been very different. Law now seemed to limit food taxes to wheat, meat and possibly dairy produce, while at the same time shifting the whole onus on to the Dominions by suggesting that the proposed duties would only be imposed if the Dominions regarded them as essential to Imperial Preference.

Though Law claimed that his speech was entirely compatible with Lansdowne's Albert Hall pledge, its effect was little short of disastrous. Almost overnight the party's prospects were set back dramatically. The Chief Whip commented:

> We are now on the defensive. A month ago we were anxious for a dissolution - today we would enter upon an election with anxiety, perhaps with dismay.[45]

Milner interpreted Law's speech as a clumsy first step to try to cut the Gordian Knot and begin a retreat from what had become an untenable position.[46] But without in any way pacifying the worries of men like Derby, Law had now succeeded in alarming committed tariff reformers such as Chamberlain and Amery. The latter read the speech with 'bewilderment and even consternation'.[47] He had

> understood we were to have a clear and simple reaffirmation of the policy of preference, coupled perhaps with some specific

announcement of what we meant to limit ourselves to and what
taxes we hoped to remit. But here we are back in all the
muddle of the old Balfourian exegetics.[48]

Designed to give the party a formula on which it could unite, the Ashton
speech merely had the effect of spreading dissension. As Fitzroy noted: 'No
opposition leader now makes a speech without giving the lie to one of his
colleagues, not infrequently to himself, and their followers are at sixes and
sevens.'[49] By appearing to indicate Law's own hesitations over the full policy
of tariff reform the Ashton speech turned what had hitherto been only latent
unrest over food taxes into an outright revolt.

Derby now found himself in an extremely difficult position. As President
of the Lancashire Division of the Unionist Association, he would have to chair
a meeting on 21 December at which motions critical of official party policy
were certain to be put forward. The Party Chairman attempted to persuade
Balfour to use his influence to prevent Derby from lending his name to the
mounting criticism.[50] Balfour admitted that the time might come when Derby
would feel obliged to express his dissent, but reminded the Lancashire leader
that 'if Bonar Law goes the Party ... is doomed'.[51] Even the avowed free
trader Hugh Cecil pleaded with Derby not to reopen the discussion over
tariffs.[52] Meanwhile Law received conflicting advice as to the course he
should adopt. While Long suggested that his best line was to 'make believe not
to hear the raging of the gale', F. E. Smith warned that the situation in
Lancashire was extremely dangerous and predicted that Salvidge would side
with Derby in opposing food taxes. He hoped to make use of the Ashton
M.P., Max Aitken, who was close to Law, to steady the wobblers since
failure to deal with the situation promptly would only lead to disaster.[53]
Similarly Garvin feared that renewed pressure on Law to drop food taxes
might bring the whole Unionist party crashing down 'in a squalid, ludicrous,
ignoble fiasco'.[54]

Derby was anxious not to split the party in any way and keen that no
hasty decision should be arrived at. A cooling-off period might have beneficial
effects. His hope, therefore, was to summon a further meeting for the
following February. If by that time no alternative policy had been prepared by
the leadership, he would no longer be able to keep silent and would publicly
declare himself against food taxes.[55] Indeed, on the very eve of the meeting,
Derby, while assuring the leader of his personal loyalty, warned Law that the
abandonment of the referendum would have a 'very disastrous effect in this

county unless some substitute is provided'.[56]

In the event, although not all observers in London were convinced of the fact, Derby's behaviour at the Lancashire meeting was thoroughly loyal to Law. As he explained:

> I would not let them come to a vote but if they had I have not
> the least doubt that they would practically unanimously have
> passed a vote asking that the question of preferential treatment
> with the Colonies should be postponed and not be a subject for
> discussion at the next General Election.

Of one fact he was certain. All present at the meeting were convinced that seats would be lost if the question of food taxes were not submitted to a referendum.[57] As it was, the delegates would not agree to adjourn for more than three weeks rather than the six for which Derby had hoped.[58] Yet while his public behaviour may have been beyond reproach, Derby made a rather desperate attempt behind the scenes to entice Balfour back into the political fray 'with a policy that did not include food taxes'. As he explained:

> I could not keep silent when I knew that, if the present policy
> is persevered with, it must mean a certain defeat at the next
> Election and a great loss of seats in this County. The feeling
> roughly is this. We have been dictated to by Birmingham for
> several years past. We have fought three elections with the
> millstone of Tariff Reform tied round our necks and each time
> we have been defeated. We are going to cut ourselves away
> from it now. Surely we have paid enough tribute to the
> Birmingham gang ? [59]

Derby was adamant that a split in the party would be inevitable unless the food taxers gave way. He was not going to be 'browbeaten ... any more'. [60]

For his part Law was unconvinced that Derby had behaved entirely properly.[61] Henry Chaplin confirmed that Derby was 'doing mischief in Lancashire'.[62] In fact the report of the meeting which Law received via the Party Chairman was highly unreliable and tended to blind him to the central truth, which Derby had fully grasped, that a political party committed to food taxes could never present itself successfully to a working-class electorate. In urging the Chief Whip to attend the next Lancashire meeting accompanied by as many of the Lancashire members as he could persuade to support him, Law was attacking the manifestation of his difficulties rather than their cause.[63] Indeed the Chief Whip later conceded that the evidence of disquiet was so sustained that there was no need to think that Derby had stimulated it.[64] In delaying the showdown until a further meeting of the Lancashire Association, Derby was allowing time for further pressure to be brought to bear on the party leadership. Though warned that to persist in his present policy might lead to the resignations of both Bonar Law and Lansdowne, with no member of the front bench able to take up the leadership in their place,[65] Derby was taking a calculated risk. He even admitted that, should Law go, there was no one in the House of Commons who was likely to make even a decent leader.[66] If the resumed Lancashire meeting carried a resolution deprecating the Ashton speech, and if this opinion was then endorsed by a party meeting, Law would have to resign. 'That means not merely a split in the party but its complete and utter disruption', commented Gwynne. 'It can only end in disaster and damnation to the Unionist cause.'[67]

In the whole-hogger camp alarm bells were now ringing. Leo Amery scathingly commented:

> three-quarters of the party are like panic-stricken sheep and temporarily beyond the reach of argument, prepared to swallow everything they have said for the last few years ... prepared to ask their leader to discredit himself ... anything rather than face a purely imaginary bogey invented by themselves and certain other old women on their local committees.

If it were not so tragically serious, 'the crisis in the Unionist party would really afford most delightful sport for anyone with a sense of humour'.[68] Austen Chamberlain, admitting that there were some difficult times ahead, urged Law to stand firm and suggested a six weeks' campaign to educate the party to the whole-hogger point of view.[69] 'For heaven's sake', he pleaded, 'don't let us allow a frightened crew to knock the captain on the head and put about! If we do the Party is d__d and deserves it.'[70] From his enforced retirement his father Joseph regarded the present crisis as an attempt to see just how far Law could be pushed.[71]

But Law's nerve was clearly beginning to fail. He had no stomach for the sort of fight which the Chamberlains wanted him to wage. Recognising now that the great majority of Unionists were keen to get rid of the food duties, he was convinced that the policy he had laid down would ultimately have to be modified. He doubted, however, whether this modification would be possible under his leadership.[72] Lansdowne, too, was depressed by the recent course of events and could see no outcome which did not involve his own resignation.[73] As a result Law proposed to summon a party meeting and give up the leadership. While Derby considered the possibility of a break-away movement if Law failed to retreat from the Albert Hall and Ashton positions, the Tariff Reform League prepared itself for a climb-down by the leader and maintained that its policy would be 'unaffected by political trimmings'.[74] But for the great bulk of opinion in the middle ground of the party the present impasse, threatening both the possibility of Law's resignation and an impediment to the Unionists' effective opposition to the government's Home Rule proposals, was quite intolerable. Put simply, if Law did resign there was no one likely to be able to lead the party through the stern parliamentary battles which lay ahead. As Lord Balcarres put it : 'we are not only in danger of losing our leaders, but equally of losing the Union, the Welsh Church and Tariff Reform into the bargain'.[75] Of the two earlier contenders for the leadership, Long's health had now deteriorated, while Austen Chamberlain could scarcely take over as the inheritor of a watered-down tariff policy which had forced Law to resign. The real difficulty was for Law and Lansdowne to find a dignified line of retreat. Robert Sanders commented perceptively upon the irony of the situation:

> For years the party jibed at Balfour for being nervous about this
> policy; now that the leader is a thorough whole-hogger it goes
> back on him at the first opportunity.[76]

Searching for an acceptable compromise, Edward Goulding had already taken tentative steps to organise a petition to Law signed by tariff reform M.P.s approving a referendum limited to food taxes - a move which Chamberlain thought would cover tariff reformers 'with ridicule and destroy every shred of character with which we are yet blessed'.[77] Meeting Law and Lansdowne at the Duke of Abercorn's funeral, Carson learnt that both leaders intended to retire. Together with Goulding, Carson arranged to get together a group of the strongest tariff reformers and prepare a letter to Law asking him to postpone food duties but retain the leadership. Hewins, McNiel and Page Croft were among the first to come forward and were soon joined by F. E. Smith and others. Ultimately only a handful of Unionist members refused to sign this memorial.[78] The fact that as committed a tariff reformer as Professor Hewins along with as staunch a free trader as Hugh Cecil could put their names to the same document revealed that it came as close as was possible to reflecting the wishes of the whole party. In urging Law to resign rather than admit of any compromise on the policy of tariff reform, Henry

Chaplin was very much in a minority.[79] The substance of the memorial was loyalty to the leaders and a determination to press ahead with Imperial Preference on the understanding that any preference which was possible without food taxes should be carried immediately the party obtained power, but that any further preference including food taxes would be subject to approval at another election. Law accepted these stipulations with some reluctance but, convinced that only his own leadership could keep the party intact, he at last admitted that 'one has to take into account the feeling of the Party'.[80] Walter Long expressed the general sentiment that the party owed Law and Lansdowne 'a big debt of gratitude for your public spirited and most unselfish action'.[81]

With the effective dropping of food taxes, to which Law gave expression in a speech at Edinburgh later in the month, a provisional division of the National Union had in practice succeeded in formulating the policy of the party as a whole - something which Law had previously described as 'unheard of'.[82] Over an issue on which the leadership and the rank and file were going in opposite directions, the grass roots of the party had been seen to triumph.[83] Law's handling of the whole crisis was strangely inept for a leader who had risen to the top largely because he epitomised the spirit and frustrations of those beneath him. As Lansdowne admitted, the Unionist agents and party managers ought to have been better informed as to the state of feeling in the country.[84] Long lamented that the real difficulty of the situation had arisen from the fact that the leaders had no means of accurately ascertaining what the views of their followers in the country were on these questions.[85] This was true. But what evidence there is suggests that Law and Lansdowne had for almost a year consistently misinterpreted the situation in making their judgement as to what was practical politics. Information on the state of feeling in the country had not been entirely lacking. Long had warned as early as June 1912 of the growing disillusionment with the whole-hogger approach,[86] and since the Albert Hall declaration he had seen representatives from London, Lancashire, Cheshire, Yorkshire and Scotland who deprecated above all else the fact that nothing had been done to consult them before that far-reaching pronouncement was made. 'It is quite clear', noted Long,

> that no steps of the kind were taken, because if any information
> had been obtained from these important centres it would have
> been known before the declaration was made that we should
> incur great odium in these parts of the country, whatever might

have been the case in the rest of the United Kingdom.[87]
Law, however, had persisted in the mistaken belief that provided there was no difference of opinion among the leaders of the party in London there would be no trouble in the country.[88] Derby had not been forcing his opinion on the people of Lancashire, but giving expression to their own very real anxieties. As he put it:

> It is in this county, in Yorkshire and Scotland that you have got to gain seats if you are going to get a majority and if you persist in the position now taken up [of abandoning the referendum] you are not going to gain anything like the number of seats you require, even if you do not as a matter of fact lose some.[89]

The decision reached by the party in January 1913 was not so much a major reversal of principle as a restatement of the Unionists' gut feeling for practical politics. It was not, asserted Long, a question of principle but of tactics - 'not a case of the Party refusing to follow their Leader, but simply that they beg the Leaders to make such a modification as will ... ensure success and avert a National disaster'.[90] Sir Almeric Fitzroy sensed a fluctuating mass of unsettled opinion in the party which was ready to crystallise into any mould which offered the prospect of success at the polls. But his scorn for a political party in 'a pitch of sombre and sordid anarchy' did less than justice to the Unionists' pragmatism and adaptability.[91] In 1909 and 1910 a similar decision had been taken but with an opposite effect. Then, in the face of the danger posed by the Liberal government's Finance Bill and the threat of constitutional legislation to come, free trade Unionists and hesitant Balfourites had been obliged to swallow the bitter pill of tariff reform to avert a graver disaster. Now, for similar reasons, the mechanics of political manoeuvring were reversed and tariff reform dealt a severe body blow. There was some insight in Selborne's cynical conclusion that the policy had been both adopted and abandoned 'out of sheer opportunism'.[92] No doubt with a certain wry satisfaction, Robert Cecil reminded Austen Chamberlain that it was now his turn to compromise and recalled 'allocutions to us to yield to the majority and the requirement then ... that we should advocate that which we disapproved' in the broader interests of the party.[93]

The fact was that, except for a hard core of zealous tariff reformers, the majority of the party at Westminster cared infinitely more for saving the Union with Ireland than for establishing a system of preference. Those extreme tariff reformers who appeared willing to sacrifice the Union sooner than abandon their commitment to food taxes were likely only to damage their own cause.[94] Chaplin's scale of priorities which placed colonial preference before the Union with Ireland as 'the larger of the two Imperial issues now before us' was not widely shared.[95] Strachey spoke for the majority:

> My feeling throughout the crisis has been that it was the supreme duty of every Unionist to help put the party in the best possible position for saving the Union at the polls and turning out the present Government. To accomplish this I was for my part perfectly willing to accept even food taxes .... When, however, it turned out ... that the general feeling in the Party was that the way to save the Union was to give up food taxes at the next general election and not to insist upon them - then it was clearly the duty of the food taxers to make the sacrifice in regard to food taxes which I and other free traders would have been willing to make in other circumstances.[96]

Such considerations could not lessen the disappointment of that minority of Unionists for whom tariff reform had always been, as it was for Joseph Chamberlain himself, an issue which transcended the more mundane loyalties of party politics.[97] For such men Law's escutcheon had been permanently stained. The one-time ardent tariff reformer, unduly influenced now by Goulding and Aitken, had given way on that issue with which he had hitherto been primarily associated. 'The horse could not be got over the fence', commented Milner, 'and when the rider himself became nervous and irresolute the case was evidently hopeless.'[98] Austen Chamberlain, 'bitterly disappointed and very depressed', spoke as one whose dearest political hopes had received a cruel blow.[99] He was very unhappy about the party's prospects, fearing that the new position combined all the disadvantages and none of the comforts of either extreme.[100] Such feelings were in no sense lessened by Law's Edinburgh speech on 24 January which appeared, if anything, still further to dilute the party's commitment to tariff reform.[101] In theory the party was still ultimately pledged to the full policy, providing public approval was forthcoming, but in Chamberlain's view, if the Unionists did not face up to food taxes immediately on coming into office, they were scarcely likely to do so three or four years later.[102] In similar vein Leo Amery was 'utterly appalled' by what had happened and what it suggested about the party's future prospects. He regarded the practical result of the compromise as damping down the enthusiasm of the party's best working-class supporters, alienating the agricultural vote and making a nonsense of all that had been said about a national economic policy for the United Kingdom.[103]

Though the crisis had been surmounted with party unity essentially maintained and without an upheaval in the leadership, scars did remain. Law was for the moment extremely dispirited and hankering 'much after his bridge and golf'. Sandars heard that 'the glory of the position is much diminished for him by reason of the discordant cries of his followers and the difficulty of satisfying his adherents and maintaining his own self-respect'.[104] The damage to Law's position might have been permanent had the party as a whole not felt the overriding need to unite behind his leadership on the issue of Ireland. A party whip concluded that although the immediate trouble was over for the time being, the party was none the better for it. 'On the whole we are not in such a good position as in October.'[105] No obvious benefit to the party was visible in February when a by-election took place in Balcarres's old constituency of Chorley. The Unionist majority was cut and a high poll saw a swing to the Liberals of 2.8%.[106] Somewhat provocatively, the new Unionist candidate, Sir Henry Hibbert, was a full-blooded tariff reformer - a fact which convinced Bowles that the Party Chairman was running the party machine less with a view to carrying out the new policy than with the aim of swinging back to a full insistence on the most extreme demands of the tariff reformers.[107] Indeed the Tariff Reform League was active during the spring of 1913 in Lancashire, trying to reinstate food taxes as party policy. 'Now to my mind', commented Derby, 'that is absolutely breaking through the bargain and it must mean war.'[108]

The decision that had been reached in January was probably the only one that was practicable in the circumstances of the time. But the corresponding loss could not be discounted and affected the whole party. While the committed tariff reformers may have been pursuing an illusory goal, they were at least a dynamic element within a party which seemed as a whole to be seeking a viable identity. Bridgeman commented that the timid members of the party had for the time being damped down the ardour of its keener spirits.[109] By April Austen Chamberlain was wondering how long it would be possible for him to remain a party man. Exhausted by the battles that he had fought, he felt that he might be far happier if he were 'quit of a Party who seem to me determined to ruin their own fortunes and most of what I hold dear with them!'[110] As the Liberal government seemed in danger of falling over the

Marconi scandal, Chamberlain viewed the prospect of office without
enthusiasm:

> And here while they are cutting their own throats and
> destroying themselves, we have been fools enough to tie our
> hands with needless pledges and when they put themselves out
> and us in ... we have deprived ourselves in advance of freedom
> to act! Oh - !![111]

Both extremes on the tariff question continued to fire sporadic shots across
the bow of party unity, but as Unionism increasingly found a new purpose in
resistance to the government's proposed Home Rule legislation, most agreed
that it would be a mistake to run unnecessary risks by provoking either wing
of the tariff debate into further disruptive action.[112] Bonar Law had to this
extent succeeded in reordering the priorities of the party.[113] It was a sign of
the times that the party's campaign guide of 1914 relegated tariff reform to its
penultimate chapter, ahead only of 'miscellaneous questions'. Law, trying to
conciliate all factions, invited the free trader Robert Cecil to join the Unionist
front bench, but was adamant that there could be no further change in policy
on the issue of tariffs while he remained leader.[114] Not in preference but in
the troubled politics of Ireland and particularly of Ulster, which had broken
and were yet to break the careers of so many other statesmen, the Unionist
leader saw the opportunity to recover and enhance both his position and that
of his party.

## NOTES

1.	Law to Balcarres 30 Dec.1911, Law MSS 33/3/38. During the Bootle
	by-election of March 1911 the Liberal candidate, Max Muspratt,
	referred to Law as 'the archangel of Tariff Reform': P. J. Waller,
	*Democracy and Sectarianism: a Political and Social History of
	Liverpool 1868-1939* (Liverpool, 1981) p.250.
2.	Amery diary 25 Jan.1913.
3.	Hewins, *Apologia* i, 268-9.
4.	Derby to Law 13 Nov.1911, Law MSS 24/3/30.
5.	Ibid 16 Nov.1911, ibid 24/3/43.
6.	Law to Derby 14 Nov.1911, ibid 33/3/4.

7.     Chamberlain, *Politics from Inside* pp.377, 392.
8.     Chamberlain to Law 11 Nov.1911 and 17 Feb.1912, Law MSS 24/3/11 and 25/2/24.
9.     Chamberlain, *Politics from Inside* p.408.
10.    Ibid p.416; Lansdowne to Law 19 Feb.1912, Law MSS 25/2/34.
11.    Chamberlain, *Politics from Inside* p.433.
12.    Curzon and Salisbury, who were absent from the meeting, would also probably have dissented.
13.    Balfour to Finlay 8 Jan.1913, Balfour MSS Add. MS 49862; Balfour to Col. J. Denny 21 Nov.1912, ibid.
14.    Chamberlain, *Politics from Inside* p.433.
15.    Salvidge, *Salvidge* p.127.
16.    Balcarres to Law 5 Sept.1912, Law MSS 27/2/7.
17.    Derby to Law 14 March 1912, ibid 25/3/32.
18.    Report by Long on the state of the party in Manchester 29 Feb.1912, ibid 26/1/76.
19.    Ibid.
20.    Report on South Manchester by-election 8 March 1912, Law MSS 26/1/76.
21.    Cecil to Law 21 Feb.1912, ibid 25/2/41.
22.    Ibid 9 March 1912, ibid 25/3/19.
23.    Salisbury to Law 1 May 1912, ibid 26/3/2.
24.    Law to Salisbury 3 May 1912, ibid 33/4/34; Blake, *Unknown Prime Minister* pp.108-9.
25.    H. Cecil to Law 16 July 1912, Law MSS 26/5/29.
26.    Strachey to H. Cecil 7 Nov.1912, Strachey MSS S/4/3/21.
27.    Law to St. Aldwyn 3 Sept.1912, Beaverbrook MSS, House of Lords Record Office, BBK C/201. Law's hesitant phraseology perhaps indicated that his commitment to the cause of tariff reform had weakened since 1910. Austen Chamberlain later ruefully reflected that 'it had been my consolation when Long and I withdrew our names and proposed Bonar Law as leader that he had made his reputation by his Tariff Reform speeches and that the cause was safe in his hands': Chamberlain, *Politics from Inside* p.506.
28.    St. Aldwyn to Law 31 Aug.1912 and Law to St. Aldwyn 3 Sept.1912, Beaverbrook MSS BBK C/201; Sanders diary 8 Dec.1912; Law to Borden 26 Oct.1912, Law MSS 33/4/61: 'this decision might have

been different were it not for what you told me of the effect a change would have on your position in Canada.'

29.   Lansdowne to Law 10 Oct.1912, Law MSS 27/3/28.
30.   Younger to Law 6 Nov.1912, ibid 27/4/7.
31.   H. Cecil to Law 7 Nov.1912, ibid 27/4/10.
32.   Chamberlain, *Politics from Inside* p.495.
33.   Sanders diary 8 and 15 Dec.1912.
34.   Memorandum by Long 9 Dec.1912, Law MSS 28/1/11.
35.   G. Bowles to Law 27 Nov.1912, ibid 27/4/57.
36.   Salvidge, *Salvidge* p.125.
37.   Salvidge to Long 28 Nov.1912 and 6 Dec.1912, Long MSS 446/5.
38.   Vincent (ed.), *Crawford Papers* p.304.
39.   Law to Strachey 9 Dec.1912, Strachey MSS S/9/8/4. Bridgeman commented that the leadership 'took no steps to ascertain the opinion of Members of Parliament ... and seemed to entertain no doubt as to the assured success of their decision'. When Bridgeman himself sounded out opinion, he estimated that something like four to one 'would willingly have thrown over these taxes ... and that if you included people who reluctantly thought it was now the only hope of winning the next election, the majority would be quite 10 to 1': Bridgeman diary 30 Dec.1912. Sykes, *Tariff Reform* p.286. Bowles estimated the number of hardline tariff reform M.P.s at no more than a dozen: Bowles to Law 27 Nov.1912, Law MSS 28/1/26.
40.   Strachey to Lansdowne 5 Dec.1912, Strachey MSS S/9/7/10; Strachey to Law 12 Dec.1912, Law MSS 28/1/26.
41.   Petrie, *Chamberlain* i, 329.
42.   Salvidge, *Salvidge* p.124. *The Times* claimed on 18 December that the present divisions within the party reflected a continuing divide between the followers of Chamberlain and those of Long. The *Manchester Guardian* implied that the Albert Hall declaration resulted from an open threat from Chamberlain to which Law had succumbed. Long regretted that such publicity encouraged the view that 'our policy and tactics are dictated from Birmingham': Long to Gwynne 19 Dec.1912, Long MSS 446/28.
43.   *Liverpool Courier* 14 Dec.1912.
44.   Amery, *Life* i,414.
45.   Vincent (ed.), *Crawford Papers* p.292.

46.  Milner to Selborne 24 Dec.1912, Selborne MSS 12/236.
47.  Amery diary 17 Dec.1912.
48.  Amery to Chamberlain 27 Dec.1912, AC 10/3/1.
49.  Fitzroy, *Memoirs* i, 501.
50.  Steel-Maitland to Balfour 18 Dec.1912, Balfour MSS Add. MS 49862.
51.  Balfour to Derby 20 Dec.1912, ibid 49743.
52.  Cecil to Derby 18 Dec.1912, cited Churchill, *Derby* p.166.
53.  Lansdowne to Law 18 Dec.1912, Law MSS 28/1/54; Smith to Law 18 Dec.1912, ibid 28/1/53.
54.  Garvin to Selborne 19 Dec.1912, Selborne MSS 73/73.
55.  Derby to Gwynne 19 Dec.1912, Gwynne MSS, Bodleian Library, 22.
56.  Derby to Law 20 Dec.1912, Law MSS 28/1/65.
57.  Ibid 21 Dec.1912, ibid 28/1/72.
58.  Derby to Long 25 Dec.1912, Long MSS 446/23.
59.  Derby to Balfour 22 Dec.1912, Balfour MSS Add. MS 49743.
60.  Derby to Long 25 Dec.1912, Long MSS 446/23.
61.  Law to Balcarres 24 Dec.1912, Law MSS 33/4/81.
62.  Chaplin to Long 26 Dec.1912, Long MSS 446/34.
63.  Clarke, *Lancashire* p.307; Law to Balcarres 24 Dec.1912, Law MSS 33/4/81.
64.  Balcarres to Law 28 Dec.1912, ibid 28/1/98.
65.  Gwynne to Derby 29 Dec.1912, Gwynne MSS 22.
66.  Derby to H. Cecil 1 Jan.1913, cited Churchill, *Derby* p.179.
67.  Gwynne to Long 29 Dec.1912, Gwynne MSS 20. Gwynne commented: 'But the worst of it is that if he goes, there is no leader who can possibly take his place, for Lansdowne, Austen, Walter Long, Wyndham and Carson are all in the same boat and if they were to consent to accept the choice of leadership when their leader had resigned it on a question to which they gave their approval, I do not see how they can have any influence in the country or with their party. That is the chief reason why I am so upset and depressed for I think the party ... is heading straight not merely for disaster, but for a splitting up into little bits which will take at least a couple of generations to piece together again': Gwynne to Amery 7 Jan.1913, Amery MSS D45.
68.  Amery to Gwynne 3 Jan.1913, Gwynne MSS 14.
69.  Amery, *Chamberlain* p.980; A. Chamberlain to Law 24 Dec.1912,

Law MSS 28/1/86.
70. Chamberlain to Gwynne 21 Dec.1912, Gwynne MSS 17.
71. Gwynne to Law 29 Dec.1912, Law MSS 28/1/99.
72. Law to Selborne 20 Dec.1912, ibid 33/4/78; Law to Chaplin 31 Dec. 1912, ibid 33/4/86; Blake, *Unknown Prime Minister* p.114.
73. Lansdowne to Law 27 Dec.1912, Law MSS 28/1/94.
74. Derby to E. Hulton 1 Jan.1913, Derby MSS 4/39; Amery diary 7 Jan.1913.
75. Vincent (ed.), *Crawford Papers* p.298.
76. Sanders diary 5 Jan.1913; Amery diary 1 Jan.1913 : '[Rupert] Gwynne said frankly that if there was to be change and wobbling we might just as well have kept Balfour who could do that sort of thing better'.
77. Goulding to Law 30 Dec.1912, AC 10/3/33; Chamberlain to Law 24 Dec. 1912, AC 10/3/34.
78. Sanders diary 12 Jan.1913. Amery noted (diary 7 Jan.1913): 'I read the thing, a long winded screed treating preference as a very subordinate issue and directly suggesting its postponement. I urged that we could not possibly agree to such a thing.'
79. Chaplin to Law 1 Jan.1913, Law MSS 28/2/2.
80. Law to Chaplin 10 Jan.1913, ibid 33/5/8; Blake, *Unknown Prime Minister* p.116.
81. Long to Law 9 Jan.1913, Law MSS 28/2/40.
82. Law to Derby 24 Dec.1912, ibid 33/4/81.
83. Sanders diary 29 Dec.1912.
84. Lansdowne to Long 19 Dec.1912, Long MSS 446/36.
85. Long to Gwynne 19 Dec.1912, Gwynne MSS 20.
86. Comyn Platt to Long 20 June 1912, Law MSS 26/4/29.
87. Long to Law 24 Dec.1912, ibid 28/1/56.
88. Ibid.
89. Derby to Gwynne 31 Dec.1912, Gwynne MSS 22.
90. Long to Lansdowne 7 Jan.1913, Long MSS 446/36.
91. Fitzroy, *Memoirs* ii, 502.
92. Selborne to Amery 21 Jan.1913, Amery MSS D 45.
93. Cecil to Law 4 Jan.1913, Law MSS 28/2/19.
94. Salvidge to Long 23 Dec.1912, Long MSS 446/5.
95. Marchioness of Londonderry, *Henry Chaplin: a Memoir* (London, 1926) pp.182-3.

96.  Strachey to Lyttelton 20 Jan.1913, Strachey MSS S/9/17/2.
97.  R. Jebb to Chamberlain 4 Jan.1913, AC 9/5/42.
98.  Milner to Amery 28 Jan.1913, Amery MSS C 25.
99.  Chamberlain to Chaplin 15 Jan.1913, AC 9/5/9; Chamberlain to Law 8 Jan.1913, Law MSS 31/1/15.
100. Chamberlain to Lansdowne 16 Jan.1913, AC 9/5/54.
101. Amery diary 25 Jan.1913.
102. Bridgeman diary 9 Jan.1913. Interestingly, when Long drew up a memorandum on Unionist policy in June 1913, tariff reform no longer figured among his priorities: Memorandum by Long 27 June 1913, Law MSS 29/5/57.
103. Amery, *Political Life* i, 416.
104. Sandars to Balfour 23 March 1913, Balfour MSS Add. MS 49768.
105. Sanders diary 16 Feb.1913.
106. Clarke, *Lancashire* p.389.
107. Bowles to Law 17 Feb.1913, Law MSS 29/1/21. See the continuing correspondence between Bowles and Law on this subject, ibid 30/1/4, 33/5/50 and 30/4/33. Robert Cecil also believed that Steel-Maitland was stretching the Edinburgh compromise too far in a tariff reform direction: Cecil to Law 15 May 1913, Law MSS 29/4/9.
108. Derby to Woodhouse 6 May 1913, Derby MSS 2/15.
109. Williamson, *Modernisation* p.69.
110. Chamberlain, *Politics from Inside* p.553.
111. Ibid pp.564-5. Joseph Chamberlain found the Unionist attitude over the Marconi case 'too bloody polite': Amery diary 25 June 1913.
112. Steel-Maitland to Derby 10 Nov.1913, Derby MSS 4/40.
113. Coetzee, *Party or Country* p.152.
114. Law to R. Hunt 5 Jan.1914, Law MSS 34/1/4.

# 9

# POLICY: IRELAND
# 1906–1914

In a period of political opposition which saw Unionists fighting as bitterly amongst themselves as they did against the Liberal government, the issue of Ireland at least gave them the opportunity for united action. In their resistance to the policy of Home Rule, the Unionists came nearer than on any other issue to a straightforward exemplification of Tierney's dictum that it is the duty of the opposition to oppose. In one sense this could not be otherwise. Though it is usual nowadays to think of Ireland as an incubus in the context of British politics, this has not always been the case. The Unionist coalition owed its very existence to the split in the Liberal ranks brought about by the introduction of Gladstone's first Home Rule Bill in 1886. This had brought the Liberal Unionists headed by Joseph Chamberlain and Lord Hartington into eventual co-operation with the Conservatives - a fusion which could not conceal the fact that, over a range of issues other than Ireland, the two wings of the coalition remained, even in the early twentieth century, fundamentally divided. Thus, if Unionists as a body could not unite in defence of the existing constitutional structure of the United Kingdom, there was really nothing to keep the party intact. The Union was, said Walter Long, 'the greatest cause ever committed to the care of mortal man'.[1] Yet this was not simply a case of Unionists joining together in an exercise of conventional parliamentary opposition. In their determination to thwart the government's legislative proposals for Ireland, Unionists went far beyond the accepted norms of political behaviour and threatened to breach the fundamental conventions of the constitution.

At the outbreak of European war in 1914 Ireland was undoubtedly on the brink of civil conflict. 'The country is now confronted', asserted *The Times* on 27 July, 'with one of the great crises in the history of the British race.'[2] Two political aims in Ireland were sustained by private armies, one threatening to block the legislative enactments of the Westminster parliament. In Great Britain political opinion was violently divided, with some prominent politicians even talking of carrying an Irish civil war to the mainland. For the development of this state of affairs the Unionist party bore considerable responsibility. Much has been made of Bonar Law's famous speech at

Blenheim Palace on 29 July 1912, in which the Unionist leader declared that if the government went ahead with its proposed legislation he could 'imagine no length of resistance to which Ulster can go in which I should not be prepared to support them and in which, in my belief, they would not be supported by the overwhelming majority of the British people'. As Lord Blake has commented:

> Undoubtedly in making a declaration of this sort Bonar Law was going far to break the conventions upon which Parliamentary democracy is based. He was in effect saying that the passing of Home Rule into law by a parliamentary majority was not decisive, that the men of Ulster had a right to resist by force and that, if they did so,they would have the Unionist Party in England whole-heartedly behind them.[3]

The following year Law gave a clear indication that his party would positively encourage and recommend a refusal by the army to obey orders if this meant implementing Home Rule.[4] Nor was Law's attitude unrepresentative of that of his party as a whole. Lord Winterton's response to the situation was typical of many:

> I was among many young Conservative M.P.s who were ready to support Ulster in a physical sense and took effective means to that end ..... For instance, I formed what would now be described as a Commando which was ready to give physical assistance to Northern Ireland and the Ulster volunteers if the need arose.[5]

Similarly Willoughby de Broke, though hoping that the government would be forced into a general election, warned in July 1913 that 'if that means of settlement is denied to us, then we must fall back on the only other means at our disposal'.[6]

This was not a case of political metamorphosis, of democratic politicians transforming themselves into anarchists. What Unionists did and said in these years accurately reflected the intensity of feeling on the Unionist side against the plans of Asquith's government. In the British parliamentary system, based upon a confrontational and often ritualised debate between government and opposition, the sincerity of a politician's stance is sometimes open to question. But no element of feigned passion was involved in the struggle over Ireland. When in February 1914 Lord Stamfordham, on behalf of the King, suggested that the violence of Unionist speeches was rendering a peaceful settlement impossible, Law felt obliged to point out that

> we might be right or wrong but that S. should understand that
> these speeches were not made in thoughtlessness or passion ....
> We were convinced that ... [Asquith's] policy must result in
> civil war and the only way to stop it was to convince Asquith
> that we were serious and that we would go all lengths in
> support of the Ulstermen.[7]

From where, then, did this conviction and commitment derive? The challenge of the government's Irish policy struck out at the two ideals for which Unionists stood above all others - the sanctity of the constitution and the integrity of the imperial edifice. The first decade of the twentieth century was one in which the once impregnable British Empire seemed to be under challenge. Such fears may be traced in the writings of Kipling and the popular obsession with 'invasion literature'. Ireland was seen as an integral part of the United Kingdom. The subversive effects of Irish nationalism had implications for India as well as for Ireland. For the diehards in particular the prospect of an independent Ireland was a strategic nightmare in the event of a European war.[8] Concern that Britain was in danger of squandering her imperial inheritance had been at the heart of Chamberlain's campaign for tariff reform, just as it had been in his determination to subdue the Boers in southern Africa. In the disturbing vision of many imperialists the new century was likely to be dominated by super-states, power units which would create a new political game in which Britain would have few credentials to participate unless she was able to draw her Empire into a closer association with herself. Men such as Edward Carson and Henry Wilson firmly believed that if Britain lost control over Ireland this would represent the first, but certainly not the last, step in the break-up of the Empire. As Carson proclaimed:

> If you tell your Empire in India, in Egypt and all over the
> world that you have not got the men, the money, the pluck, the
> inclination and the backing to restore order in a country within
> twenty miles of your own shore, you may as well begin to
> abandon the attempt to make British rule prevail throughout the
> Empire at all.[9]

Many imperialists believed that the Empire derived its strength from the unity of Britain itself and Balfour for one would never admit 'that the Irishman is one race of inhabitants and England or Scotland or Wales is another race'.[10]

Similarly, Unionist concern for the preservation of the constitution was no hollow platitude. Unionists persuaded themselves that the government had no electoral mandate for Home Rule and that such a measure should therefore not be enacted until a general election had given the formal sanction of the British public. Though their own use, or perhaps abuse, of the constitution was open to criticism, and their contention that Home Rule lacked the sanction of the electorate was at least questionable, Unionists sincerely believed that the Liberal government's behaviour after 1909 was thoroughly reprehensible. To the modern observer such an attitude may smack of political double standards, but it needs to be seen in the context of the increasingly bitter atmosphere created by the apparent advance of left-wing politics and latterly the passing of the Parliament Act in 1911. Unionists held that the methods employed to put this legislation on to the statute book had strained the constitution to breaking point, thus justifying them in taking up postures and attitudes which might otherwise have been unacceptable. As Bridgeman wrote in 1912: 'Every standing order of the House is to be overridden - and I do not see what is to be left as a weapon against tyrannical Govt. except sheer force.'[11] Unless this fact is grasped, little sense can be made of statements like that of the generally moderate George Wyndham in the wake of the passing of the Parliament Act: 'When the King wants loyal men, he will find us ready to die for him. He may want us. For the House of Lords today - though they did not know it - voted for revolution.'[12]

The Liberal government, moreover, made no gesture towards redeeming the pledge contained in the preamble to the Parliament Act to carry out a reform of the upper chamber. Unionists therefore argued that, in this transitional phase before the reconstruction of the Lords took place, the government was not justified in introducing any further constitutional measures.[13] Exasperated by what many regarded as the pusillanimity of their own leaders over the preceding months - if not years - and frustrated by the loss of three successive general elections, Unionists, as defenders of the existing order, were resolved that they would give way no further. If a stand could not be made on the Union, what other issue would be left to justify their political existence? Many believed that Ireland might incidentally offer the party its best prospects of returning to power. Certainly for Law and others it offered welcome relief from the internecine strife which any consideration of tariff reform inevitably entailed. They could, moreover, justify their ultimate appeal to force on the grounds that the destruction of the House of Lords' veto had deprived the opposition of its constitutional means of compelling a general election. The attempt to put Home Rule on to the statute book could be portrayed as the worst example of 'single chamber tyranny'. Though at a distance of eighty years the Unionists' rationale may no longer impress or convince, it is not necessary to question the sincerity, at least by their own standards, of the stance which they took up.[14]

For some Unionists such gut reactions against Home Rule were underpinned by more hard-headed considerations. The importance of Irish Unionists, particularly Southern Unionists, acting as a pressure group within the British Unionist party should not be ignored. These were men who often had much to lose from the destruction of the British ascendancy within Ireland. Being well-placed among the policy-making section of the party, they worked through such leading figures as Long, Lansdowne and Carson to ensure the effective presentation of their case. They were also well represented and organised in both houses of parliament and acted with great persistence and methodical organisation within the constituencies of the mainland.[15] But this sort of influence was always of secondary importance. The passion and conviction with which Unionists defended their case do not smack of a policy shaped first and foremost by pressure groups and vested interests. This was a heart-felt response by a political grouping which owed its very existence to the Irish issue. Great Irish landowners such as Lansdowne may have had additional reasons for concern, but Unionists with no obvious Irish connection were ready to fight to the last with equal vehemence against Home Rule - and without the need for Irish Unionist propaganda to spur them on.

That the Irish issue should have come to dominate British politics after 1911 to the almost total exclusion of all other issues could not have been apparent when the Unionists first went into opposition in 1905. The story of the way in which members of the Liberal cabinet took little notice of the worsening international situation in July 1914 because of their total immersion in the problems of Fermanagh and Tyrone has been immortalised in the writings of Winston Churchill. After 1911 the Irish question tended to obscure all other issues and served to submerge the more progressive elements in both main parties.[16] In terms of national political development the trend of the previous decade went into reverse as the progressive move towards class-based politics and the on-going advance of collectivism slowed down and traditional nineteenth-century issues reasserted themselves. Defence of the Union and, to a lesser extent, the Established Church [17] largely replaced 'socialism' and tariff reform as the dividing lines of British politics. Yet in 1906, after less than a year out of government, Austen Chamberlain had commented that 'just now, for an Englishman at any rate, a speech on Home Rule is like flogging a dead horse', while Cawdor suspected, albeit wrongly, that Joseph Chamberlain considered the Irish issue as 'dust in the balance'.[18] Though in earlier decades the programme of Gladstonian legislation had ensured that the maintenance of the Union had been a central issue of the Unionists' last two periods in opposition, and while the party had again placed Ireland in the forefront of its campaign in 1906, the reality of electoral politics served to render the issue largely irrelevant once the election was over. Though there undoubtedly remained Liberals for whom Home Rule was a vision and a crusade, a matter of conviction and principle, by the beginning of the twentieth century most had come to recognise that the issue had become, as Joseph Chamberlain had long before predicted, 'death and damnation' for the party as a whole. Such a question would be reluctantly resuscitated only under the dictation of parliamentary arithmetic.[19]

In November 1905 Campbell-Bannerman revealed his cautious step-by-step approach when informing Redmond and O'Connor, the Irish Nationalist leaders, that, while he would not pledge his party to full Home Rule in the new parliament, he did intend to enact 'some serious measure which would be consistent with and lead up to the other'.[20] Similarly Bryce wrote that

> no one thinks it possible to bring into the next Parliament a bill
> like that of 1893. But probably there may be further steps
> towards granting local powers and removing topics from the
> British Parliament while retaining ultimate control.[21]

The idea was to try to satisfy the Irish with minor reforms while preparing the electorate for the possibility of Home Rule some time in the future. When, however, the Liberals grasped the immensity of their electoral victory of 1906 it was apparent that the numerical factor which had complicated Gladstone's parliamentary horizon in 1886 and 1892 was no longer in play.[22] As a result, only once before 1910 did the Irish question re-surface into prominence with the Irish Councils Bill of 1907, designed to provide more local participation in and a measure of local responsibility for some parochial administrative affairs. That the government soon dropped the bill was perhaps less surprising than that they had bothered to introduce it in the first place.[23] There remained nonetheless abundant evidence that for many Unionists there lay just beneath the surface a volcano of intense feeling on the Irish question which would erupt if ever circumstances beyond their control once again made Home Rule an issue of practical politics. The strange case of the Wyndham-MacDonnell affair, fostering the belief that some Unionists might themselves be toying with the idea of a limited measure of Irish devolution, bore witness to the passions which could be effortlessly aroused even when there was no evidence that the matter was one of inter-party dispute.[24] The shadow cabinet, moreover, contained men such as Long and Londonderry who, because of their strong Irish connections, could always be relied upon to remind their colleagues of the potential priority in the party's affairs of opposing Home Rule. Such elements ensured that there was a dispute within the shadow cabinet in February 1909 over the formulation of the opposition's amendment to the King's Speech between those who wished to give priority to the fiscal issue and those who preferred to deplore the government's administration in Ireland.[25]

That Ireland re-emerged as a live issue in British politics was the direct result of two factors. The first was the outcome of the two general elections of 1910, which recreated the parliamentary position of 1886 and 1892 by leaving the Liberal administration dependent upon the Irish members at Westminster for its continued survival. Such electoral statistics were, wrote George Dangerfield, 'like historical graffiti, the naughty calligraphy of Fate itself'.[26] The result of 1906 was now revealed to be an aberration, as party politics resumed their more typical format of the late nineteenth century. Liberals needed the support of Irish Nationalist M.P.s in the lobbies of the House of Commons if Lloyd George's ill-fated budget of 1909 was going belatedly to make its way on to the statute book. But the price of such succour would be a renewed commitment by the government to yet another Home Rule Bill. Though Liberal ministers had not made much of Home Rule during the campaign of January 1910, they were now obliged to restore this issue to the forefront of their legislative programme in order to get the remainder of that programme enacted. Ironically, the relative success of the Unionists in 1910 had only succeeded in bringing back to the immediate political agenda that issue which they were most concerned to avoid.[27]

The second factor was the passing of the Parliament Act in August 1911. This ensured that the third Home Rule Bill would not in the long term fall victim, as had its Gladstonian predecessor of 1893, to the immovable Unionist majority in the upper house. Indeed the destruction of the Lords' veto added an element of almost eerie certitude to the parliamentary progress of the bill, since contemporaries could now work out with accuracy and precision the cumbersome yet inevitable timetable by which Home Rule would find its way into law. It could indeed be argued that the Liberals had bungled their showdown with the upper chamber and the ensuing constitutional legislation to the extent that the government's programme was to be encumbered for almost an entire parliament by the treadmill of Irish Home Rule.[28] Under the limited prerogatives now remaining to the House of Lords, Ireland would become self-governing by the summer of 1914 even if their lordships exercised their powers of delay in 1912 and 1913. The law of the land now dictated that a bill would become an act, despite being rejected by the Lords, provided it was passed in the Commons in three successive sessions and provided not less than two years elapsed between the bill's second reading in the first session and its third reading in the third session. With the Parliament Act on the statute book, Unionists saw their only option being to obstruct its operation by forcing a general election before either Home Rule or any other contentious issue could be passed three times through the House of Commons.

When, in the summer of 1910, the leaderships of the two main parties came together in an attempt to resolve the constitutional deadlock by negotiation, it was the issue of Ireland which played a leading role in preventing an agreed solution emerging from the conference. The movement advocating a federal resolution of the Irish impasse - 'home rule all round' as it was sometimes called - had won many converts within the Unionist ranks including the influential Austen Chamberlain and many of the party's leading publicists, prompting even Jack Sandars to question whether 'home rule - Parnellite home rule - [was still] the issue and nothing else', or whether it was not possible to move the debate 'on to this new ground'. But Balfour was not prepared to contemplate such heresy. Like many traditional Unionists Balfour refused to believe that there was any real half-way house between the Union and a complete separation in Anglo-Irish relations, while his overriding concern remained, as it always had been, to preserve the unity of his party. In this respect nothing had happened to convince him that a new stance on the Irish question could carry with it a united party.[29] Balfour's misgivings were almost certainly well-founded. One group of Unionist M.P.s had got together to issue a manifesto condemning federalism, while at the annual conference of the National Union on 17 November a resolution was passed entreating 'all Unionists throughout the United Kingdom to maintain unimpaired their unalterable opposition to the policy of Home Rule'.[30]

As Unionists juggled with their own proposals for reforming the upper chamber, their dominating thought was that any reshaped house should still be capable of resisting Home Rule.[31] Similarly, by the time in 1911 that control of the constitutional issue had moved irretrievably out of the hands of the opposition, there were those like Walter Long who wished to see the government's Parliament Bill safely enacted because its terms would at least prevent the *immediate* passing of Home Rule legislation and thereby allow Unionists the time to rally their forces.[32] Though the country as a whole may have been 'amazingly apathetic about this parliament bill either way',[33] the prescient within the Unionist ranks were only too aware that, in determining the party's best tactical approach to this piece of constitutional legislation, they were playing with the fate not only of the House of Lords but also of the Irish Union. To the delight of many of his colleagues Bonar Law dubbed the Parliament Bill the 'Home Rule in Disguise Bill'.[34]

Once the Parliament Act was safely on the statute book it was clear to everyone that Ireland would be the next great issue of British politics. For the remainder of 1911 the Unionist leadership actively prepared its anti-Home Rule campaign, while Ireland figured prominently in the thoughts of the Halsbury group throughout the autumn and winter. In his letter to Lord Curzon of 21 August which merits extensive quotation because of the prominence he was soon to assume in Unionist politics, Sir Edward Carson[35] gave a remarkably frank expression of his thoughts on the Irish question in the wake of the passing of the Parliament Act:

> The Home Rule fight will be a very difficult one for many reasons and everything will in my opinion depend on how far we appear to the country to be in earnest and prepared to fight it. I have to make up my mind as regards the North of Ireland to what extent I am prepared to go and to encourage them in actual resistance. I believe that a vast number of the working classes there are prepared to resort to force and violence in opposing Home Rule, but if we are to have on this side a 'moderate party' who will criticise our action and disavow us the position will become one not only of difficulty but probably of rupture. I do not want to enter into a game of bluff and become ridiculous which I think leads the most stalwart supporters into a false position. I am really sick of trying to fight great questions as if they were Parish Council Bills and I believe there is a very large following in the country which

> fails to understand why we do not show more resentment over
> the way we are kicked and knocked about in the House of
> Commons ... in my opinion, unless dramatic action is taken
> even to the extent of damaging the parliamentary machine, we
> cannot under existing circumstances get any fair play .... I do
> think the time has come of making it clear in our statements
> that we are entering upon a straight fight to the finish.[36]

The fact that Carson was prepared to confide in Curzon in this way, when
the latter was so reviled in other quarters for the part he had played in
securing the passage of the Parliament Bill, cannot pass without notice. It
perhaps reflects Carson's realisation that Curzon's attitude to the Parliament
Bill had been based on shrewd calculation rather than abject cowardice. An
upper chamber, deprived of its power of veto but retaining its Unionist
majority, would still be better placed than one swamped by newly created
Liberal peers to resist the inevitable Home Rule Bill whenever it should be
introduced.[37] At all events Carson's letter accurately encapsulates the
motivating forces in Unionist policy at this time.

Of the Unionist hierarchy only Lansdowne seems to have had serious
doubts about the wisdom of the anti-Home Rule cry, fearing that it would not
secure the popular support that it had enjoyed in 1886 and 1893: 'People have
got much more used to the idea than they were', he argued, 'and there is an
intense desire to relieve the Westminster Parliament of some of the work
which it now does so badly.' Lansdowne believed that the Unionists' best
tactics would be to propose completing the Land Purchase policy begun when
George Wyndham had been Irish Secretary. Showing that he was fully alive
to the constitutional difficulties into which the party might run, the leader of
the Unionist peers argued that if the Home Rule Bill were to survive a two or
three year struggle in both Houses of Parliament and 'if the majority of the
electors declared themselves in favour of it, I do not see how we could resist
further or encourage Ulster to do so'.[38] Despite his misgivings Lansdowne
had thus singled out what was to become the centrepiece of Unionist strategy -
to secure the verdict of the British electorate in a general election held
specifically on the Home Rule issue.

Before resorting to more drastic measures, Unionists were anxious to
exhaust all possibilities allowed them under the constitution. By the beginning
of 1912 the new Unionist leader, Andrew Bonar Law, was toying with a
novel, if spurious, piece of constitutional doctrine. Much to the alarm of the

King, Law argued that because the Parliament Act had removed the veto powers of the upper house, the royal assent to government legislation could no longer be regarded as a formality. It was now the only check on the otherwise unfettered power of the House of Commons. The King would therefore have to decide on his own initiative whether the Home Rule Bill should become law.[39] At this early date many Unionists had also clearly perceived that the most effective opposition to Home Rule would come from the province of Ulster, since only there were Unionists in sufficient numbers to make Home Rule unworkable. But at this stage Ulster was seen primarily as a means of thwarting the government's legislation rather than as the basis for a possible compromise. Unionist leaders were as concerned about the Southern Unionists as they were about Ulster. Leo Amery assured Law that the Ulstermen were absolutely reliable,

> quietly working out all their plans for keeping order and carrying on the local administration within their own area - not encroaching upon the sphere of the Imperial authorities, but simply exercising whatever powers the Home Rule Bill will confer on the Irish Executive.

He also hoped that Law would be able to reframe the party's tariff reform policy in such a way as to favour the needs of Ireland.[40] Similarly Carson had already tried to persuade the less numerous but very influential Southern Unionists that their best hope lay in the resistance of the North since, apart from the effect which partition would have on the nationalist concept of 'Ireland', he believed that it would be impossible to finance Home Rule without the taxable resources of Belfast. 'To stop Home Rule in Ulster therefore would prevent it for all Ireland.'[41] By March Carson had in his own mind resolved the doubts he had felt the previous summer. He had now decided to recommend 'very drastic action in Ulster during this year and also in the House when the H.R.Bill is on .... I certainly think this is the critical year and am prepared for any risks.'[42]

By the spring of 1912 the government's bill, announced in the King's Speech in February, was ready and on 11 April Asquith introduced it in the House of Commons. The Unionists had had plenty of time to work out their response and Law, already emphasising that Ulster was the rock upon which the proposed legislation would come to grief, replied in terms which foreshadowed his later Blenheim speech:

> We can imagine nothing which the Unionists in Ireland can do

which will not be justified against a trick of this kind .... I say
to the Government ... you will not carry this Bill without
submitting it to the people of this country and if you make an
attempt you will succeed only in breaking our parliamentary
machine. [43]

Party tempers ran high as a member of the Carlton Club proposed that the
Union Jack should remain flying on the roof of the club's premises until the
Home Rule Bill was defeated or withdrawn. In an atmosphere of frenzied
vilification civilised communication across party lines became a hazardous
occupation.[44] The King expressed the hope that the parliamentary session
would witness no scenes of violence, but Law countered by reiterating his
point that because of the government's actions the King was now inextricably
caught up in the political debate. The monarch's options would be either to
accept the bill or to dismiss his ministers and choose others who would support
him in vetoing it. In either case, argued Law, half the King's subjects would
feel that he had acted against them.[45] Law's intention was less to involve the
King in politics than to use the monarch's dilemma as a moral lever to induce
Asquith to rescue him from his predicament by either withdrawing the bill or
submitting it to the verdict of the electorate.[46]

   Though the bill inevitably passed its first reading with a comfortable
majority, the Unionist opposition fought valiantly throughout 1912 to thwart
its progress, particularly during the committee stage, and it was not until 16
January 1913 that the House of Commons gave it its third reading by a
majority of 110. As the debate proceeded Unionist rhetoric became
increasingly violent and unashamedly negative. Lansdowne's proposed
alternative policy was now lost from sight. The Unionist peer, though feeling
qualms about the virulence of some of Law's language, was nonetheless fully
behind his uncompromising opposition to Home Rule. 'Although I do not
mean to shoulder a musket, I certainly should not think of snubbing the
Ulstermen or of dissociating myself from Bonar Law.'[47]

   To begin with, the main thrust of the Unionist campaign was conducted
within the parliamentary forum. Unionist lawyers searched for flaws in the
Parliament Act, with Selborne even coming up with the ingenious notion that
the Lords could force a dissolution by adjourning themselves indefinitely, thus
preventing the King from giving his assent to the bill since constitutional
practice demanded that the royal assent be given in the upper house in the
presence of the Lords Spiritual and Temporal.[48] Law toyed with the idea that

it might be possible to force an election if, at a given time, the House of Lords simply declared that it did not regard the cabinet as the legitimate government and would refuse to pass any further legislation.[49] As the year progressed, however, it became increasingly clear that, whatever parliamentary devices the Unionists employed, the government's majority in the Commons would in the last instance prevail.

Especially when the government began to make use of the guillotine to curtail parliamentary debate, Unionist leaders realised that the customary means of constitutional opposition could not in the long term help their cause. By the late summer of 1912 Unionist speakers had taken their case to the country and were campaigning against Home Rule throughout the land, culminating in Law's great gathering at Blenheim. The 'grammar of anarchy' soon spread to the parliamentary forum.[50] In the autumn rowdy scenes in the Commons cost the Unionists the support of some staunch constitutionalists.[51] Meeting on 12 November, Unionist leaders decided that, unless the government gave a pledge to submit the Irish question to the electorate before the legislation became law under the terms of the Parliament Act, they would seek to wreck the whole process of parliamentary government. All speakers on both sides of the House, with the sole exceptions of Asquith, Law and Austen Chamberlain, would be shouted down. 'This is a drastic policy', commented Alfred Lyttelton, 'but I think it stands on solid reasons.'[52] In such a situation Unionist eyes became more and more fixed upon the province of Ulster as the hope of their salvation. This was partly explicable in terms of the assumed ability of Ulster to thwart the Home Rule policy altogether and partly in that the Unionist party's stance over Ulster looked far more reasonable than when related to Ireland as a whole, where there existed a large nationalist majority. Such considerations would be important if the Unionist party was ever successful in forcing the government into a dissolution. If the nationalist aspirations of Irish Catholics merited sympathy, so too did those of Ulster Protestants. Yet for Unionists of the South and West of Ireland this growing concentration on Ulster was potentially dangerous, for Ulster's case effectively conceded that of Irish nationalism. While the province itself continued to drill and to arm, Law reminded the government benches that 'they know that if Ulster is in earnest, that if Ulster does resist by force, there are stronger influences than Parliamentary majorities'.[53] Austen Chamberlain was also confident that resistance would be successful if Ulstermen

will keep cool, resolute and, as far as may be, silent as to their

exact intentions .... The cooler, nay the colder, the resolution
of Ulster is, the more impressive it will be and the more
terrifying to the Government. [54]

Ulster thus came to occupy a twofold position in Unionist calculations. In
the first instance it remained the obstacle which might make the whole scheme
of Home Rule unworkable. Such thoughts were clearly to the forefront of
Unionist minds when in June 1912 the party supported the Agar-Robartes
amendment to exclude certain counties from the operation of the bill and again
the following January when Carson himself proposed an amendment to remove
the whole of the province from the bill's remit.[55] But the Agar-Robartes
amendment created an acute dilemma for the party. To support it invited the
charge of deserting loyalists in the rest of Ireland, while to oppose it might
later lay Unionists open to the charge of rejecting the only viable compromise
likely to emerge. The Union and nothing but the Union was undoubtedly the
preferred ground, since the opposition of Unionists to Home Rule was not
based simply upon calculations of the unacceptability of the policy to those
sections of the Irish population where Protestants were in a majority.
Moreover, the influence of the Unionists of the three southern provinces was
out of all proportion to their numerical strength, and they never tired of
impressing their case upon the party in England. As one Southern Unionist
told Walter Long:

To us Southern Unionists the idea of Exclusion - partial or
complete, of Ulster - is an abomination. We believe the
principle of the Union is the real thing not only for Ireland but
for Great Britain and that if the Unionist Party gives up the
principle the Unionist Party will be smashed for ever.[56]

But the Ulster fixation was not a purely tactical or cynical posture on the
part of the Unionist party.[57] In reality the possibility of compromise had
entered the party's agenda if not its vocabulary. If the Union could not be
preserved intact, there existed a genuine fall-back position, since the rights of
Ulstermen to determine the government under which they lived appeared to
most thinking politicians a more easily justifiable and more readily attainable
goal than the preservation of the Union pure and simple. As Law recognised,
if the matter were ever placed before the British electorate, 'they are so sick
of the whole Irish question that they would vote in favour of trying an
experiment so long as the Ulster difficulty was solved'.[58] Even Carson, who
originally envisaged the Ulster card solely in terms of thwarting the

government in its wider designs, came to champion the province more and more in its own right.[59]

For some Unionists, however, the possibility of a compromise based on the exclusion of Ulster from the operation of a scheme of Home Rule was always an unacceptable option. To Leo Amery, for example, it meant endangering the more important issue of the Union by implying that a concession over Ulster would be an acceptable solution. As he warned Bonar Law, the danger existed that by steadily focusing public attention on Ulster the party might lead the electorate to forget that 'the only thing for which we can really be asked to face civil war - is not Ulster but the Union'.[60]

When the Home Rule Bill embarked upon its second parliamentary excursion there was inevitably an element of *déjà vu* about the whole proceedings. The government's unassailable majority ensured the completion of its progress through the Commons by July 1913, but once again the House of Lords summarily threw the measure out by 302 votes to 64. Parliament was prorogued on 15 August and remained in recess for the rest of the year. Behind the facade of formal parliamentary business, however, Unionist preparations went on apace. In Ulster the machinery of a provisional government steadily took shape, ready to assume control of the affairs of the province should the need arise.[61] In mainland constituencies the campaign of the Union Defence League and the Unionist Association of Ireland continued, educating the country so that, in the event of a general election or of the bill coming into operation without being submitted to the opinion of the people, 'the country will thoroughly understand the evils of the Home Rule Bill and in the latter case appreciate the unconstitutional procedure that has been adopted'.[62] In March 1912 Willoughby de Broke had founded and become chairman of the British League for the Support of Ulster and the Union, which gained the immediate adherence of 120 M.P.s and a hundred peers. The League had close links with the Ulster Volunteer Force which recruited half-pay and reserve officers and got involved in clandestine gunrunning operations.[63] Curzon was also among those ready to see the issue being 'allowed to solve itself in battle on the soil of Ireland'.[64] There was, of course, something profoundly ironic about members of the Unionist party, the great exemplar of constitutional propriety, adopting such a position. Selborne accurately captured their dilemma:

> I will never say that it is always wrong to take up arms. I
> should myself take up arms without any hesitation for the

Monarchy against a republic, and I have already said that I think Ulster is wholly justified in her present attitude. But civil war is the ultima ratio and the last party in the world that ought to turn to arms if it can possibly avoid it or go outside legal and constitutional forms is the Conservative and Unionist Party.[65]

Yet despite the apparently inevitable drift towards violence, by the time that the Home Rule Bill had completed its second parliamentary circuit many people on both sides of the debate were prepared to argue for compromise. The alternative - the inexorable working of the Parliament Act coming up against the steely determination of the Ulster Protestants to fight rather than submit - seemed altogether too dreadful to contemplate. The prospect of civil war breaking out by the summer of 1914 obliged the party leaders to reconsider their entrenched positions. Most importantly, the King had come to see it as his duty to bring the apparently irreconcilable factions together.

Each side was ready to accuse the other of using the King for its own purposes and, as Esher appreciated, 'if the situation remains unchanged and the controversy in the newspapers upon the use of the King's prerogative continues, the King's personal position will become intolerable and the Monarchy itself endangered'. There was a growing feeling that Unionists 'should not sulk behind the Throne'.[66] Lansdowne was anxious to assure the King that Unionists were not going to ask him to revive the royal veto last used by Queen Anne, but he and Law had submitted a memorandum to the monarch which, in addition to urging him to request Asquith to call an election, also insisted upon the now questionable royal prerogative of dismissing his existing ministers.[67] The King's position was, of course, a delicate one and his burden was not lightened by the barrage of advice to which he was subjected by leading Unionists during his summer stay at Balmoral. As Balfour - whose status as an elder statesman gave him an influence with the monarch which other Unionists lacked - pointed out, the King could not avoid responsibility. Whatever he did, half his subjects would condemn it. But Balfour clearly led the King to believe that he was not bound to accept the advice of his existing ministers, but could summon others who would 'accept the responsibility of advising him differently'.[68] The government, on the other hand, understandably insisted that the monarch had no power to dismiss his ministers before the reopening of parliament or to insist upon a dissolution, nor could he withhold his signature from the bill should it be presented to him the following summer.[69]

In conversations with Churchill at Balmoral in September, Law indicated a new willingness at least to consider a compromise since 'the position for both parties was becoming impossible'. The cabinet's legislative programme would lead to civil war, while Unionist resistance would probably include making government at Westminster unworkable and encouraging the army to disobey orders. It was not an attractive prospect. But, Law argued, the only grounds for any discussions between the parties would be either a general scheme of devolution or the exclusion of Ulster from Irish Home Rule. Of the two Law clearly believed that exclusion offered the greater prospect of success since an examination of the larger question of general devolution would involve a discussion, 'for instance, of the House of Lords and probably other questions and would really be impossible, I think, unless there were something in the nature of a coalition'.[70] In the event of an exclusion-based settlement, however, Law insisted that a large measure of consent among the loyalists of the South and West of Ireland would be imperative. By now this rider reflected less a hope on Law's part that such a qualification would render exclusion unworkable than his genuine fear that he would not be able to sell such a scheme to the Southern Unionists. Would they or would they not regard it as a betrayal? Carson, who had ruled out the possibility of compromise the previous May, was now prepared to agree with Law that exclusion might just provide the basis for a settlement, though he personally preferred the idea of a general scheme of devolution for the whole of the United Kingdom.[71] Significantly, Carson already recognised that the case for excluding the six plantation counties might be more compelling than that of excluding the whole province of Ulster.[72]

From their conversations at Balmoral both Balfour and Curzon gained the impression that nothing that could be done, or was likely to be done, would prevent the bill becoming law. Accordingly, Balfour seems to have encouraged the King to think that a restricted conference was now the only door left open to avoid bloodshed in Ulster and serious trouble in the army.[73] With commendable clarity Balfour set out, for Law's benefit, the possible courses of action in descending order of desirability from the Unionist point of view. A dissolution advised by the government was the only thoroughly satisfactory course. A dissolution forced on the government was the next best alternative. If both of these were rejected there was no other plan which was not surrounded by the gravest difficulties and dangers, though the separation of

Ulster from the rest of Ireland might be the least calamitous of all the calamitous options which still remained open.[74] But when the King's secretary suggested that the Unionists themselves should propose a conference based on acceptance of the general principle of the present bill but with Ulster excluded from its operation, Law dug in his heels. Fearful of a 'wild outburst' of resentment in the South of Ireland which would be reflected with almost equal violence in England, Law insisted that no conditional promise of support for the Home Rule Bill could be given.[75] His position, in fact, was becoming increasingly difficult. Though his trusted confidant, Max Aitken, assured him that almost all his parliamentary supporters favoured a conference on the Irish question,[76] elements on the right of the party were beginning to voice their concern. Willoughby de Broke, feeling he could not trust a leadership which had already 'given away the Constitution and countenanced the Parliament Act', spoke for those who would 'not let them out of our sight if we can help it'.[77] Many Unionists also recalled the unpromising precedent of inter-party discussions in 1910 and Maxse was preparing to use the *National Review* to argue against the whole idea of 'another Conference trap'.[78]

Of more significance than the attitude of the diehard right was the view of Lord Lansdowne, Unionist leader in the upper chamber. He was 'inclined to think' that the practical difficulties of an arrangement under which 'a sort of Home Rule' would be given to Ireland, while Ulster would remain an integral part of the United Kingdom, would be even greater than Law supposed. Unionists, after all, 'want[ed] something quite different and must strive to get it'. Lansdowne, himself a great landowner in Southern Ireland, doubted whether such a scheme could ever secure the requisite approval of Unionists in the South and West, and argued that the form of local government which would be given to the rest of Ireland under such a plan would fall far short of Nationalist ideals.[79] Apart from the personal commitment which his Irish estates gave him, Lansdowne shared the conviction of many Unionists with no comparable involvement in the land of Ireland, that a compromise based upon exclusion would betray the broader historical interests for which Unionism had always stood.[80] Not surprisingly, therefore, the idea of a conference based on the assumption that the only matter open for discussion was the exclusion of Ulster filled him with alarm. He was careful to remind Law of his commitment that such a project could not be entertained unless it were consented to by the loyalists of the South and West and added that 'some kind of authorisation' from mainland Unionists, 'many of whom would ...

regard us as guilty of a betrayal' would also be necessary.[81] While the apparent conversion of Carson to the principle of exclusion had perhaps convinced the King that a solution had been found, Lansdowne argued that 'the path is ... a very dangerous one and I hope we shall be extremely careful how we allow ourselves to be inveigled into it'.[82] He did not yet believe that a settlement based upon exclusion was inevitable.[83] 'We may', Lansdowne conceded, 'have to fall back upon it, but only when we are in our last ditch and we are not there yet.'[84] At all events it was not, he felt, the Unionists' business to make offers or suggestions.[85] He doubted whether the King and his Secretary really grasped the difference between what they called 'leaving out Ulster' and the kind of settlement which Carson could afford to consider or the leadership to discuss.[86] The distinction, it must be admitted, had apparently also escaped Bonar Law. Nonetheless, Lansdowne's attitude seems to have been the crucial factor in determining Law's cool response to Stamfordham on 4 October.[87]

But Law's conscience was clearly troubled. The royal intervention had brought home to him the dangers of the course upon which his party was set. If the action of the government was so monstrous that Unionists were prepared to countenance civil war to resist it, the party was honour bound to take every means in its power to force an election to prevent such strife. This might involve making the conduct of business in the House of Commons impossible and utilising to the full the residual powers of the House of Lords. But the consequences of using such means were 'appalling' and, even if successful, would 'destroy perhaps for a generation our whole Parliamentary Institutions'. The conclusion which Law therefore drew was that if it were possible to secure a settlement by consent he ought to pursue it, even if it were a settlement which he basically disliked - especially as Carson now seemed to believe that such a settlement, based on exclusion, could be carried without any serious attack from the Unionists in the South and West.[88] From an electoral point of view, moreover, nothing could be worse for the party than being put in the position of refusing an offer which the electorate would regard as fair and reasonable.[89]

Though a formal conference seemed out of the question for the time being, Law and Asquith did agree to open informal conversations between themselves. If these proved fruitful a conference could then be called. At a first meeting between the two party leaders on 14 October Law seems to have pledged his party to accept the implementation of Home Rule, providing that

Ulster - as yet undefined - was excluded and so long as this provoked no general outcry in the South and West of Ireland and met with the general agreement of Law's colleagues. Each of these qualifications was important. No one could be sure of the reaction of the Southern Unionists, while several senior party figures including Salisbury were 'getting a little restless'.[90] As regards the exclusion of Ulster, Carson had now made it clear that he could not assent to any proposition other than the exclusion of the whole of the ancient province of nine counties.[91] The danger from the Unionist point of view, as Law was quick to appreciate, was that Asquith might offer to exclude the four overwhelmingly Protestant counties and allow plebiscites to be held in two others. Though such a compromise might be totally unacceptable to Carson, it would appear so reasonable to the average voter that the Unionists would be left in a hopelessly exposed position if they had to refuse it. Conscious of this difficulty both Law and Lansdowne counted on the outright opposition of Irish Nationalists to what would be a dilution of their aspirations to take away from Unionists the onus of rejecting any such proposals.[92] Lansdowne, who throughout this episode remained somewhat warier than Law of the government's real intentions and who had hoped to obtain a clear written statement of any terms Asquith might offer, suspected that the Prime Minister's overriding aim was to put the Unionist party 'in the wrong by offering us terms which will seem reasonable to the ill-informed public, but which we should find it impossible to accept'.[93] Law was therefore reluctant to press Asquith to define the area to be excluded and the conversations drifted inconclusively.

Lansdowne was evidently not entirely happy at the way in which Asquith seemed to be winning a tactical battle with Bonar Law. The central problem, he believed, was the 'Ulster red herring ... being trailed backwards and forwards across the track'. So long as Unionists had been fighting for a general election they were on solid ground, but from the moment that the focus was changed and they began to talk about the exclusion of Ulster, 'we found ourselves in a quagmire'. To Austen Chamberlain Lansdowne confided that he would prefer to contemplate a general scheme of devolution for Ireland, Wales and Scotland, which would make no separate provision for Ulster, than an exclusion-based compromise on the Irish question.[94] Feeling among the party leadership as a whole, on the other hand, remained firmly opposed to a federal solution and Chamberlain's hope that the devolution option could be taken up to thwart Asquith came to nothing.[95]

When Law and Asquith came together for a second meeting on 6 November, the Unionist leader took a somewhat firmer line. He reminded the Prime Minister that the Unionist party contained all the elements for a diehard revolt should any compromise be attempted. Asquith agreed to put the question of the exclusion of a 'part' of Ulster to his cabinet colleagues, though Law now clearly hoped that this would be rejected by the Irish Nationalists, for otherwise Unionists would lose their best electoral card.[96] From Walter Long came an unequivocal warning that the unanimous opinion of a 'great many of our most reliable men' was that the acceptance of any compromise would be 'absolutely <u>fatal</u>' to the party.[97] He was afraid that

> events have marched too quickly for us and that the time has gone by now for any arrangement .... The result of this has been to force our Party throughout the United Kingdom to face the Civil War prospect and prepare for it and consequently public opinion amongst our supporters now runs very high indeed.[98]

Though Long's opinion could not be ignored, neither could Law disregard evidence of the cabinet's plans. From Churchill he learnt that the government was prepared to envisage some compromise based on the exclusion of Ulster.[99] But if Law's position was difficult, so too was the Prime Minister's. It was impossible for Asquith to dismiss the resistance of Ulster as mere bluff when the massed Ulster Volunteer Force was plain for all to see and when it was known that 5,000 rifles and 95,000 rounds of ammunition had been smuggled into Ulster. The War Office, moreover, believed that up to a third of all army officers would resign their commissions rather than take military action against Ulster loyalists.[100]

Austen Chamberlain later criticised Law for failing to hold Asquith to the commitment, which the Prime Minister gave at their second meeting, to lay a proposal for exclusion before the cabinet and let Law know the result in a matter of days.[101] Such strictures take no account of the delicate position Law would have faced had the government offered a compromise which, though on the surface eminently reasonable, did not go far enough to satisfy Carson. In fact five weeks elapsed before the two leaders met again. By the time that Law and Asquith held their third discussion on 9 December it was clear that the gap between the two sides was widening and that the fragile basis for a possible compromise was crumbling away. It was now evident that the cabinet would only contemplate exclusion for a fixed term of years - a proposition which held no attraction for Law.[102] The only alternative which Asquith was able to offer was a form of Home Rule for Ulster within Home Rule, but this was equally unacceptable.[103] Law countered that the one possibility of a settlement lay in the permanent exclusion of Ulster and a modification of the government's bill as it applied to the rest of Ireland, involving the removal of the Customs Service, the Post Office and the Judiciary from the jurisdiction of the Dublin parliament. Asquith promised to consider these proposals but Law's impression was that the chance of a settlement was now very small. Asquith 'simply means to drift'.[104]

Lansdowne favoured making the conversations between the two party leaders public. If Asquith could be brought to state clearly in writing what changes he was prepared to make to the bill, his response would probably form the basis upon which negotiations could be safely discontinued without damage to the Unionist party.[105] Long and Chamberlain were also convinced that the moment had arrived for the inter-party dialogue to be broken off.[106] Both on the front bench and within the party at large there was considerable anxiety as to what had been going on over the previous two months. Though Law had never come near to a sell-out, it was inevitable that the clandestine nature of his discussions with Asquith - they were held in the isolation of Max Aitken's country house at Cherkley - should have bred suspicion and mistrust.[107] When, therefore, Asquith made it clear to Carson that the cabinet could not advance beyond its offer of Home Rule within Home Rule, this particular episode in the Irish question came to a halt. Law delayed making a formal announcement, perhaps giving the Prime Minister who, he was convinced, was 'quite at sea and does not in the least know what he can do', the time to make a final concession.[108] At last, on 15 January in a speech at Cardiff, Law officially declared that the negotiations for a compromise were at an end. The fight, it seemed, would be to the bitter end with the highest possible stakes. As Leo Amery reminded Law:

> We shall have to do some very hard thinking as to the most effective kind of measures to take in England and a lot of organising to make those measures a success. Whatever they are they will be measures that nothing but success could justify. And even success won't save us from some of their undesirable consequences.[109]

This protracted attempt to bring about a compromise is interesting chiefly for the light it throws upon Law's role in the whole Irish question. The rigid fanatic revealed in some of his public utterances emerges from the Asquith negotiations as a far more reasonable statesman, readier to compromise than the majority of his senior colleagues and consciously seeking a peaceful solution to a problem which otherwise appeared to lead inexorably towards bloodshed. Between Law's public language and his private views there was a considerable gap. Whatever his outward appearance Law was far less certain of his own ground than many contemporaries believed.[110] Though his terms would have been high, it would be wrong to suppose that Law did not genuinely seek an agreement with Asquith and that he merely entered into negotiations as a cynical and insincere expedient. Though he recognised that Redmond's concurrence was extremely doubtful, Law *was* prepared to settle on the sort of terms which he presented to Asquith on 9 December.[111] In other words, he did not regard the problem of the Southern Unionists as insurmountable. As he later told Strachey, 'If Asquith honestly tries to arrange a settlement I should feel bound to help him, however much it might be distasteful to some of our supporters.'[112]

Though observers such as Joseph Chamberlain, removed from the political stage, could afford to talk of 'fight[ing] it out to the finish',[113] Law was always hesitant about endangering the canons of constitutional practice, no matter how justified he felt his party's stance to be and how abhorrent that of the government. He had always to maintain a delicate balance between his own political principles, the unity of his party and protecting the essential social fabric of the realm. Balfour put into words of total clarity what was undoubtedly the dilemma facing his successor:

> There are bound to be great divisions of opinion in the Party on this point; but I cannot help thinking that the opinion of the majority will turn upon this : If they believed that the Government could not be compelled to dissolve, and that, as a result, there would be a rebellion in Ulster with all its collateral tragedies, I think they would favour a compromise. If, on the other hand, they thought that, either by skilful negotiation, or by the very necessities of the position, the Government would be forced to go to the country before such a catastrophe occurred, then I think they might be inclined to resent a compromise, which, on that hypothesis, was unnecessary and which would sacrifice (as they would think) much of what they had fought for in their Anti-Home Rule campaign.[114]

*      *      *

'Have any of us', asked Lansdowne rhetorically, 'an idea of what the new year will bring? The only prophecy upon which we can safely venture is that no one is likely to have a good time.'[115] Lansdowne, ignorant of the international crisis now only months away, could have had no idea of the magnitude of his understatement. But British political eyes were firmly fixed upon Ireland rather than the continent of Europe for the first six months of 1914. Not even Lloyd George's controversial budget succeeded in shifting the political debate on to fresh ground.[116] So grave was the situation that Lord Esher wondered whether the time had not come when it was the duty of the sovereign, at whatever risk to himself, to insist upon a dissolution. The moment was bound to arrive 'when the mass of the King's subjects will expect him to throw down his truncheon and cry "hold"'.[117]

The failure of the attempt at a compromise inevitably gave a fillip to the Unionist right wing, for whom the prospect of a successful outcome to the Asquith-Law negotiations had been a genuine nightmare. Willoughby de Broke had been ready to rekindle the glowing embers of the diehard movement of 1911 had the inter-party discussions resulted in a compromise agreement.[118] With Amery and Broke to the fore, plans for resisting the government's bill, which would make its way on to the statute book before the year was out, grew apace.[119] Broke, who prayed 'every day that we may have a straight fight for the Union as it stands and nothing but the Union', claimed to have 10,000 men who were prepared to seize rifles and fight in Ulster.[120] Only, asserted Amery, if the government realised in time that their opponents were really serious was there any chance of averting civil war in Ireland and probably Britain too.[121] By the end of February preparations were ready for the launching on the mainland, under the leading signatures of Lord Milner and Lord Roberts, of a declaration in which individual signatories would announce that, if Home Rule were carried without reference to the electorate, they would feel justified in taking or supporting any action which might be effective to prevent its being enforced.[122] Esher recognised that the forces of resistance in Ulster itself were now so large and well-organised that resistance would mean not a riot or a protest but civil war.[123] No longer did Liberals greet any reference to Ulster's preparations with 'sneers and jeers'.[124] Law himself had given his backing to the British League for the Support of Ulster and the Union, though he remained anxious that its organisation should be kept separate from that of the Unionist party.[125]

The opening of the new parliamentary session of 1914 brought to a head a debate which had been going on for over a year inside the Unionist ranks - usually in guilty whispers - as to whether the party should dare to tamper with the Army Annual Bill. This venerable piece of legislation, a legacy of the Glorious Revolution of the seventeenth century, regulated annually the army's code of disciple. It gave to parliament formal authority over the armed forces of the crown and, if it were not passed, the government would have no legal powers over the army, which would effectively cease to exist. Selborne had suggested to Law as early as July 1912 that the government might be brought down if the Lords failed to pass the bill,[126] but not until the end of 1913 was the matter taken seriously. The most likely option was to amend the bill in the House of Lords in such a way as to exclude the employment of the army in Ulster until after a general election. By this stage, with so many other avenues apparently blocked to them, some Unionists were prepared to consider almost any expedient, and even Balfour had come to regard the idea of amending the bill as an 'ingenious suggestion'.[127] Similarly, Hugh Cecil, who had 'some scruples about running civil war very fine', felt that Unionists were duty bound to save the men of Ulster from having to resort to force, 'if by any manipulation of constitutional machinery we can possibly do so'.[128] That some army officers might, when it came to the crunch, prefer to resign their commissions rather than act against Ulster loyalists to enforce the government's legislation had also been realised. Milner was among those who hoped for a Unionist declaration that the party, when returned to power, would reinstate any officers who had resigned in such circumstances.[129]

Law was careful not to adopt a policy which flew in the face of the spirit, if not the actual letter, of the constitution, without first consulting his senior colleagues. To introduce political purposes into the question of military discipline was obviously playing with fire.[130] By the end of January 1914, however, despite some misgivings from Lansdowne, Law was clearly moving in the direction of a radical departure from normal political practice.[131] Increasingly the prisoner of his own rhetoric, the Unionist leader was running out of peaceful options for the salvation of the Union - or at least of Ulster - and was now ready to embrace 'the least of a choice of evils'.[132]

The shadow cabinet, meeting on 5 February in an atmosphere of 'considerable uneasiness',[133] seemed anxious to postpone a decision for as long as possible and the question was delegated for further consideration to a

committee consisting of Finlay, Carson, Cave, Halsbury and Robert Cecil.[134]
It was also agreed that the opening of the new parliamentary session should
be accompanied by a dramatic gesture to emphasise that the exceptional nature
of the crisis justified exceptional action. As soon as the King's Address had
been moved and seconded, Long would move an amendment to the effect that
it would be disastrous to proceed further with the Home Rule Bill without a
general election.[135] In the event, though the opening day of the new session
was 'more interesting' than usual, 'public expectations were disappointed',
largely because Asquith did not, as predicted, outline government proposals
for a scheme of Home Rule for Ulster within Home Rule.[136]

By the middle of March, Law had the backing of two distinguished
military figures - Earl Roberts, the victorious hero of the Boer War, and Sir
Henry Wilson, Director of Military Operations - for the proposal to amend the
Army Annual Act.[137] By this stage, however, misgivings within the party
were beginning to grow, even among erstwhile diehards. The opposition of the
majority of the party whips was perhaps indicative of the attitude of backbench
M.P.s.[138] Though the shadow cabinet finally gave the plan its approval,
Curzon, Salisbury and Selborne dissented, while Austen Chamberlain, who
missed the meeting, found himself 'rather shaken' by Selborne's arguments.
In the latter's view it was now clear that Asquith could not coerce Ulster, so
the imperative urgency for the proposed action had gone. If the bill were
amended, Asquith would be able to claim that the Unionist party was
endangering the safety of the realm at a time of international uncertainty,
while the power of the Court would bear down on the House of Lords. 'So
much depends on how public opinion would be affected by our action and it
is extremely difficult to forecast its effect.'[139] Lansdowne feared that the
government might persuade the King to appeal to his army to rally to his
support in order to preserve discipline and good order until the act could be
renewed. The cry of 'King and People against the Peers' would be more
damaging than anything the Liberals had been able to chant in 1911.[140] Even
the King's Secretary intervened to try to dissuade Lansdowne from moving an
amendment in the upper house.[141]

The Unionist leaders no doubt had one eye on the electoral implications
of any action they might take. The trend of by-elections, though moving in the
party's favour, could not 'be called a great wave'.[142] Strachey believed that
the government might lose a few seats but would win a general election held
in the wake of an amendment to the Army Annual Act. The coercion of Ulster

would then proceed and 'the great heat' that would have been generated would spread to England and Scotland. He feared that Law, motivated above all by his horror of bloodshed, was reaching the point of exasperation when what was really needed was 'equability of mind no matter how provocative the situation'.[143] By 20 March Law was writing that it would be 'quite fatal' to amend the bill if there were any serious opposition to it in the party's ranks and 'I think there is a sufficient amount of that feeling at present to make it impossible to do it'.[144] On that very day, however, the deliberations of the Unionist leadership were overtaken by the course of events in Ireland. News filtered through of the so-called mutiny at the Curragh.[145]

The complicated developments which culminated in the Curragh incident have been described in detail elsewhere and the story need not be retold here.[146] In the context of Unionist politics two points should be underlined. In the first instance, if Law needed any further persuasion, there was now no likelihood that the Lords would amend the Army Bill. The Curragh provided graphic evidence that the army would prove an impotent weapon for the coercion of Ulster.[147] Secondly, though the truth remains to this day somewhat obscure, Law and other leading Unionists were convinced that the government had been engaged in an outrageous plot designed to create a crisis in which the coercion of Ulster could take place. Unionists believed that a plot had been hatched by Churchill, Seely, the Secretary for War, and possibly Lloyd George, to rush troops into Ulster from the Curragh, send more over from England and support them with a squadron of ships from Lamlash. The aim, it was assumed, was either to provoke Ulster into a rash act of aggression and then attack the province with troops, or else to get such a grip on it that the Ulster volunteers would be cornered.[148] As the dust from the Curragh incident began to settle, Walter Long wrote to Carson:

> We are convinced here that (a) warrants were signed for the arrest of political people, such as you and me and (b) that a deliberate plan was arrived at to attack Ulster on Saturday last with a considerable force. The news that I cabled you to this effect last week came from an absolutely reliable source and is, I know, trustworthy. [149]

The starting point for this further deterioration in inter-party relations towards a new low point of bitterness and animosity must be seen as the offer made by the government in the House of Commons on 9 March, after consultation with the Nationalist leadership, to give a separate option to each county of Ulster to exclude itself from Home Rule for a period of six years. At the end of this time the whole province would be included automatically unless, in the meantime, the Westminster parliament had decided otherwise. Though from a Nationalist point of view it might be argued that this was, historically speaking, a fatal concession,[150] it was no more acceptable to the Unionist leadership than any previous government offer had been. Indeed, it prompted a contemptuous dismissal by Carson in the celebrated words 'a sentence of death with a stay of execution for six years'.[151] Only if the proposal of exclusion were made permanent would Carson be prepared to submit it to his followers in Ulster.[152] But the government's offer was evidently a clever political ploy since, as Lloyd George observed, it removed the immediate justification for armed resistance in Ulster unless loyalists were prepared to rebel against a hypothetical act of oppression which could not occur for six years.[153] Selborne and Milner urged Law to counter the government's tactics by proposing that the question of exclusion should be decided by a referendum.[154]

In the light of the Unionist refusal to countenance fixed-term exclusion, the attitude of the government, and particularly of Churchill, became noticeably more belligerent, leading to the creation of an atmosphere of deep suspicion in which talk of plots and counter-plots was rife. Carson himself left for Ulster on 19 March convinced that there was a real prospect that he would be arrested, while on the government side it was widely supposed that he was about to proclaim a provisional government. Into this situation the Curragh incident entered with explosive force. Though Law was in no sense responsible for the actions of General Gough and his fellow officers, except to the extent that they may have been influenced by rumour of the proposed amendment to the Army Act, the Unionist leader was kept fully in touch with the unfolding drama through the indiscretions of Sir Henry Wilson.[155] The latter's crucial position within the War Office gave him intimate knowledge of what was going on and he had no compunction about passing such information on to Law if he believed that it might be of use in the struggle against Home Rule.

Meeting to consider what action they ought now to take, senior Unionist leaders decided that Law should write to Asquith stating the necessity of either at once omitting Ulster from the bill or else of consulting the electors by a referendum or general election. Additionally it was agreed that a future Unionist government would be pledged to reinstate the dismissed officers.[156] As the seriousness of the Curragh incident emerged, it was clear that the initiative was passing back once again to the Unionist party. Some Unionists were almost gratified to think that the government had descended to the same level of unconstitutional behaviour that had previously been the preserve of their own party. As H. A. Gwynne, editor of the *Morning Post*, put it:

> We had to find arguments and reasons for what was, in a manner, illegal though highly justifiable. Now the position seems to me to be changed. Whatever Ulster has done, she has done nothing so diabolical as the Junta in the Cabinet very nearly succeeded in doing. Wherefore we can now take the offensive with all vigour.[157]

Strachey was in a buoyant mood:

> If we keep our heads and are cool, Asquith is certain to come to grief. His only chance now is in our taking some foolish step and helping him get out of the awful morass into which he has floundered.[158]

Debates in parliament over the next few weeks were dominated by Unionist attempts to induce a confession from the government front bench of complicity in the supposed plot. Wilson was confident that the disclosure of the government's orders to Paget, the Commander-in-Chief in Ireland, would 'ruin Winston, Lloyd George, Birrell, Seely and (I think) Asquith'.[159] But the sort of gaffe which Strachey had feared occurred on the night of 24 April when the 'Mountjoy', carrying 35,000 rifles for the Ulster volunteers, successfully landed its cargo at Larne. By the time, therefore, that Law moved a vote of censure on the government four days later, Churchill was able to compare it to one 'by the criminal classes upon the police', while Asquith calmly announced that he would answer no further questions on the Curragh incident.[160] The debate left Amery convinced, more strongly than ever, that there was no real possibility of any settlement, tolerable or intolerable, as long as the present government remained in office.[161]

While the balance of party political advantage continued to shift from one side to the other, one fact remained constant and apparently inescapable. Under the government's parliamentary timetable the Home Rule Bill would pass into law in a matter of weeks. This was a prospect which neither party leader could view with enthusiasm, since the inevitable corollary seemed to be the outbreak of civil war in Ireland and possibly on the mainland as well. The pressure on both Asquith and Law to seek a way out of the impasse was therefore intense, despite the lack of success which had accompanied previous attempts at a compromise settlement. Divisions of opinion inside the Unionist party as to the best way to proceed became increasingly evident. The party witnessed 'serious discontent', and there was considerable dissension within the shadow cabinet.[162] It was now difficult to see how the government could be forced into calling a general election before Home Rule was placed on the statute book, although if the government did agree to go to the country Law was prepared to guarantee an easy passage for the bill in the event of the Liberals winning.[163] Law was still inclined to think that the government would have to make a further offer - probably the exclusion of the six counties. Without this he could see no chance of peace.[164] By contrast Austen Chamberlain was still keen to revive his father's abortive scheme of Provincial Councils and 'escape the dangers of a single practically independent parliament by a general system of equal devolution'. But he appreciated that Balfour, Law, Lansdowne and Curzon all disliked the idea to one degree or another, and he hesitated about dividing the party's ranks by pushing it too hard.[165] Chamberlain's fear nonetheless was that, between the party's very understandable dislike of any sort of compromise and its reluctance to envisage a federal solution, it would drift until such time as the Unionists, confronted by the reality of civil war, would be forced by public opinion to accept some other scheme of Irish government not compatible with British national unity and strength.[166]

These divisions of opinion came to a head on 5 May when Asquith invited Law and Carson to a further private discussion of the problem. Prior to the meeting the two Unionists wisely sought the counsel of Chamberlain, Balfour and Lansdowne. The discussion among the Unionist hierarchy revealed that Law was alone in believing that, if Ulster were excluded, the Unionist party would have to accept the rest of the bill as it stood. Chamberlain, still keen to float the possibility of a federal solution, reminded his colleagues that he and Lansdowne had from the first laid more stress than Carson and Law on the Imperial aspect of the Home Rule Bill and had therefore been anxious to prevent the impression growing that 'you had only to cut out Ulster in order to make the bill safe'. Not fully confident of Law's negotiating skills,[167] Chamberlain later reflected that it would be a miracle under the circumstances if the party did not drift either into civil war or into some form of compromise 'which will be hardly less bad than the original Bill'.[168] But when Law and Carson met Asquith later in the day, the Prime Minister produced an unexpected initiative which the Unionist leaders had not previously considered.[169] His proposal now was to pass the Home Rule Bill in its existing form under the provisions of the Parliament Act, but simultaneously to introduce an Amending Bill in the Lords to deal with the question of Ulster.[170] Though Law and Carson responded that this was the worst of all solutions, Asquith repeated his proposal in the Commons on 12 May and Lord Crewe introduced the new bill on 23 June.

Pressure against accepting any form of compromise was, however, mounting in the Unionist ranks.[171] Garvin, anxious for 'vigorous, determined leadership', stressed that the introduction of the Amending Bill would create a totally altered position.[172] Throughout May and June Milner busily urged Unionist peers to organise themselves to defeat the new bill on the grounds that it was no more than a device to ease the government out of its difficulties.[173] Some, like Willoughby de Broke, needed little persuasion. This diehard peer gave Lansdowne due warning that he did not think it right to agree to the repeal of the Union in any shape or form, or to the promotion in parliament of any new scheme which had not been submitted to the electorate.[174] Lansdowne himself now believed that the party should steer clear of any further dealings with the government and warned that the diehard movement 'might become formidable'.[175] His plan was to allow the Amending Bill a second reading, but insert drastic amendments including provision for the protection of Southern Unionists, insist upon them and thus wreck the bill. 'If this were to lead to a dissoln. we should have a very tenable position to defend.'[176] Amery thought that any compromise would have to be on the basis of federalism or devolution and would involve a start *de novo*. His real hope, however, was that the government would collapse when it came to the point of coercing Ulster and he urged Law and Lansdowne to commit the party on the third reading of the Home Rule Bill 'to repeal it lock, stock and barrel' the moment the Unionists were returned after an election.[177]

As Unionists debated furiously amongst themselves how the House of Lords should treat both the Home Rule Bill, now nearing the end of its long parliamentary journey, and the Amending Bill, the danger clearly existed that Law would lose control of the situation. Hugh Cecil summed up the range of options which was being canvassed:

> Some people really wish in one way or another to destroy the
> Amending Bill: some people want to pass it with amendments
> sufficient to avoid civil war: some people want federalism:
> some people, like myself, want to take the course most likely

to wreck Home Rule subject to the supreme moral obligation of
avoiding unjustifiable bloodshed.[178]
The Commons third reading debate on 21 May degenerated into an unseemly
row as backbench Unionists failed to elicit from Asquith details of the
forthcoming Amending Bill, but Law did much to restore his own authority
when he curtly and successfully rebuked the Speaker for enquiring whether the
demonstration had the Unionist leader's approval.[179] When the Amending
Bill was introduced in the Lords after the Whitsun recess, it was clear that its
provisions were virtually the same as those already offered by Asquith - a
separate option for each Ulster county to exclude itself from the provision of
the act for a period of six years, followed by automatic inclusion unless
parliament had meanwhile decided otherwise. A complete impasse seemed to
have been reached.

Amery now proposed giving the government a fourteen-day ultimatum
that, unless the people were consulted before Home Rule was submitted for
royal assent, the Ulster provisional government would take over the
administration of the province.[180] Milner too, concerned that any 'attempt
to patch things up will fail', favoured setting up a provisional government
under Carson's authority.[181] By early July rumours abounded that the
government intended to make further and far-reaching concessions to Ulster;
others believed that a general election was imminent.[182] In fact Asquith had
begun to explore once again the possibility of a compromise, using the former
government Chief Whip, Lord Murray of Elibank, as an intermediary. Though
these negotiations failed to reveal any grounds for optimism,[183] Asquith tried
again in the middle of the month. Murray was now permitted to make minor
concessions, but discussions broke down on the question of the area of Ulster
to be excluded.[184] Only the renewed intervention of the King kept alive the
faint hope of ultimate agreement. It was reported that George V had insisted
that his ministers should reach a settlement, otherwise he would only sign the
bill on condition that it was followed by an immediate general election.[185]
Out of deference to the wishes of the monarch Law agreed to attend a
conference at Buckingham Palace under the chairmanship of the Speaker of the
House of Commons, but he was careful to express the view that the meeting
offered 'little prospect of agreement'.[186] Indeed the predominant opinion in
the Unionist ranks was that Law and Carson should have refused to meet the
other side.[187] 'You can hardly conceive the anger and the excited state of our
people in the Lobby immediately after the announcement that there was to be

a conference', noted Amery.[188]

In such inauspicious circumstances failure was almost inevitable. Two fundamental questions formed the conference agenda - the area to be excluded and the time limit for such an exclusion. Only the former was discussed. On 23 July negotiations came to an end with no agreement reached. Though most of the discussions had focused on the possibility of partitioning the county of Tyrone, the area of disagreement was far broader than this might suggest; and the question of the time-limit, had negotiations ever advanced to that point, would almost certainly have posed an insurmountable stumbling-block. The problem of selling any compromise to Unionist hard-liners was another bridge that had not been crossed. 'I could never follow Bonar Law', confessed Lord Selborne, 'in accepting the present Government of Ireland Bill with the complete exclusion of the six Ulster counties as a final settlement of the Irish constitutional question.'[189] For most Unionists the news of the deadlock came as a relief. For Amery it provided a golden opportunity for 'cleansing ourselves completely from the entanglement of the Ulster exclusion idea' and reverting to the simple notion of the Union and nothing but the Union.[190] He urged Law to propose an amendment to the effect that the House declined to waste its time on a discussion of the Amending Bill, thus giving him a 'great opportunity of dismissing the whole boundary question, Tyrone etc., and of stating the broad case of principle'.[191] Failing this, Amery predicted 'a regular revolt' in the Commons, complete discouragement among Unionists in the country and defeat whenever the election came.[192]

\*   \*   \*

At the end of June 1914 Joseph Chamberlain gave one of his last recorded opinions on the political situation. To Leo Amery he asserted, 'Amery ... if I ... were the ... House of Lords ... I would ... fight'.[193] Each word was a physical effort, but the passionate intensity of emphasis was unmistakable. On 2 July Chamberlain died, but though his death caused considerable national comment and even provoked a brief pause in the prevailing political confrontation, history has seen it overshadowed by the death, four days earlier, of the Austrian Archduke, Franz Ferdinand, murdered by a Serbian nationalist in the Bosnian town of Sarajevo. So effectively did the authorities in Berlin and Vienna conceal their true intentions that British statesmen felt little inclination to divert their attention from matters nearer to hand. On the very day of the breakdown of the Buckingham Palace Conference, however, the Austrian government presented its ultimatum to Serbia, the terms of which revealed the potential magnitude of the international crisis. The Amending Bill, itself crippled by amendments from the Lords, was due to be discussed in the Commons on 30 July. Prompted by Law and Carson, Asquith agreed that the bill should be postponed. By 4 August the country was at war and the bill was never discussed. The entire context of the party political debate was to be transformed for more than four years. As Grey declared to the House of Commons:

> The position in Ireland - and this I should like very clearly to
> be understood abroad - is not a consideration among the many
> things we have to take into account now.[194]

Notwithstanding the wartime efforts of Lloyd George and others to effect a settlement, the resolution of the Irish imbroglio was effectively postponed for the duration of hostilities. It would be idle to speculate as to the development of the situation had not graver matters on the continent intervened. Both sides had modified their positions since 1912, but their remaining differences still seemed intractable. Austen Chamberlain somewhat dejectedly remarked: 'things are so grave abroad that a way of peace at home must be found, and if it must, it will!'[195] Law had at least escaped from an apparently hopeless political dilemma. An issue which at first had seemed to proffer welcome relief from the stale and apparently ceaseless debate over tariff reform had turned into a political nightmare. Law had consistently tried to steer a precarious course between responding to the clamour of his rank and file (and many of his senior colleagues as well) for a straightforward, hard-hitting and unequivocal defence of the Union, and his own concern not to see the party drift into an intransigent position from which the only exit would be civil war. By 1914 his priority was to find a way out of the Irish problem which did not destroy the confidence of his followers. Law's uncompromising language was maintained, but only as a way of forcing the government into offering a settlement. Yet Law's tactics risked breaching that party unity which the re-emergence of Ireland as a political issue had secured. He thus faced the danger of the same sort of dissension which had plagued Balfour's leadership, when the political focus had centred upon issues where no party consensus existed. As Leo Amery, who unequivocally rejected all idea of compromise, spelt it out:

> The fact is, and everything I see and hear makes one feel it

more strongly every day, that the policy of excluding Ulster, and inferentially in effect accepting Home Rule for the rest of Ireland, has been absolutely detested by the rank and file of the Party and, if it had succeeded, would have led to something like an open explosion.[196]

Yet Law did regard exclusion as a viable option, although even he had probably come to despair of the prospects of a solution by the time of the Buckingham Palace Conference.

More than two years of obsessive concentration on the Irish question had thus failed to produce a resolution. In the context of the continued failure of politicians in more recent times to bring about a final settlement, this may seem no surprise. In the context of the development of Unionist politics, on the other hand, it might well have proved a disaster, for, irrespective of short-term electoral advantage, the Irish preoccupation diverted the party from tackling more basic questions - questions which would determine its fitness to survive as a viable party of government in twentieth-century Britain.

## NOTES

1.  *The Times* 30 Aug.1906. Hugh Cecil went even further, reminding Bonar Law that 'we are the Unionist Party - that is we exist to oppose Home Rule': Cecil to Law 11 Sept.1914, cited J. O. Stubbs, 'The Unionists and Ireland, 1914-18', *Historical Journal* 33 (1990), p.867.
2.  *The Times* 27 July 1914.
3.  Blake, *Unknown Prime Minister* p.130. Law tried to justify his Blenheim declaration in a speech in Glasgow in June 1914 on the grounds that (a) 'in any event no doubt Ulster would resist' and (b) 'we believe not as a matter of opinion, but as a conviction which stirred the deepest feelings of which we are capable, that they would be right in resisting': *National Union Gleanings* July 1914.
4.  Law to Carson 18 Sept.1913, Law MSS 33/5/57.
5.  Winterton, *Orders* p.38.
6.  G. D. Phillips, 'Lord Willoughby de Broke and the Politics of Radical Toryism, 1909-1914', *Journal of British Studies* 20 (1980), p.219.
7.  A. Chamberlain to M. Chamberlain 28 Feb.1914, AC 4/1/1079.

8.  Phillips, 'The Diehards' p.149.

9.  B. Bond, *British Military Policy between the Two World Wars* (Oxford, 1980) p.18. Joseph Chamberlain had used the same argument during the heated 1886 election campaign when Home Rule first appeared on the legislative agenda: S. H. Zebel, 'Joseph Chamberlain and the Genesis of Tariff Reform', *Journal of British Studies* 7 (1967), p.133.

10. *The Times* 7 Jan.1910.

11. W. Bridgeman to C. Bridgeman 13 Nov.1912, cited Williamson, *Modernisation* p.63. After the disappointments of the previous years Ireland perhaps offered disgruntled Unionists the chance of a final engagement in which lost ground could be recovered: D. G. Boyce, 'British Conservative opinion, the Ulster question, and the partition of Ireland, 1912-21', *Irish Historical Studies* 17 (1970), p.91.

12. Egremont, *Balfour* p.237. Many Liberals found the Unionist rationale quite spurious. Churchill wrote: 'What is this miserable quibble on which the Conservative Leader seeks to justify doctrines of rebellion? That Home Rule was not mentioned in the election addresses of certain Ministers; that the preamble to the Parliament Bill has not yet been carried into effect. Can such a slender fabric really span the gulf between constitutional action and civil war?': Churchill, *Churchill* vol 2, companion pt.3 (London, 1969) p.1395.

13. Ramsden, *Balfour and Baldwin* p.78; Petrie, *Long* p.164.

14. Not all Unionists, of course, thought in these terms. The party's candidate for Rochdale wrote : 'Conservatism - to my mind - is disgraced with this policy of supporting rebellion and the use of force against a law which the British Parliament may pass .... The course now taken by Conservatives is, in my judgement, unEnglish, unlawful and ought never to have been fastened upon its members': N. Cockshutt to Derby 20 May 1913, Derby MSS 2/18. Other Unionists pursued curiously double standards. Lansdowne, for instance, though staunch for the Union and opposed to any compromise based on exclusion, was 'a little horrified' at the commitment of some of his colleagues to violent action in Ulster and saw some advantage in 'our being able to say ... that we are in no sense responsible' for the activities of Carson and his followers. Yet 'we should indeed be shabby fellows if we allowed Carson to do the rough work for us without helping him so far as help can legitimately be given':

Lansdowne to Law 23 and 25 Sept. 1913, Law MSS 30/2/21,25.

15.    P. J. Buckland, 'The Unionists and Ireland : the Influence of the Irish
       Question on British Politics, 1906-1914', University of Birmingham
       M.A. thesis (1965) esp. pp.507-8.

16.    See below, chapter 10.

17.    A bill for the Disestablishment of the Welsh Church accompanied the
       Home Rule proposals along the legislative route dictated by the
       Parliament Act. This was introduced in 1912, followed a very similar
       course to the Home Rule Bill and was still being examined by a select
       committee of the House of Lords when war was declared on 4
       Aug.1914. See P. M. H. Bell, *Disestablishement in Ireland and Wales*
       (London, 1969).

18.    A. Chamberlain to M. Chamberlain 30 Nov.1906, AC 4/1/122;
       Cawdor to Balfour 8 Feb.1906, cited R. Fanning, 'The Unionist Party
       and Ireland, 1906-10', *Irish Historical Studies* 15 (1966), p.160.

19.    Compare Buckland, 'Unionists and Ireland' p.72: 'To rebut the charge
       that these [Liberal] principles were a convenient reflection of the
       British political situation, to gain the political support of Irish
       nationalism for purely party reasons, there is the evidence of the
       application of these principles in South Africa ... where little Party
       advantage could be found.'

20.    B. K. Murray, *The People's Budget 1909-10: Lloyd George and
       Liberal Politics* (Oxford, 1980) p.54.

21.    H. W. McCready, 'Home Rule and the Liberal Party, 1889-1906',
       *Irish Historical Studies* 13 (1963), p.341.

22.    Fanning, 'Unionist Party' p.149.

23.    A. O'Day, 'Irish Home Rule and Liberalism' in O'Day (ed.),
       *Edwardian Age* p.131.

24.    Sir Antony MacDonnell was appointed Under-Secretary in Dublin in
       1902 with the primary task of drawing up a scheme to encourage land
       purchase in Ireland as part of the Unionist government's policy of
       killing Home Rule by kindness. His negotiations with the Irish Reform
       Association seemed to envisage a measure of Irish devolution which,
       when not nipped in the bud by the Chief Secretary, George Wyndham,
       fostered the belief that some members of the government were
       considering a modification of the Union. A crisis of confidence
       developed within the Unionist party in 1904-5, and revived the

following year when MacDonnell re-emerged as one of the architects of the Liberal government's proposed scheme of devolution.

25.   Chamberlain, *Politics from Inside* pp.140-1. In November 1906 Long became leader of the Irish Unionist party in parliament, a position he held until he was elected for a London seat in 1910. Thereafter he remained vice-chairman of the party, chairman of the Union Defence League and vice-president of the Irish Unionist Alliance.

26.   G. Dangerfield, *The Damnable Question* (London, 1979) p.53.

27.   J. Campbell, *F. E. Smith, First Earl of Birkenhead* (London, 1983) p.215.

28.   Grigg, *People's Champion* p.360.

29.   Fanning, 'Unionist Party' pp.165-9; Buckland, 'Unionists and Ireland' p.694; P. J. Buckland, 'The Southern Irish Unionists, the Irish Question and British Politics 1906-14', *Irish Historical Studies* 15 (1967), p.229.

30.   Buckland, 'Unionists and Ireland' p.20.

31.   Salisbury to Lansdowne 6 Sept.1910, cited Fanning, 'Unionist Party' p.164.

32.   See correspondence in Long MSS 448.

33.   Selborne to Lady Selborne April 1911, cited Egremont, *Balfour* p.233.

34.   Waller, *Democracy and Sectarianism* p.250.

35.   Carson, who became leader of the Irish Unionists in succession to Walter Long at the beginning of 1910, remains an enigmatic figure notwithstanding the efforts of his biographers. Despite the violence of his oratory and the stern austerity of his manner, Carson was a much more complex individual than his surface appearance may have suggested. Certainly he was at times less fanatical in his beliefs and readier to compromise than his public utterances implied and it remains difficult to assess how he would have reacted had Home Rule become a reality in 1914.

36.   Carson to Curzon 21 Aug.1911, Curzon MSS Eur.F 112/18.

37.   Research has shown that Curzon did not, as was once thought, vote with the government in the crucial division on 10 August 1911, but abstained. Working behind the scenes, Curzon helped Lord Newton to persuade enough Unionist peers to vote for the bill to ensure its passage: Southern, 'Lord Newton' pp.334-40. The subtlety of Curzon's tactics did not free him from contemporary criticism. One indignant

correspondent labelled him 'a most infamous traitor, a cowardly swine, a liar and a cad': A. Spencer Cragoe to Curzon 12 Aug.1911, Curzon MSS Eur. F 112/89.

38. Lansdowne to Curzon 25 Sept.1911, Curzon MSS Eur. F 112/18, emphasis added.

39. Brett, *Esher* iii, 117; Nicolson, *George V* p.200.

40. Amery to Law 17 Jan.1912, Law MSS 25/1/33. Amery found the Ulstermen 'a solid determined looking lot ... no more Irish than they are Chinese and with not much more use for "Papishes" that they have for "Chinks" or niggers': Amery to Mrs. Amery 5 Jan.1912, cited Barnes and Nicholson (eds), *Amery Diaries* i, 84.

41. I. Colvin, *The Life of Lord Carson* (3 vols, London, 1932-6) vol.ii (1934) p.101.

42. Carson to Lady Londonderry, cited Hyde, *Carson* p.310.

43. House of Commons Debates, 5th Series, vol xxxvii, cols. 300-1.

44. Petrie, *Carlton Club* p.156. The atmosphere inside the House of Commons inevitably worsened as the months passed and Home Rule crept ever nearer the statute book. Bridgeman commented of 1914: 'The bitterness between the parties ... was intense. This made Whips' work difficult, as one could find out nothing because one did not feel on speaking terms with any opponent': Diary review of 1914, 10 Aug.1914.

45. Chamberlain, *Politics from Inside* pp.486-7; Nicolson, *George V* p.200.

46. Memorandum by Law for the King on the latter's position in relation to the Irish question, Sept.1912, Law MSS 39/1/6. See also memorandum of July 1913, ibid 39/1/10.

47. Lansdowne to Curzon 13 Sept.1912, Curzon MSS Eur. F112/19. To Austen Chamberlain Lansdowne wrote : 'I feel just as strongly as Bonar Law does about Ulster, although I should personally have used language rather less suggestive of readiness to carry a rifle in her defence': Lansdowne to Chamberlain 22 Aug.1912, AC 12/28.

48. Selborne to Law 27 June 1912, Law MSS 26/4/39; Selborne to Lansdowne 27 June 1912, Selborne MSS 77/7.

49. Law to Selborne 19 July 1912, Law MSS 33/4/50. Later Robert Cecil argued that bills could not be passed under the Parliament Act if the Lords, instead of rejecting them, simply adjourned without considering

them: Cecil to Law 23 Nov.1913, ibid 30/4/48.

50.   The phrase is Asquith's, cited Blake, *Unknown Prime Minister* p.134.
51.   Dicey to Strachey 14 Nov.1912, Strachey MSS S/5/6/6.
52.   Lyttelton to Balfour 13 Nov.1912, Balfour MSS Add. MS 49775.
53.   House of Commons Debates, 5th Series, vol.xxxix, col.1560.
54.   Chamberlain to Lansdowne 26 Aug.1912, AC 10/2/22.
55.   As late as March 1914 Strachey still hoped that the exclusion of only the four overwhelmingly Protestant counties, Antrim, Armagh, Down and Londonderry, would be sufficient to wreck the bill: Strachey to Milner 9 March 1914, Strachey MSS S/10/11/4.
56.   A. W. Samuels to Long 15 March 1914, Long MSS 947/343.
57.   But there were those Unionists for whom the exclusion of Ulster was never more than a tactical diversion. After the final collapse of the Buckingham Palace Conference in July 1914, Selborne commented : 'It never could possibly have been considered a policy and it has done a great deal to kill the Liberal conception of a National Parliament for Ireland': Selborne to Amery 27 July 1914, Amery MSS D45.
58.   Law to J. P. Croal 18 Oct.1913, Law MSS 33/6/84.
59.   For a different analysis see Buckland, 'Southern Irish Unionists' p.232.
60.   Amery, *Political Life* i, 437.
61.   Sir C. E. Callwell, *Field Marshal Sir Henry Wilson* (2 vols, London, 1927) vol.i, p.124.
62.   Long to Derby 18 Feb.1913, Derby MSS 4/39.
63.   Phillips, 'Willoughby de Broke' p.219.
64.   Brett, *Esher* iii, 135.
65.   Selborne to Comyn Platt 19 Sept.1912, Selborne MSS 77/18, cited D. G. Boyce (ed.), *The Crisis of British Unionism* (London, 1987) p.92.
66.   Brett, *Esher* iii, 134-5.
67.   Lansdowne to Law 28 Aug.1913, Law MSS 30/1/29; Blake, *Unknown Prime Minister* pp.152-3.
68.   Note by Balfour of conversation with King 16 Sept.1913, Balfour MSS Add MS 49693.
69.   Note of conversation with King 16 Sept.1913, Curzon MSS Eur. F112/95. Esher confirmed that the King had to give way to the recommendations of his ministers even if he disapproved of them: Lees-Milne, *Enigmatic Edwardian* p.245.
70.   Colvin, *Carson* ii, 205; compare Blake, *Unknown Prime Minsiter*

p.154 : 'upon this [exclusion] Bonar Law was far more sceptical [than upon general devolution]'.
71.   Law to Lansdowne 18 Sept.1913, Law MSS 33/5/56; Carson to Law 20 Sept.1913, ibid 30/2/15; Blake, *Unknown Prime Minister* p.156; Colvin, *Carson* ii, 198.
72.   Hyde, *Carson* p.339.
73.   Lansdowne to Law 23 Sept.1913, Law MSS 30/2/21.
74.   Balfour to Law 23 Sept.1913, ibid 30/2/20.
75.   Stamfordham to Law 1 Oct.1913, ibid 30/3/1; Law to Stamfordham 4 Oct.1913, ibid 33/5/66; Blake, *Unknown Prime Minister* p.159.
76.   Aitken to Law 20 Sept. 1913, Law MSS 30/2/16.
77.   Willoughby de Broke to Cecil 21 Sept.1913, Cecil MSS Add. MS 51161.
78.   Maxse to Law 27 Sept.1913, Law MSS 30/2/30.
79.   Lansdowne to Law 20 Sept.1913, ibid 30/2/17.
80.   Blake, *Unknown Prime Minister* pp.157-9.
81.   Lansdowne to Law 23 Sept.1913, Law MSS 30/2/21.
82.   Ibid 27 Sept.1913, ibid 30/2/29. F. E. Smith had given the King an over-optimistic estimate of the chances of an agreement.
83.   Lansdowne to Law 26 Sept.1913, Law MSS 30/2/27.
84.   Ibid 2 Oct.1913, ibid 30/3/3.
85.   Ibid 4 Oct.1913, ibid 30/3/4.
86.   Ibid 30 Sept.1913, ibid 30/2/37.
87.   Law to Stamfordham 4 Oct.1913, ibid 33/5/66.
88.   Carson had recently spoken to a delegation of Southern Unionists who had indicated that they did not intend to take their opposition to Home Rule too far for fear of intimidation and damage to their economic interests.
89.   Memorandum to Lansdowne 8 Oct.1913, Law MSS 33/5/68.
90.   Note of conversation 15 Oct.1913, Balfour MSS Add. MS 49693; Lansdowne to Law 10 Oct.1913, Law MSS 30/3/17.
91.   Carson to Lansdowne 9 Oct.1913, ibid 30/3/23.
92.   Law to Lansdowne 15 Oct.1913, cited Blake, *Unknown Prime Minister* p.163; Lansdowne to Law 16 Oct.1913, Law MSS 30/3/31.
93.   Lansdowne to Law 13 and 27 Oct.1913, ibid 30/3/29 and 30/3/56.
94.   Lansdowne to Chamberlain 31 Oct.1913, AC 11/1/47. For many Imperialists in the Unionist ranks the federal option seemed to offer not

only a viable solution to the Irish problem but also a step towards the consolidation of the Empire: J. E. Kendle, 'The Round Table Movement and "Home Rule All Round"', *Historical Journal* 11 (1968), pp.332-53.

95.   P. Jalland, 'United Kingdom devolution 1910-14 : political panacea or tactical diversion?', *English Historical Review* 94 (1979), pp.781-2. Amery was later to write rather misleadingly of 'the failure of Unionist leadership against Home Rule' in shrinking 'from committing itself irrevocably to the alternative policy which it professed to favour ... a complete recasting of the United Kingdom on federal lines': Amery, *Political Life* i, 461.

96.   Memorandum on the second meeting 7 Nov.1913, Law MSS 33/6/93; Law to Long 7 Nov.1913, ibid 33/6/94. For Asquith's version of this meeting see David, *Asquith's Cabinet* p.149.

97.   Long to Law 7 and 9 Nov.1913, Law MSS 30/4/11 and 30/4/18.

98.   Memorandum by Long 20 Nov.1913, ibid 30/4/46.

99.   Note by A. Chamberlain of conversation with Churchill 27 Nov.1913, ibid 31/1/3.

100.  Colvin, *Carson* ii, 254.

101.  A. Chamberlain to M. Chamberlain 11 Feb.1914, AC 4/1/1069.

102.  Memorandum on the third meeting 10 Dec.1913, Law MSS 33/6/111.

103.  Lansdowne to Law 11 Dec.1913, ibid 31/1/25.

104.  Law to Curzon 13 Dec.1913, Curzon MSS Eur. F 112/95.

105.  Memorandum by Lansdowne 16 Dec.1913, Law MSS 31/1/38.

106.  Lansdowne to Law 21 Dec.1913, ibid 31/1/46.

107.  R. Cecil to Law 24 Dec.1913, ibid 31/1/54; Lansdowne to Law 30 Dec.1913, ibid 31/1/65.

108.  Law to Selborne 22 Dec.1913, Selborne MSS 77/64.

109.  Amery to Law 27 Dec.1913, Law MSS 31/1/57.

110.  Compare Long's later assertion that Law 'never wavered' in his defence of the Union: Viscount Long of Wraxall, *Memories* (London,1923) p.212.

111.  Sanders diary 7 Dec.1913.

112.  Law to Strachey 14 Feb.1914, Strachey MSS S/9/8/12.

113.  Colvin, *Carson* ii, 232-3.

114.  Balfour to Law 8 Nov.1913, Law MSS 30/4/16. Law's relative moderation was still evident at the customary Unionist dinner on 9

February 1914, before the opening of the new parliamentary session. He was 'very much impressed with the delicacy of the situation. If we go in for compromise on Ulster we desert the rest of Ireland but avoid civil war: is it right for the sake of avoiding civil war to ignore the loyalists in the S. and W. of Ireland?' By contrast Austen Chamberlain 'deprecated too much finesse and advocated as plain a policy as possible which would leave the party in the Country under no delusions and make it clear that we stood for the Union': Chamberlain, *Politics from Inside* pp.608-9; Bridgeman diary 9 Feb.1914.

115. Lansdowne to Law 23 Dec.1913, Law MSS 31/1/51.
116. B. B. Gilbert, 'David Lloyd George, the Reform of British Landholding and the Budget of 1914', *Historical Journal* 21 (1978), p.140.
117. Brett, *Esher* iii, 148-50.
118. Willoughby de Broke MSS WB/7. As a sign of his determination not to be bound by the decisions of the party leadership, Broke - much to Lansdowne's annoyance - organised an independent initiative on the debate on the Address at the beginning of 1914: Lansdowne to Broke 7 Feb.1914, Willoughby de Broke MSS WB/8/24.
119. Amery diary 12 and 13 Jan.1914. See also H. A. Gwynne's pledge to place his services at the disposal of Carson's provisional government if the need arose: Gwynne to Carson 18 Feb.1914, Gwynne MSS 17.
120. Broke to Law 21 Jan.1914, Law MSS 31/2/52.
121. Amery to N.Chamberlain 16 Jan.1914, cited Barnes and Nicholson (eds), *Amery Diaries* i, 98; Amery to R. Cecil 16 Jan.1914, Cecil MSS Add. MS 51072.
122. Amery to M. Chamberlain 27 Feb.1914, AC 4/11/11.
123. Brett, *Esher* iii, 154.
124. Winterton, *Orders* pp.70-1.
125. Amery, *Political Life* i, 440-1; Amery diary 13 Jan.1914.
126. Selborne to Law 20 July 1912, Law MSS 26/5/34.
127. Lewis Coward to Ailwyn Fellowes, forwarded to Law 2 Dec.1913, ibid 31/1/7.
128. H. Cecil to A. Chamberlain 31 Dec.1913, AC 11/1/8.
129. Gollin, *Proconsul* p.196.
130. Balfour summed up the dilemma which confronted constitutionally-minded Unionists : 'in revolutionary times I suppose revolutionary

measures are necessary. I confess, however, that they are rather against the grain': Balfour to Lansdowne 13 March 1914, Balfour MSS Add. MS 49730.

131. Lansdowne 'rather dreaded the step', but could not see 'any other way out': Lansdowne to Law 1 Feb.1914, Law MSS 31/3/1.

132. Law to Balfour 30 Jan.1914, Balfour MSS Add. MS 49693; Law to Lansdowne 30 Jan.1914, Law MSS 34/1/25; Blake, *Unknown Prime Minister* p.176.

133. Salisbury to R. Cecil 6 Feb.1914, Cecil MSS Add. MS 51085.

134. Blake, *Unknown Prime Minister* p.177; A. T. Q. Stewart, *The Ulster Crisis* (London, 1967) p.136. Law took advantage of the meeting to brief his colleagues on his three meetings with Asquith.

135. A. Chamberlain to M. Chamberlain 5 Feb.1914, AC 4/1/1062. Balfour, who was unable to attend the shadow cabinet, had expressed misgivings about such tactics: Balfour to Law 3 Feb.1914, Law MSS 31/3/7.

136. A. Chamberlain to M. Chamberlain 11 Feb.1914, AC 4/1/1069.

137. Callwell, *Wilson* i, 138; Blake, *Unknown Prime Minister* pp.178-80.

138. Sanders diary 19 March 1914.

139. Chamberlain to M. Chamberlain 15 March 1914, AC 4/1/1090.

140 Ibid 16 March 1914, AC 4/1/1091.

141. Ibid 18 March 1914, AC 4/1/1092.

142. Sanders diary 24 Feb.1914.

143. Strachey to Curzon 19 March 1914, Curzon MSS Eur. F 112/95.

144. Law to J. P. Croal 20 March 1914, Law MSS 34/2/44.

145. The word 'mutiny' is certainly a misnomer, since the army officers were merely responding to a choice put before them. The word will, however, be difficult to erase from the historical record. See, for example, Dangerfield, *Damnable Question* p.86 : 'mutiny it was'.

146. Sir J. Ferguson, *The Curagh Incident* (London, 1964); D. R. Gwynn, *The Life of John Redmond* (London, 1932) chapter 8; Blake, *Unknown Prime Minister* chapters 11-12.

147. The party leader's conclusion was widely shared in Unionist circles, though not by Lord Milner: Gollin, *Proconsul* p.203.

148. Bridgeman diary 21-23 March 1914.

149. Colvin, *Carson* ii, 352-3.

150. Dangerfield, *Damnable Question* p.81, has written of 'the first

Nationalist obeisance to that principle of Partition which afterwards became a great stumbling block to peace in Ireland'.
151. House of Commons Debates, 5th Series, vol.lix, col.934.
152. Winterton, *Orders* p.71.
153. Gwynn, *Redmond* pp.256-8.
154. Milner to Law 17 March 1914, Law MSS 31/4/30; Selborne to Law 18 March 1914, ibid 31/4/33.
155. Callwell, *Wilson* i, 141. See also Amery to Law 23 March 1914, announcing that Gough had secured a written assurance that his troops would not be used 'to coerce Ulster to accept the present Home Rule Bill': Law MSS 32/1/46; and 'Message from General Wilson' 23 March 1914, ibid 32/1/50, indicating that Gough had sensed a possible loophole in the government's assurances in that, if the bill became law, the army might still be called upon 'to enforce it upon Ulster in the name of law and order'.
156. A. Chamberlain to M. Chamberlain 21 March 1914, AC 4/1/1096.
157. Gwynne to Law 11 April 1914, Law MSS 32/2/29.
158. Strachey to Curzon 23 March 1914, Curzon MSS Eur. F 112/95.
159. Callwell, *Wilson* i, 146.
160. Blake, *Unknown Prime Minister* pp.203-4.
161. Amery to Law 30 April 1914, Law MSS 32/2/68.
162. Sanders diary 30 April 1914.
163. Selborne regarded it as 'almost impossible' that the government would yield on this point: Selborne to Lansdowne 1 May 1914, Law MSS 32/3/2; Selborne to Law 5 April 1914, ibid 32/2/18. There were, however, those who believed that Ulster 'would not and ought not' to yield even if a general election were to go in favour of the government: Brett, *Esher* iii, 163-4.
164. Law to Selborne 7 April 1914, Selborne MSS 77/100.
165. A. Chamberlain to M. Chamberlain 2 April 1914, AC 4/1/1110.
166. Ibid 2 May 1914, AC 4/1/1128.
167. 'Law seems to me so much afraid of having to take any definite decision that he just lets matters drift along and never brings anything to a point': Ibid 11 May 1914, AC 4/1/1133.
168. Ibid 5 May 1914, AC 4/1/1131.
169. Interestingly Selborne had already put forward the idea of an amending bill as an acceptable arrangement because it could be passed by the

Unionists without their incurring any responsibility for the main
Government of Ireland Act: Selborne to Lansdowne 1 May 1914, Law
MSS 32/3/2.
170.  A. Chamberlain to M. Chamberlain 6 May 1914, AC 4/1/1132.
171.  Long to Law 9 May 1914, Law MSS 32/3/20.
172.  Garvin to Amery 14 May 1914, Amery MSS D 45.
173.  Gollin, *Proconsul* p.218.
174.  Willoughby de Broke and Ampthill to Lansdowne 13 May 1914,
      Willoughby de Broke MSS WB/10/10.
175.  Lansdowne to Law 27 May 1914, Law MSS 32/3/55.
176.  Lansdowne to Salisbury 29 May 1914, Salisbury MSS S(4) 74/244.
177.  Amery to Chamberlain 4 May 1914, AC 11/1/2; Amery to Law 13
      May 1914, Law MSS 32/3/25.
178.  H. Cecil to Salisbury 29 June 1914, Salisbury MSS S(4) 75/123.
179.  Hewins, *Apologia* i, 311; Fitzroy (*Memoirs* ii, 550) commented that
      Law's reply to the Speaker 'won him more fame than three years of
      laborious tactics'.
180.  Amery to Carson 22 June 1914, cited Barnes and Nicholson (eds),
      *Amery Diaries* i, 100-1.
181.  Milner to Law 15 July 1914, Law MSS 33/1/28; Gollin, *Proconsul*
      p.219.
182.  Sanders diary 6 and 16 July 1914; Derby to Woodhouse 10 July 1914,
      Derby MSS 2/15.
183.  Gwynn, *Redmond* pp.327-30.
184.  Memorandum by Law, Law MSS 39/E/43.
185.  Gwynne to Law 19 July 1914, ibid 33/1/37.
186.  Law to Stamfordham 20 July 1914, ibid 34/2/85. For a discussion of
      the Buckingham Palace Conference see J. D. Fair, *British Interparty
      Conferences* (Oxford, 1980) pp.114-9.
187.  Note by Gwynne 20 July 1914, ibid 33/1/39.
188.  Amery to Law 25 July 1914, ibid 33/1/46.
189.  Selborne to A. Chamberlain 12 Aug.1914, Selborne MSS 77/184.
190.  Amery to N. Chamberlain 25 July 1914, cited Barnes and Nicholson
      (eds), *Amery Diaries* i, 101.
191.  Amery to Law 25 July 1914, Law MSS 33/1/46.
192.  Amery to Selborne 25 July 1914, Amery MSS D 45.
193.  Amery, *Political Life* i, 465.

194.   House of Commons Debates, 5th Series, vol.LXV, col.1824.
195.   A. Chamberlain to M. Chamberlain 2 Sept.1914, AC 4/1/1139.
196.   Amery to Law 25 July 1914, Law MSS 33/1/46.

PUNCH, OR THE LONDON CHARIVARI.—January 6, 1909.

THE NEW YEAR'S GIFT.

## . 10 .

### POLICY: SOCIAL POLICY 1906–1914

That social reform should have emerged as a key issue in the politics of Edwardian Britain was in some ways surprising and in others entirely predictable. It was surprising to the extent that the new Liberal government had not really signalled its innovative intentions by making social reform a prominent issue in the election campaign of 1906. Yet longer-term factors pointed in a different direction. The most important, perhaps, was the progressive extension of the franchise in the later decades of the nineteenth century. The Earl of Derby put the point very clearly as early as 1875 when he said of the working man: 'He is master of the situation. His class can, if it chooses, outvote all the other classes put together.'[1] On the whole this class of voters faced difficult times during the Edwardian era as a result of a steady rise in the cost of living, after a period of growing prosperity in the last quarter of the nineteenth century. Yet it would not necessarily be correct to draw a direct correlation between a mass working-class electorate and the inevitable emergence of questions of social reform on to the political agenda. To many working men the idea of state intervention was synonymous not with beneficial welfare measures but with the hated Poor Law and the forces of law and order. It is a striking fact that most of the reforming legislation of the 'New Liberalism', apart from the introduction of old age pensions, was viewed with wary suspicion rather than unbridled enthusiasm. There is, for example, clear evidence from by-election results that Lloyd George's health insurance measures of 1911 were far from popular.

There had, nonetheless, emerged within both political parties a growing body of opinion which recognised the need to court the working-class vote in the interests of political survival. For Unionists this had not necessarily meant engaging in a competition with radical Liberals, but rather putting fresh energy into traditional stances.[2] After the Boer War, however, with its apparent revelation of physical deterioration, there was a growing feeling, not confined within party boundaries, that the national interest might have to involve a greater state involvement in the welfare of the population than had hitherto been thought appropriate. This belief gave birth to the cult of 'National Efficiency' to which all the political parties made some form of contribution.

When the electoral power of the working class is appreciated, the long-term success of the British Conservative party in the twentieth century as a whole becomes apparent. It is no small achievement for a party which has remained overwhelmingly dominated by the upper and middle classes that the Conservatives and Unionists have, since the passing of the Second Reform Act in 1867, governed Britain alone or in coalition for approximately three quarters of the time. Keir Hardie maintained that 'when once the working man is found who is a Conservative from honest, intelligent conviction,he should either be sent to Barnum for exhibition, or he should be stuffed and put under a glass case in the British Museum'.³ Yet the Conservative working-class voter is no rarity. The party's electoral achievement is in large part explained by its success in winning at least one third of the working-class vote at most general elections. Or, to put the point another way, the party, despite its own social composition, has consistently drawn half its support from the working classes.⁴

As the twentieth century opened, however, there seemed signs that the Unionist party was, if anything, veering away from the course which pioneer Tory democrats had begun tentatively to chart. During the years which immediately preceded the Unionist *débâcle* of 1906, efforts to cultivate working-class support were visibly declining. In some ways this was surprising. When the Liberal Unionists left the Liberal fold in 1886 they took into the Conservative ranks middle-class men from industrial areas, infusing business and Nonconformist strength into the new Unionist party.⁵ Indeed most Liberal Unionists saw themselves as belonging to the camp of progress rather than that of caution.⁶ But the Unionists' electoral victory of 1895, though it brought Liberal Unionists into a Conservative cabinet for the first time, also revealed that their importance had sharply declined. 'A majority of 152 seats was the most effective counter to any view that Unionists needed progressive leaders with progressive policies.'⁷ Thereafter the reforming zeal of men like Joseph Chamberlain had been largely stifled beneath the weight of other governmental work. The Liberal Unionist spirit never captured the party as a whole. In 1912 Lord Selborne complained that 'the present flabbiness lies mainly with the Tories by origin'.⁸ Indeed not even all Liberal Unionists were imbued with a commitment to reform. The dissenting Liberals of 1886, who by the 1890s were appearing as members of a Unionist government, included not only radicals but right-wing Whigs. Not surprisingly, then, the decade of Unionist government which began in 1895 was not characterised by any particularly progressive spirit. Sidney Low, writing in the *Nineteenth Century* in 1902, drew attention to a reactionary trend in the party, noting the absence of the progressive and vitalising contribution made earlier by such figures as Pitt, Peel, Disraeli and Randolph Churchill.[9] One hero of the early years of Tory Democracy, John Gorst, constantly bemoaned the fact that Unionists had exchanged the legacy of Disraeli for a mess of pottage, by which he meant the South African War and Chamberlain's crusade for tariff reform.[10] As a Unionist contributor to the *Fortnightly Review* recalled a decade later, Balfour's government of 1902-05 had 'relapsed into a state of moral limpness when its energies should have been usefully employed in dealing with old-age pensions' and similar measures.[11]

The electoral catastrophe of 1906 and the political developments of the following years inevitably forced at least some Unionists to reconsider their stance on social questions. Unionists from all sections of the party were conscious of the loss of working-class support.[12] It was not simply that the magnitude of the party's defeat suggested to many that all was not well with its public image. The emergence now of an independent working-class party with a substantial representation at Westminster showed to the prescient in both traditional parties that they might themselves not be able indefinitely to share a monopoly of political power. In the years which followed, moreover, the unfolding of a substantial body of social legislation by the Liberal government indicated that the future debate within British politics would focus on the role of the state in society and the respective merits of collectivist and individualist responses to society's problems. It would of course be wrong to present Edwardian Britain as a golden age of individualism, shattered only by the arrival of European war in 1914. Most practising politicians were prepared to accept an increasing role for the state long before the demands of total war removed any option to argue otherwise. The question was, how far should this role go and in which areas should it develop? Since Gladstone's death many Liberals had been steadily abandoning their strict adherence to the doctrines of Manchester *laissez-faire*. Indeed it was now often Conservatives whose instincts seemed to recoil from intervention in the free working of the market.[13] After 1906 the Liberal government seemed ready to intrude into matters which most Victorians had assumed to be beyond its range. These were developments which Unionists could not indefinitely ignore. Indeed the posture taken by them was of crucial importance in the development of the party in this period, helping to determine its electoral fortunes in a way that had long-term implications for the party's future within the democratic state. Yet, as will emerge, the party was deeply divided on this issue. Before 1914 no single coherent attitude towards the role and limits of the state became apparent.[14]

In the immediate wake of the election, however, it was the sight of a solid body of Labour M.P.s which caused Unionists most concern. 'Fact is', concluded Lord Newton, 'that working classes have at last recognised their power.'[15] In similar vein Balfour himself sensed

> the faint echo of the same movement which has produced
> massacres in St. Petersburg, riots in Vienna and Socialist
> processions in Berlin .... We are face to face, (no doubt in a
> milder form), with the Socialist difficulties which loom so large
> on the Continent.[16]

Balfour's dramatic pronouncement signalled what developed into a marked apprehension in Unionist circles over the growth of 'socialism'. The word socialism became a convenient umbrella description for a variety of developments which Unionists viewed with distaste and disquiet. It could be used to cover not only the activities of a few committed ideologues in the Labour party, but also the increasing self-assertion of the trade union movement. Just as often, however, Unionists damned as socialistic the legislation of the governments of Campbell Bannerman and particularly Asquith, which was pictured as deliberately designed to arouse class animosities.[17] As one observer noted:

> It is not a libel but a truth to say that Socialism by instalments,
> Socialism, more and more self-consciously pursued, is now
> bound to become and is, in fact, becoming the creed of one of
> the great parties in the State.[18]

Unionists seldom referred to the members of the government as 'Liberals'. They were 'Radicals' and, as a Central Office publication noted in 1910, 'it is becoming harder and harder to draw any line of distinction between the radicals and the Socialists'.[19] Similarly, Austen Chamberlain commented that 'our danger now is not Liberalism but "Labour" working with and through Liberalism'.[20]

Balfour's assessment of the 'Socialist difficulties' apparent after the election of 1906 presented Unionists with the need to come to grips with a political climate which contained both new problems and new dimensions to old ones. The first decade of the twentieth century, which saw a growing realisation that the Pax Britannica and its economic counterpart, world industrial supremacy, were things of the past, brought exacerbated social, economic and industrial difficulties which no party, granted the enlarged and increasingly active electorate, could afford to ignore. The Unionists' problems were heightened by the danger that even limited success on the part of any other party in drawing away working-class support would threaten their very survival as a potential party of government. With the patent advance of the Labour party and the apparently new course being charted by Liberalism, the Unionist opposition after 1906 needed to define its attitude to the recently enfranchised masses and their aspirations - indeed to recast the party's image as presented to the whole electorate. As the newspaper editor, R. D. Blumenfeld, noted, 'the day has gone by when the legitimate aspirations of the people can any longer be ignored'.[21]

In carrying out the necessary processes of adaptation the Unionists possessed, in theory, positive advantages. They were not committed to an ideological stance which would inhibit the flexibility of their response to those problems which came to typify twentieth-century society. *Laissez-faire* had never become for Unionists an enshrined article of faith as it had once been for Liberalism. Not hampered by adherence to a fixed economic system, Unionists could face the challenge of collectivism with some confidence. With justice Lord Hugh Cecil wrote in 1912 that Conservative social reform need not proceed on purely individualist lines. 'There is no antithesis between Conservatism and Socialism .... Conservatives have no difficulty in welcoming the social activity of the State.'[22] A year later Keith Feiling noted:

> We are not sworn either to State control or to the rights of the
> individual: by our judgement of facts and of the history of the
> English people, we lay the onus of proof on the State, but our
> sole criterion is the well-being of the commonwealth, tested by
> the Moral Law.[23]

Yet whatever the electorate was looking for from the political parties - and it may well not have been greater state intervention[24] - the evidence of the 1906 election, particularly in working-class areas of Lancashire and London, suggested that the Unionists' popular image remained unconvincing. A further difficulty for the party was that of maintaining Disraeli's classless one-nation appeal in such a way that any gestures towards the working class did not serve to alienate middle- and upper-class voters whose financial assistance was increasingly crucial. Though, as Garvin recognised, 'we shall never come back to power by the support of the middle class,'[25] the Unionists' long term financial viability could not be ignored.

The problem, then, was clear. But while Balfour apparently recognised the nature of this problem as it confronted his party, his approach to it seemed to look back to a political age that had now passed. The man who in 1895 had argued that social legislation was not merely to be distinguished from socialist legislation, but was its direct opposite and most effective antidote,[26] now preferred to base his response to the reform measures of the Liberal government upon the obstructive powers of the hereditary peerage sitting in the Unionist-dominated House of Lords.

*          *          *

In the immediate aftermath of the 1906 election, it was, of course, by no means certain that it would be Arthur Balfour who would be setting the tone of the Unionist party in opposition and its response to the new political situation. Lacking a seat in the Commons and obliged to make substantial concessions over policy in the Valentine letters, Balfour was in some danger of being eclipsed by a man who could genuinely claim popular appeal - indeed the very man who had already tried and failed two decades earlier to move the Liberal party out of its unpromising Gladstonian mould. In Joseph Chamberlain Unionism possessed a politician who had already made that jump from aristocratic paternalism to popular politics which many of the more traditional members of the Unionist alliance seemed reluctant to make. Having made his fortune in the screw-manufacturing firm of Chamberlain and Nettlefold, the Birmingham leader had gone on to become a radical reforming mayor of the city. In that capacity he helped alleviate some of the most glaring abuses of Victorian industrialisation. As a result, after his entry into national politics, Birmingham repaid Chamberlain with an electoral loyalty - irrespective of his own party affiliation which not even the violent political winds of 1906 could undermine. Indeed Dr. Pelling has drawn attention to the way in which Chamberlain's distinctive influence not only obtained a new lease of life after 1903 but also widened its geographical extent. 'It was strengthened in the Black Country and spread outside it to the urban and rural areas beyond.'[27]

Even before the election of 1906 this 'prophet and architect of British democracy at the close of the patrician era'[28] had been anxious to do something to popularise the party's representative associations and secure the involvement in them of the working classes. Now, with the election lost but with his personal position within the party probably stronger than ever before, Chamberlain intended, or so Beatrice Webb at least believed, 'to try to outbid the Liberals by constructive social reform', which would at the very least put 'pressure on the Liberals to do something for raising the standard of life of the very poor'. [29] What Chamberlain might have achieved, what his continued presence might have meant for the way in which the Unionist party responded to the challenge of Radical Liberalism with its policies of social reform, and that of advancing Labour and its quest for the working-class vote must, of course, remain a matter of speculation. Within five months of his apparent triumph over policy, Chamberlain was effectively removed from the inner councils of the Unionist opposition when a severe stroke paralysed the right side of his body.

The campaign for tariff reform to which Chamberlain had devoted almost all his political energies since 1903 did not disappear with its creator, but under less inspiring leadership, such as that of his son Austen, the crusade inevitably lost some of its momentum. In other hands, moreover, the policy itself was never quite the same again. With tariff reform Chamberlain had hoped to achieve a number of aims : to hold the British Empire together and ensure that Britain remained a great world power; to enable the government to safeguard British industry and maintain full employment; and to provide the revenue to finance measures of social reform. It meant claiming that Unionists would be able to improve the material condition of the working man, an aspiration which implied a competitive conflict with the architects of the New Liberalism. Yet those who came after him and adopted tariff reform for a variety of practical and tactical reasons did not necessarily embrace the whole of Chamberlain's vision.

Whatever its drawbacks - and, as the 1906 election showed, these were by no means negligible - tariff reform was at least a positive policy which could form the basis of a constructive programme to be placed before the electorate, posing a viable alternative to Radical Liberalism. The two ideologies offered alternative remedies to the social problems of the day, with tariff reformers placing emphasis upon increased production and Radicals upon wealth redistribution as the basis of their solution. Chamberlain's policy was designed to build a new mass base of support among the industrial working

LOYAL OPPOSITION

class, who were expected to be attracted by the irresistible combination of
patriotism and economic advantage. As regards the latter, the essential
argument was that reforming legislation could only be financed from the
revenue provided by a general tariff.[30] The National Union Conference
resolved in 1907 that

> the Socialist movement can be met by the insistence upon the
> constructive policy of the Unionist party, and especially upon
> fiscal reform, as the only practical means of carrying out a
> scheme for the provision of pensions for the aged deserving
> poor and other social reforms.[31]

In this way Chamberlain sought to recapture for the party the leadership in
domestic reform. Though the details of this were often left vague, the promise
about which tariff reformers felt most confidence was the part to be played by
their economic doctrine in the return of full employment. The slogan 'Tariff
Reform means work for all' was central to the whole campaign. Social reform
and Imperialism could also be linked in another way. Many Unionists, shocked
by the evidence of physical deterioration revealed by the Boer War, thought
of social legislation primarily in terms of the contribution it could make
towards the Empire's survival in a more difficult future. One noted that 'the
difficulty of breeding an Imperial race in the foul deeps of the town slums
raises a problem that has to be attacked as tropical medicine attacked the
mosquito pools'.[32]

The debate over tariff reform thus highlights a fundamental struggle which
went on inside the Unionist ranks in the years before the First World War to
determine what sort of party it was going to be and how successfully it could
cope with the challenges of a new era. The central point was not the intrinsic
merits or fallacies of tariff reform, colonial preference and imperial union.
Whether Chamberlain's programme did or did not offer Britain the road to
salvation, in the face of a relatively declining power-base in world affairs and
the growth of competitors in Europe and beyond, is not now of primary
concern. But the proponents of tariff reform, whether they fully recognised the
fact or not, were moving to make the Unionist party something it had not been
before. Tariff reform heralded a break with traditions going back into the
nineteenth century and raised the possibility of redefining Unionism in a way
that made sense in terms of the demands of the twentieth century. It meant a
significant development in the collectivist approach to government and society.
Tariff reform was not the only, or as history has perhaps shown, the best way

of achieving this end, but it was one way. Inevitably, therefore, the debate over tariff reform reflected not only a disagreement over fiscal policy but also a struggle between the forces of change and reaction within the party.

Attempts to categorise Unionist tariff reformers and free traders into convenient stereotypes are inviting but somewhat unrewarding. For one thing, by about 1910 all leading Unionists, with varying degrees of both commitment and comprehension, professed to support tariff reform. The unlikeliest figures, including aristocratic backwoodsmen, sometimes turned out to be ardent protectionists. While stalwart old-style Tories like the Cecils were predictably free traders, Walter Long, a representative figure of the party's landed interest, was a moderate tariff reformer. But at the two extremes the protagonists had difficulty in believing that they were really members of the same political movement as one another. Lord Balfour of Burleigh, for example, wrote with distaste of the Chamberlainite faction as 'that tribe who have no pretence to represent the Conservative side of politics to which I gave the allegiance I still retain'.[33] In general, many of Chamberlain's more ardent disciples tended to be among the younger members of the party and often had industrial or commercial interests. At all events the outcome of the tariff reform debate was bound to have profound implications in determining the sort of party which emerged to face the problems of the new century.

The deterioration in the country's economic climate around 1908 helped the tariff reform argument that a modern state could no longer be run on the basis of free-trade finance - to which, protectionists rather misleadingly asserted, the government was still committed. But the presentation of Lloyd George's famous budget the following year served to bring into focus a clear-cut alternative between the rival strategies of tariff reform and, as Unionists now portrayed it, the government's 'socialism'. Hence the Central Office argued:

> While their Budget piles up on British shoulders new burdens of taxation, which would certainly increase unemployment and could not possibly make 'life easier', a tariff would create fresh fields for British industry and thus increase the demand for British labour and make 'life easier' for thousands of British workmen.[34]

Nonetheless, it could clearly no longer be argued that tariff reform was the only way of financing social reform. The question now was which of the two competing strategies would succeed in capturing the allegiance of the electorate. The Unionists' difficulty was that Lloyd George's proposed methods of raising revenue were inherently more attractive to the mass of the electorate than tariff reform, whose impact would be to place the overwhelming burden upon the working classes, not least through the imposition of food taxes. Just as it was the landed rich who squealed at the proposals of the People's Budget, so in 1906 it had been the ordinary working man who had taken fright at food taxes increasing his cost of living. Indeed by 1909 tariff reform could be portrayed by its enemies as a rich man's device to avoid taxation. As Lord Derby pointed out in 1911, industrial unrest could largely be attributed to the failure of wages to keep pace with the rise in the cost of living. Yet Unionists could still be accused by their political opponents of intending to raise the price of food.[35] To run food taxes against land taxes might turn out to be a disastrous mistake for the party.

The difficulties of convincing the working man that his long-term interests depended upon the introduction of fiscal reform were well illustrated by the relative failure of the Trade Union Tariff Reform Association founded in 1904. Leo Amery hoped that this body would 'gradually dispute the tyranny of the present official Labour representatives', encourage working-class Unionists to play a greater part in the running of the party, and produce perhaps thirty members of parliament.[36] His hopes were to be severely disappointed. Years later Amery recorded that the Association 'never secured from Conservative headquarters the attention or support which it deserved'.[37] It is a striking fact that throughout the first decade of the twentieth century the parliamentary Unionist party contained not one manual worker.[38]

The social composition of the party suggested that it was not yet ready to accept Chamberlainite concepts of democratisation. In the last years before the First World War the Liberal and Unionist parties in the House of Commons did not significantly diverge in terms of socio-economic composition. Both showed the advance of industrial and trading interests, though 'landholding' continued to be predominantly associated with the Unionists. Yet the largest single group within the post-1906 Unionist parliamentary party has been categorised simply as 'gentlemen'.[39] In other words, at the higher levels of personnel the party had not succeeded in making any noticeable gestures towards the country's expanded electorate which now included, as a result of the Reform Acts of 1867 and 1884, a substantial section of the working class. Such a social composition was bound to be reflected in the realm of policy formulation. When it came to the introduction of working men into the

Unionists' parliamentary ranks or even into prominent positions within local party organisations, there was a marked gap between the party's rhetoric and its achievement. It needed more than pious declarations of intent to secure a significant change in the party's social composition. Six working men stood as Unionist candidates in December 1910, but their constituencies were not among the party's more likely electoral gains and none was successful.[40] In 1913 Feiling wrote cynically of 'the Tory working-man candidate, whom the Central Office permits to stand in the Orkneys'.[41] Indeed if the Unionist leadership had been really serious about the question of working-class representation, its continuing opposition to the payment of M.P.s becomes difficult to comprehend. The fact that members were not paid was bound to nullify the apparent equality of opportunity for the working man which party leaders proclaimed. Prominent Unionists such as Balfour and Austen Chamberlain only began to show some sympathy for the idea of paid M.P.s when they saw it as an alternative to the reversal of the Osborne Judgement of 1909. Independent working-class M.P.s were seen to pose a lesser threat than a party of members backed by trade union funds.[42]

Even had Joseph Chamberlain not been removed from the political stage in the summer of 1906 his task would have remained a daunting one. The policy of tariff reform and its foremost champion both aroused feelings of deep suspicion among many Unionists, even those who for tactical reasons came to espouse the policy itself. George Wyndham sensed that Imperialism was purely incidental to Chamberlain's aim which boiled down to 'protection of manufactures plus a surplus revenue to be devoted to reconciling Agriculture by doles and fostering advanced Domestic legislation'.[43] He was, he added, opposed to the raising of 'superfluous millions' for dubious projects at a time when the reduction of taxation was the first need of the country and opposition to 'socialistic vagaries' the first duty of the party.[44] Robert Cecil reacted in similar vein, fearing that tariff reform was only the first step in a policy distinguishable in name only from 'State Socialism'.[45] His elder brother added a note of electoral caution which summed up the difficulties which reforming Unionists faced:

> And our supporters are Conservatives. Anything like sweeping
> change is in fact repugnant to a large and influential proportion
> of them. I believe the advocacy of almost any sweeping change
> will lose you enough votes to put you into a minority.[46]

Discussion of the sort of problems Chamberlain might have encountered had he survived to determine the tone of the Unionist opposition remains academic. The fact was that as a semi-paralysed spectator of the political scene he was unable to prevent Balfour from shaping the party in the latter's own image. Though Balfour was obliged to take on board the policy of tariff reform as a party commitment, there was no possibility that in his hands it would be the same policy with the same implications that Chamberlain had envisaged. Balfour's methods would not be Chamberlain's and Balfour's style of leadership would not be Chamberlain's either. This was particularly noticeable at the time of the contest over the People's Budget. Chamberlain might have been able to compete with Lloyd George in terms of popular appeal; but Balfour most certainly could not. Balfour was a confirmed believer in the *status quo* who tended to admit the need for change only in order to maintain the essence of that *status quo*.

Balfour in fact had clear views about what the Unionist party should do now that it faced an extended period out of office. He believed that, notwithstanding the enforced pre-eminence of the fiscal issue, the duty of His Majesty's Opposition was to oppose rather than to formulate policy. His recognition that the Unionists were still, twenty years after the Irish crisis which had brought them together, an inherently unstable coalition of forces inevitably confirmed him in this opinion. This accounted in part for his initial wariness in regard to the whole question of tariff reform. When confronted with the two sides of the fiscal debate, Balfour found it difficult to understand how anyone in his senses could wish to decide between two policy options, 'neither of which has the smallest chance of taking practical shape until the end of this Parliament at the very earliest'.[47] Having had to live with a divided party in government for three years after 1903, Balfour was ready to welcome a spell in opposition to the extent that it at least freed him from the pressing requirement to formulate policies for immediate implementation. This attitude also helps to explain his reluctance to commit the party to a detailed social policy. After he had spoken at Edinburgh in October 1910 - 'a courageous and sincere speech but one of complete scepticism on the constructive side' - Beatrice Webb came away convinced that Balfour had 'done for the chances of a Tory Party at the next election'.[48]

In general terms it is certainly true that an opposition leader who emphasises the shortcomings of the government rather than risking disagreements among his own ranks through the formulation of an alternative policy stands an enhanced chance of maintaining party unity. But such a strategy of blurring over controversial issues cannot be maintained indefinitely, particularly with a party as restless as the Unionists were after 1906. Robert Cecil argued that the effect of Balfour's tactics was deplorable:

> If anyone could reconcile the irreconcilable it would be he. But it cannot be done. And any attempt to do it merely taints the party with a suspicion of dishonesty, the most fatal of all accusations in English politics.[49]

Similarly St. John Brodrick noted that the strategy of trying to keep a party together by minimising its differences 'leaves us without anything for which our side can shout'.[50]

For Balfour, then, the short-term goal of party unity was the first and overriding priority of political leadership. His chance of achieving this depended to some extent on the kind of issue upon which he succeeded in concentrating his party's attention. If the emphasis shifted away from the Unionists' traditional and safe ground of Irish and Imperial questions and towards social policy, there was inevitably an enhanced chance of the disintegration not only of the Unionist alliance, but also the actual Conservative party.[51] Forced, largely against his will, to pronounce on the fiscal issue, Balfour remained determined to avoid similar excursions into the hazardous realm of policy formulation in other spheres. Thus, as Austen Chamberlain commented, with the single exception of tariff reform Unionist policy was 'purely critical and negative'.[52] Balfour's hope was that the party could rely on the natural swing of the electoral pendulum rather than a series of policy pledges to cancel out the Liberal gains of 1906 and return the Unionists to office in the not too distant future. The problem was whether party morale could be sustained as the months and years of opposition dragged on with what was almost entirely a negative platform. As Henry Page Croft complained, 'at present there is no heart in platform work because we simply don't know where we are'.[53] The negativeness of Unionist strategy was reflected in some of the party's institutional responses to the spread of socialism. The Liberty and Property Defence League and the Anti-Socialist Union were dominated by Unionists, but offered little that was constructive. The A.S.U., despite an avowed intention to advocate positive policies, opposed almost all suggestions for social reform. Walter Long, who became vice-president of the Union in 1909, argued that it was pointless to try to counter socialism without answering its economic and political arguments, and he clashed with the Union's chairman, Claude Lowther, over the content of the Union's pamphlets.[54]

Thus, with Balfour rather than Chamberlain at the helm, the Unionist party in the years after 1906 showed little awareness that there now existed a mass working-class electorate whose living standards had apparently ceased to rise and whose allegiance needed to be courted if the party was to remain a viable aspirant for office in the changing political environment of the early twentieth century. It may not have been necessary to detail specific policies of social reform. Indeed it would perhaps have been unwise to have done so, granted the widespread working-class mistrust of the extension of state activity. But it was surely vital to portray the Unionist party as one with which working people could readily associate and this Balfour conspicuously failed to do. As early as October 1907 Austen Chamberlain warned that, despite the government's unpopularity, it was not the official opposition but the socialists who were taking advantage of this situation, largely, he believed, because of their support for positive policies.[55] By the end of 1909 J.L.Garvin was convinced that

> nothing but a much greater constructive programme ... will save us now .... I see that unless there is a complete reformation soon in our methods and spirit the vast social movement of the future will sweep right past us.[56]

Even Walter Long wanted to see the party's resources thrown into the fight against socialism with a policy that included social reform 'in connection with Poor Law and other cognate schemes'.[57]

While Balfour hesitated, the Liberal government's chief success was in getting a scheme of old-age pensions enacted, an achievement which must have been particularly galling for the side-lined Chamberlain, who had for long dreamed of introducing such a reform. The official Unionist attitude, however, remained cautious, emphasising the principle of payment in accordance with the benefits received. If a particular group in society wished the state to provide certain benefits, then they should contribute, if not the whole cost, then at least such a proportion of it as the scale of benefit demanded.[58] Balfour remained curiously unresponsive both to the example of his opponents and the warnings of his colleagues, despite the success achieved at a local level by some Unionists in winning over working-class support.[59] Only months before Balfour gave up the leadership of the party, and after more than five years in opposition, his shadow cabinet colleague, Walter Long, could still declare that the party had not yet given close enough attention to social questions.[60]

In this respect the general elections of 1910 offered the party few grounds for satisfaction. Unionists may have had some success in reclaiming middle-class support, but the Liberals still had a strong hold on the working-class vote, especially in areas such as Lancashire and London where Unionists had once done well. Indeed there is evidence that in 1910 the Liberals were still gaining ground in working-class constituencies not won even in the landslide of 1906.[61] Professor Hewins concluded that 'Conservatism divorced from its historic policy of social reform had no chance whatever in the country'.[62]

With the change of leadership in November 1911 and the selection of Andrew Bonar Law to spearhead the Unionist opposition, there could be no doubt that the party had a wholly different type of leader. In terms of social background the choice of Law represented a significant departure. As Long noted, Unionists now had a leader 'who has been trained in the best of business circles .... I believe this will be of far-reaching importance to our Party.'[63] In his readiness to take the battle to the Liberal government and substitute fighting invective for Balfour's sophistry, Law certainly satisfied a patent need within the party. Now that his sustained campaign to free the Unionists from Balfour's kid gloves approach had met with success, Leo Maxse asserted that

> the one demand of the Party ... is that the White Flag ... shall
> be hauled down: that our parliamentarians shall cease running
> away from the positions they are pledged to hold and that the
> Party in the country shall receive a clear and unhesitating call
> to arms, so that we may know precisely where we are.[64]

But while the tone of the Unionist opposition clearly changed under Law's direction, its essential content did not. Its emphasis remained negative and the vast majority of the party's pent-up energy released by the new leader was directed into the purely destructive campaign to defeat the government's proposed Irish Home Rule legislation. Whatever is said about the party's recovery in the period before the outbreak of war, 'it was by no means an entirely healthy recovery .... The party had little that was positive to offer.'[65]

Law did show some awareness of the social problems of the age and of the challenge they posed to the Unionist party. He had, moreover, for long been regarded as an enthusiastic supporter of tariff reform, believing that 'in the troubles ahead of us connected with labour we are moving very fast in the

direction of revolution' and hoping that 'by Tariff Reform ... we might ... get
the train, for a time at least, shifted on to other lines'.[66] But by the time that
Law became leader, tariff reform had been forced to share its priority in
Unionist thinking with constitutional questions, brought to the fore when the
House of Lords had rejected Lloyd George's budget two years earlier. In
dealing with the constitution Unionists were returning to the safe bedrock of
their ideology, but there was some doubt whether the electorate as a whole
would be similarly enthused. The constitutional crisis which came to a head
in 1911 probably never captured the popular imagination to the extent that
political activists expected or desired. A legalistic debate about the
prerogatives of the upper chamber was bound to exercise only a limited
electoral appeal. Unionist enthusiasts might continue to devise complex
schemes of constitutional reform, fondly imagining that the prevailing apathy
of the electorate could be countered by an educational campaign organised by
the Central Office, and the creation of a 'League of the Constitution' to arouse
enthusiasm and commitment where none existed.[67] But Professor Dicey,
whose knowledge of the constitution was probably unrivalled, more wisely
concluded that these issues did not interest the wider electorate, whose
attention had been 'directed to social questions [and] the pecuniary advantage
they can gain from the state'.[68]

   While Unionists became increasingly absorbed by the issue of Ireland, the
cause of tariff reform was delivered a perhaps mortal blow by the decision of
the party leadership in January 1913 to postpone food taxes as an immediate
item of policy.[69] One historian has concluded from this development that 'the
failure of tariff reform [in 1913] was the failure ... of radical Unionism itself.
By 1913 it was clear that the Liberals would be the party of change and the
Conservatives the party of resistance in social as well as constitutional
questions.'[70] Even though tariff reform had been seen by Chamberlainites as
the vehicle for a range of progressive policies, the simple equation between it
and constructive politics cannot go unchallenged. On the one hand, the divorce
was not permanent. Tariff reform and the Unionist party renewed their
troubled relationship a decade later. More importantly, the party's subsequent
history and its successful transformation in the inter-war years into a force
which could offer a combination of domestic stability and moderate social
reform raises an important question mark over Dr. Sykes's conclusion. An
analysis of the crisis of 1912-3 which led to the party's modification of policy
confirms the weakness in his argument. The fortunes of the Unionist party as

a party of progress were not inextricably linked with the policy of tariff reform and its promised consequences of social betterment. It was precisely because influential Unionists began to see that the whole-hogger policy of tariff reform carried with it insuperable handicaps in terms of popular electoral appeal that they determined to modify the party's stance. It was to this pressure that Law finally succumbed in 1913.[71] Lancashire Unionists were convinced that the maintenance of food taxes could cost their party up to fifty seats nationally, thereby postponing indefinitely its return to power.

After the eclipse of Joseph Chamberlain in the summer of 1906, moreover, how close was the connection between tariff reform and social policy? As has been argued, some advanced tariff reformers were among the most progressive Unionists when it came to using the power of the state to improve social conditions. But the motives of tariff reformers varied. Many of the diehard peers of 1911, for example, had adopted tariff reform as an essentially conservative measure in order that they 'could preserve something akin to the *status quo* in internal affairs'.[72] The majority of tariff reformers were extremely vague when it came to formulating social policy. Even Joseph Chamberlain had declared in 1905:

> I do not propose to make the question of old-age pensions a part of the programme of Tariff Reform. The latter will secure ... additional revenue, but I have said that the disposal of this revenue must be left for later consideration, when the working classes ... will be able to make their wishes known as to the use to which it shall be put. [73]

Dr. Sykes himself notes that the Unionists' difficulty was that they had, by and large, no agreed social policy worthy of the name to add to tariff reform.[74] Austen Chamberlain, who effectively became leader of the tariff movement after his father's removal from the political stage, was in no sense the harbinger of a new style of constructive Unionism committed to policies of state intervention. Considering the proper role of government in relation to the wave of industrial unrest in 1912, Chamberlain concluded that 'state interference is bad'.[75] Over the previous two years he had objected to Balfour's adoption of a referendum partly because he was 'frightened' that it would 'not be a conservative measure if applied to social reform'.[76] He had in fact been anxious not to 'discredit the practical reforms we can make by leading people to expect the impossible'. The simple cries of 'cheap food' and 'work for all' were his texts. Significantly the third slogan which Chamberlain 'might have added' was 'no income tax'.[77] But it could well be argued that while the Unionist party remained wedded to a policy of indirect rather than direct taxation, its capacity to draw upon the resources of the country to the extent needed to make a significant contribution in the field of social policy was bound to be limited. Tariff reform fitted easily into the traditional argument that general benefit for all classes would derive from an increase in the nation's wealth. As Bonar Law argued in 1912:

> We believe that the greatest of all social reforms ... would be
> a general rise in the level of wages in this country ... we know
> - at least we believe we know - that such a rise is impossible
> without a change in our fiscal system.[78]

But constructive Unionism was more likely to flow from the espousal of income tax than tariff reform. Direct taxation was the only realistic means of paying for social reform and yet throughout the period before the First World War the Unionists remained opposed to the whole concept of income redistribution through progressive taxation.[79]

It is difficult then to argue that it was the eclipse of tariff reform in 1913 which prevented Law from emerging as a champion of Unionist social policy. The fact was that, like his predecessor before him, Law tended to believe that social reform was not, generally speaking, a profitable line for Unionists to pursue. If social reform was really what the voters wanted, then they would turn to Liberal or Labour candidates. Earlier hopes that Law might change the direction of Unionist politics on social questions soon evaporated. In November 1913 Hewins despaired that

> unless we rapidly reorganise on the lines of Disraelian Toryism,
> adapted of course to modern conditions, we cannot now stop
> revolution .... But what can be done with a leader who makes
> speeches like that of Bonar Law at Norwich?[80]

Even had Bonar Law been personally more enthusiastic, he would not in all probability have had the opportunity to promote social questions to any great extent. Until the passing of the Parliament Act, or at least until the introduction of the People's Budget, the Unionists had succeeded, despite their weakened position in the House of Commons, in setting the agenda of their own political preoccupations. Thereafter it was the Liberal government which held the whip hand and which, by introducing a third Irish Home Rule Bill, fixed the central focus of national politics in the months and years before the Sarajevo assassination. Since the Unionist party owed its very existence to the issue of Ireland, its almost total absorption in that country's problems after 1912 is entirely explicable. The passion and conviction which Home Rule and the Ulster question introduced into the conduct of Unionist politics were for the most part spontaneous and genuine, and left little room for anything else. As one party official noted in the last year of European peace:

> In the first place everything except the Irish question became absolutely dull and all other business including the Finance Bill was quite perfunctory. Our leaders would or could think of nothing but Ireland and would not decide on any course of action on other subjects and the rank and file became very restless ....[81]

If it is the central purpose of political opposition to secure a party's return to government, then the Unionists' campaign against Home Rule should not be dismissed out of hand. The evidence of by-election results, as Unionist leaders were quick to appreciate, suggested that the majority of the electorate backed the party's stance on this issue. But a commitment to resist Home Rule could never develop into any sort of far-reaching constructive policy designed to wed a significant section of the working class loyally to the party's cause. The campaign to thwart the government's legislative designs might have borne fruit, but such an achievement would have been limited in scope and have had little to offer in the longer term. Henry Page Croft, representative of the party's radical right wing, warned:

> It seems to me that we are making the same grave mistakes that we made prior to the 1906 election. We are out of touch with the working classes who are absolutely indifferent to either Home Rule or the Welsh [Disestablishment] Bill; they are concerned with one question and one question only which is the wage question and unless we grapple with it fearlessly ... an enormous number of our working-class supporters will go over to the Labour Party.[82]

Another observer concluded that Home Rule interested none but the Irish, and Disestablishment none but the Welsh. 'They are steps to political dominance, but not part of the social war that now holds the people's mind.'[83] Looking towards the next election, Hayes Fisher noted:

> There are a number of seats in London which will depend on the turn-over of just a few hundred votes, and however strongly we may endeavour to force the electors to vote on the Home

Rule issue only, they will not be deterred from supporting a
candidate who promises them speedy relief from a position of
financial injustice, while the other candidate refuses to
recognise in his address or in his speeches that they have any
grievances for which any remedy can be found.[84]

So while Bonar Law may have represented a welcome change from Balfour as
far as many grassroots party activists were concerned, and although in
spearheading the campaign against Home Rule he played a role which Balfour
would have found well-nigh impossible, there were few signs before the
outbreak of war that he was ready as leader to grapple with the deeper
problems which threatened the long-term interests of the Unionist party in the
modern state. Pressurised by party extremists on the Ulster question, his vision
was, in its own way, as blinkered as that of his predecessor.

*       *       *

In concentrating upon the shortcomings of Balfour and Bonar Law, it
would be wrong to give the impression that the entire Unionist party was
oblivious to the development of the democratic state and the urgency of social
issues. One of the continuing strengths of the twentieth-century Conservative
party has been its unwillingness, unlike some of its continental counterparts,
to wed itself totally to reaction. Writing in 1922, E. G. Knollys affirmed that
'all present-day Conservatives, except those most bigoted, are Tory
Democrats, principally by conviction, but partly by necessity, for they know
that they could not hold power by merely "conserving" the institutions of the
country'.[85] Such a comment would certainly have been more difficult to make
in the decade before the First World War. After a year of opposition *The
Times* leader writer thought it opportune to remind his readers that back in
1895 Conservative working men had given the party a parliamentary majority
because of its programme of social reform.[86] At much the same time Fabian
Ware commented that

Murmurs are, indeed, heard from rank and file, complaining
that it was because the Conservative leaders lost sight of the
essential principles of Tory Democracy that they so utterly
failed to command the confidence of the people at the recent
elections.[87]

He was convinced that only the restoration of these principles could restore the party's fortunes.

Not all Unionist politicians ignored such warnings as these. Even Austen Chamberlain - at least according to Jack Sandars - wanted Balfour to adopt 'an elaborate programme of Social Reform - some replica of [Gladstone's] Newcastle scheme'.[88] The imperialist Lord Milner publicly criticised the party for missing the bus. The proposal to introduce old age pensions, about which Unionists had talked for so long, had now become part of the Liberal government's legislative programme. The party, he argued, needed to do more than simply attack socialism. It should produce a policy to deal with those economic evils which socialism claimed to be able to eradicate. Social reform would thereby become the Unionists' most effective antidote to revolutionary socialism. To neglect this fact would be unworthy of the Unionists' 'own best traditions from the days of *Sybil* and *Coningsby*'.[89] It was noticeable that a higher percentage of Unionist than Liberal candidates listed social reform among their priorities in the second election of 1910.[90] The Reveille movement of that year and some of the Diehards of 1911 also tried to emphasise the constructive side of Unionism and gave considerable attention in their policy discussions to social questions.[91]

Contemporary publications revealed some particularly hopeful signs. *The New Order* appeared in 1908. This was an attempt by some of the party's younger elements to present the sort of modern image that had been lacking in 1906, by incorporating policies of moderate social reform. Its editor, the Earl of Malmesbury, insisted that

> however difficult it may be for the more rigidly Conservative
> cast of mind to accept it, the necessity for new institutions and
> new movements in harmony with the changing spirit of the time
> has never been more imperative ... and just in proportion as the
> Unionist Party proves itself capable of this adjustment will be
> its power of continued usefulness to the Country.[92]

Sections of the Unionist press were also active. In October 1908 the *Morning Post* published a statement of constructive policy drawn up as the result of an exchange of views during the previous twelve months among some of the 'most active supporters and influential members of the Unionist Party, both in and out of Parliament'.[93] Four years later the paper's editor, H. A. Gwynne, was still hopeful that Bonar Law would come forward as the champion of the workers with 'a definite policy of Social Reform'.[94] In like vein the proprietor of the *Observer* urged his editor to use that paper to stimulate

Unionist interest in social questions. This was something which Garvin, conscious that 'without a great social policy programme the Conservative and Unionist parties have never long prospered', was very ready to do.[95]

Perhaps the most significant figure within this more constructive side of prewar Unionism was F. E. Smith, one of the few new men to break into the party's hierarchy during the years of opposition. As an M.P. for Liverpool Smith recognised that Unionists ran a grave risk if they chose to leave the whole field of social policy to their political opponents. On the same day that Lloyd George's famous budget was finally passed by the House of Lords, Smith called upon his party to accept the challenge of social reform, a challenge which the Liberals might well now neglect in their entanglement with constitutional questions. From this initiative there eventually emerged the Unionist Social Reform Committee, of which Smith acted as chairman.[96] But Smith's most notable contribution was probably his collection of essays published in 1913 under the title *Unionist Policy*. Here he sought to refute the idea that Conservatism was synonymous with *laissez-faire* individualism. Instead he presented Conservatism as a pragmatic middle way between unfettered individualism and Marxist socialism.[97] The implication seemed to be that, since the eclipse of Joseph Chamberlain, Unionists had jettisoned an essential element of their political creed. The party would never 'conquer a majority adequate to its purpose until it re-establishes itself in the confidence of the great industrial centres'.[98]

The Unionist Social Reform Committee was set up in February 1911. Though unofficial, it employed a full-time staff and enjoyed the full facilities of the Central Office. It proceeded to divide up the major social issues of the day, including welfare insurance and small ownership, for examination by sub-committees and selected individuals. Observers were even sent abroad to assess the effectiveness of social legislation on the continent. For the first time the party was attempting systematically to devise coherent policy programmes on a wide range of pressing social problems. The result was the publication between 1912 and 1914 of a number of detailed reports on such matters as Poor Law Reform, schools and housing.[99] The Committee's membership was largely composed of relatively little-known backbenchers of progressive inclination. But a conspicuous and significant feature was the involvement of some of those men such as Stanley Baldwin and Samuel Hoare who would dominate Unionist politics after the war and give to the inter-war party a more acceptable image than it had enjoyed prior to 1914. Observers became aware that at least on the party's backbenches there was a growing consciousness of social issues. In April 1911, for example, Winston Churchill drew the King's attention to two private members' bills concerned with police pensions and hours of work in asylums which 'were prepared by the young Conservative Members who take an interest in social reform'.[100]

The report produced by the sub-committee investigating the great wave of industrial unrest of 1911-12 - in itself a clear reflection of the severe social and economic tensions inherent in this period - may be taken as illustrative.[101] This stressed that the Unionist party had never believed that the state should remain indifferent to conditions of work. It was the state's duty to supervise conditions of employment in the interests of the state as a whole and to intervene in disputes 'to protect the interests of the community and especially those of its weaker members'. The report therefore urged that power should be given to the Board of Trade to establish tribunals of arbitration in the event of industrial disputes. The findings of these tribunals would not be legally binding, but would, it was thought, win acceptance through the backing of intelligent public opinion. The *National Union Gleanings* concluded that the Unionist Social Reform Committee was inviting the party finally to abandon 'the principles of the Manchester School of *laissez-faire* without going to the other extreme of officialdom to which Radicalism is tending'.[102]

The spirit of the U.S.R.C. seemed to be in evidence on the party's benches in both houses of parliament when the Liberal government came to introduce its National Insurance Bill in 1911. The Committee was able to counter 'the efforts of the reactionary and old-fashioned elements in the Party who wanted to fight such measures'.[103] Churchill sensed a considerable body of Unionists who were genuinely friendly to the bill and that this might become more apparent during its committee stage.[104] From the opposition front bench Austen Chamberlain congratulated Lloyd George on introducing the bill and suggested that the legislation ought not to become the subject of party strife.[105] This mood, however, seemed not to envelop Bonar Law, since the party leader assured the Commons that the next Unionist government would repeal the Insurance Act - an unfortunate impression only partly removed by a subsequent letter to *The Times*.[106] When it began to appear that the measure was electorally unpopular, Unionists were understandably confused as to what their attitude should be.

The division between Law and his more advanced followers on the question of National Insurance well illustrates the problems which faced the U.S.R.C. and its protagonists. There is conflicting evidence as to how much had been achieved by the outbreak of war. On the one hand the Campaign Guide for 1914, setting out the party's programme for the election, which was anticipated in 1915 at the latest, did show clear signs of the Committee's influence.[107] But there is a suggestion of window dressing in all this and it is noticeable that Smith was the only member of the shadow cabinet who really became involved in the Committee's activities. Interestingly, the majority of the Committee's members sat for industrial constituencies where social reform propaganda could be concentrated for their particular benefit.[108] Overall, and especially once the anti-Home Rule campaign had got underway, this more positive and constructive side of Unionism was not the abiding image presented to the outside world in the period before the coming of European war. When in 1913 Keith Feiling published a fictional dialogue between archetypal Unionists, representative of the differing shades of opinion within the party, it was perhaps significant that Bellinger, the Tory Democrat, did not have the best of the argument.[109] F. E. Smith's biographer concludes that 'there is little ground for imagining the Tory party coming to power in 1915 pledged to an advanced social programme'.[110]

In the last years of peace it became clear that the Liberal government, particularly in the person of David Lloyd George, had succeeded in making the land question an issue of considerable political importance. Again, the Unionist party's response was slow and uninspiring. Its major problem lay in the danger that to adopt a policy designed to alleviate the lot of the rural working class ran the risk of alienating the farming community, upon whose support the party could generally rely. The Land Taxes imposed by the 1909 budget were not seriously challenged by the Unionist party once the Finance Act itself had found its way on to the statute book, despite the efforts of E. G. Pretyman's Land Union to commit the party to a policy of repeal. But it was the government which had seized the initiative. Walter Long had earlier made strenuous efforts to get a scheme of state-aided land purchase by tenant farmers, on the lines of Jesse Collings' unsuccessful Land Purchase Bill of 1905, adopted as official Unionist policy, but efforts to convert Balfour had proved unsuccessful.[111] In 1910 Balfour did create a Small Ownership Committee under Gilbert Parker. The latter wrote that the party and the country were presented with 'the opportunity of our generation',[112] but it was the Liberals who succeeded in presenting themselves as the constructive party of reform in this field. By 1912 Lloyd George, setting up his Land Enquiry Committee, was clearly about to launch a new political crusade. Meanwhile the Unionist opposition lagged far behind, with many even sensing benefit for themselves in the fact that Lloyd George might be 'outrunning a large section of his party in the country and probably in the cabinet'.[113] Long summed up the problem from the Unionists' point of view:

> For years we have heard Unionists talking about occupying ownership as a policy, but when the subject comes up in a definite form in the House of Lords or House of Commons what do the leaders say? ... Nothing but vacillation and havering .... Assuming the atmosphere to be good, I do think that the Unionist Party can regain their hold of rural constituencies by a bold policy connected with land.[114]

Bonar Law and Long did organise a Unionist Land Committee in 1912, but with confusion and dissension again evident and the party's real preoccupation by this date lying on the other side of the Irish Sea, little attention was paid to the crucial proposal for a legislative minimum wage. Lord Salisbury's committee, reporting in 1913, isolated many of the central problems of the countryside, but without providing any concrete remedies. Indeed the crucial issue of a minimum agricultural wage was side-stepped with the decision to postpone this question for future discussion.[115] By July 1913 the Central Office was giving its official blessing to a purely negative campaign against 'Home Rule, Socialism and Radical Land Robbery'.[116] It was indicative of the party's problems that Lord Lansdowne, though recognising the importance of the agricultural labourer's vote, concluded that there was little to be gained from attempting to run a Unionist land policy against that of the government. Rather, he believed, the opposition's chance would come when the Liberals attempted to put their own schemes into operation.[117] Thus after seven years in the political wilderness the Unionists were still relying on a policy of negative opposition rather than constructive alternative as the means whereby to regain political power.

At the end of 1913 a group of younger Unionists wrote despairingly to Bonar Law to try to alert him to the fact that an attempt simply to ignore the land problem could not in the nature of things meet with success. They were quite prepared to accept the priority of the Ulster question in Unionist thinking but feared that, if no lead were given over land policy, the typical agricultural voter might conclude that he was being asked to choose between sacrificing

Ulster and sacrificing his own self-interest.[118] But the Party Chairman still found it impossible to extract Law from the Irish imbroglio for a sufficient length of time to elicit a clear statement of policy on the land question.[119] In January 1914 Long announced Unionist plans for compensation for improvements, extended leases and a new land court. By the following June, however, Steel-Maitland conceded that the party had completely lost the initiative on the land question and that Unionist prospects for the coming autumn looked extremely unfavourable.[120] Some recognised that it was not enough for the leadership to issue pious declarations of its intent to secure a substantial increase in the number of owner-occupiers of land. In an influential and widely circulated memorandum Lord Milner argued that

> if the present Social Order is to endure it is simply necessary,
> at whatever cost, to effect a great increase in the number of
> people who have a direct personal interest in the maintenance
> of private property.

He asserted that such degree of recovery as the Unionist party had made in rural constituencies since 1906 was largely due to the promise of land legislation.[121] But in trying to pursue the matter any further Milner came up against 'the stickiness and stupidity of the old Tories and the trop de zèle of some of our younger reformers'.[122]

*    *    *

In sum it seems that during the long years of opposition after 1905 the Unionist party largely forgot the critical lessons taught by earlier figures such as Disraeli and Lord Randolph Churchill. In these years the Liberal government's legislative programme helped forge that pattern of political society which became characteristic of twentieth-century Britain. Taken as a whole, however, Unionists seemed reluctant to admit that a mass electorate might come to regard social security as a legitimate aspiration of state policy. The party's policy priorities were almost certainly misguided as far as its longer-term interests were concerned. The leadership could not see that 'unless you put yourself straight with the people on Social questions all your Tariff Reform, Home Rule and Constitutional thunderbolts will be discharged in vain'.[123] Feiling captured the essence of the problem:

> Will you make the cotton-spinners weep for the Peerage or the
> railwaymen sigh for the sorrows of Ulster? Will the robbery of

God's Church in Wales wring the hearts of the unemployed
who cry out in vain to God and are not regarded of man? [124]
   The candidature of Sir John Gorst as a Liberal in the first general election
of 1910 was perhaps symbolic of the passing of the great days of Tory
democracy. Gorst explained his *volte-face* in terms of the changed attitude of
the two parties to the question of social reform. [125] With European war only
months away, Sir James Fortescue Flannery, a veteran of five general
elections, warned his party leader that unless the Unionists offered a policy of
social amelioration at the next general election 'things will go hard with us'.
The idea that the 'Commonsense of the People ... would be sufficient to
enable them to recognise that the Unionist Policy of maintaining the
Constitution was the safe one and that recognition would sufficiently draw
them together to support us' was totally unfounded. [126] Yet as the Home Rule
Bill neared the statute book the Unionists remained obsessively concerned with
the situation inside the Commons to the exclusion of the impact of their
policies in the country. As the Party Chairman warned:

> If we do nothing for the people in the ways immediately
> touching their lives, while the Radicals and Socialists profess to
> do all, then the masses as a whole ... will gallup to socialism
> as hard as they can. It will be a rush, a stampede .... We may
> see the Social Revolution carried out through the ballot-box
> with appalling rapidity and ease. [127]

It has been justly written that over the past century as a whole,

> the Conservatives have managed both in their political
> propaganda and in their performance in office to present an
> image of themselves and of the society they believe in that is
> more consistently attractive to the electorate - and to
> working-class voters in particular - than their opponents have
> ever seemed able to realise.[128]

Yet the period between 1905 and 1914 showed few traces of this recipe for
electoral success. The main focus of historical attention on Edwardian politics
has been the struggle to determine whether the Liberal or Labour party would
emerge as the chief alternative to the Conservatives in a political system which
favoured the existence of only two parties of government. In this analysis the
ultimate survival of Conservatism as the party of the right is largely taken for
granted. But the decade after 1905 may also be viewed as a battleground in
which the two traditional nineteenth-century parties sought to shake off the last

remnants of *laissez-faire* individualism and grapple with the social problems
of the day. Just how well the Liberal party was doing in this process of
transformation remains a matter of some debate. While many historians now
point to a successful period of adaptation, others still insist that the objectives
of the New Liberalism remained severely circumscribed. Even C. P. Scott of
the *Manchester Guardian* admitted, just before the outbreak of European war,
that the existing Liberal party was played out and needed to be reconstituted
'largely on a labour basis'.[129] Furthermore there certainly were those
Liberals who still clung to the *laissez-faire* traditions of Cobden and Bright,
and who were deeply troubled by the path charted by men such as Lloyd
George and Churchill.[130] In the case of the Unionist party there seems less
room for debate. The period prior to 1914 provides little evidence to suggest
that Unionists had enjoyed even the level of success of their Liberal rivals in
coming to terms with the demands of governing a mass democracy.


## NOTES

1.    Speech by Derby in Edinburgh 17 Dec.1875.
2.    M. Pugh, *The Tories and the People 1880-1935* (Oxford, 1985) p.6.
3.    I. McLean, *Keir Hardie* (London,1975) p.11.
4.    R. McKenzie and A. Silver, *Angels in Marble* (London, 1968) p.v.
5.    M. Pugh, *The Making of Modern British Politics 1867-1939* (Oxford, 1982) p.96.
6.    Boyce, *British Unionism* p.xvii. It is difficult to endorse Dr. Fforde's contention that there were no significant differences of outlook towards social and economic life between Liberal Unionists and Conservatives: M. Fforde, *Conservatism and Collectivism 1886-1914* (Edinburgh, 1990) p.vii.
7.    Jay, *Joseph Chamberlain* p.344.
8.    Selborne to Law 19 Dec.1912, Law MSS 28/1/64.
9.    *The Nineteenth Century* vol.52, pp.682-3.
10.   W. Wilkinson, *Tory Democracy* (New York, 1925) p.239.
11.   *Fortnightly Review* vol.100, p.44.
12.   A. Sykes, 'The Radical Right and the Crisis of Conservatism before the First World War', *Historical Journal* 26 (1983), p.670; Green,

'Radical Conservatism' pp.682-3.

13.   Campbell, *F. E. Smith* p.364.
14.   G. C. Webber, *The Ideology of the British Right 1918-39* (Beckenham, 1986) p.94.
15.   Newton diary 16 Jan.1906, cited Southern, 'Lord Newton' p.835.
16.   Balfour to Knollys 17 Jan.1906, Balfour MSS Add. MS 49685.
17.   G. R. Searle, 'Critics of Edwardian Society : the Case of the Radical Right', in O'Day (ed.), *Edwardian Age* p.81; P. Kennedy and A. Nicholls (eds), *Nationalist and Racialist Movements in Britain and Germany before 1914* (London,1981) p.23.
18.   Note on the necessity, the method and the limits of social reform, n.d., Steel-Maitland MSS GD 193/80/5.
19.   'The Radicals - they can no longer be called Liberals.' Lord Roberts to M. Chamberlain 8 Jan.1910, AC 4/11/208; 'Radicalism means Socialism', National Union publication 1910.
20.   Chamberlain to M. Chamberlain 25 May 1907, AC 4/1/195.
21.   Blumenfeld to Long 22 Aug.1910, Long MSS 947/438.
22.   Cecil, *Conservatism* p.195.
23.   K. Feiling, *Toryism: a Political Dialogue* (London, 1913) p.115. Compare R. A. Butler's statement made in March 1947 : 'We are not frightened at the use of the State. A good Tory has never been in history afraid of the use of the State.'
24.   The qualification is an important one. Dr. Pelling has argued that the working class as a whole feared that the changes which would result from state intervention would be likely on balance to worsen their lot: H. Pelling, *Popular Politics and Society in Late Victorian Britain* (London, 1968) pp.1-18. But while social reform may not have bulked large among the issues which apparently moved the working-class voter, he was 'always concerned about unemployment and higher prices and often expressed this in [his] political behaviour': Ibid p.13. To be seen to be generally in sympathy with the needs of a working-class voter was probably important for the electoral appeal of a political party at the beginning of the twentieth century, even though to enunciate specific proposals involving the extension of state intervention and interference might in the short term alienate that voter. Some social reforms proved to be popular once they had been enacted.
25.   Garvin to Maxse 4 April 1906, cited Sykes, *Tariff Reform* p.118.

26. Scally, *Lloyd George Coalition* pp.97-8.
27. H. Pelling, *The Social Geography of British Elections 1885-1910* (London, 1967) pp.201-2.
28. P. Fraser, *Joseph Chamberlain* (London, 1966) p.311.
29. Webb, *Our Partnership* p.331. Interestingly, Chamberlain himself doubted whether 'the principles of socialism [had] made or [were] likely to make much way with the English working classes': Chamberlain to Northcote 14 Sept.1907, Northcote MSS PRO 30/56.
30. B. Semmel, *Imperialism and Social Reform* (London, 1960) p.26. As early as 22 May 1903 Joseph Chamberlain had insisted in the House of Commons in reply to a personal attack by Lloyd George that the level of income tax was already exorbitant and that the funds needed to finance a scheme of old age pensions could only be secured if the country revised its fiscal system: Zebel, 'Genesis of Tariff Reform' p.149.
31. *National Union Gleanings* Dec.1907.
32. Note on the necessity, the method and the limits of social reform, n.d., Steel-Maitland MSS GD 193/80/5. See also J. R. Jones, 'England' p.41 in H. Rogger and E. Weber (eds), *The European Right* (London, 1965).
33. Balfour of Burleigh to R. Cecil 5 Dec.1909, Balfour of Burleigh MSS 38.
34. 'Tariff Reform versus Radical-Socialist Tradition', National Union publication 1909. See also Coetzee, *Party or Country* p.119.
35. Churchill, *Derby* p.147.
36. Barnes and Nicholson (eds), *Amery Diaries* i, 63-4.
37. Amery, *Political Life* i, 298.
38. Thomas, *House of Commons* p.46.
39. Jenkins, *Balfour's Poodle* p.7.
40. Ramsden, *Balfour and Baldwin* p.55.
41. Feiling, *Toryism* p.155.
42. Balfour to A. Chamberlain 21 Sept.1910, AC 8/6/12; Chamberlain to Balfour 23 Sept.1910, AC 8/6/16.
43. Mackail and Wyndham, *Wyndham* ii, 517.
44. Ibid p.520.
45. Cecil to Balfour of Burleigh 2 May 1910, Balfour of Burleigh MSS 37. Hugh Cecil held very similar views. See Sykes, 'Radical Right' p.664.

46. Salisbury to Selborne 12 Sept.1911, Selborne MSS 6/116.
47. Balfour to Sandars 26 Jan.1906, Sandars MSS c.751/124.
48. Webb, *Our Partnership* p.461. Balfour appears not to have changed his views on the role of an opposition party as late as December 1912. Lord Ashbourne recorded : 'Bonar Law asked A.J.B. what he thought, and A.J.B. said he did not think it was for an opposition to formulate a programme of more than general views, leaving details for any future Cabinet that might be formed': A. B. Cooke and A. P. W. Malcomson, *The Ashbourne Papers 1869-1913* (Belfast, 1974) p.32.
49. Cecil, *All the Way* p.109.
50. Brodrick to Selborne 10 Nov.1905, Selborne MSS 2/108.
51. J. P. Cornford, 'The Parliamentary Foundations of the Hotel Cecil' in R. Robson (ed.), *Ideas and Institutions of Victorian Britain* (London, 1967) p.307.
52. A. Chamberlain to Balfour 24 Oct.1907, Balfour MSS Add. MS 49736.
53. Page Croft to Hood 12 Sept.1910, Sandars MSS c. 761/67.
54. K. Brown, 'The Anti-Socialist Union 1908-49' in K. Brown (ed.), *Essays in Anti-Labour History* (London, 1974) pp.247-50.
55. A. Chamberlain to Balfour 24 Oct.1907, Balfour MSS Add. MS 49736.
56. Garvin to Goulding 5 Dec.1909, Wargrave MSS A/3/2.
57. Long to Blumenfeld 7 Sept.1910, Blumenfeld MSS LONG/W5.
58. H. V. Emy, 'The Impact of Financial Policy on English Party Politics before 1914', *Historical Journal* 15 (1972), p.113.
59. For Lancashire see Salvidge, *Salvidge,* passim, and D. J. Dutton, 'Lancashire and the New Unionism: the Unionist Party and the Growth of Popular Politics, 1906-14', *Transactions of the Historic Society of Lancashire and Cheshire* 130 (1981), pp.131-46.
60. *Yorkshire Post* 18 March 1911. Rather surprisingly in view of his enthusiasm for land reform, Long is described by Dr. Sykes as 'generally hostile ... to constructive politics': Sykes, *Tariff Reform* p.219.
61. Pugh, *Modern British Politics* p.137.
62. Hewins, *Apologia* i, 251.
63. Speech to party at Law's election, Long MSS 451.
64. Maxse to Law 11 Nov.1911, Law MSS 24/3/9.

65. Peele and Cook (eds), *Politics of Reappraisal* p.16.
66. Law to Salisbury 3 May 1912, Law MSS 33/4/34.
67. Memorandum by Selborne Sept.1911, Selborne MSS 76/162.
68. Dicey to Strachey 7 Jan.1912, Strachey MSS S/5/6/2.
69. See above pp.183-193.
70. Sykes, *Tariff Reform* p.6.
71. Dutton, 'Lancashire' pp.141-6. Long commented: 'All [the information] that I can get - coming as it does from thoroughly representative men, who speak for the working classes - points to the fact that so long as we have Food Taxes as a compulsory part of our policy we shall not command the support of the working men of the North': Long to Gwynne 19 Dec.1912, Gwynne MSS 20. Robert Eccleshall recently - and correctly - wrote of the decision of some Unionists after 1910 'to detach social reform from protectionism': R. Eccleshall, *English Conservatism since the Restoration* (London, 1990) p.129.
72. Phillips, *Diehards* p.119.
73. *National Union Gleanings* Dec.1905.
74. Sykes, *Tariff Reform* p.206.
75. A. Chamberlain to M. Chamberlain 16 March 1912, AC 4/1/790.
76. Chamberlain to Salisbury 22 March 1911, Salisbury MSS S (4) 69/129.
77. A. Chamberlain to M. Chamberlain 29 May 1908, AC 4/1/284.
78. Speech at the Albert Hall 26 Jan.1912.
79. Emy, 'Financial Policy' passim.
80. Hewins, *Apologia* i, 304.
81. Bridgeman diary 10 Aug.1914.
82. Croft to Law 8 Nov.1913, Law MSS 30/4/17.
83. Feiling, *Toryism* p.8.
84. Hayes Fisher to Lansdowne 16 Dec.1913, Long MSS 947/441.
85. *Nineteenth Century* Dec.1922.
86. *The Times* 9 Feb.1907.
87. *Nineteenth Century* 61 (1907), p.405.
88. Sandars to Douglas 10 Nov.1907, Akers Douglas MSS c. 478/9.
89. Wilkinson, *Tory Democracy* pp.248, 297.
90. Blewett, *Peers, Parties* p.326.
91. Croft, *Life of Strife* pp.54-5; Lansdowne to Willoughby de Broke 11

Oct.1910, Willoughby de Broke MSS WB/1/8; Hood to Sandars 10 Oct.1910, Sandars MSS c.761/170; Amery, *Political Life* i, 395-6.

92. Ramsden, *Balfour and Baldwin* p.30; Phillips, *Diehards* p.112.
93. *Morning Post* 12 Oct.1908.
94. Gwynne to Law 4 Oct.1912, Law MSS 27/3/7.
95. Gollin, *Observer* p.326; Garvin to Northcliffe 4 Aug.1909, Sandars MSS c.759/64.
96. Campbell, *F. E. Smith* pp.217-8.
97. Ibid pp.356-8.
98. F. E. Smith, *Unionist Policy* (London,1913) p.15.
99. J. W. Hills and M. Woods, *Poor Law Reform, a Practical Programme* (London, 1912); S. Hoare,*The Schools and Social Reform* (London, 1914); M. Woods, *The History of Housing Reform* (London, 1914).
100. Churchill, *Churchill* vol.2, companion pt.2 p.1068.
101. J. W. Hills, W. J. Ashley and M. Woods, *Industrial Unrest: a Practical Solution* (London, 1914).
102. *The Times* 16 June 1914; *National Union Gleanings* July 1914.
103. Winterton, *Orders* p.60.
104. Churchill, *Churchill* vol.2, companion pt.2 p.1084.
105. Wilkinson, *Tory Democracy* pp.254-5.
106. Winterton, *PreWar* p.248; H. Hyndman to Blumenfeld 5 Nov.1913, Blumenfeld MSS HY/3.
107. J. Ridley, 'The Unionist Social Reform Committee, 1911-14: Wets before the Deluge', *Historical Journal* 30 (1987), p.391.
108. Ramsden, *Balfour and Baldwin* p.77. Steel-Maitland, who attended meetings of the shadow cabinet as Party Chairman, was active in the U.S.R.C.
109. Feiling, *Toryism* especially pp.xi-xii (introduction by F. E. Smith).
110. Campbell, *F. E. Smith* p.363.
111. Correspondence between Long and Collings, Long MSS 947/438.
112. G. Parker, *The Land for the People* (London, 1909) p.8, cited E. Bristow, 'Profit sharing, Socialism and Labour Unrest', in Brown (ed.), *Anti-Labour History* p.283.
113. H. Cecil to Law 20 July 1912, Law MSS 26/5/32.
114. Long to Law 8 Aug.1912, ibid 27/1/28.
115. Undated memorandum by Steel-Maitland on the land question, Steel-Maitland MSS GD 193/119/5; J. F. Hope to Steel-Maitland 1

Jan.1914, Law MSS 31/2/3. See also complaints of E. G. Pretyman, President of the Land Union: Pretyman to Law 28 Oct.1913, ibid 30/3/64. For a recent assessment of the Unionist response to the Liberal government's land campaign, see Fforde, *Conservatism and Collectivism* pp. 131-59.

116.  A. J. P. Taylor (ed.), *Lloyd George: Twelve Essays* (London, 1971) p.54.
117.  Observations on Lord Milner's memorandum on land policy April 1913, Balfour MSS Add. MS 49862.
118.  S. Baldwin, P. Lloyd-Graeme, E. Wood and others to Law 8 Nov.1913, Law MSS 30/4/12.
119.  Sanders diary 13 Nov.1913.
120.  Gilbert, 'British Land-holding' p.129; Steel-Maitland to Law and Lansdowne 23 June 1914, Law MSS 39/4/40.
121.  Memorandum on land policy by Lord Milner 1913, Curzon MSS Eur. F112/93.
122.  Milner to Steel-Maitland 29 Oct.1913, Steel-Maitland MSS GD 193/119/5.
123.  M. Woods to Willoughby de Broke 16 Aug.1911, cited Ramsden, *Balfour and Baldwin* p.76.
124.  Feiling, *Toryism* pp.10-11.
125.  Clarke, *Lancashire* pp.403-4.
126.  Fortescue Flannery to Law 2 April 1914, Law MSS 32/2/5.
127.  Note on the necessity, the method and the limits of social reform, n.d., Steel-Maitland MSS GD 193/80/5.
128.  McKenzie and Silver, *Angels* p.15.
129.  D. Read, 'Crisis Age or Golden Age', in D. Read (ed.), *Edwardian England* (London, 1982) p.25.
130.  See, for example, D. J. Dutton (ed.), *Odyssey of an Edwardian Liberal: the political Diary of Richard Durning Holt* (Gloucester, 1989) pp.xviii-xxvi.

. 11 .

## *POSTSCRIPT:*
## *WAR 1914—1915*

   Until the very last days of July 1914 few figures among the British
political elite appreciated the seriousness of the diplomatic crisis which had
been developing in Europe since the assassination of the Austrian Archduke
Franz Ferdinand on 28 June. Yet once war had broken out it was not long
before the face of British domestic politics was transformed. 'Everything',
wrote William Bridgeman only a week into the conflict, 'fades into distance
and flees from memory with the War in full swing.'[1]  Nine months later the
last purely Liberal government in British history came to an end. By the close
of the war, after more than four years of unprecedented national effort and
sacrifice, the Unionist party was again the leading political force in the land,
its pre-war problems little more than a fading memory. Meanwhile the great
Liberal party of Campbell-Bannerman and Asquith lay divided and ruined,
never again a serious aspirant for government.
   To explain this dramatic reversal of fortunes simply in terms of the effects
of the ever-increasing challenge of collectivism generated by the demands of
total war would fly in the face of much that has been written above. As has
been seen, at least as far as the party leaderships were concerned, pre-war
Liberals were probably ahead of their Unionist rivals in shaking off the legacy
of nineteenth-century individualism. Few Unionists had emerged as natural
interventionists prior to 1914. Yet this traditional thesis is not without its
merits. The demands of war and its ever increasing encroachments did serve
to heighten the latent *laissez-faire* sensibilities of many Liberals. The war
required them to cross boundaries which had not really confronted them before
1914, in a way that convinced them that they were in danger of betraying their
deepest beliefs. As one Liberal M.P. put it after two years of warfare:
      All the old principles of the Liberal party have been virtually
      abandoned by its leaders .... The betrayal has been cruel. War
      seems to arouse so many bad passions that Liberalism cannot
      live in its atmosphere.[2]
Such developments ensured, at the very least, divisions within the Liberal
ranks which were bound to work to the advantage of the Unionist party. The
latter, moreover, had fewer doubts about the imperative need to win the war

at no matter what cost. Whatever their reservations about the use of the power
of the state in peacetime, Unionists reacted without hesitation in the very
different context of international danger. Particularly after Lloyd George
became Prime Minister in December 1916, British wartime politics were
driven by the needs and demands of what contemporaries, both critics and
supporters, regarded as Conservatism.

The contrast between the two parties was apparent at the outbreak of
hostilities. Only the fortunate arrival of the issue of Belgian neutrality enabled
the Liberal government to enter the war with a minimum of resignations from
the cabinet and a parliamentary party still largely united behind it. By contrast
the Unionist opposition responded to the crisis with a single-minded
patriotism, strengthened by the belief that their pre-war warnings about the
German menace had now been justified. Unionist dissidents at this moment of
national peril were few and far between.[3] As Bonar Law and Lansdowne told
Asquith on 2 August, 'any hesitation now in supporting France and Russia
would be fatal to the honour and to the future security of the United
Kingdom'.[4] Their letter was far less important in deciding the cabinet for war
than Unionists believed at the time, though the fear of being forced into a
Unionist dominated coalition seems to have had some effect on cabinet
waverers such as the Attorney- General, John Simon. It did, however, indicate
the conviction of a united party. Liberal rebels soon gave up the idea that they
could look for any significant support among the ranks of the opposition for
a policy of standing aside from the European conflict. 'The overwhelming
mass of the Tory party', concluded one dissenting Liberal, 'seem to regard
war as inevitable and some seem to be eager to take the best chance of
smashing Germany.'[5]

That the war would have a long-term beneficial impact on the fortunes of
the Unionist party was not immediately apparent. One possibility, of course,
was an immediate coalition government. Fearful of a split within his own
party, Churchill made overtures about such a development, but Law refused
to respond and made no moves on his own initiative.[6] Yet if the Unionists did
not enter the government, they could scarcely carry on with the functions of
opposition as if nothing had changed. Partisan politics in wartime ran the risk
of incurring a charge of disloyalty at a time when the safety of the realm was
at stake. It was almost inevitable that a political truce should be declared. This
resulted in the suspension of by-elections and the cessation of normal party
conflict in the constituencies.

At least as far as the Irish question was concerned, the war deprived the opposition of the tactical advantage which it had seemed to enjoy earlier in the year. Indeed Ireland provided the clearest illustration of the way in which the war transformed the domestical political scene. Having been the pre-eminent obsession of most Unionists in the years immediately preceding hostilities - indeed the force which had kept them together - the Irish issue receded by the end of the war 'below the domestic political horizon'.[7] To begin with, however, leading Unionists could not bring themselves to believe that Asquith would proceed with controversial issues such as Home Rule and Welsh Disestablishment. As Lord Selborne wrote to his wife:

> I shall never believe that Asquith is capable of playing such an
> infamous trick on us as to pass these bills during this truce of
> God and after what pledges have passed between the two sides
> about it, until he does it.[8]

But negotiations between government and opposition failed to produce an acceptable compromise with the result that Asquith went ahead with his two contentious bills. Home Rule was enacted without an accompanying Amending Bill, though its operation was suspended for the duration of the war. Unionists were genuinely outraged by the government's actions. 'How is it possible', asked Balfour, 'to let political warfare run riot within H[ouse of] C[ommons] and proclaim the truce of God everywhere else?'[9] With theatrical flourish, Unionist M.P.s signalled their disgust by walking out of the House of Commons. They were, thought Asquith, 'a lot of prosaic and for the most part middle-aged gentlemen trying to look like early French revolutionists in the Tennis Court'.[10]

But it was difficult to see how much further Unionists could take their opposition. 'We cannot fight the Government now,' concluded Bonar Law. 'They have tied our hands by our patriotism.'[11] After registering this token protest over Asquith's handling of the Home Rule legislation, Unionists proceeded for the most part to give the government steady support during the early months of the conflict in all questions concerning the prosecution of the war effort.[12] It was a necessary but difficult stance to adopt. As Bridgeman recorded:

> It has been a very high trial of the patriotism of Unionists to
> support them through all on the War. But we have certainly
> done it wholeheartedly, going on tour with little-navyites,
> traducers of the Army and peace-at-any-price men to raise

recruits and explain the war to the people.[13]
Ireland had provided an extremely tentative first step towards national unity in the changed political climate created by the war.[14]

Even in the absence of coalition some leading Unionists came close to entering the decision-making processes of government. As a long-standing member of the Committee of Imperial Defence, Balfour was invited to meetings of the War Council which Asquith established in November 1914, while at the invitation of Lloyd George the two surviving former Unionist Chancellors of the Exchequer, Austen Chamberlain and the seventy-seven years old Lord St. Aldwyn, took up semi-official posts at the Treasury.[15] But as many Unionists were quick to realise these arrangements did not necessarily work to the party's advantage. Both Chamberlain and Robert Cecil argued that the government was not making concessions and sacrifices commensurate with those of the opposition.[16] Government spokesmen were quick to claim that the opposition had been informed of, and by implication were partly responsible for, decisions that were being made. Law and Lansdowne, feeling that the Liberals were taking unfair advantage of the opposition's enforced good behaviour, were obliged to try to draw a not always discernible distinction between cooperation with the government and partial accountability for its policies.[17]

Unionists would have found it easier to sustain their self-denying ordinance had predictions about the short duration of the conflict proved accurate. But as 1915 opened with no obvious military victory in prospect, the opposition's impatience became increasingly apparent. Law faced calls from senior colleagues such as Long and Curzon either to insist upon more confidential consultations with government ministers or else to renew parliamentary opposition. Curzon's criticism of government policy in the House of Lords drew from Lord Crewe the predictable claim that Unionists bore a joint responsibility for war policy. Law tried to defuse the situation by insisting that the opposition bore no such responsibility, but privately advised Curzon that should the government attempt to enact further controversial legislation, such as the Plural Voting Bill, the opposition might well be forced to declare that the political truce was at an end. For the time being Law could see no alternative to the party's present course save coalition, a prospect which 'I should certainly be against'.[18] But at much the same time Long circulated to his colleagues a clear statement of where the balance of advantage lay as regards the party truce. It amounted to a crushing indictment of the policy pursued since the outbreak of hostilities:

> It is not too much to say that all the advantages of the Party truce remain with the Government and all its disadvantages with the Opposition. The Opposition has given up contesting by-elections and propaganda work in the country. The Government pursues its course of domestic legislation, retarded and truncated it is true, but nevertheless by no means entirely suspended. It expects from the opposition entire acquiescence in its war policy, resents criticism of its actions in connection with the war, hints indeed at a joint responsibility when mistakes are pointed out, but takes great care that all praise for success shall be showered exclusively upon itself.[19]

By January 1915 almost 140 Unionist M.P.s had joined the armed services. Nonetheless there were clear signs that many of those who remained were ready to resume the normal activities of parliamentary opposition. The tradition of backbench pressure groups which had originated during the early years of the tariff reform controversy was continued with the setting up of the Unionist Business Committee with Walter Long as its chairman. By March Churchill sensed that Law was surrounded by figures who wished to revive party bitterness at the earliest possible moment.[20] If this was indeed the case, they did not have the opportunity for very long. The origins of the first coalition of May 1915 have never ceased to be a matter for historical debate, but one which lies outside the scope of the present study. Suffice to say that the privately expressed misgivings of leading Unionists at the prospect of entering Asquith's government offer support to those who have argued that the Prime Minister was far more in charge of the process of governmental reconstruction than was once supposed. If Unionists really did force their way into office in May 1915, their leaders reacted curiously to their success in doing so. For Curzon the coalition was 'long expected' but 'much dreaded'. Long was even more forthright. 'I loathe the very idea of our good fellows sitting with these double-dyed traitors.'[21] But Austen Chamberlain probably spoke for many. If the government asked for help, the Unionists had no option but to give it:

> God knows each one of us would willingly avoid the fearful responsibility; but the responsibility of refusing is even greater than that of accepting, and in fact we have no choice ... we cannot shirk this job because we don't like it or because we

think the risks to ourselves too great.[22]

In the distribution of posts in the new government the Unionists did very badly. Most of the major offices of state remained in Liberal hands. Against the advice of several of his colleagues, Law accepted the Colonial Office, something of a ministerial backwater in the context of a major European war and scarcely commensurate with his standing as leader of the Unionist party. There is little doubt that Asquith was still in charge. The Unionist leaders had joined the government because it seemed right to do so, but had made no stipulation as to the policy to be pursued. Also, as Leo Amery later put it, they had 'abdicated for themselves and very largely for their followers the essential function of active and authoritative criticism'.[23] Not for some time would the Unionist party be able to resume its old dominance of British politics. But at least, after nearly a decade out of power, the days of opposition were finally over. Gradually, as the Liberals began to divide over the conduct of the war, the problems of pre-war Unionism would recede from the political stage.

## NOTES

1.   Bridgeman diary 10 Aug.1914.
2.   Holt diary 6 Aug.1916, Dutton (ed.), *Edwardian Liberal* p.45.
3.   An exception was Lord Hugh Cecil, who wrote to Churchill to urge complete neutrality: C. Hazlehurst, *Politicians at War, July 1914 to May 1915* (London, 1971) pp.41-2.
4.   Petrie, *Chamberlain* i, 373.
5.   Hazlehurst, *Politicians* p.42.
6.   Ibid pp.50, 135.
7.   Stubbs, 'Unionists and Ireland' p.867.
8.   Selborne to Lady Selborne 6 Aug.1914, Selborne MSS 102/156.
9.   Undated memorandum, Law MSS 34/3/16.
10.  H. H. Asquith, *Memories and Reflections 1852-1927* (2 vols, London, 1928) vol.i, p.33.
11.  *National Union Gleanings* Oct.1914. 'Whatever happens there should be no controversy in the House': Sir G. Younger to Law 5 Sept.1914, Law MSS 34/5/16.

12.    For an analysis of this stage of the Irish issue in British politics, see P. Jalland and J. Stubbs, 'The Irish question after the outbreak of war in 1914: some unfinished business', *English Historical Review*, 96 (1981).
13.    Bridgeman diary 29 Nov.1914.
14.    Stubbs, 'Unionists and Ireland' p.870.
15.    Dutton, *Austen Chamberlain* p.114.
16.    Chamberlain to Lloyd George 3 Sept.1914, Lloyd George MSS C/13/14/4; Cecil to Grey 11 Sept.1914, Cecil MSS Add. MS 51073.
17.    Hazlehurst, *Politicians* p.159.
18.    Law to Curzon 29 Jan.1915, Selborne MSS 93/36.
19.    Memorandum by Long 27 Jan.1915, ibid 93/26.
20.    Churchill to F. E. Smith 7 March 1915, cited M. Gilbert, *Winston S. Churchill* vol.3, companion pt.1 (London, 1972) pp.652-3.
21.    Hazlehurst, *Politicians* p.286.
22.    Chamberlain to Law 17 May 1915, Law MSS 37/2/37.
23.    Amery, *Political Life* ii, 66.

PUNCH, OR THE LONDON CHARIVARI.—July 1, 1914.

## THE EMERGENCY EXIT.

Scene—*A Tight Place.*

Child Herbert (*to "Wicked Baron"*). "MY LORD, I HAVE EVER REGARDED YOU AS A PESTILENT VILLAIN—NAY WORSE, AN HEREDITARY IMBECILE. I THEREFORE RELY ON YOUR BENEFICENT WISDOM TO FIND ME A WAY OUT OF THIS SINISTER WOOD."

## *CONCLUSION*

When, towards the end of 1905, Jack Sandars had urged Balfour to resign and make way for a minority Liberal administration 'at the earliest possible moment',[1] he was in effect showing his acceptance of the contemporary doctrine that the fortunes of the two leading parties were bound to alternate. It was safe to assume that the exclusion of the Unionists from office would not be of long duration. The swing of the pendulum which had marked the electoral verdicts of 1868, 1874 and 1880 - contests which had some claim to be the first characteristically modern general elections in the country's history - had gone far to establish in the public mind a general expectation that government and opposition would normally succeed one another in office. In the circumstances of the early years of the twentieth century, however, this was not necessarily the case. To suggest that any given period is of crucial transitional importance in the development of modern British political history is to risk elevating the normal process of historical chronology into something altogether too complex. But a case can be made out for the notion that the first years of the new century did witness a political climate posing problems which were rather different from those which had characterised the preceding decades. The new age was marked by the mounting challenge of collectivism, the emergence of a new political force in the shape of the Labour party and the growing polarisation of political attitudes along class lines. All this took place against a background of mounting economic difficulties.

Joseph Chamberlain, while sharing Sandars' basic assumption that the Unionists' exclusion from power would not last long, showed in other respects somewhat greater vision. In one of the last public speeches he ever made, Chamberlain said this:

> We must not make the mistake of thinking that we can or ought to ride back to power on a policy of mere negation .... The policy of resistance, of negation, is not sufficient answer to that Socialist opinion which is growing up among us - that Socialist opinion the objects of which are, after all, worthy of earnest and even favourable consideration. But the means by which those objects are promoted are open to serious objections. We can only meet Socialism ... by pointing out in all true sympathy

the impossibility, the impracticability of the methods chosen,
and by suggesting other and better methods of securing all that
is good in the object sought for. [2]

As he contemplated the 1906 election result, Chamberlain had 'no conception
of such an unprecedented revolution. Even now I do not fully understand it
nor can I foresee all that it portends.' But, providing the right steps were
taken, he was not convinced that Unionism as a political force had been
destroyed, believing rather that 'Labour ... thrown into the scale entirely
against us ... at the next opportunity may prove a weapon against our
opponents'. [3]

Historians have in fact for a long time been prepared to accept that the
Edwardian era was one of political crisis. The whole context of the party
political struggle, characteristic of the nineteenth century, was changing. The
halcyon days of the late Victorian age when politics for the last time 'turned
to any serious extent on the conflict between the Church of England and the
Nonconformists' had all but passed. [4] But ever since the days of Halévy and
Dangerfield, most historians of the Edwardian years have tended to place the
Liberal party in the centre stage, concerning themselves with the impact which
this altered political setting had upon the contest which now ensued between
the established Liberal party and the embryonic Labour challenge. In
particular, the state of health of British Liberalism as it prepared to face the
trials of the First World War has been treated as a question of critical
importance. There has been altogether less recognition that the Unionists too
were engaged in what was really a triangular contest. It could in fact be
argued that all three parties were in serious difficulties in the years
immediately prior to the outbreak of war. Thus the whole British party
political system in the first years of the new century was extremely fluid, with
the parallel concerns of Fabian Socialists and the Radical Right giving some
indication of this.

Ever since the Home Rule crisis of 1886 the two traditional parties had
remained inherently unstable coalitions, owing their fundamental shape to the
Irish question but unable because of internal diversity fully to work out their
policies in relation to a wide range of other issues. This meant that a major
political realignment remained, even in the first decade of the twentieth
century, a distinct possibility. [5] The intrusion of democratic trends after 1867
and 1884 added further complications for Liberals and Unionists. Both parties
had made gestures in the direction of the expanded electorate, particularly in

relation to their national and local organisations, to move themselves into more democratic channels. But these concessions and shifts of emphasis had proved only partially successful. Had they succeeded completely in assimilating the working classes into the existing party structure, there would not, presumably, have been the need for a new working-class political movement to emerge in the 1890s.

Thus the transition from the pattern of Victorian politics in which Unionists opposed Liberals to that of the post-war era in which the Unionists faced Labour was by no means inevitable. 'Britain', writes Dr. Pugh, 'did not develop a system ... in which Liberal and Labour forces contended for power; but one sees no fundamental obstacle to the emergence of such patterns.'[6] It is indeed surprising that any objective observer could escape the conclusion that Edwardian Unionism was in a state of crisis. Only an overwhelming obsession, confirmed by the benefit of hindsight, with the condition of the Liberal party can obscure this reality. Contemporaries had a clearer picture. In 1907 J. L. Garvin warned that the Unionist party 'threatens to become the sick man of domestic politics'.[7] By 1914 the party had been out of office for eight years and had lost three consecutive general elections. It had effectively forced out one leader and narrowly avoided losing another less than two years later. On many of the issues on which the party was most clearly divided from its Liberal opponents, it had failed to establish internal conformity within its own ranks.

The problem was that the Unionist coalition, owing its existence to little more than the issue of the Irish Union, as yet lacked a sufficient identity of purpose and sense of direction to meet the challenges of the new age. The result, therefore, was not a temporary removal from office but one of extended duration which ended only in the exceptional circumstances of the formation of a coalition government in wartime. 'All oppositions', wrote Feiling in 1913, 'are conducted in an atmosphere of dissatisfaction. The longer the period of opposition the more acute does the dissatisfaction become.'[8] This was as true of the Unionists before the First World War as it was of any other opposition party in the twentieth century. Searching for a political *raison d'être*, Unionists prior to 1914 seemed unsure what sort of party they belonged to. 'It is because we have lost sight of first principles', commented Willoughby de Broke, 'that we have got into all this trouble.' He was not asking for 'the terrible thing called a programme; or even for a concrete policy', but for 'a doctrine and reaffirmation of national principles'.[9]

Glickman has identified two strains in British Conservatism - a doctrinal strain and a positional element of trimmers and realists.[10] The supremacy of the latter has tended to be the basic recipe for electoral success. But throughout its quest for identity during the years under examination, the role and voice of the doctrinal strain - both the evangelism of the tariff reformers and the fundamentalism of the diehards - was inevitably much in evidence and produced profound discord. The struggle over tariff reform, which so preoccupied Edwardian Unionists, epitomised the party's almost desperate quest for electoral salvation. In itself the issue symbolised a new development in the party's history. Its emergence while the Unionists were still in government, and more particularly their failure to make up their minds about it before they were again in opposition, meant that unlike previous periods out of power the party was absorbed with an issue of constructive policy rather than being able to content itself with opposing the measures of the government. As Dr. Ramsden has written: 'The effect of the tariff agitation was to liberate the Party from its previously negative attitude to policy making'.[11]

Upon this question of policy, however, no consensus was to emerge. For some it offered the prospect of transforming the party into a radical movement of the right, able, as Chamberlain hoped, both to resist socialism and yet offer the advances of which socialism professed a monopoly. For others it was characteristic of a trend within the party which, if it became dominant, would destroy the traditional principles of old-fashioned toryism to which they adhered. For a third group it was little more than an electoral liability which would prevent the party from ever winning the votes of industrial Britain in sufficient numbers to return to the seat of government. The last was an important consideration. By the second decade of the twentieth century the narrowing class basis of Unionism was a matter of some concern. Even in 1905 Chamberlain had recognised that 'unless I have the support of the working people, clearly my movement is already condemned ... a failure'.[12] Yet it was a striking fact that after 1910 no less than 78% of Unionist seats were situated south of a line drawn from the Humber to the Dee, while areas north of the line and including Wales accounted for 64% of the parliamentary strength of the other parties.[13] Even in the class structure of its own parliamentary membership the party was showing few signs of moving with the new century. The landed interest made up more than a quarter of Unionist M.P.s in 1910 - a level not matched since 1880.[14] Indeed it has been argued that

> a Law Government in 1915 would have included hardly any
> more M.P.s from a business background than Disraeli's 1874
> Ministry or Salisbury's of 1895. Not all members would have
> been aristocratic or from the gentry, but the fastest route to the
> top was still through the law rather than through commerce.[15]

Balfour, in his quest to retain a central position in the political spectrum, probably succeeded in thwarting a Chamberlainite takeover of the party, but at the same time he proved incapable in the longer term of moulding Unionism in his own image. The consequence, in the words of Lord George Hamilton, was that the 'dunderheads in the Conservative party ... combine[d] to push him out because he would not insist upon promoting a revolution'.[16] Balfour's successor, Bonar Law, after burning his fingers on the smouldering embers of the tariff controversy, succeeded only in confusing the fundamental issues by shifting the focus of Unionist attention to that single question of Ireland on which the party could present a convincing image of unified intent. By this time some of the other basic tenets of Conservatism such as the constitution and the Anglican establishment had come under attack. Negativism seemed the only viable response. Thus the real legacy of the immediate prewar years was 'a united and cohesive party with partisan politics embedded in its soul',[17] rather than a party which had come to grips with the essential crisis of identity with which the twentieth century challenged it. Though the decade revealed evidence of elements of Unionism that were progressive and constructive, it was only under an old-fashioned banner of retrogressive reaction that the party emerged as a united and coherent force within the body politic. Maurice Woods, secretary of the Unionist Social Reform Committee, might claim in 1914 that 'the manifest interest taken by the Unionist Party in social evils and the sane and practical nature of the remedies put forward should go far to convince the electorate ... that the best friends of the people are to be found in the Unionist ranks',[18] but what he was describing was characteristic of the Unionist periphery only. Indeed, the party's experience after 1906 had perhaps shown the dangers of leaving their Liberal and Labour opponents to make the running in this area.

Signs of Unionist recovery prior to 1914 should therefore be viewed with some caution. It has been suggested that 'by 1913, the Conservatives had rarely been stronger in the Councils of the land, or indeed more poised for success in the forthcoming general election'.[19] Indeed it cannot be questioned that the Unionists, who in terms of parliamentary seats had drawn level with the Liberals in 1910, had made up more ground since then. By-election gains were recorded at Oldham and South Somerset in November 1911; a further success was achieved at Ayr North the following month, with five more gains in 1912. This pattern continued, with the result that by the outbreak of war the party had 287 M.P.s, thirty more than the Liberals and approaching the combined strength of Liberal and Labour members.[20] Appropriately, it was only the Irish members, whose attitude would remain permanently hostile because of the Unionist stance on Home Rule, who were keeping the party in a minority. In only one by-election during 1914 was there a small decrease in the Unionist vote and that was one of the cases which were complicated by a three-cornered contest.[21] Thus there are grounds for suggesting that, had a general election taken place in 1914 or 1915, the Unionists might have emerged victorious. By-election statistics together with local government election results give weight to such a conclusion and to this extent Unionist fortunes were improving at the outbreak of the First World War. One observer has even written of 1912 and 1913 witnessing 'the strange revival of Tory England'.[22] Certain reservations need, however, to be made. In the first place the slump in the Liberal party's fortunes may have passed its trough by 1914. The government experienced a markedly smaller swing against it after November 1912. The cabinet, moreover, was attempting to create an advantageous electoral climate by passing a bill to abolish plural voting and would probably have got this measure on to the statute book but for the outbreak of war. Elections tend, of course, to be lost by governments rather than won by oppositions. In any case the majority of voters were always less excited about the issue of Ulster than were leading Unionist politicians. The whole Home Rule issue probably never exercised more than a marginal impact on the party's fortunes. But with the politics of the New Liberalism far from exhausted by 1914, it is perhaps not surprising that some Unionist leaders were privately anticipating a fourth electoral defeat. Such an eventuality might well have destroyed the party's credibility as a potential party of government.

Even had such predictions proved unnecessarily pessimistic, the winning of a single general election would not have provided conclusive evidence that the long-term future of the Unionist party was assured. This is particularly the case when it is remembered that prior to the Representation of the People Act of 1918 the electorate was not one of universal male suffrage. The total of those entitled to vote in 1910 stood at just under 7.7 millions - some 28% of the adult population. Put another way, no woman could vote in a general election before the war, nor could four out of every ten men.[23] Furthermore the six million men added to the electoral register in 1918 represented that section of the population for whom the absence of constructive Unionist policies may have had most significance, but who would have been unable, before the war, to express their feelings at the ballot box. Such men may not have been automatic supporters of the Labour party, as was once thought.[24] But it seems unlikely that they would have felt drawn to Unionism as it existed in 1914. Finally, it needs to be noted that in three of the eight seats lost by the government between 1910 and 1912 Liberal and Labour candidates opposed one another but between them polled a majority of the votes cast, and this also happened in five of the seven seats lost in the next nineteen months. If this pattern had continued, the outcome of the next general election would have been determined by the development of relations between the Liberal and Labour parties, rather than by the performance of the Unionists. Nor was it by any means certain that Labour would be the inevitable victors in any contest with Liberalism. Ramsay MacDonald for one did not expect his party to retain all its seats in a 1915 general election, even if it were able to renew its electoral pact with the Liberals.[25]

So there was far from universal optimism in the Unionist ranks as the unwanted European war rather than the anticipated general election drew near. Austen Chamberlain, admittedly saddened by the apparent eclipse of his father's socio-imperial vision, commented in March 1913:

> The fact is I think our present position illogical and indefensible, our recent history cowardly and disgraceful, our prospects of winning poor, and our prospects if we do win, alarming; and I say to myself that it would be better that we should be beaten again and learn in that fiery trial to find faith and courage and leadership such as may deserve victory first and be able to use it afterwards.[26]

With the Sarajevo assassination less than two months away, Walter Long sensed 'a great deal of unrest among those who are our best supporters' over a wide range of issues.[27] The coming of war, of course, transformed the situation because it changed the whole basis of the political debate. 'No-one', commented Winston Churchill, 'can foresee the shape in which the political parties will emerge from the struggle.'[28] This was no doubt true as far as the majority of contemporaries were concerned, though a prescient few might have been able to foretell that the war, in creating problems which traditional Liberalism would have difficulty in resolving, afforded to Unionists far fewer dilemmas. During and indeed after the war government was sucked into unfamiliar realms - areas of the economy and society from which both Liberals and Unionists had tended to steer clear before 1914. The pragmatism of the latter enabled them to cope with this development more effectively than their Liberal opponents - or at least a substantial number of them - could do. The war also gave Unionists the opportunity to wear again the telling Disraelian vestments of patriotism and nationalism with their irresistible wartime appeal. From this new beginning the party would emerge as the dominant partner in the coalition government which brought the conflict to a successful conclusion.

The reactionary and negative excesses which had characterised the party's approach to the Irish issue were largely assuaged by the nationally shared commitment to the war effort. But not all the internal wounds within the party could be healed immediately by the soothing balm of European war. At the beginning of 1915 Hugh Cecil wrote in these terms to his brother Robert:

> No doubt as far as concerns Bonar Law - and I think, now that his father is dead, we may add Austen Chamberlain - there is nothing very serious which divides us from them except the decayed barrier of Tariff Reform. But there is a section of their supporters with whom I do not think it would be ever possible for me to work; and past experience shows that that section has had great influence with both Bonar and Austen and may still exercise a dangerous power over them .... The particular point about which we have disagreed with these in the past is Tariff Reform; but it is not a single issue but the whole attitude they adopt towards politics which is intolerable. I cannot read either the *National Review* or the *Morning Post* without being driven into violent antagonism.[29]

Interestingly, Cecil thought that these continuing party divisions were a factor which should encourage Unionists of similar persuasion to himself to regard a coalition with the Liberals as desirable. Only gradually would a new sense of purpose and identity emerge within the Unionist ranks. From the perspective of 1918 and beyond the party's prospects were bright indeed. Yet if, for a moment, the cauldron of war could be removed from the historical canvas, might there not emerge the most tantalising of scenarios - that of the 'Strange Death of Tory England'?

## NOTES

1.  Sandars to Balfour 22 Nov.1905, Balfour MSS Add.MS 49764.
2.  Speech at the inaugural dinner of the 1900 Club, 25 June 1906, cited Amery, *Chamberlain* p.893.
3.  J. Chamberlain to Mrs. Endicott 30 Jan.1906, AC 1/8/8/30.
4.  R. Blake, *The Conservative Party from Peel to Churchill* (London, 1970) p.167.
5.  Sykes, *Tariff Reform* especially chapter 7.
6.  Pugh, *Tories and People* p.1.
7.  Green, 'Radical Conservatism' p.669.For one interpretation of the crisis of Edwardian Unionism see Sykes, 'The Radical Right'. See also E. H. H. Green, 'The Strange Death of Tory England', *Twentieth Century British History* 2 (1991), pp.69, 83.
8.  Feiling, *Toryism* p.viii.
9.  Willoughby de Broke to Law 5 May 1912, Law MSS 26/3/11.
10. H. Glickman, 'The Toryness of English Conservatism', *Journal of British Studies* 1 (1961-2), p.116.
11. J. Ramsden, *The Making of Conservative Policy* (London, 1980) p.15.
12. Speech in London 17 May 1905, cited C. W. Boyd (ed.), *Mr. Chamberlain's Speeches* (2 vols, London, 1914) vol.ii,p.316. See also Green, 'Radical Conservatism' pp.686-92.
13. P. Cain, 'Political Economy in Edwardian England : the Tariff Reform Controversy' in O'Day (ed.), *Edwardian Age* p.57.
14. P. Clarke, 'The Edwardians and their Constitution' in Read (ed.), *Edwardian England* p.48.
15. Ramsden, *Balfour and Baldwin* p.96.
16. Hamilton to Balfour of Burleigh 11 Nov.1911, Balfour of Burleigh MSS 25.
17. Peele and Cook (eds), *Politics of Reappraisal* p.17. As one scholar has recently argued, 'that very sense of retrenchment, of assuming a purely defensive or negative posture, troubled those who feared that without a positive initiative the Unionists would inevitably be doomed to a permanent minority by the sheer weight of numbers against them': Coetzee, *Party or Country* p.154.
18. *Our Flag* June 1914, cited Ramsden, *Conservative Party Policy* p.18.
19. C. Cook, 'Labour and the downfall of Liberalism' in A. Sked and C.

Cook (eds), *Crisis and Controversy: Essays in honour of A. J. P. Taylor* (London, 1976) p.63. Yet granted the very high turn-out in the general elections of 1910, and the fact that Unionists polled a higher percentage of the electorate than ever before in the period since the passing of the Third Reform Act, it could be argued that the Unionist vote had reached a natural ceiling and that the prevailing electoral system threatened to condemn the party to a role of permanent opposition: Green, 'Radical Conservatism' pp.670-1.

20. Ramsden, *Balfour and Baldwin* p.85.
21. *National Union Gleanings* Aug.1914.
22. W. L. Arnstein, 'Edwardian politics : turbulent spring or Indian summer?' in O'Day (ed.), *Edwardian Age* p.78.
23. N. Blewett, 'The franchise in the United Kingdom, 1885-1918', *Past and Present* 32 (1965), p.31.
24. D. Tanner, 'The Parliamentary Electoral System, the "Fourth" Reform Act and the Rise of Labour in England and Wales', *Bulletin of the Institute of Historical Research* 56 (1983).
25. Read, 'Crisis Age' in Read (ed.), *Edwardian England* p.25.
26. Chamberlain, *Politics from Inside* p.534.
27. Note by Long 6 May 1914, Salisbury MSS S(4) 74/200.
28. Churchill to R. Cecil 8 Sept.1914, Cecil MSS Add. MS 51073.
29. H. Cecil to R. Cecil 10 Jan.1915, Cecil MSS Add. MS 51157.

# SOURCES

## A  Manuscript Collections

| | |
|---|---|
| Akers-Douglas MSS | Kent County Record Office. |
| Amery MSS | In possession of the Rt. Hon. Julian Amery, M.P. |
| Arnold-Forster MSS | British Library. |
| Balfour, A. J., MSS | British Library. |
| Balfour, Gerald, MSS | In possession of Lord Balfour. |
| Balfour of Burleigh MSS | In possession of Lord Balfour of Burleigh. |
| Beaverbrook (Aitken) MSS | House of Lords Records Office. |
| Blumenfeld MSS | House of Lords Records Office. |
| Bridgeman MSS (diary) | Seen when in possession of Lord Bridgeman; now published, see below. |
| Cecil, Robert MSS | British Library. |
| Chamberlain, Austen, MSS | University of Birmingham Library. |
| Chamberlain, Joseph, MSS | University of Birmingham Library. |
| Curzon MSS | India Office Library. |
| Derby MSS | Liverpool Central Library. |
| Gwynne MSS | Bodleian Library. |
| Halsbury MSS | British Library. |
| Hewins MSS | University of Sheffield Library. |
| Law MSS | House of Lords Record Office. |
| Lloyd George MSS | House of Lords Record Office. |
| Long MSS | Wiltshire County Record Office. |
| Northcote MSS | Public Record Office. |
| St. Aldwyn MSS | Gloucestershire County Record Office. |
| Salisbury (4th Marquess) MSS | In possession of the Marquess of Salisbury. |
| Sandars MSS | Bodleian Library. |
| Sanders (Bayford) MSS (diary) | Conservative Party Research Department; now published, |

| | |
|---|---|
| | see below. |
| Selborne MSS | Bodleian Library. |
| Steel-Maitland MSS | Scottish Record Office. |
| Strachey MSS | House of Lords Record Office. |
| Wargrave (Goulding) MSS | House of Lords Record Office. |
| Willoughby de Broke MSS | House of Lords Record Office. |

## B  Newspapers etc.; Hansard

*Daily Express*
*Fortnightly Review*
*Liverpool Courier*
*Manchester Guardian*
*Morning Post*
*National Review*
*National Union Gleanings and Memoranda*
*Nineteenth Century*
*Observer*
*The Times*
*Yorkshire Post*

*House of Commons Debates* (Hansard)

## C  Published Diaries, Papers and Memoirs
(place of publication London unless otherwise stated)

L. S. Amery, *My Political Life*, 3 vols (1953-5)
H. H. Asquith, *Memories and Reflections 1852-1927*, 2 vols (1928)
J. Barnes and D. Nicholson (eds), *The Leo Amery Diaries*, 2 vols (1980-88)
W. S. Blunt, *My Diaries*, 2 vols (1919-20)
D. G. Boyce (ed.), *The Crisis of British Unionism: the Domestic Political Papers of the Second Earl of Selborne 1885-1922* (1987)
C. W. Boyd (ed.), *Mr. Chamberlain's Speeches*, 2 vols (1914)
M. V. Brett (ed.), *Journals and Letters of Reginald, Viscount Esher*, 4 vols (1934-8)

Viscount Cecil of Chelwood, *All the Way* (1949)
Sir Austen Chamberlain, *Politics from Inside* (1936)
A. Clark (ed.), *A Good Innings: The Private Papers of Viscount Lee of Fareham* (1974)
A. B. Cooke and A. P. W. Malcomson (eds), *The Ashbourne Papers 1869-1913* (Belfast, 1974)
H. Page Croft, *My Life of Strife* (1948)
E. David (ed.), *Inside Asquith's Cabinet* (1977)
D. J. Dutton (ed.), *Odyssey of an Edwardian Liberal: the Political Diary of Richard Durning Holt* (Gloucester, 1989)
Sir Almeric Fitzroy, *Memoirs*, 2 vols (1923)
D. Lloyd George, *War Memoirs*, 2 vols (1938)
W. A. S. Hewins, *Apologia of an Imperialist*, 2 vols (1929)
Viscount Long of Wraxall, *Memories* (1923)
Lord Midleton, *Records and Reflections 1856-1939* (1939)
J. A. Ramsden (ed.), *Real Old Tory Politics: the Political Diaries of Robert Sanders, Lord Bayford 1910-1935* (1984)
Lord Riddell, *More Pages from my Diary 1908-1914* (1934)
Viscount Samuel, *Memoirs* (1945)
Lord Swinton, *Sixty Years of Power* (1966)
J. Vincent (ed.), *The Crawford Papers* (Manchester, 1984)
B. Webb, *Our Partnership* (1948)
P. Williamson (ed.), *The Modernisation of Conservative Politics: the Diaries and Letters of William Bridgeman 1904-1935* (1988)
Lord Willoughby de Broke, *The Passing Years* (1924)
Lord Winterton, *Orders of the Day* (1953)
Lord Winterton, *PreWar* (1932)

## D  Biographies

J. Amery, *Joseph Chamberlain and the Tariff Reform Campaign* (1969)
Lord Askwith, *Lord James of Hereford* (1930)
D. Ayerst, *Garvin of the Observer* (1985)
Lady Frances Balfour, *A Memoir of Lord Balfour of Burleigh* (1924)
Lady Victoria Hicks Beach, *Life of Sir Michael Beach*, 2 vols (1932)
Lord Birkenhead, *Frederick Edwin, Earl of Birkenhead*, 2 vols (1933)

R. Blake, *The Unknown Prime Minister: the Life and Times of Andrew Bonar Law, 1958-1923* (1955)

Sir C. E. Callwell, *Field Marshall Sir Henry Wilson: his Life and Times,* 2 vols (1927)

J. Campbell, *F. E. Smith, First Earl of Birkenhead* (1983)

Viscount Chilston, *Chief Whip : the Political Life and Times of Aretas Akers-Douglas* (1961)

R. S. Churchill, *Lord Derby: 'King of Lancashire'* (1959)

R. S. Churchill [and M. Gilbert], *Winston S. Churchill,* 8 vols and companion volumes (1966-88)

I. Colvin, *The Life of Lord Carson,* 3 vols (1932-6)

B. E. C. Dugdale, *Arthur James Balfour,* 2 vols (1936)

D. J. Dutton, *Austen Chamberlain: Gentleman in Politics* (Bolton, 1985)

M. Egremont, *Balfour* (1980)

A. Wilson Fox, *The Earl of Halsbury, Lord High Chancellor 1823-1921* (1929)

P. Fraser, *Joseph Chamberlain* (1966)

B. B. Gilbert, *David Lloyd George: the Architect of Change 1863-1912* (1987)

A. M. Gollin, *The Observer and J. L. Garvin* (1960)

A. M. Gollin, *Proconsul in Politics* (1964)

J. Grigg, *Lloyd George: the People's Champion 1902-1911* (1978)

D. R. Gwynn, *The Life of John Redmond* (1932)

B. Holland, *The Life of Spencer Compton, Eighth Duke of Devonshire,* 2 vols (1911)

H. M. Hyde, *Carson: the Life of Sir Edward Carson, Lord Carson of Duncain* (1953)

R. Jay, *Joseph Chamberlain: a Political Study* (Oxford, 1981)

D. Judd, *Balfour and the British Empire* (1968)

D. Judd, *Radical Joe* (1977)

S. Koss, *Asquith* (1976)

J. Lees-Milne, *The Enigmatic Edwardian: the Life of Reginald, Second Viscount Esher* (1986)

Marchioness of Londonderry, *Henry Chaplin: a Memoir* (1926)

J. W. Mackail and G. Wyndham, *Life and Letters of George Wyndham,* 2 vols (1924)

R. F. Mackay, *Balfour: Intellectual Statesman* (Oxford, 1985)

I. McLean, *Keir Hardie* (1975)

L. Masterman, *C. F. G. Masterman: a Biography* (1939)
Lord Newton, *Lord Lansdowne: a Biography* (1929)
H. Nicolson, *King George the Fifth* (1952)
Sir Charles Petrie, *The Chamberlain Tradition* (1938)
Sir Charles Petrie, *The Life and Letters of the Rt. Hon. Sir Austen Chamberlain*, 2 vols (1939-40)
Sir Charles Petrie, *Walter Long and his Times* (1936)
R. Pound and G. Harmsworth, *Northcliffe* (1959)
Lord Ronaldshay, *The Life of Lord Curzon*, 3 vols (1928)
S. Salvidge, *Salvidge of Liverpool* (1934)
T. J. Spinner jnr., *George Joachim Goschen: the transformation of a Victorian Liberal* (Cambridge, 1973)
A. J. P. Taylor (ed.), *Lloyd George: Twelve Essays* (1971)
H. A. Taylor, *The Strange Case of Andrew Bonar Law* (n.d.)
M. Thomson, *David Lloyd George* (1949)
K. Young, *Arthur James Balfour* (1963)
S. H. Zebel, *Balfour: a Political Biography* (1973)

## E Other books

R. Barker (ed.), *Studies in Opposition* (1971)
P. M. H. Bell, *Disestablishment in Ireland and Wales* (1969)
R. Blake, *The Conservative Party from Peel to Churchill* (1970)
N. Blewett, *The Peers, the Parties and the People: the General Elections of 1910* (1972)
G. D. M. Block, *A Source Book of Conservatism* (1964)
B. Bond, *British Military Policy between the Two World Wars* (Oxford, 1980)
K. D. Brown (ed.), *Essays in Anti-Labour History* (1974)
G. Butler, *The Tory Tradition* (1914)
Lord [R. A.] Butler, *The Conservatives : a History from their Origins to 1965* (1977)
Lord Hugh Cecil, *Conservatism* (1912)
P. F. Clarke, *Lancashire and the New Liberalism* (Cambridge, 1971)
F. Coetzee, *For Party or Country: Nationalism and the Dilemmas of Popular Conservatism in Edwardian England* (Oxford, 1990)
G. Dangerfield, *The Damnable Question* (1979)

G. Dangerfield, *The Strange Death of Liberal England 1910-1914* (New York, 1935)

R. Eccleshall, *English Conservatism since the Restoration* (1990)

R. C. K. Ensor, *England 1870-1914* (Oxford, 1936)

J. D. Fair, *British Interparty Conferences* (Oxford, 1980)

K. Feiling, *Toryism: a Political Dialogue* (1913)

J. Ferguson, *The Curragh Incident* (1964)

M. Fforde, *Conservatism and Collectivism, 1880-1914* (Edinburgh,1990)

I. Gilmour, *Inside Right: a Study of Conservatism* (1977)

J. W. Hills, W. J. Ashley and M. Woods, *Industrial Unrest: a Practical Solution* (1914)

J. W. Hills and M. Woods, *Poor Law Reform: a Practical Programme* (1912)

S. Hoare, *The Schools and Social Reform* (1914)

R. R. James, *The British Revolution: British Politics 1880-1939*, 2 vols (1976)

R. Jenkins, *Mr. Balfour's Poodle* (1954)

P. Kennedy and A. Nicholls (eds), *Nationalist and Racialist Movements in Britain and Germany before 1914* (1981)

R. B. McDowell, *British Conservatism 1832-1914* (1959)

R. T. McKenzie, *British Political Parties* (1963)

R. T. McKenzie and A. Silver, *Angels in Marble* (1968)

B. K. Murray, *The People's Budget: Lloyd George and Liberal Politics* (Oxford, 1980)

A. O'Day (ed.), *The Edwardian Age: Conflict and Stability 1900-1914* (1979)

G. Peele and C. Cook (eds), *The Politics of Reappraisal 1918-1939* (1975)

H. Pelling, *Popular Politics and Society in Late Victorian Britain* (1968)

H. Pelling, *The Social Geography of British Elections 1885-1910* (1967)

Sir Charles Petrie, *The Carlton Club* (1972)

Sir Charles Petrie, *The Powers behind the Prime Ministers* (1958)

G. D. Phillips, *The Diehards: Aristocratic Society and Politics in Edwardian England* (1979)

M. Pugh, *The Making of Modern British Politics 1867-1939* (Oxford, 1982)

M. Pugh, *The Tories and the People 1880-1935* (Oxford, 1985)

R. M. Punnett, *Front-Bench Opposition* (1973)

J. A. Ramsden, *The Age of Balfour and Baldwin* (1978)

J. A. Ramsden, *The Making of Conservative Party Policy* (1980)

D. Read (ed.), *Edwardian England* (1982)

R. Rempel, *Unionists Divided: Arthur Balfour, Joseph Chamberlain and the*

*Unionist Free Traders* (Newton Abbot, 1972)

R. Robson (ed.), *Ideas and Institutions of Victorian Britian* (1967)

H. Rogger and E. Weber (eds), *The European Right: a Historical Profile* (1965)

P. Rowland, *The Last Liberal Governments: the Promised Land 1905-10* (1968)

P. Rowland, *The Last Liberal Governments: Unfinished Business 1911-14* (1971)

A. K. Russell, *Liberal Landslide: the General Election of 1906* (Newton Abbot, 1973)

R. J. Scally, *The Origins of the Lloyd George Coalition* (Princeton, 1975)

G. R. Searle, *The Quest for National Efficiency* (Oxford, 1971)

A. Sked and C. Cook (eds), *Crisis and Controversy: Essays in Honour of A. J. P. Taylor* (1976)

A. T. Q. Stewart, *The Ulster Crisis* (1967)

A. Sykes, *Tariff Reform in British Politics 1903-1913* (Oxford, 1979)

J. A. Thomas, *The House of Commons 1906-1911* (Cardiff, 1958)

J. A. Thompson and A. Mejia (eds), *Edwardian Conservatism : Five Studies in Adaptation* (1988)

P. J. Waller, *Democracy and Sectarianism: a Political and Social History of Liverpool 1868-1939* (Liverpool, 1981)

G. C. Webber, *The Ideology of the British Right 1918-1939* (Beckenham, 1986)

W. Wilkinson, *Tory Democracy* (New York, 1925)

M. Woods, *The History of Housing Reform* (1914)

## F  Articles

N. Blewett, 'The Franchise in the United Kingdom, 1885-1918', *Past and Present* 32 (1965), p.27-56.

N. Blewett, 'Free Fooders, Balfourites, Whole Hoggers: Factionalism within the Unionist Party, 1906-1910', *Historical Journal* 11 (1968), pp.95-124.

D. G. Boyce, 'British Conservative opinion, the Ulster question and the partition of Ireland, 1912-21', *Irish Historical Studies* 17 (1970), pp.85-112.

P. J. Buckland, 'The Southern Irish Unionists, the Irish Question and British Politics 1906-14', *Irish Historical Studies* 15 (1967), pp.228-255.

P. F. Clarke, 'British Politics and Blackburn Politics,1900-1910', *Historical Journal* 12 (1969), pp.302-327.

J. P. Cornford, 'The Transformation of Conservatism in the Late Nineteenth Century', *Victorian Studies* 7 (1963), pp.35-66.

D. J. Dutton, 'Lancashire and the New Unionism: the Unionist Party and the Growth of Popular Politics, 1906-14', *Transactions of the Historic Society of Lancashire and Cheshire* 130 (1981), pp.131-148.

D. J. Dutton, 'Life beyond the Political Grave: Joseph Chamberlain 1906-14', *History Today* 34 (1984), pp.23-28.

D. J. Dutton, 'The Unionist Party and Social Policy 1906-1914', *Historical Journal* 24 (1981), pp.871-884.

D. J. Dutton, 'Unionist Politics and the Aftermath of the General Election of 1906: a Reassessment', *Historical Journal* 22 (1979), pp.861-876.

H. V. Emy, 'The Impact of Financial Policy on English Party Politics before 1914', *Historical Journal* 15 (1972), pp.103-131.

R. Fanning, 'The Unionist Party and Ireland 1906-10', *Irish Historical Studies* 15 (1966), pp.147-171.

P. Fraser, 'Unionism and Tariff Reform: the Crisis of 1906', *Historical Journal* 5 (1962), pp.149-166.

P. Fraser, 'The Unionist Debacle of 1911 and Balfour's Retirement', *Journal of Modern History* 35 (1963), pp.354-365.

B. B. Gilbert, 'David Lloyd George: Land, the Budget and Social Reform', *American Historical Review* 81 (1976), pp.1058-1066.

B. B. Gilbert, 'David Lloyd George, the Reform of British Landholding and the Budget of 1914', *Historical Journal* 21 (1978), pp.117-141.

H. Glickman, 'The Toryness of English Conservatism', *Journal of British Studies* 1 (1961-2), pp.111-143.

E. H. H. Green, 'Radical Conservatism: the Electoral Genesis of Tariff Reform', *Historical Journal* 28 (1985), pp.667-692.

E. H. H. Green, 'The Strange Death of Tory England', *Twentieth-Century British History* 2 (1991), pp.67-88.

P. Jalland, 'United Kingdom devolution 1910-14: political panacea or tactical diversion?', *English Historical Review* 94 (1979), pp.757-785.

P. Jalland and J. Stubbs, 'The Irish question after the outbreak of war in 1914: some unfinished business', *English Historical Review* 96 (1981), pp.778-807.

R. B. Jones, 'Balfour's reform of party organisation', *Bulletin of the Institute of Historical Research* 38 (1965), pp.94-101.

J. E. Kendle, 'The Round Table Movement and "Home Rule All Round"', *Historical Journal* 11 (1968), pp.332-353.

Z. Layton-Henry, 'Democracy and Reform in the Conservative Party', *Journal of Contemporary History* 13 (1978), pp.653-670.

H. W. McCready, 'Home Rule and the Liberal party, 1889-1906', *Irish Historical Studies* 13 (1963), pp.316-348.

H. W. McCready, 'The Revolt of the Unionist Free Traders', *Parliamentary Affairs* 16 (1963), pp.188-206.

B. K. Murray, 'The Politics of the "People's Budget"', *Historical Journal* 16 (1973), pp.555-570.

G. D. Phillips, 'The "Diehards" and the Myth of the "Backwoodsmen"', *Journal of British Studies* 16 (1977), pp.105-120.

G. D. Phillips, 'Lord Willoughby de Broke and the Politics of Radical Toryism, 1909-1914', *Journal of British Studies* 20 (1980), pp.205-224.

R. Rempel, 'Lord Hugh Cecil's Parliamentary Career 1900-14: Promise Unfulfilled', *Journal of British Studies* 11 (1972), pp.104-130.

J. Ridley, 'The Unionist Social Reform Committee, 1911-14: Wets before the Deluge', *Historical Journal* 30 (1987), pp.391-413.

W. D. Rubinstein, 'Henry Page Croft and the National Party 1917-22', *Journal of Contemporary History* 9 (1974), pp.129-148.

D. Southern, 'Lord Newton, the Conservative Peers and the Parliament Act of 1911', *English Historical Review* 96 (1981), pp.834-840.

J. O. Stubbs, 'The Unionists and Ireland, 1914-18', *Historical Journal* 33 (1990), pp.867-893.

A. Sykes, 'The Confederacy and the Purge of the Unionist Free Traders 1906-10', *Historical Journal* 18 (1975), pp.349-366.

A. Sykes, 'The Radical Right and the Crisis of Conservatism before the First World War', *Historical Journal* 26 (1983), pp.661-676.

D. Tanner, 'The Parliamentary Electoral System, the "Fourth" Reform Act and the Rise of Labour in England and Wales', *Bulletin of the Institute of Historical Research* 56 (1983), pp.205-219.

C. C. Weston, 'The Liberal Leadership and the Lords' Veto 1907-1910',
    *Historical Journal* 11 (1968), pp.508-537.
S. H. Zebel, 'Joseph Chamberlain and the Genesis of Tariff Reform', *Journal
    of British Studies* 7 (1967), pp.131-157.

## G  Unpublished Theses

P. J. Buckland, 'The Unionists and Ireland: the Influence of the Irish Question
    on British Politics, 1906-14', University of Birmingham M.A. (1965)
G. A. Jones, 'National and Local Issues in Politics: A Study of East Sussex
    and the Lancashire Spinning Towns, 1906-10', Sussex D.Phil. (1965)
R. B. Jones, 'The Conservative Party 1906-1911', Oxford B.Litt. (1960)
A. K. Russell, 'The Election of 1906', Oxford D.Phil. (1963)

# INDEX

Abercorn, Duke of : 192
Agar-Robartes amendment : 216
Aitken, Max : 133,165,167,189,
  195,220,224
Amending Bill (1914) : 233-6,287
Amery, Leopold S. : 34-5,48,51,
  60,86,100,103,133,135,156,
  164,188,191,195,213,217,224,
  226,233,234-6,260,290
Anti-Socialist Union : 263
Army Annual Bill (1914) : 124,
  227-30
Ashbourne, Lord : 119,122
Ashton-under-Lyne : 165,188,192
Asquith, Herbert H. : 57,73,81,
  85,97,99-102,119,125,150,
  171,204-5,213-5,218,221-6,
  228,230-4,236,254,285-90
Asquith, Margot : 168

Balcarres, Lord : 11,37,39,
  122-3,131,133,140,151,158,
  165-7,190,192
Baldwin, Stanley : 272
Balfour, Arthur J. : 14-15,20,80,
  87,122,133,164,189,236,261,
  265; and Army Annual Act
  (1914), 227; and Central
  Office,130; and Confederacy,
  52; and Constitutional
  Conference (1910), 81-3,85-6;
  and disputed leadership (1906),
  21-32; and First World War,
  287-8; and General Election
  (1906), 19; and Halsbury
  Club, 154,156-8; and House of

Lords, 47,69-70,78-9; and
  Ireland, 205,210,218-9,225,
  232; as opposition leader,
  33-40,91,94,123-5,149,151,
  154-5,161-2,168-71,262-3,
  297; and Parliament Bill
  (1911), 96-103,149-50,153;
  and party organisation, 12,
  128-9,132,135-8,140; and
  People's Budget (1909), 71,
  73-5; and referendum, 78,
  88-91,93-4,149,181-3,185-6;
  and resignation as party leader,
  157-63,166,181; and resignation as Prime Minister, 1,7,12,
  293; and shadow cabinet,
  118-21; and social reform,
  53,264,270-1,274; and
  socialism, 254,256; and tariff
  reform, 8-11,13,48-51,53-7,
  59, 61,63,72,74,185,190,262;
  as second Robert Peel, 9,
  36,85,162; speeches (Albert
  Hall, Nov. 1910), 92; (Bingley
  Hall, Sept. 1909), 74;
  (Birmingham, Nov. 1907),
  54-5,59,62; (Devonport, Dec.
  1907), 55; (Edinburgh, Oct.
  1904), 10; (Edinburgh, Oct.
  1910), 262; (Hull, Feb.1907),
  49; (Savoy Hotel, Feb.1907),
  54; (Wrexham, Dec.1910), 93
Balfour, Betty : 13,27
Balfour, Gerald W. : 12,29-30,39
Balfour of Burleigh, Lord : 56,
  74,259

*The Times* : 28,71,85,100,
130,139,188,203,270,273
Tory Democracy : 253,270
Trade Union Tariff Reform
Association : 260
Trades Disputes Bill (1906) : 70
'Truce of God' : 80,86
Tyrone : 207,235

Ulster, exclusion of : 213,215-7,
219-27,230,232-7
Ulster Volunteer Force : 217,223
Union Defence League : 217
Union with Ireland : 3,13,76,85,
88,95,163,184,186,192,194-6,
203,205,207-8,216-7,226-7,
235-6,266,295,297-300; see
also Home Rule
Unionist Association of Ireland :
217
Unionist Business Committee :
289
Unionist free traders : 7-8,11-15,
20,23-4,26,30-1,51-9,61-2,72,
77,88,91,128,194
Unionist Land Committee (1912)
: 275

Unionist Organisation Committee
(1911) : 133,135-9
Unionist party, class structure of :
260-1,296-7
*Unionist Policy* : 272
Unionist Social Reform
Committee : 272-4,297

Valentine Compact : 30-2,48-9,
55,128,256

Ware, Fabian : 181,270
Webb, Beatrice : 32,90-1,257,262
Wells, Lionel : 126
Welsh Disestablishment : 152,
184,192,269,287
Westminster, Duke of : 99
Wilson, Sir Henry : 205,228,
230-1
Winterton, Lord : 204
Woods, Maurice : 297
Worcester : 129
Wyndham, George : 14,40,51,63,
100,122-5,152-3,155-6,162-3,
206,212,261
Wyndham-MacDonnell affair :
209

Younger, George : 186